Communal Organization
and Social Transition

American University Studies

Series XI
Anthropology and Sociology

Vol. 46

PETER LANG
New York • Washington, D.C./Baltimore • Boston
Bern • Frankfurt am Main • Berlin • Vienna • Paris

Barry Laffan

Communal Organization and Social Transition

A Case Study from the Counterculture of the Sixties and Seventies

PETER LANG
New York • Washington, D.C./Baltimore • Boston
Bern • Frankfurt am Main • Berlin • Vienna • Paris

Library of Congress Cataloging-in-Publication Data

Laffan, Barry.
Communal organization and social transition: a case study from the
counterculture of the sixties and seventies / Barry Laffan.
p. cm. — (American university studies. Series XI, Anthropology
and sociology; vol. 46)
Includes bibliographical references.
1. Communal living—United States—Case studies. 2. United States—Social
conditions—1960–1980. I. Title. II. Series.
HQ971.L34   307.77'4'0973—dc20   90-19209
ISBN 0-8204-1193-0
ISSN 0740-0489

Die Deutsche Bibliothek-CIP-Einheitsaufnahme

Laffan, Barry:
Communal organization and social transition: a case study from the
counterculture of the sixties and seventies / Barry Laffan.
–New York; Washington, D.C./Baltimore; Boston; Bern;
Frankfurt am Main; Berlin; Vienna; Paris: Lang.
(American university studies: Ser. 11, Anthropology and sociology; Vol. 46)
ISBN 0-8204-1193-0
NE: American university studies / 11

Maps are not drawn to scale and are by the author.

The paper in this book meets the guidelines for permanence and durability
of the Committee on Production Guidelines for Book Longevity
of the Council of Library Resources.

© 1997 Peter Lang Publishing, Inc., New York

Printed in the United States of America.

Dedication

This book is dedicated to my wife, Joanna A. Mauer, and daughter, Brooke Laffan Ciraldo.

Joanna and Brooke, in turn, rededicate it to Barry, beloved late husband and father.

Acknowledgments

Barry Laffan died suddenly after a two year long illness before this book was published. He did not read the Preface, Introduction nor Epilogue and it had been some time since he had reviewed the book. Also, he did not review the final camera ready copy. I, who deeply loved and admired him, in his stead, with the help of his closest friend and colleague, the sociologist, Gerald Levy, and with the kind and helpful production assistance of Marj Jacques, prepared the final version of his book for publication. Indeed, I relied heavily on Professor Levy because he was the only one alive who knew this work from its inception through its various manifestations over the years. But, I guess I am somewhat co-responsible for any errors and omissions.

This book was very dear to Barry's heart and it represents some of the best of his intellectual mettle. He knew its merit and value to academe and to the larger society, and, I know, would be happy that at least one version is now published.

On behalf of my late husband, I offer the following acknowledgments. First, I know Barry would acknowledge his stalwart parents, James and Jennie. Barry often spoke of how loving and supportive they were in all his endeavors. They, too, have passed away, but for the sake of his grandchildren, Jacqueline Claire and Natalie Michele Ciraldo, their memories continue to be preserved by acknowledgment here. Second, his sister Yvonne, now also dead, and her very much alive daughter, Kim Romano, provided love that nurtured a committed scholar. Last but not least, one close family member to whom Barry was always grateful must be acknowledged: his dear and humorous son-in-law, Michael Ciraldo, who often cheered Barry on.

Turning next to those folk who initially pushed, cajoled, and advised Barry to turn part of his Ph.D. thesis into the present book because they thought it an exemplary work of ethnographic scholarship, he would acknowledge gratefulness to his thesis committee: Charles Harrington, the late Conrad Arensberg, Lambros Comitas, Herbert Passin, and Janet Dolgin, and to his late mentors and teachers Margaret Mead and George Z. F. Bereday. Special thanks goes to Charles Harrington for writing an apropos introduction that places the work in context.

Other prominent scholars in the social sciences who became familiar with all or parts of Barry's thesis, earlier versions of this book, and this version, such as Marvin Harris, Arthur Vidich, Laurin Raikin, David Harvey, and Steven Dandaneau, provided assistance and encouragement. Barry was also especially grateful for the support that Marvin Harris provided. Professor Harris was an extremely strong influence in Barry's anthropology and on this work. Friends and colleagues including Marty Jezer, Paul Cantrell, and Jeffery M. Jacques, are to be thanked for providing information and good wishes.

I also want to thank the kind and helpful people at Peter Lang Press and Andrew Kouroupis and Marj Jacques for producing the typescript.

I am very grateful to our dear friends Susan Cook, Gerald Levy, and J. Anthony Paredes, who provided me with love and support and substantive suggestions during posthumous productions. Professor Levy was also the first dissertation editor, the one Barry told that his task was to leave out nothing! Barry would have been profuse in his thanks to Professor Levy for his support and I am extremely grateful for his friendship and assistance to me in preparing this book, and for writing such an excellent preface.

Barry would have also acknowledged Professor Paredes for the pleasure of a close intellectual friendship and I thank him for his important suggestion to me to find a former communard to write an epilogue for this work. Thank you Howard Lieberman, for your friendship to Barry and to me and for writing such a wonderful Epilogue.

Finally, Barry would have thanked all the people who participated in this study and who he interviewed. As well he would have wanted acknowledged the eight young people (and perhaps more) from Jackson's Meadows who suffered premature and unnatural death.

And, finally, I am thankful for the love and support from James Parker, III, during this gratifying but also difficult posthumous production process.

Joanna A. Mauer
Panacea, Florida
1997

Contents

Figures

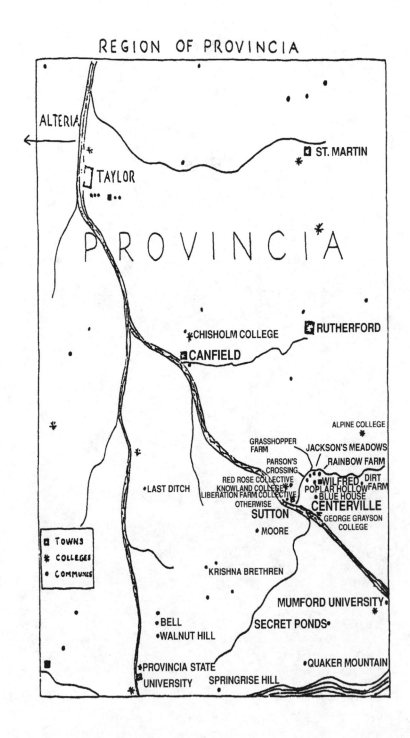

REGION OF PROVINCIA

ALTERIA

TAYLOR

PROVINCIA

ST. MARTIN

CHISHOLM COLLEGE

CANFIELD

RUTHERFORD

ALPINE COLLEGE

GRASSHOPPER FARM   JACKSON'S MEADOWS

PARSON'S CROSSING   RAINBOW FARM

RED ROSE COLLECTIVE   WILFRED   DIRT FARM
KNOWLAND COLLEGE   POPLAR HOLLOW
LIBERATION FARM COLLECTIVE   BLUE HOUSE
OTHERWISE   CENTERVILLE

LAST DITCH   SUTTON   GEORGE GRAYSON COLLEGE

MOORE

TOWNS
COLLEGES
COMMUNES

KRISHNA BRETHREN

MUMFORD UNIVERSITY

BELL   SECRET PONDS
WALNUT HILL

PROVINCIA STATE   QUAKER MOUNTAIN
UNIVERSITY   SPRINGRISE HILL

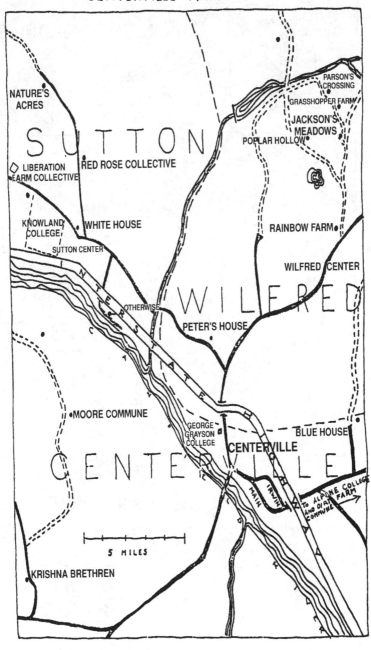

CENTERVILLE AREA

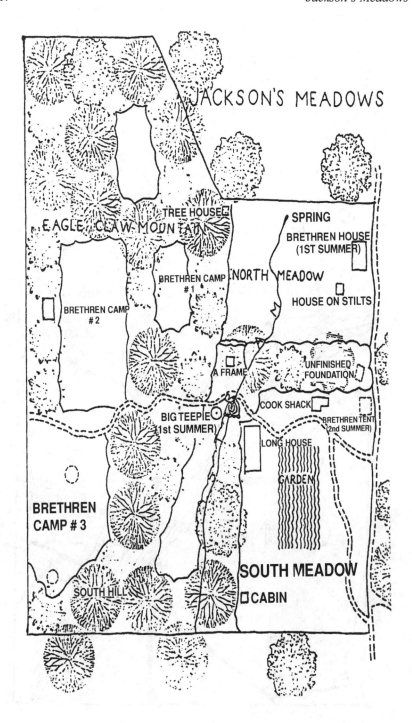

Preface

With the publication of *Communal Organization and Social Transition*, Barry Laffan's study of a 1960s and 1970s counterculture is now available more than two decades after it was completed in 1975. Focusing on the Jackson's Meadows Commune, but anchored in a description of a regional counterculture, Laffan's portrait of community life traces the evolution of a post-1968 urban migration to a New England rural "Mecca." Placing youth who were caught up in the turmoil of the 60s and 70s under an ethnographic microscope, the author describes their class, status, and life-style diversity, their communal politics, and their relationship with the so-called straight society. This more pervasive urban to rural migration that Laffan's case-study illustrates was a consequence of an ongoing conflict between traditional and liberal classes over civil rights, the new lifestyles, the welfare state, and the Vietnam War that escalated in 1968 with the Tet offensive, the assassination of Martin Luther King and Robert Kennedy, the urban riots, the debacle at the 1968 Democratic Convention, and the election of Richard Nixon. The youthful responses to this crisis described in Laffan's study not only aggravated an already activated conservative backlash but, as the author points out in his conclusion, contributed to the formation of a resistance to that backlash which survives today in New England and elsewhere. From the vantage point of the 1990s, Laffan's portrait of a regional counterculture captures what would become America's central domestic problem in its formative stages.

For much of his childhood, Laffan worked as a professional actor on Broadway and with touring companies until the age of 13 when he informed his parents that he wanted a more normal life. Interrupting what must have been a promising acting career, Laffan eventually enrolled at the University of Colorado where he joined a fraternity and majored in zoology. After teaching high school biology, he embarked on a career as a freelance international journalist, traveling in over 50 countries before returning to the United States to study anthropology at Columbia University where he became involved in the 1968 student rebellion. Despite an opportunity to study in Japan where he had already lived for two years and despite the advice of Margaret Mead that there was "no future in communes," Laffan was intent on researching the by then burgeoning commune movement, convinced that it offered a unique opportunity for exploring the dynamics of rapid social change while it was happening. In the spring of 1970, Laffan took up residence in the Jackson's Meadows commune where he engaged in participant observation research.

Throughout his fieldwork, Laffan was continuously cross-checking his own observations with those of numerous informants who cooperated in his research. This approach to gathering information was especially fruitful because the ongoing crises which characterized Jackson's Meadows during its two and a half year history were invariably accompanied by discussions which included all of the various status group perspectives on specific events. Furthermore, because attempts to assuage these crises necessarily involved the routine compiling of intelligence concerning every facet of life in the commune and the wider counterculture, this relentless pursuit of information was considered normal activity and thus coincided with Laffan's research strategy. After concluding the resident period of his fieldwork, Laffan conducted in-depth interviews often lasting 6-8 hours with most of the commune's major participants as well as key figures in the counterculture. This conscientious exploration of his informant's perspectives and his attention to detail enabled Laffan to capture the nuances of countercultural status groups and the complexities of Jackson's Meadows' history.

Laffan's research sets an ethnographic standard in its illumination of the class, social-psychological, and lifestyle dimensions of the counterculture. His descriptions of the various economic, political, religious, artistic, gender, and erotic orientations of individuals, groups, and specific communes reveals a culturally diverse and deeply stratified community. The array of street people, bikers without bikes, back-to-the-land hippies, revolutionary politicos, ex-political contemplative artists, aging academic seekers, resilient commune mothers, libertarian mystics, and eclectic religious fundamentalists provides the ethnographic basis for an analysis of counterculture politics which has not been matched. What is particularly significant in Laffan's study and what appears to have escaped the notice of other scholars is the high proportion of working and poverty class youth, some of whom were assimilated into the mainstream counterculture but many of whom were rejected and marginalized by their middle and upper class brethren. The author's sensitivity to class and status distinctions transcends stereotypes and dispels some of the myths surrounding the counterculture. Reading like an epoch novel, yet crafted with an attention to factual detail that reeks with authenticity, Laffan's example demonstrates that social research can have real value for those who would understand the world as it is.

The posthumous publication of this definitive community study provides an historical and ethnographic record of a phenomenon that has been widely discussed but largely unrecorded at the time that it was happening in the terms that Laffan's study indicates is possible. Those who participated in this social experiment can ponder the long-term consequences of their actions. Those who are considering such experiments in the future might profit from his legacy. Those who need to bask in 60s nostalgia might temper their imaginations with a tinge of reality. And those who are attempting to understand why a nation so endowed with resources and what appears to be an unlimited capacity for action is unable to address its fundamental problems can learn much from this case study. For, in its portrait of youthful class and cultural conflict, the historical trajectory of the United States in microcosm is brought into sharper focus.

Gerald E. Levy
Marlboro, Vermont

The author and his daughter at Jackson's
Meadows during the period of this study.

Introduction
Jackson's Meadows: A Retrospective Foreword

In the summer of 1975, Barry Laffan, then one of my doctoral students, called me at my weekend home in Columbia County, New York, to tell me that he had at last finished a draft of his dissertation, and to ask if he could drop it off as he travelled from Vermont to his own summer home near Catskill, New York. I said that I wouldn't be home that day, but that he could leave it in the mailbox. He said that he wasn't sure it would fit, and sensing that he might be anxious about leaving his precious document in a road side rural mailbox, I made arrangements for him to leave it with the town justice, my next door neighbor, where some one was always home. She called the day after the drop off date to say that someone had left a case of liquor for me. Puzzled I drove over and found a Dewar's White Label liquor carton. Inside was a document which filled it fairly well: Barry's "thesis" was 2,000 typed pages long.

I spent the rest of the summer reading what Barry had written. I concluded that he had actually written three different books: one was a study of a particular commune which he called Jackson's Meadows, the other was a descriptive, historical, and comparative account of all the communes in the area he called Provincia, and the third, as I recall, was a historical treatise on the subject of communes in the United States from the 18th century to the present. Worried that Barry would be unwilling or unable to do so, I spent days that summer walking around my study sorting the manuscript into the three piles, and sorting each pile into its own beginning, middle and end. I then read each separately and made a judgment about which would be the most defensible to a committee of anthropologists.

I chose the first pile about Jackson's Meadows because it was the one that was most traditionally anthropological: it dealt ethnographically with a particular community over time, and was informed by extensive fieldwork and participant observation on site with the people of the community. It told their story, and the data upon which the story was based included first hand observation, detailed interview data with all the participants over time about their own and others behavior, and their hopes, feelings and aspirations. I called Barry and told him to come over and meet his new thesis. We spent the weekend together discussing his thesis, and he left in agreement that he had indeed written three publishable works, and that this was the one most likely to get him his Ph.D. degree in anthropology and education from Columbia. The present book is a revision of that dissertation; parts of the second "book" have been incorporated, especially in Chapters 8 and 9.

Since this book makes arguments that people are located in their own particular cultural time, and that persons are malleable over time, it might help the reader to know more about Barry and the academic milieu in which he matured. I will, therefore, briefly explore the time and setting in which Dr. Laffan prepared for this study. The Columbia University anthropology and education program was then embedded in Teachers College's Department of Philosophy and the Social Sciences; a collectivity which included other programs—sociology, history, philosophy, economics, and politics of education, and the college's programs in comparative education. In 1967 Barry was enrolled in this department in the Ed.D. program in comparative education. His adviser was George Z.F. Bereday, a prominent figure in that field, and a charismatic teacher, whose scholarly interests were in comparative sociology. Barry's interests reflected a previous experience in Japan where Bereday had also worked, and he was then on a career trajectory which would have led to a dissertation involving Japanese education patterns.

I came to the Columbia anthropology and education program in 1967 immediately following my own graduate work in psychological anthropology at Harvard's Department of Social Relations. I was a specialist in a relatively new field, the anthropology of contemporary American society, and had studied sex-role and political socialization. William Dalton joined the program at the same time. Trained at Manchester University for his doctorate, he was from Boston and was a social anthropologist whose area of specialization included Libya and the Middle East. We joined the other anthropologist* on the program faculty, Lambros Comitas, a Columbia University trained cultural anthropologist and a well-known Caribbean specialist. My own interests in the anthropology of contemporary United States society were shared by Conrad Arensberg, a true pioneer in such efforts by virtue of his membership on the research team studying "Yankee City". Arensberg was a senior member of the GraduateSchool of Arts and Science's (GSAS) Department of Anthropology, with whom Barry would also study. Barry also studied with Margaret Mead, an adjunct professor in both the Teachers College and GSAS departments, who shared interests in psychological anthropology, but who managed to bring anthropology to policy-makers and other non-anthropologists through her mass-media activities.

It was an exciting time. Comitas, then 40, Dalton, 30, and I, at 25, shared a desire to change the field of anthropology to increase its relevance to contemporary society and we proposed a new Ph.D. program in applied anthropology which, with Arensberg, Mead, and Marvin Harris, became a joint program between the Teachers College and GSAS departments. We were the first Ph.D. program in applied anthropology in the country. Whatever opposition

*Solon Kimball had departed the year before for the University of Florida

purer academic colleagues may have had to this development was overwhelmed by the riotous events of the Spring of 1968 at Columbia. With the campus shut by police responses to student sit ins, and the semester's classes effectively suspended, students, anthropology students among them, demanded to know the relevance of their academic programs to understanding the events of the day: academic power structures, politics, and, of course, the war in Vietnam. Even GSAS critics of applied science soon learned to point to the applied program when students demanded they do something about anthropology's relevance to real world concerns. There couldn't have been a better fit between a new academic program and a political moment.

During this period Barry was active in the political events of that spring, and channelled his energy into helping create a student government at the college, which he was quickly elected to lead. Calls for change seemed to be everywhere. It seems natural, in retrospect, that Barry became increasingly attracted by anthropology as a discipline: we had a critical mass of faculty who seemed to be moving more rapidly than those in other disciplines toward policy and relevance to larger political issues. If the faculty thought, in differing ways, we could change the world for the better, Barry came to believe our vision that anthropology was an effective means to that end. We were also anti-authority in our orientations, though we differed in style. Dalton was confrontational and more of a Marxist. I maintained a more conventional persona but had similarly impatient and unconventional beliefs, though I was more Weberian liberal than Marxist. Barry was the political activist, and was attracted by Marxism, but seemed intellectually more influenced by Anthony Wallace, and the later work of Victor Turner.

Paradoxically, in light of these political leanings, Barry, Dalton and I also shared many personal characteristics which were decidedly mainstream. He was also just 30; he had married young (by 20) as had we, and he had a child, as we had children. We maintained stable marriages, took child rearing responsibilities seriously, owned rural homes, and had strong career orientations. We also could all trace some Irish ancestry. Barry cast his lot with us, and left comparative education behind, though this was, I thought, a difficult decision for him because he was closely linked to Bereday, and their daughters were the best of friends.

Our programs attracted a splendid group of students in both anthropology and education and applied anthropology which also would have attracted Barry. They were diverse, energetic, intelligent, and motivated. His fellow alumni from that period include MacArthur Fellows Shirley Brice Heath and Ruth Watson Lubic, prominent applied anthropologists like Tony Barclay, Twig Johnson, John Carleton Kelley, Joyce Lewinger Moock, Claudia Rogers, and Frances Schwartz, and academic anthropologists like Carol Ascher, Joan Cassell, Melanie Dreher, and Glenn Hendricks.

Barry was a competent and hardworking student, but his true love was people. His gregariousness brought life to a gathering. He loved to talk, was equally adept at being a host or a guest, and he listened just as well as he talked.

He had an irreverent sense of humor, and puns abounded. He remained very active in student politics, and politics used up a lot of his time.

As his course work with us came to a close, he began to see the possibility of a dissertation involving fieldwork in contemporary America, and ultimately planned a study of the rebellions underway in parts of the country, and which he had experienced first hand at Columbia in the spring of 1968. He owned land in a number of rural areas, and heard about the communes developing near one in Vermont. He proposed, and we accepted, the idea of a dissertation studying such a commune. While he and we shared sympathy with the goals of such efforts, we were also professionally skeptical, and we were all far too mainstream to join them. Barry, and we, could have been charged with voyeurism for our interest in such counter culture phenomena, but all anthropology is inherently voyeuristic. Even if more true in this instance than others, it was only a part of the motivation. Unique, ephemeral, and possibly non-repeatable events were happening. Applied, or even policy relevant, anthropology had to be there. The main point of the study was to describe what was happening.

The study took over his life for years. It is not fair to say that he went native. He always maintained some physical distance—in the field, e.g., he usually lived in his VW camper, not in the communal houses. As his comments about his field notes in the Prologue indicate, Barry maintained intellectual distance as well. He was deeply troubled by the immaturity, the conflicts, and the pettiness that he observed. His anti-authority stance also made him leery, if not critical of self-proclaimed leaders, messianic or otherwise, like James and Roy. He remained in the field until the outcome of Jackson's Meadows had traveled its full cycle, and continued to follow up this research for years afterwards.

But the intellectual paradox of studying Jackson's Meadows was that to study it you had to join it. The boundaries were fairly vague, and it didn't take much to join, but Barry was in fact a member of the group he was studying as much as most of the people described in his research. His way of handling the inevitable split between Laffan as researcher and Laffan as *de facto* member was novel. He acknowledged that on several occasions he had an impact in a definite way on what he was studying: he stopped a fight, mediated a conflict, told DT he had to leave, etc. As ethnographer he assiduously reported his role, but gave the name Patrick to the actor he wrote about. This was never a deception on his part; I do not recall any effort to pretend to me or others that Patrick was anyone else. It was simply that this community required membership if you were to study it, and when he was acting as member, or solely as actor in this social milieu, not as an anthropologist, he was Patrick. It was the anthropologist Barry who would go back to his camper and type his fieldnotes every night, no matter how much "Patrick" had drunk during the evening. I came to see this as a necessary defense for him regarding the conflict inevitable between the participant and the observer that this setting intensified by insisting on membership. He separated them: Barry is the author: one of the people he observes, and dispassionately speculates about, is Patrick. Readers can judge for themselves how this works.

Since Barry's fieldwork, some writers in our discipline urged us to become "the Other," not just study the other, in order to gain true understanding. This position has led some to formulate a sharp answer that becoming like your subjects is not a reasonable goal of the fieldwork process. Most of us today would argue that any anthropologist who claimed to have "become a native" or to understand his group as a native would, was engaging in self delusion. How in 12-18 months of fieldwork could anyone accomplish what socialization had taken decades for the others to accomplish? Further, how could the anthropologist pretend one's previous life experiences were no longer operative?

In Barry's case, however, he was studying people who had grown up in the same society as himself, and some had backgrounds similar to his. The community which was unique to them—and which he was to study—was itself only months old and still in formation throughout his fieldwork. If Barry claims an understanding as an insider, the claim would have more legitimacy than if he were to have studied Pukapuka. Finally, I think Barry was also always aware that he had an outsider perspective—his analysis sections are clearly outsider perspectives—and that these have shaped his understanding of what these people are about.

As a work in anthropology when it was done, the study was respectful of, and provided careful description of, the words and models of the participants. Barry's use of their words for many of his categories in this book, e.g., street kids, over 30s, IBMs are good examples. To this essentially emic frame, he also uses etic concepts and frames: social class, family of origin characteristics, etc. These constitute a kind of dialectic between Patrick and Barry, between participant and observer, between the other and the ontological frame.

Some readers may be troubled by Barry's poetic writing style in this version which occasionally puts you in someone else's head as if those dialectics had not taken place: "Peter thought that...Jessie believed that.., etc." Methodologically these are indeed quite troubling: we can't ever know what is claimed to be known. But he would write this only when the individual involved had in fact told him what he remembered thinking at the time, and that most of the participants so described had in fact read parts of the manuscript and vouched for it. While I would argue that this still told us nothing about what they were actually thinking at the time of the action, I take the descriptions as based upon self report data. Readers can make this correction for themselves. If you see "Peter thought that...", simply read it as "Peter said he thought that."

When Barry and I parted that weekend in 1975, the third of his manuscript which became his dissertation was still almost 600 pages long, and by the time his dissertation typist—no computers in those days—followed marginal requirements for the library the dissertation was over 1,000 pages. Dalton had become so anti-authority that he avoided perishing by, in the words of this book, moving from SS academics to Alteria to seek alternatives in a provincial college. The final defense committee consisted of me as sponsor, Conrad

Arensberg, Lambros Comitas, Herbert Passin (a GSAS sociologist of Japan from Barry's earlier life), and Janet Dolgin (a young symbolic anthropologist who joined the faculty after Barry had begun fieldwork). Some of them were disturbed by the length of the document—longer than any of them had seen in their careers, and they complained to me in various ways; they were mollified when I told them that more than two thirds had been cut! Since it told a story that was complete, but had various stages, they had no cuts to suggest either. It was still a work on a grand scale, and the depth of data was seen as overwhelming whatever problems were in the manuscript. The committee not only approved the dissertation as written, but they nominated it for the Bancroft Award, the highest award for dissertations on topics relating to American history, and which would have come with assured publication. The Bancroft trustees award that year went instead to Elizabeth P. McAughey for her study of *William Samuel Johnson: Loyalist and Founding Father*.

After his defense Barry put the manuscript aside. I think he was actually fonder of some of the material we had taken out than what was included, and while I urged him to publish all three volumes, nothing happened. After all, the question of "was it anthropology" was not relevant anymore, and he agreed that what was most defensible for his committee was not necessarily synonymous with what was most important to publish. He talked about getting them ready for publication. He took a job teaching at Marlboro College and devoted increasing time to students and other applied projects, while continuing to update material on individuals.

After many years, he left Vermont, and resettled in Florida, teaching at Florida State University and becoming involved in many novel applied projects, many of which concerned community development in rural areas. I remember him calling me after the first year there to express delight in having left winter and mud season behind forever. In the end, the only manuscript he prepared for publication was this one, and he died before it came out. Joanna Mauer told me that she has found what looks like the remains of the other manuscript pieces and that they may be published in the future.

So this book could have and should have been published more than twenty years ago. Had it been, the events described would have been closer to their own time, and, I suspect, not as surrealistic as they appear with hindsight. Readers are about to embark on a unique journey to a time not so long ago, in a place not so far away. For those of us who lived as adults during that time it will be a reminder of that time, for those not alive then, I wonder what you will make of it. Will you find Jackson's Meadows a very foreign place, or will you recognize these data as exemplifying more general human themes that render the bizarre familiar and predictable?

Charles Harrington, Ph.D.
Professor of Anthropology, Psychology and Education
and Chairperson of the Department of Scientific Foundations
Teachers College, Columbia University
April 2, 1997

Communal Organization and Social Transition

A Case Study
from the Counterculture
of the Sixties and Seventies

Prologue

This book is based on a participant observation field study I conducted of a commune located among a cluster of other communes that thrived in Northern New England in the early 1970s. Since over twenty years have passed since its completion, it is in a sense an historical work. But it is also more than that. It is a detailed account written from a social scientific perspective of fast moving, urgent events in intensely hopeful and fearful times. As such, it provides the critical kinds of detail in an instance of rapid American social change that were often neither noticed or remembered by the active participants, nor available to scholars seeking to reconstruct the dynamic afterwards. Because I tried to organize the accounts of events systematically and put them into some context along the way, I believe they can also yield some insights into our society's present and future conditions as part of an ongoing evolutionary process.

Although I had planned research as a graduate student in other areas at the time, in 1968 I was suddenly swept away like many others there by the student rebellion at Columbia University. My head swam with the ideas and attitudes that exploded in the throes of institutional and neighborhood, and eventually nationwide, catharsis. Simultaneously seduced by the utopian promises, yet repulsed by the runaway fantasies that accompanied them, I watched the rebellion unfold to include communalism and collectivism as positive ideals, along with negative stances regarding racism, war, corporate capitalism, and after the police riots at the Democratic National Convention in Chicago, the established political process. If this incipient "cultural revolution" was to succeed, it would have to be able to propose genuine alternatives to current institutions it was attacking. Because the social and political issues appeared so vast and important, because communalism appeared to me to be the all-inclusive phenomenon that embodied the alternative values and ideals being proposed, and because communes could manifest themselves in very tangible and testable ways, I determined that I would apply my research skills there instead.

Using contacts gained through the Liberation News Service, which was the foremost underground news organization of the time also springing from the Columbia rebellion, I set out to gain entry to a commune only three hours away in Western Massachusetts. Tainted as part of the establishment academic world, I was refused entry as a possible informer and/or exploiter of this deliberately seditious, revolutionary enterprise. But shortly afterward, through a different part of the Columbia underground network, I was invited to make a trip to a non-political, back-to-the-land commune situated in southern Vermont; a half hour's drive further north. I was to remain associated with this commune and, through it, all the surprisingly many other communes in the area it was associated with (including the one that initially rejected me) for many years.

The field study was concentrated in the period from early 1970 through late 1972; earlier events being articulated through many hours of cross-referencing interviews, and later events monitored regularly through 1975. The fieldwork and interviews encompassed all communes in the area and their related goings-on, many of which were known superficially by the general public at the time through spotty news coverage. A first draft was completed in 1973, but because of its large size and broad scope, it was cut down to manageable proportions in 1975 by focusing primarily on the commune I knew best: Jackson's Meadows. The deleted material, which in my opinion and in the views of others who know it contains some very interesting historical as well as social scientific material, still sits in unpublishable form.

This current book, however, is the result of further editing designed to eliminate the worst instances of dissertationese in an effort to make it more readable, and was completed in 1976. Because by then academic as well as popular interest in communes had waned, the publishing industry had significantly altered its practices, and I had gone on to other projects, it too sat unpublished. Only now, after a rebirth of some interest in the phenomenon, new developments in publishing, and circumstances which have allowed me the time to add some more editorial touches, has its publication been possible.

This recent editorial work did not include an update* or a reinterpretation based on twenty years of subsequent hindsight, though I must say that hindsight has not caused me to wish I had come to conclusions different from the ones I did. In fact, I believe they were surprisingly on the mark. Accordingly, a follow-up study of the people, institutions and region would be fascinating to undertake now in order to put the analysis to the test nearly a generation later, but that must wait. More important, I felt, was to get this volume out first, capturing the flavor and complexity of the times. To the best of my knowledge, no other similar study was published then or has been since.

The editorial work also did not involve changing any of the fictitious names given to people and locations back to their actual names. The pseudonyms were originally employed to prevent identification at the time, thereby protecting people from future legal problems, discrimination, embarrassment, retribution, and the like. These people, many of whose names were not their real ones in the first place, were indeed wanted by law enforcement authorities, targeted for harassment by former acquaintances, or sought for various other reasons, and for all I know, still are. Others are now well known and respected in their areas of activity and they might not appreciate parts of their past lives being exposed in

_____

* *An epilogue was added posthumously.*

such a raw manner. Because sufficient time has passed and overall danger has receded, some relaxation in identity protection is called for, however, at least in terms of the geographical area. "Provincia," the name given to the region in the text, actually refers to Vermont and nearby parts of western Massachusetts and New Hampshire. "Centerville," the town around which many key events occurred, is actually Brattleboro, Vermont, and the foreign country, "Alteria," is of course Canada; specifically Quebec province.

The general approach to the text has also remained untouched. It was designed to avoid certain forms of scholarly protocol that I regarded then, and still do now, as needing counterbalance. It addresses excessive social scientific specialization and compartmentalization by taking the traditional anthropological, holistic, integrated approach, aimed at a broader, multifaceted understanding, even if necessarily somewhat less precise. Accordingly, it takes on an entire sociohistorical event; not just certain slices of it for possible piecemeal comparisons elsewhere, monitoring the interplay of the many factors that always impinge on real life situations. It also incorporates and reconciles various possible alternate interpretations rooted in a number of different relevant disciplines, such as microeconomics, political philosophy, psychology, and sociology. The analysis is mostly qualitative rather than quantitative, in that statistical reliability concerning the kinds and levels of phenomena observed was either impossible or irrelevant to achieve. It is essentially a community study (mixed in with a little network analysis), something increasingly rarely undertaken these days usually for reasons other than those concerning intellectual or scientific rigor. While its findings cannot be applied to all societies, communities, movements, and collective organizations everywhere, it is a relevant case study, for reasons made clear in its concluding pages, and certainly is representative of similar situations elsewhere, perhaps revealing some subtle principles common to all.

Participant observation, so often criticized by other social science disciplines for the bias it engenders as a research method, is still probably the best way to understand human behavior in context, which is to say, in real life. I tried to minimize my biases by checking my own subjectivity in a number of ways. The description of events is deliberately separated from my analysis, thereby facilitating the portrayal of events as objectively as possible, while freely acknowledging that any analytical framework, including my own, is a ultimately a subjective choice for interpretation. But, I also happen to believe, of course, that my choice in this regard was the best I could make in approaching empirical accuracy. Thus each chapter (except chapters 1 and 2) is divided into two distinct descriptive and analytical sections. This format will also allow the reader to choose the manner in which he or she prefers to read the book, focusing on "story line," or discussion, or both.

Also, the account is written in the third person so as to make it more difficult for me to slide into less careful observation and more egocentric perspectives that first person writing more easily permits. Like so many anthropologists in the field who struggle with the objectivity issue, I kept two sets of notes, one of which was my "content" set, which is the basis for this book. The other, the "research process" set, consisted of personal railings and musings about people and events and dealt with various other issues. These included problems of my exhaustion of keeping pace with and recording so much activity, the sometimes extremely dangerous situations I had to face, research ethics, and gaining access to underground or secret organizations. Of special concern were problems arising from participant observation research in one's own society and in close knit groups where everyone, including me, was regarded as either part of a problem, or part of a solution, but never free to be even remotely uninvolved. As my research training did not adequately prepare me for all of this, these notes could also someday become the basis for another book. Where I was obligated to play an important active participant role in events I refer to myself in the text as "Patrick."

Finally, the people who were the subjects of the study provided an acid test of any biases I might have expressed. During the exhaustive interviews that followed the intensive fieldwork period, I often organized my questions around what I indicated were my necessarily limited perceptions and interpretations of past events. Eliminating as much as possible any unconscious prompting, I asked my respondents to contrast their own perceptions and interpretations of events with mine to point out my possible errors. Because of the extreme diversity of backgrounds and interests among people in the milieu, there was little danger of skewed results due to some kind of monolithic defensive collective consciousness, and this became increasingly clear as I proceeded with each interview to refine fact and synthesize opinion. At the end, I felt that nearly everyone had been honest with themselves and with me, many painfully facing up to their failed expectations and false assumptions that would have been so easy to deny. In fact, some experienced outright catharsis during the interviews; one proclaiming that it was the least expensive, shortest and most effective therapy he had ever had.

After the study had been completed and written up, with no small amount of anxiety, I circulated copies to some of my potentially toughest critics for their reaction. Unlike most anthropologists in the field, my work had to survive the scrutiny of a study population that included published authors, social essayists and Ph.Ds. Although never intending to change any major conclusions on the basis of their criticism, I nevertheless was greatly relieved when they all admitted there was nothing in it they could really argue with, and that it gave them a kind of overview they had never had before.

But the road to the finished project was a long and difficult one.

I began with what amounts to journalistic kinds of questions: what was the counterculture developing as a model for its alternative society, how well would it meet real human needs, and what would be the likelihood for its success? With neat, compartmentalized preconceptions in tow, derived from media reports and from debates within university circles, I arrived in the field to find utter chaos. There was no order I could find or hold onto long enough against which to measure and compare any general notion. The first day alone, I had unwittingly participated in a burglary, nearly got into a wreck on the interstate as my contacts in my car were exchanging drugs with the occupants of a speeding tractor trailer truck that had pulled along beside us, and had to sleep on an uninsulated shack floor that was so painfully cold I was certain I would get frostbite. And the reason I was forced to sleep there was because, to my horror, I had arrived to find that the main building had burned to the ground the previous night, incinerating four people alive. That was only a taste of things to come, which included death threats, sorcery, security checks by revolutionary groups, surveillance by the FBI who intended to make me testify in a grand jury investigation, riotous celebrations, and constant coming and going and moving in and out of different communes and projects.

The only way to get a handle on it all was to take the hippie advice, consummately adaptive in that environment, to "let go" of preconceptions and agendas, and "go with the flow." Once I had become accustomed to my kaleidoscopic field environment, I began to see patterns in the motion and commotion; kinds of systematic repetitions and nuances detectable only with the passage of time. Accordingly, chronology became the first organizing principle, and careful notation of systematic phenomena within it, the next. Eventually, the dynamics could be sufficiently articulated such that basic social and behavioral scientific concepts, once reworked so as to make them more amenable to a state of constant motion, could be dropped successfully into the stream of events.

All this led me to a general systems theory orientation. Through exposure to the field situation, I eventually became convinced, because of the accelerated rate of social time and structural change I was witnessing, that I had stumbled into a discernible, tangible burst of social micro-evolutionary process. It was a field scientist's dream: a naturally occurring virtual laboratory in which observable applied experiments would be devised and tested on their own. All I had to do was to keep up with them all.

In writing this book, I had to significantly modify this and other simplistic notions, but nevertheless outlined what I believed then and believe now to be an important, pivotal instance of a fundamental shift in American society through a process that generally remains underrecognized or underappreciated. With the subsequent concerns and issues of the intervening years, interest has faded even further, except perhaps as popularly restimulated by 60s nostalgia in the mass media targeted at aging hippies-turned-yuppies.

This general unawareness is unfortunate. I would argue that counter cultures are with us more than ever, proliferating particularly in the 80s. Only now they tend to be fragmented, visionless, and self-concerned, and thus are often more sinister, such as in new events surrounding social service availability, drugs, white supremacy, homelessness and high finance. Rather than proposing uplifting, even if naive, alternatives for everyone, they are more a means of coping and self preservation by different isolated, struggling segments of society responding to ever greater pressures. They are the signs and artifacts of needed fundamental adaptive adjustments for the society as a whole, and closer examination of parallels with the communal and counterculture movements would make clear how that is so.

It is also unfortunate that interest in the communal/countercultural phenomenon has waned. Closer examination would make it clear that many of the more positive elements of current American life actually have their roots in them. Among the most notable of these would be greater opportunity for women, environmental sensitivity, reduced nuclear risk, more open relations in the workplace, health awareness, and the availability of broader life choices. In these instances, the movements of the late 60s and early 70s led in the effort to make fundamental societal readjustments necessary to relieve the growing problems and strains of those times.

Jackson's Meadows and its surrounding groups and institutions played of course, only a very small role, but it is an illustrative one nonetheless. Although it was finally formally dissolved in 1987, many of its former members and friends continue to be active and influential in various ways in the area and elsewhere. The fields, forests, and buildings still exist with entirely new people living there who themselves profess commitment to applicable and more workable original counterculture ideals and practices. The quality of life has improved significantly in Brattleboro, Vermont and Western New England through the 70s and 80s in no small measure, I would argue, due to the impact and ripple effect that Jackson's Meadows and others in its milieu had. And while much of the rest of the country has experienced a conservative backlash since, this region shows no signs yet of changing the overall course set in motion back then. The following pages will attempt to show how the process began, follow the surprising and sometimes terrible twists and turns it took, and point out, at least in part, how it has come to be part of a legacy important to the region and beyond.

Barry Laffan
1990

1. Confusion: The Local Counterculture in Provincia

One evening in March, 1970, Jesse, one of the founding members of Jackson's Meadow Commune, lit up a joint and proceeded to write a piece for a newspaper later to be distributed throughout the quiet countryside. He began:

"Cities are burning. Youth is rising up against the monster. Tearing down the walls that separate us—tearing down the machinery with a new force—People Power. Sisters and brothers are beginning to move from every direction. Students are turning on to drugs and to each other. The working class is making demands on the bosses to meet the needs of the people by equal share of resources. Third World Vanguard movements saying, 'off our backs pig power structure—up against the wall.' Now is not the time for reform, but the time to piss on the Pentagon, paint the White House red, avenge the death of Fred Hampton, avenge the murder of Che.

We have begun to avenge the murder of the mind. Kids turning against their parents. Workers stealing from their bosses and not from each other. Bosses, the ones with the controlling interest in this country. Those are the cats that make us slaves, gettin' a huge slice of what should be our pie. Those are the cats that want us to believe materials breed pure happiness under this Fascist state. It is like looking for the end of a bag of grass. You see the material up front. You hope to make it yours; profit from it. Well, all you really have to do is get stoned and dig on the way you feel. No end in sight, only dreams that will come true when we are together. If you don't like the State's product, don't buy it."

It began an article that went on to describe how a commune movement had already begun and how it should continue to embody a viable psychosocial alternative to a collapsing society, serving as a spearhead of constructive change for everyone. Although sounding historically outdated and naive just a few years later, it accurately reflected the mood of the time, at least in his milieu. And though the rhetoric has quieted since, and along with it many assumptions, much of the malaise and turmoil is still present in American society. In these two paragraphs, Jesse touches on the central themes of social change; from mass uprisings to alterations of individual consciousness, industrial production to biological function, vested interests to ephemeral fantasies, being together in life to being alone in death. Deep and fundamental changes in any society must affect every avenue of human experience, and Jesse's article only began to describe some of the ramifications.

Jackson's Meadows was one of the communes established in the midst of all this turmoil. The story of its inception, growth, decline, rejuvenation, and transition, it can be argued, recapitulates in microcosm the history of the "cultural revolution" of the late 1960s and early 1970s. Similarly, a careful analysis of the dynamics in and around JM (Jackson's Meadows) gives insight into the whys, hows, and whos of this deep societal transformation that generated many common social forms and practices taken for granted not too many years later. Although later manifestations and permutations largely masked the exploratory roots illustrated by JM at the time, the case study of JM demonstrates the complexity of factors, ideas, and emotions involved when a collection of individuals faced and made critical decisions to transform their individual lives. And viewed in the aggregate, it shows the way the composite of these decisions and actions constituted social process and change.

In order to better understand the "counterculture" (CC) phenomenon and the society that gave birth to it, and which was subsequently significantly altered by it, many specific questions about JM must be asked. Why was this commune formed? How was its organizational form supposed to correct the ills of society, and to what extent was it only symptomatic of larger changes already underway in America? What were the special opportunities for individual change and growth that it opened up, and what were the inherent problems and dangers? Who were the people drawn to it, and why? What experiences did they share before getting involved, and how did their different backgrounds concerning sex, age, education, or socioeconomic class affect the dynamic outcome of the JM experience in terms of new statuses, skills, and self-concepts? Indeed, what does Jackson's Meadows tell us in general about special environments conducive to radical behavior change; about the interplay between social situation and the personalities of the people involved in that situation; about the similarities and differences between psychological and sociological interpretations of the same events?

There are also questions concerning the manner in which the internal dynamics of the commune and the life trajectories of the individuals in it fit into a larger picture. Why did the communal form emerge from a general movement for social change, and how did it become a catalyst for further change? More specifically, how did JM as a certain kind of commune interact with others—including religious, political, psychotherapeutic, and artistic—to affect the fates of certain organized movements within the overall CC? In fact, how does it help explain the development of the CC in the first place and the subsequent conflict with the mainstream "straight society" (SS)? Ultimately, did JM as a manifestation of the CC really succeed or fail as a causative agent for social change?

Going beyond specific sociocultural phenomena, what does JM tell us about the relationship between ideologies (the way the human mind sets personal and social goals and rationalizes behavior) and ecologies (the way external material and societal forces channel behavior and constrain social form)? And what is the function of altered states of consciousness in achieving altered states of sociopolitical organization? What does it say about the simultaneous and interdependent roles of conflict, cooperation, and competition in human affairs; about the appearance of centers of power and social hierarchy even in ostensibly egalitarian groups; about the dynamics of change in postindustrial societies and the evolution of all social systems?

Of course JM is not going to provide complete answers to these questions, nor will it even concern them all to the same extent. But the details of the sometimes chaotic events depicted here eventually weave themselves into a coherent fabric with few loose ends. The fabric can only be complete and integrated if contexts as well as focal phenomena are presented. In fact, without context, any extrapolation of the meaning of JM events to broader areas of our society would be impossible. Accordingly, before the account of JM begins, the region in which JM is located, the structure of various subcultures concerned, and the mood of the times are described.

Provincia and the Centerville Area

Provincia is the name given to one of a limited number of regions in America that attracted numerous active and formerly active hippies, radicals, new religion converts, artists, and intellectuals from 1968 to 1972 and beyond. During this period, there was a virtual migration underway. Those who had seen the failure of the Haight-Ashbury Summer of Love, the debacle of the Chicago demonstrations at the Democratic National Convention, the futility of the efforts to halt the invasion of Cambodia, and even the inability of the urban environment in general to permit a less than frenetic lifestyle, headed for the open countryside. In rural areas there was more room for nonconformist or experimental behavior, and fewer watchful eyes to observe it.

Why did Provincia become a center of activity for activists and dropouts from urban areas and university settings? The answer lies in the quiet and aesthetics of the natural environment, the low population density, yet the proximity to stimulating urban zones, and a long tradition of self-sufficiency coupled with community-oriented attitudes and lifestyles that appealed to evolving CC ideals. The specific vehicles that brought them there, besides some early communal experiments, were the relatively large number of colleges in the region, underutilized or vacant country homes owned by wealthier, older relatives, and inexpensive land made available by the shrinking farm economy.

The sketch of the region offered here is deliberately scrambled to help protect the identities of participants, many of whom in both the CC and SS were breaking laws and accepted ethical codes at the time, and are still living there. The region can be described as roughly rectangular, 250 miles across by 330 miles long, containing 825,000 square miles in all. Its boundaries do not coincide with state lines, but are instead formed by geographical features. It consists of rather hilly and mountainous areas cut by river valleys, particularly one large valley that runs through the entire region. The north's boundary is a region in which the hills gradually diminish into flat land. The south edge is also characterized by lowlands, but has a series of waterways in addition, making the boundaries more exact. A widening river valley and rolling topography continue to the east, while a very flat and extensive region lies to the west. Also further to the west is the border with a foreign nation that will be called Alteria.

Provincia has boundaries near larger population concentrations, particularly to the east and north where there is extensive manufacturing and commerce. The flat lands to the west are agricultural. Only to the west is the population equally as sparse, for beyond the flatlands there lies another mountainous region. There are two large urban centers located within a day's drive: one to the northeast and one to the southeast.

Life in Provincia has always been rough for its settlers. The growing season is short and the soil thin and rocky. Snow covers the ground several months of the year, and freezing temperatures can occur early and extend late into spring. There is a spring thaw season, when most of the dirt roads turn to mud and are often impassable. In addition to snow and mud, rough terrain has usually made travel and communication between farms, settlements, and towns difficult. Despite the harsh winters and muddy spring, Provincia is regarded as a very scenic region attracting many tourists and sportsmen each year. It is a four season recreational area with resorts and camping in the summer, hunting and colorful foliage in the fall, skiing in the winter, and fishing in the spring. Many vacation homes and much acreage was, and still is, owned by residents of the high population density centers to the north and east, causing a weekend ebb and flow into and out of the region.

In contrast to the vacationers are the natives whose income, employment, and style of life then reflected a condition that was far from affluent. Provincia was characterized by a high rate of rural and small town poverty and unemployment with relatively high welfare expenditures. Older industries were folding, especially with the inflation/recession of the late 60s and early 70s, but new manufacturing and subsidiaries of large corporations such as GE and IBM had been started because of tax concessions and cheap labor. Labor requirements were mostly unskilled, with almost all management positions being filled by migrants. Small locally owned machine industries were being bought up by large corporations who then operated them as subsidiaries. So did most of the mining, skiing, and lumbering operations. As of 1973 there was little organized labor of any consequence.

Much of the native population was supported by small business and family enterprises. A significant portion was involved in small scale independent agricultural operations, but this sector was rapidly shrinking. There were in the mid-1950s more than 20,000 farms present, but by the early 1970s the number declined to around 5,000. Families who held farm and forest acreage for generations began selling their land to ski interests, real estate developers, and timber and paper companies, such as International Paper, Weyerhauser, and Boise-Cascade who were and still are moving into the resort and recreation business.

The cost of living was high and wages were well below the national average. Unemployment was particularly high in the one part of the region where older industry used to be concentrated. Taxes were high in one administrative region to support tax incentives for new industry, while in another, taxes at the town level supported virtually all public services. The level of reading comprehension of children in schools was comparable to urban ghetto areas. One third of Provincia's population lived below the federally established poverty line. If Provincia were comparable to an entire state, it would rank as the sixth poorest in the union in terms of annual income at the time.

Political and administrative organization was decentralized, with the bulk of decision making and financing falling at the local rather than county or state levels. Town councilmen were powerful figures, but all citizens could actively participate in local governments at town sponsored meetings. Political independence had always been a hallmark of Provincia; its history marked by rebellion, moves toward independence, and querulous negotiations with the federal government. Provincia also contributed more than its share of mystical prophets and religious leaders. Before the Civil War, a number of historically documented communes were formed in the area, while individuals born and raised there began what is still a major American religious sect. Both innovation and deep conservatism characterized the region's family life. On the one hand, a few multigenerational farm families survived, while in the past, social activists openly experimented with group marriage, polygamy, and free love relationships. In short, the region has served as a kind of social laboratory in which new and old forms have been permitted to flourish with relative immunity from the influence of national norms.

Most of Provincia's CC activities occurred in and around a town given the name Centerville. The most frequent contact between communes and other alternative institutions occurred here. Only one commune had regular contacts outside this area, while Jackson's Meadows functioned almost totally in and around Centerville. Relatively small, the town had a population of 12,000 in 1970. The entire 40 square-mile area in and around Centerville had an estimated population of 35,000. Much of the area was involved in small scale farming and forest operations in the rural sectors. Two ski areas were situated on the northeast fringe. In addition to the many small businesses, there were 11 factories and institutions that employed over 100 people each, two related to agriculture, two hospitals, and the rest manufacturing. In a town near Centerville was a recently completed power plant. Only four of Centerville's 31 factories and institutions were unionized. The average wage for manufacturing was $2.45 an hour and there had never been a labor strike.

Educational institutions played a significant role in the Centerville area. An institution referred to here as Knowland College was private and nonsectarian with 800 students and 61 faculty. Noted for its liberal policies toward students (students belonged to the board of trustees) and the sense of community that small colleges aspire toward, it was also known for its low standards of scholarship. But it did have high tuition, attracting youth from well-to-do families who failed to make it into more prestigious colleges. Knowland College also had its share of radical students dismissed from other schools and other varieties of dropouts who attempted to survive there. There was also a small avant-garde graduate school of education and an administrative and training center for foreign and student exchange programs. The area also boasted an exclusive private school for boys and girls from wealthy families.

In the mountains outside Centerville, located near the ski areas, was another college. Also private, nonsectarian and accredited, this school was even smaller than Knowland, with 150 students and 30 faculty in 1970. Its size rather than its liberalism went further than Knowland in creating a sense of community. In fact, the college referred to itself as "the community," and it was partly administered through democratic "town meetings" in which students, faculty, staff, and their families all participated. Some students, however, found the intensity, isolation, and constant pressure of small community living very restrictive. Like other small colleges, it relied heavily on the arts and humanities, and was widely known for a summer music festival held there.

Inside Centerville itself was an even smaller college, begun in 1964, struggling to survive with thirty-five students and five faculty, called George Grayson College in this study. From this tiny institution, caught in the throes of a student rebellion, Jackson's Meadows commune was born.

Rounding out this portrait of the Centerville area is an outline of the public administration network. Most of the surrounding towns sent their high-school students to the Centerville Union School, which had an enrollment of over 1500. All the younger children went to local town schools. The school district was reputed to be one of the best in the region.

There was a state police barracks in the area and a county sheriff's office. Centerville itself had a police staff of 24 with three patrol cars. There was one judge for a criminal court that handled everything from traffic tickets to burglary, and there were six small law firms, none of whose members were trained in the region. The county had one district attorney, and the smaller towns elected peace officers who were authorized to issue summonses and make arrests. A regional employment security office in Centerville kept track of job openings and issued unemployment checks. The unemployed registered at the office, particularly those wishing to receive welfare or food stamps. Also located in Centerville, the welfare center played a central role in the lives of many area "longhairs" (a name often applied to CC types). Centerville's Memorial Hospital had 100 beds, while the 350-bed Centerville Sanitorium served the emotionally disturbed from all over the region. There were 18 churches in town with a number of others in small surrounding towns. Church people coordinated a series of youth centers that followed one another into and out of existence over the period of four years covered in this study.

Centerville had a salaried town manager selected by a town council that consisted of five members. Much of the administrative bureaucracy for the town, such as agencies concerned with water, sewage, or tax collection and assessment, was located in the police station/courthouse. Centerville had had a planning commission since 1932 and a zoning ordinance since 1948.

Wilfred, the name given to the town in which JM was located, was typical of the smaller rural towns. It had no town manager, but did have two councilmen and a chief councilman elected every two years. Other elected officials were the road commissioner, town clerk, peace officer, and health commissioner. Wilfred also had a five-member planning commission that was created in 1969. This late inception was finally brought about for two reasons. The first stems from the fact that regional authorities became increasingly aware of the encroachment of urbanization and pollution into their land, and Wilfred was forced to conform. The second reason was the growing fear that the "hippie invasion" and communes in the town would get out of control. On September 1, 1969, the Wilfred commission came up with a stop-gap set of interim zoning regulations due to expire in two years, when more permanent ones could be formulated and voted on. The interim regulations were fearfully and hurriedly installed after only four months of Jackson's Meadows' tumultuous existence.

CC Populations

Because the concept and reality of the counterculture that existed then is central to this study, an attempt at defining it is necessary. It can perhaps best be approached by pinpointing certain subpopulations in a semi-amorphous social sphere that consisted of a hard core of participants with increasingly less defined inner and outer layers of affiliates and sympathizers surrounding it. At the periphery were the most ill-defined and fluid groups; many individuals from which could easily be considered "straight" and, as such, members of the SS.

College and student populations constituted one of these groups. While many students and CC people not in school shared similar lifestyles and basic antagonisms toward American society, actual student contact with hard-core "freaks" (another term commonly applied to CC people) was a surer indicator of inclusion in the CC. Students often had non-student freak friends living with them off-campus, whose lifestyle easily rubbed off on them. The off-campus freaks tended to cluster around colleges usually had the same intellectual and aesthetic interests. Thus student and non-student CC people engaged in the same activities outside the college context, which drew them into a common network.

The "street scene" constituted another, but less peripheral population. The majority of street people dressed hip and hung out with their friends under relatively uncontrolled circumstances. Unlike the college crowd, they tended to be poor and disinterested students, coming from borderline low-middle-class backgrounds, with a sizable sprinkling of blue-collar and poverty-class youth thrown in. This clearly distinguished them from the teenyboppers of the mid-sixties who often came from upper-middle-class suburbs with expensive pseudobohemian clothes to weekend in urban hippie centers. The street-people group also contained what in former days would have been called juvenile delinquents, who in turn had a close affiliation with the SS down-and-outers who frequented Centerville's honky-tonk bars and billiard parlors.

Just as there were hard-core college-oriented freaks, there were also hard-core street freaks. These people were older or had already dropped out of school. Most were unemployed or part-time workers, either by choice or by circumstance, leaving them with little money. Many drifted from town to town looking for a niche. Like residents of urban ghettos, they were street-wise, flirting with an underworld life, instinctively fending for themselves while trying not to expose any vulnerability. They were resourceful in scrounging up spending money and places to stay. The most successful, with a disarming friendliness, could charm the most reticent acquaintances and could get people who were just as poor as they were to lend them a few dollars. They could also be quite violent and abusive when the situation called for it.

In one spot downtown, on warm summer afternoons, as many as 30 youth, some barely pubescent and others in their early twenties, sat on the park bench, stretched out on the grass, and sprawled over the church steps. Although marijuana was not openly smoked on Main Street, cheap wine and malt liquor was sipped from vessels concealed in paper bags. A public town building served as the location for Hotline, a youth drug crisis center. LSD and other drugs were easily obtained in this scene; some people getting theirs from a supposed drug counselor inside the Hotline building. Tabs of acid (LSD) were inconspicuously "dropped" in the shadow of the old church steeple.

Carloads of freaks passed by on the street, frequently waving and loudly yelling to one another. This eventually ruffled the dignity of elderly passersby, who either lectured them on good manners or complained further on down the street. Occasionally, shiny cars with loud exhaust pipes pulled up in front of the group to drop someone off or to pick up "the town whore." The people from the communes, students from the colleges, and youth from outside Centerville occasionally dropped by to exchange gossip. Hitchhikers with backpacks straggled into town and joined the scene, asking: "Where can I get a cheap meal? Where can I cop some dope? Is there any place around here I can crash tonight? Can you tell me how to get to Jackson's Meadows?"

These hitchhikers formed part of the hip circuit population. It consisted of people who drifted from street scene to street scene, commune to commune, college town to college town, coast to coast. Some were veteran street people, others touring college kids, some runaways, and others fugitives from the police. Many were older people leaving jobs or family situations who were searching for new direction in their lives. This drifting was not a haphazard affair. A kind of floating social circulation system ran through all areas of the country where there were communes, large or progressive colleges, urban bohemian centers, and certain wilderness camping areas. By jumping into the flow and asking for recommendations as to where to go and who to contact, CC neophytes could locate these circulation centers. Veteran freaks also traveled on the hip circuit constantly, often having a home base, or two, or three. These flow channels passed through Provincia bringing many strangers and old friends into the region while taking others away.

Another segment of the CC consisted of hip entrepreneurial enterprises. These were usually small business ventures run by individuals, couples, or a small group of friends. Known as "hip capitalists" or "hippie rip-offs" within the CC, these people were often accused of having sold out the ideals of the new society. The most common hip businesses were arts and crafts shops, health food stores, clothing boutiques, music and record stores, and emporia known as "head shops" that sold assorted hippie paraphernalia. Much of hip enterprise clientele were longhairs or former longhairs, thus accounting for much of the animosity existing between antimaterialist freak customers, who were indeed materially deprived, and their profit-making, store-owning counterparts. While some freaks didn't mind if hip businesses just ripped off SS customers, many were critical of hip capitalists co-opting creations of the freak culture for distribution into the SS, thereby destroying the identity of the CC. Another segment of the freak community supplied goods to be sold, however. This wholesaling was another important source of income for many in the CC.

Most of these enterprises performed social services for the CC. Many carried literature providing information on such things as crafting techniques, cooking methods, or growing one's own marijuana. Bulletin boards were maintained, serving as communication centers in their communities. A few served as distribution centers for regional food cooperatives. Occasionally, hip facilities were made available for cultural, political, or entertainment events. Sometimes these services were rendered with a mix of guilt and resentment, however. In Centerville, there was a clothing boutique owner who had organized events at Knowland college while a student there. But when he became a hip businessman, radicals called him a "pig," and hippie women browsed in his store to rip off anything they could get away with. His losses, he claimed, chewed up 40% of his profits. At the height of his troubles, he made available to the hip community an empty back room for use as a "free store," an enterprise in which donated goods could be distributed free of charge. No one accepted his offer.

A list of these small businesses in the Centerville area will give some idea of the role they played in the local overall economy. In 1972 there were seven health food stores, one of which did a volume of business second only to three large chain supermarkets in town. Called The Soft Touch, it sold quality wines and cheeses at reasonable prices, in addition to vitamins, organic foods and grains, and provided an outlet for exotic items that would otherwise never have found their way into the region.

Seven craft-manufacturing and sales establishments sold items made on the premises or hand crafted elsewhere by friends and acquaintances. Furniture, leather goods, pottery, candles, jewelry, wall-hangings, clothing, and artwork were the typical commodities. Two music stores specialized in acoustic and electric guitars, drums, electric organs, and crafted string instruments. Two head shops sold records, posters, hashish pipes, cigarette papers, shoulder patches, and the like.

There were a few interesting but maladaptive variations on these common themes. One started up when a longhaired couple drifted into town, saw a small empty diner with a "for rent" sign on it, and decided to open a restaurant called "The Blues." It played blues music over a loudspeaker, had a small, quality menu at inexpensive prices, and offered a variety of wines. This modest forerunner of the wine bar was soon forced out of business when the landlord terminated the lease under another pretext after seeing the hippie clientele it drew.

A honky-tonk bar attracted youthful street freaks and blue collar workers. Its juke-box and weekend band divided their musical selections between funky rock and funky country. It was operated by a father and son team; the old man passing as a hard-hat and the son looking like a hippie. Both were arrested in 1971, charged with selling drugs in their establishment. The grandest effort occurred when a nineteen year old freak appeared in Centerville claiming he was a millionaire wishing to invest in the town. He bought one of the town's movie theaters and proceeded to show classic art and avant garde films at reasonable prices and to stage occasional rock concerts. But by 1973, after increasing losses due to overestimation of a paying audience, theater ownership had passed back to more conservative hands.

While craft and health-food stores had existed in Provincia before 1960, all the enterprises mentioned here were established in the late 60s and after. The big boom followed 1970, when the region became widely known throughout the country as a CC stronghold. The Centerville area also had nine alternative projects of a business or service nature not yet described. These, added to the eighteen businesses just outlined, constituted twenty-seven enterprises; not an insignificant number for a population of around 16,000 people. When compared to the number of established straight enterprises and businesses in the same area, hip enterprises comprised between eight and nine percent of the total; one for every fifty-nine people.

For lack of a more precise term, there were people who were referred to as regular freaks, having no other particular means of identification. Most were not hip businessmen, students, communards, or street people. They camped out in the hills, rented old houses, visited friends, and repaired old farmsteads for free rent. In battered pickup trucks and VW buses, they frequently drove into town for food and supplies. Those not independently wealthy or receiving welfare, food stamps, or checks from home, worked at add jobs to make ends meet. One household repaired Volkswagens while another built dry wall foundations, and another did painting and roofing. Although not really communes, these clusters of people differed little except in size. A common living arrangement consisted of a hetero or homosexual couple, or two or three friends, or a couple and a friend or two. In fact they functioned very much like nuclear families except that they were not necessarily biologically related, had no jurolegal status, and tended to be temporary arrangements.

While it is almost impossible to estimate the regular freak population (because census, tax, employment, or welfare records did not distinguish between freaks and straights), there is no question but that local freaks numbered in the thousands. Jesse, the fellow whose article on youth rebellion was quoted earlier, claimed that 10,000 freaks per year were moving into the region to live, but this figure is probably inflated. Nevertheless, in 1971, the influx of hippies became so apparent that a conference of community leaders and law authorities from the entire region concluded that their primary concern was the officially-anticipated invasion of 100,000 summer freak visitors. In Wilfred, with a sedentary 1970 census population of 1,110, there were approximately 200 longhairs, including communards, who claimed to be residents.

Communes and Communal Networks

Communes were by far the most pivotal institutions of the burgeoning CC movement in the region. The reasons for this will become clear through the specific account of JM. At this point, however, a general overview will provide a sense of scale and scope with respect to the communal phenomenon in the region as a whole.

As of 1972, Provincia had at least sixty-two recognized communes. The region's intercommunal newsletter broke down its mailing list in such a way that any addressee was considered a commune if it was either named as a collective entity, such as Jackson's Meadows, or listed four or more individual names. A considerable number of communes were not on the mailing list, but the fact of their existence was learned through piecemeal reports from hitchhikers and visitors passing through. In addition, there were undoubtedly a significant number whose existence was not even known by the newsletter staff. An estimate of one hundred communes in Provincia in 1972 would be safe, even conservative. A survey of communes in the Centerville area revealed that outside of one with three hundred, the number of members per commune ranged most often between eight and twelve: an average of ten. Given an excess of one hundred communes in the region, ostensibly between one and two thousand people in the area were members of some commune.

In the Centerville area there were sixteen communes which had contact with Jackson's Meadows. Their life cycles, along with JM's, told in microcosm the story of the CC: the different influences that went into creating it, the forms it took, the conflicts, syntheses, new directions, and finally the repetitions of old patterns with new twists. These sixteen groups were not exactly representative of the other eighty-odd communal forms and processes, however, since each was in a way a unique social experiment. While there was no single typical commune, those in the Centerville area offered a fairly representative cross-section.

Communes that sprang up around Centerville proper had diverse beginnings, involving different kinds of people brought together under different sets of circumstances. There were essentially six separate "starts" from which a total of at least twenty-two additional communes developed, tying them loosely into an overall supernetwork. So as not to confuse individual networks with communal networks, the term "karass," borrowed from Kurt Vonnegut's *Cat's Cradle*, will be used to denote a communal network. The names that follow are for purposes or reader identification and are not the actual names.

The first commune to appear in the 1960s, Last Ditch Farm, did not give rise to a karass. It was founded in 1967 by a group of intellectuals in their 30s to test the visibility of anarchist principles. Although at the outer edge of JM's circle of contacts, informal links were established by two JMers leaving to join Last Ditch, but returning for visits.

By contrast, Parson's Crossing, born in 1968, led directly to the founding of six other communes, two of which were important in JM's development. Located in Wilfred, just down the road from JM, it was begun by somewhat younger people, perhaps less intellectually oriented but more radical than Last Ditch. The founders had been involved in the underground media and widely recognized in the national protest movement. They moved to Provincia in response to repressive measures by the SS and to equally extreme countermeasures by the anti-Vietnam War Movement. A sister commune, Walnut Hill, was founded a few miles away shortly thereafter by friends from the same media outfit. In 1970, another offshoot, Grasshopper Farm, appeared down the road from Parson's Crossing (even closer to JM), and still another, Bell, was begun not far from Walnut Hill. The sixth was located out of the region altogether. Former members of JM joined the first four groups in this karass, and JM in general had frequent, though not too friendly, intercourse with the first three. This group of communes and friends will be referred to as the Parson's Crossing Karass.

A completely different set of friends set up JM in 1969 and by mere coincidence bought the land in Wilfred close to Parson's Crossing and Grasshopper Farm. The founders were neither radicals nor intellectuals, for the most part consisting of early college or high school dropouts. Mixing drugs with spiritualism, they could be called hippies. JM had a large turnover in membership, with former JMers joining eleven other already established regional communes and establishing four others directly.

Also in 1969 yet another distinct network of individuals coalesced around a young charismatic spiritual leader in a group called the Krishna Brethren. Not only a commune, but a religious movement in itself, it eventually split into five separate residential foci. One early member of the Brethren left under unfriendly circumstances and later co-founded a psychotherapeutic community named Secret Ponds. The history of the Krishna Brethren is intimately tied to that of JM. The leaders of both groups shared a special relationship and the groups occasionally shared some common land.

Also coalescing in 1969, as a direct result of dissident response to the Cambodian invasion and the Kent State killings in early 1970, was Red Rose Collective, a group of seasoned political organizers. Largely coming from an underground media background similar to Parson's Crossing, but visual rather than print, its members represented the radical activist wing that the Parson's Crossing karass found so repugnant. They too had originally come to Provincia to slow down their pace of life and to reexamine strategies for sociopolitical change, but rather than withdraw into farming or literary activities, they unexpectedly found a new potential for active change in the rural poor, older leftist intellectuals, and thousands of recently arrived longhairs. They rode the crest of the same wave of rebellion in Provincia that they had in the past ridden in Washington, New York, Berkeley, and Chicago.

Red Rose had its hand in the initiation of five other communal groups: two subsidiary groups deliberately set up in another part of Provincia and three affiliates in Centerville by the names of Liberation Farm, Blue House, and Otherwise. Otherwise, a lesbian collective, had virtually no connection with JM, but Liberation Farm and Blue House played an important part in JM's survival struggle. Red Rose was also responsible for creating many of Provincia's alternative institutions. Their karass, like that of the Krishna Brethren, really constituted a formal social movement. However, Red Rose was significantly more loose, more democratically organized, and politically oriented. The regional manifestation of the Red Rose efforts was named Free Provincia.

A group known as Quaker Mountain grew out of the same turmoil and meetings that Red Rose did. The people who joined this group, however, quickly broke with Red Rose because of their educational and pacifist leanings and opposition to militant activism. Shortly afterward, Quaker Mountain moved to another part of the Centerville area to set up a combination school and conference center.

Composed of student friends from the same university outside Provincia, Moore Commune focused its activities around a rock band and settled near Centerville when a large house with low rent became available. Although outside any karass, it did maintain sporadic relations with JM, and two JM members eventually joined it.

In 1970, Rainbow Farm was founded by a small group, most of whose members, like Parson's Crossing and Red Rose, had been connected with the underground media, and included nationally known radical journalists. Renting the house of a member's family relative in Wilfred, Rainbow Farm settled in geographically and ideologically between the Red Rose and Parson's Crossing karasses and developed casual ties to JM. It later evolved into a women's collective; one of whose members eventually joined JM.

In addition to the communes, collectives, farms, and groups mentioned above, were two dispersed "new age families," whose bases of operations were located elsewhere, but whose members had important relationships with JM. One group, the IBM, had its beginnings in the Haight-Ashbury Summer of Love. Originally composed of prototypical love-and-peace hippies, the IBMs changed as the Haight changed from starry-eyed pacifists to hardened (at times violent) street people who eked out a tough existence. Ranging in age from mid-teens to late twenties, a high proportion of its members were orphans, high school dropouts, and virtual illiterates.

Beginning at the opposite ends of the country and the ideological spectrum, a group fondly known as the Mother Humpers coalesced on the Lower East Side of New York when political activism moved from the colleges to the streets. In addition to being political and physical, it also included third world blacks and Alterians. It too underwent a transformation, away from ideologically based challenges to law and authority toward petty crime, heroin addiction, and expressive violence. By 1970, not only had its members come to closely resemble the IBM people in background and attitudes, but they actually intermingled; traveling and living together across the country.

The Local Protest Movement and Projects

In the summer of '69, the Centerville area was in a state of turmoil. The embers of frustration, indignation, and rebellion fanned by media coverage of Columbia University, Chicago, and Vietnam had finally burst into flames in Provincia. The liberal community was threatening to go beyond words to action, while many high school students were growing long hair and turning on to dope. Longhairs were pouring into the region in significant numbers because word had circulated in the nationwide hip circuit that Provincia was a beautiful place to live. Many college students had opted to remain in the region after graduating or dropping out. There was no CC conspiracy to settle in the region; just a number of different aspects of social shifting coinciding at one time and place.

The local town fathers were alarmed by what was going on, while some of the lower working class elements became angry and aggressive toward these "disruptive influences" entering the region. Church leaders called for programs to occupy the youth, while factory workers set up road blocks on the highway between Centerville and Sutton, forcibly giving haircuts to hippies they dragged out of cars. Retired radicals were equally surprised by the new state of affairs;

some lamenting that they had left that whole scene behind only to have it follow them there, and others considering coming out of retirement to participate. Local youth began visiting communes, such as Parson's Crossing (who turned them away) and JM, eager to express their resentment against America. This rural youthful resentment had been largely disregarded up until then by Movement heavies, who assumed the revolution had to happen in the cities.

Youth pacification programs sprang up financed by enlightened "establishment" money. One 1968 project to bring ghetto youth to Provincia was disbanded when the money for the program was cut off in the fall of '69. While operating, however, it employed a young woman who had been a political science major specializing in high school unrest, and who was a member of the local SDS chapter. Through her summer job she met Bill MacDonald, the owner of the house in Sutton that eventually became the home of Red Rose Collective.

A local minister started a teen center to get kids off the street. The center's manager was a dropout from Alpine College who was a classified conscientious objector and needed an alternative service job. At first enthusiastic and hopeful, he began to realize that was causing more harm than good. Designed as a cooperative enterprise, the youth were supposed to help make decisions. But this lesson in adult responsibility was being learned only by those already overburdened with it; the high school elite who held student body offices were college bound and weren't heavy drug users. They had a sense of direction. The only ones who actually used the center were confused and had trouble in school, but had no interest in running the place. They came in wrecked from smoking dope every night, and while the manager did not want to throw them out, he felt he was doing no good by having them there either. By mid-winter, he suggested to the youthful board of directors that they take responsibility for their own actions, and consider closing the place down. They heartily followed his advice, and terminated the project.

The manager of the teen center was living at the MacDonald House with the young woman who had organized a film project with high school students she had met at the teen center. The project attracted the most hostile and alienated middle class youth at school and involved making a film portraying Centerville High School as the oppressive institution they felt it to be. Out of this a rebellious movement within the school evolved a cadre that fought against dress codes, regulations regarding haircuts, and the school's refusal to let students participate in a peace march. Thus, the teen center that was intended to co-opt frustrated youth served as the springboard for their radicalization.

By fall of '69, a loose network of anti-war liberals, radicalized students, and old radicals began to form around the MacDonald House. One of the famous Chicago Eight was living there while writing a book, and so many visitors dropped by that he decided to give weekly talks. Prestigious area liberals from the local Unitarian Church formed an anti-war committee that was in touch with the teen center as well as with the MacDonald House. But anti-establishment feeling in the area really hardened with the November 1969 March on Washington. The liberals organized a local contingent for the Washington

March and were infuriated when the bus company reneged on its promise to provide buses. Previously apolitical Alpine college students went to Washington in private autos, were caught in the police tear gas attack in front of the Justice Department, and returned fiercely politicized. Students also started organizing a political group at Knowland College. But the main articulation point for all the frustration was the MacDonald House. Only here were there experienced Movement people to look to for some kind of guidance.

Thus, the process of building a revolutionary community began. Instrumental was a local peace march in which a thousand people walked from Sutton to Centerville and sixty high school students, defying school authorities, left the building to participate. The marchers were also protesting the construction of a huge power plant in the area. The MacDonald House gave firm support. The group also traveled around Provincia showing films they and others had made. One of the films was a fictionalized account of the impending armed revolution in America that was praised by the "New York Times" as the only American film that approached the subject with any credibility. Colleges were frequently haunts on their travels, especially Chisholm College in central Provincia, where MacDonald House people made contacts with an ongoing media project and some radical faculty members who were doing research on Provincia's "colonial" status. After more thought on the potential for a revolutionary movement, mostly by Charles, the maker of the aforementioned film, the idea was presented as the Provincia Project to the White Panther convention, where it was highly praised.

A breakthrough came with Moratorium Week in spring of 1970. Some people from the MacDonald House, such as the former manager of the teen center, had been reluctant to see social change as a process requiring outright revolution, though they were slowly becoming disillusioned with do-good liberal efforts. Many went to Washington demonstrations where they were finally radicalized by the police. Others were angered to the point of desperation. Finally, the woman conducting the high school film project decided to call a meeting at the MacDonald farm. About a hundred people showed up: students, liberals, longhairs and short-haired revolutionaries. There were numerous questions. How could they break the back of government repression of dissent? What would be necessary to change the entire sociopolitical system to one responsive to the needs of the people?

The liberals talked about changing the political system by getting people elected to office. But a very articulate commentary was offered by Charles, who was later to become the de facto leader of the Red Rose Collective and the Free Provincia movement. Charles argued effectively that the political and economic structure in the area would have to be bypassed in order to bring about real change. While many of the election-oriented liberals retreated to the privacy of what others labeled as individualistic or familistic lives, six local projects for radical social change were begun by the people attending this meeting.

The Alpine College students formed a regional student party which later merged with a statewide party of older radicals to form the united third party alternative to the Democrat and Republican parties. The vacated quarters of the teen center was rented and an office for the new political party was set up in one room while a restaurant was started in the other.

The previously mentioned group from the education school used the MacDonald House meetings to develop a plan to start a school-community to help liberate future generations. Originally intending to set it up in Sutton, the group eventually moved because of an opportunity to use already existing facilities located elsewhere, but also because of a growing awareness of deep ideological differences with the MacDonald House.

A day-care center aimed at Centerville's poverty class was undertaken by some local women with the help of an Alpine College student involved in the new political party. Its organization was attempted under the auspices of the meagerly funded community action center. Although greatly influenced by CC people, it made significant headway in getting welfare and low income mothers to act in a community context for the first time. There was, however, stiff resistance to it by the borderline working people in the neighborhood who claimed the longhairs were feeding drugs to their children and teaching them un-American things. Finally, one of the women working with the day-care groups was physically threatened by a neighbor. Scared by the unexpectedly hostile opposition, most participants backed off, and the project was terminated.

The MacDonald House people decided to focus on two projects: a newspaper and a garage. The paper publicized facts about the injustices of local and regional government, pointed out vast differences between the rich and the poor, and provided examples of school administration repression of students. At a more abstract level, it introduced new left ideas concerning women's liberation, the national CC Movement, and the war in Vietnam. Aimed at welfare people, rural poor, high school and college students, and liberals, with later issues focusing on CC activities in the region, it offered testimonials by oppressed people as well as research exposing little known facts about Provincia. A thick copy filled with solid information, movement rhetoric, and eye-catching graphics was distributed throughout Provincia. Supposedly selling for $.25 a copy, many were given away. Particularly after calling itself "Free Provincia," it was regarded in many radical circles as an exemplary revolutionary undertaking toward the goal of securing semi-autonomous revolutionary regions throughout the country.

A liberation garage was started to teach people, especially women, to repair their own cars cheaply. People were encouraged to work on their own cars, and garage regulars advised them as they worked. Because there were more females than males from the MacDonald House involved, it deliberately tried to teach the sexes to work together as equals. It was anticipated that auto mechanics would be particularly attractive to poverty and lower working class youth known as "greasers." Through the establishment of such an institution it was hoped that genuine proletarian elements could be drawn in and politicized.

By early summer of 1970, Liberation Garage was fulfilling its aims and then some. Men were indeed working side by side with women, easily taking instructions from them when necessary. A number of greasers began to hang around the garage, using its space and tools to repair their jalopies and bikes. An ex-Marine sergeant who only six months previously was beating up hippies became one of the crew. Others shortly followed his example. Longhairs were regular customers, and people from the communes dropped by when they needed help, such as towing some vehicles stuck in the mud. Drifters and easy-rider types, however, made up most of the clientele, maintaining the machines that carried them in perpetual movement around the country. Although it didn't happen often, liberals and low income people brought their cars too. The biggest surprise, however, was the number of children who gathered at the garage, which was located in a dilapidated building in the poor section of town. Accordingly, some of the MacDonald House people discontinued car repair in order to work with young people, involving them in reading, art, and discussions of ecology. The garage became an informal day-care center.

Problems also beset the garage as time passed. Some people were turned off by the revolutionary slogans painted on the walls and the sign outside vividly depicting an angry, red clinched fist holding a wrench. Sometimes the garage was so crowded with people sitting around "rapping" and drinking beer that it was impossible to get any mechanical work done. Parts got lost, oil was spilled and left on the floor, tools were stolen, and garbage piled up to the point where the landlord complained. To make matters worse, those working at the garage were hesitant to charge fees because it seemed counterrevolutionary to do so, and although the garage was actually losing money, the MacDonald house people kept it going. At that point, it was felt that the spread of new ideas was more important than working out the bothersome details of fiscal responsibility.

The Alpine College students, who enthusiastically started the macrobiotic restaurant, soon discovered the work quite unrewarding. They had an increasingly difficult time paying the bills, and they developed an irresistible urge for travel. Already spread thin by its involvement in the paper, the garage, and the film making and showing, the MacDonald House people saved the restaurant by replacing the students who were dropping out. Called "Vital Victuals" and difficult to find, the second story restaurant sprouted a sign with an angry, red, clenched fist holding a spoon. Anyone could scribble on the walls and paint pictures. Some of the artwork was good and some offended the sensibilities of middle class upbringing. People breaking bread and slurping soup could look around to read in bold letters "Free Bobby, Free Erika," "All Power to the People," "Smoke Dope and Smash the State," and "Free the Panther 21." In a lighter mood, someone wrote in pencil, "Free the Indianapolis 500."

The restaurant became the center of the hip community which was growing by leaps and bounds. Summer transients found this to be the only indoor place they could hang out in, some stretching out on the floor to sleep. Despite the political flavor, just about everyone from the hip community found this was the only place in town they could regularly find each other and trade gossip, whether the people be Krishna Brethren missionaries, Parson's Crossing recluses, JM hippies, visiting radicals, hardened street people, and even local greasers. The restaurant also provided a place in the evenings to hold meetings on hip community problems, to show films, and to have weekly women's meetings.

As a result of all this activity, the air was electric with intensity around Centerville and elsewhere in the region. Both CC challengers and the SS establishment anticipated an inevitable explosion of events and the unleashing of powerful new energies for change in the towns and surrounding hills. But whereas traditional residents often feared an ominous, foreboding future, cultural revolutionaries reveled with joy in the thought of a new age they knew must dawn.

In the midst of this volatile mix of commitment, fear, and confusion on all sides, Jackson's Meadows sprang up to take an important, even if unpremeditated role. It came to embody in many ways the competing and conflicting forces at work in the CC movement, the resistance to the CC, and in microcosm, the evolving society that subsumed both.

2. Fusion: Coming Together at the Dobson House

Jackson's Meadows as a communal entity can trace roots back to very small George Grayson college in Centerville. While all its short existence it had struggled to survive, its future looked brighter in the mid-sixties with the influx of students at the time due to the greater numbers of youth as a result of the post World War II "baby boom," the readily available funding for educational programs in President Johnson's "great society," and an overall awareness that going to college was better than going to fight in Vietnam. Colleges in Provincia were particularly popular because of their only partially deserved reputations for locations in idyllic rural settings and policies that encouraged liberal experimentation.

But in the words of one student, George Grayson College "was the end of the road; it was for the desperate." It was either for students who had flunked out, or had not been admitted to other colleges. They were all trying to justify themselves in the eyes of society and live up to their parents' expectations by attempting to get a college degree. At first they felt their lives depended upon graduation, but after arriving at college, it turned into a joke. The absurdity became clear for one applicant after the interview for admission. Wracked by anxiety, he met a student outside the office who told him not to worry because "no applicant has ever been turned down." Much of the course work was independent study, and the courses that one student took, for example, included only music, theater, and crafts. The operation of the school turned out to be so flexible and spontaneous that the pretension that serious higher learning was taking place could not be maintained.

A close friendship was struck between three male students. One, a 20 year old ex-speed freak who had the dubious distinction of being the first student ever expelled from Yale because of drugs, came to be respectfully known as Yale. Another, Bill, was 20 and had been one of the original street speed freaks in New York's East Village hippie Mecca. The third was Jesse, 21, a dropout from four previous colleges and former pool hall hustler and actor. Each was outspoken, interpersonally aggressive, and outwardly self-assured. They also had high academic ratings at this college because where there were no objective measures of achievement; there remained only charismatic impression and friendship with the faculty, which they intentionally cultivated. In addition, they had a social reputation at the school for being the most vibrant and the closest of friends. Being the center of attraction, and each in his own way admittedly a con artist, they schemed for and received free dope from other younger students less versed in the ways of the world.

They grew close to the political science instructor, a prestigious law school graduate and former government employee who had "flipped out," was divorced, and ended up in a mental institution for awhile before coming to the college. The four of them, plus another fellow and two female students decided to rent a house. They found one known as the Dobson House that was located near Wilfred. After moving in, they spent most of the time partying, but still went to classes, even conducting seminars in the Dobson House. They contended that a better learning atmosphere than standard classroom practice was created by lounging around on the floor sipping wine and smoking dope. Developing a more critical view toward politics in American society through one in-house course, their awareness of their own personal needs shifted to what they saw as political consciousness.

This consciousness was finally exercised in the early spring of 1969 when the college had its rebellion. If Columbia and Harvard could do it, why not George Grayson? The rallying point was the very real problem of the college president's extreme autocratic attitude. Leading the rebellion, the three students privately acknowledged that they were rebelling as much for the excitement, involvement, and a sense of efficacy as anything else. Jesse, the most politically conscious ring leader, saw human behavior as largely constricted by sociopolitical institutions controlled by an elite; in this case the president who ruled the college by decree. In the heat of confrontation, Jesse, who before coming to college had some dealings with the Mafia, got carried away to the point of threatening the college president's life. The college closed down, students went home, and the president resigned.

That accomplished, life at the house returned to a series of parties. Word circulated in the area that the house was a focal point of activity for local and transient hip people. Because town officials were disturbed by this, the police also dropped in unannounced; once ostensibly looking for a stolen camera, but also looking for drugs. Everyone kept dope stashes hidden in snow banks outside the house, but one person forgot that he had a small piece of hash hidden in his camera case. The police found it, but instead of arresting them all, he warned them to cool down their future activities or else they would be in serious trouble.

Some visitors to the house never left, becoming full-fledged residents. One arrived by way of another college in a distant town. Jesse, who was having a relationship with a theater instructor there, met the theater instructor's roommate's boyfriend and invited him to visit the Dobson House. He showed up apparently to stay. The two of them didn't get along, as Jesse was always active and political while the other fellow was a quiet macrobiotic Buddhist who made astrology charts. The Buddhist remained at the Dobson House after he had broken up with his girlfriend, waiting to collect insurance money from a previous near-fatal auto accident that triggered his current search for life meaning. He would use the money eventually to explore India.

Jesse also made trips back to the city where he grew up. On one of his visits, he ran into an old high school friend who had dropped out of college in a severe state of depression. The friend had joined the local SDS chapter, engaged in demonstrations, been jailed and beaten, and within a period of six months had withdrawn from political action entirely. In order to cheer him up and give him a new outlook, Jesse suggested he visit the Dobson House. However, instead of regaining direction or composure, the ex-SDSer moved into heavy drug use at the house. Saying little to anyone, he tripped for days on end searching for meaning and someone to give him the direction and security he needed. Although he had become a permanent resident of the Dobson House, he nevertheless maintained contact with an SDS ex-leader, Elliot, who was undergoing a similar though less traumatic withdrawal from student politics.

Elliot was also invited to stay at the Dobson House and began to consider it his home away from home. He did not drop entirely from the college scene, however, traveling frequently back and forth and eventually returning to the school to graduate. It was through his continued participation in the academic world that many students and faculty at his university would later learn about and visit the commune at Jackson's Meadows.

At this time, however, the Dobson House people could not be considered communards searching for new modes of living and ways of relating to one another. Instead, the house was a refuge; a place where weary, defeated young people who saw no future for themselves could retreat. Perhaps the only exception was the Buddhist who was only using the place as a temporary stopover on the way to the Orient. The natural rather than the social environment was the primary factor that drew them all there. A house in the country, away from urban noise and confusion, provided an opportunity for walks in the mugger-less out-of-doors in clean air that made life appear less confusing than it otherwise seemed to be.

As more people dropped by for longer periods of time, though no one deliberately sought it, the growing social life began to offer some of the most tangible rewards. As the Dobson house became a prestigious center of hip activity, more people moved in, and the house activities spread from Wilfred to Centerville. One of these newcomers had earlier quit school, pooled some money with a young couple, and opened up Centerville's first head shop that spring. To save money, the couple moved into the house in Wilfred where they drew others into a relationship with the store. The Buddhist made astrological charts for it, while others crafted artwork, and Yale, with his fluid prep school verbal manner, made an excellent salesman. Having tripped together on acid many times, they felt a vaguely deeper attachment for each other than they felt for other friends, yet acid also made them feel curiously alone at times, sometimes frightfully alone. Outside of activities concerning the headshop, there was little common experience to reinforce the potential bonds established by drugs.

The unity of focus that eventually developed in the house was centered around Peter and Candy, a couple who came to the Dobson house at the suggestion of a woman acquaintance who lived in Sutton. She and Candy had been students at a progressive boarding school where Peter was the handyman. Peter and Candy contacted her, consciously hoping to set up a commune. After looking for land in Provincia, and not finding any, they decided to remain in the region anyway. Candy, who was eight and one half months pregnant, necessitated their settling down quickly. Visiting the Dobson House, they asked to stay for a short while, eventually indicating they wanted to remain until the child was born. Because there was no formal decision making and there were no objections, they did. Peter found a job as a carpenter's apprentice in Wilfred, allowing them to contribute financially to the upkeep of the house.

Since adolescence, Peter had been observing what he regarded as the inhuman, careless, and selfish ways people treated one another. Although he did well in school, he hated educational institutions for the way they constricted people, and despite having practically no friends (or because of it), contemplated the ways in which people could befriend and help each other while helping themselves. During the Summer of Love when San Francisco and the Bay Area was electric with ideas of peace, cooperation, and ways to foster all these attributes, Peter made his way to this "hippie Mecca." Inspired by such people as Ken Kesey of the Merry Pranksters and Lou Gottlieb, the founder of one of the first Bay Area communes, Morningstar Ranch, Peter returned home determined to create a community.

A vehement argument with his father (who took the position that people, if not governed by institutions and management elites, would soon destroy themselves), was followed the next day by his father's death from a heart attack. This triggered Peter into action. He wanted to prove he was correct in his faith in human nature (perhaps also wanting to relieve himself of some guilt as possibly having something to do with his father's death), and by setting up a viable anarchistic community he would vindicate himself. Having a small inheritance from his father, he was prepared to invest it in the creation of a school/community. Initially, not communicating many of his underlying motivations to others in the house so as not to appear overly premeditative, Peter and Candy quietly and imperceptibly became the stable axis of the raucous group of housemates.

Although Peter was the only one who had previously concluded that a commune would free people to explore their full potentials, some Dobson House people were slowly moving in that direction before Peter arrived. Peter only helped accelerate the process. Jesse thought of interpersonal material reliance in somewhat sociopolitical terms, concluding that such bonding was necessary for survival as a way to replace human exploitation through corporate government and business institutions. Elliot, on the other hand, was in the process of depoliticizing, coming to the conclusion that only good friendships, rather than institutions, could significantly positively affect people's lives.

The last significant member of the original core group at the house was Mary, who arrived with her two young children. She was a friend of Peter's, whom Peter had invited to help deliver Candy's baby. Coming from New York's East Village, she had delivered her own children by herself after leaving her husband. She was still in a deep crisis, hating the life of a housewife, yet finding herself alone and friendless in the Village. Arriving too late to help with the delivery, she nevertheless remained, having found people who were willing to care for her children, and Bill, with whom she developed a relationship.

As it turned out, it was only a few weeks after Candy's arrival at the Dobson House that she had her baby. Waiting for Mary to arrive while going into labor, she refused to have the baby in the hospital where the atmosphere was sterile and hostile, where babies had chemicals poured in their eyes, and where fathers were made to feel irrelevant to the birth process. Not trusting established medical facilities either, Yale saddled up a horse and galloped through the night to another house in Wilfred full of longhairs where a midwife might be found. This other hippie house later became known as the Parson's Crossing commune, and the father of one of its members who was visiting there happened to be a GP with obstetrical experience who agreed to help deliver the baby.

Everyone gathered in the room where Mary was, astounded at the miracle they were watching for the first time. According to most of those present, a sense of awe and rejuvenation came over them from observing a new life enter the world. They all had helped deliver the baby, and in a sense he belonged to all of them. Through the birth, the house established a firm identity in the Centerville hip community. The delivery was, by every participant's account, the first major internal step toward the formation of a communal group. Parson's Crossing, with its writer's flair for imagination and labeling, realizing the child was the first born into the New Age in the area, started calling the Dobson House "The Baby Farm."

But even with the greater closeness precipitated, the house was still filled with people marking time, withdrawing from past bad experiences, ready to embark on the road to redemption, but not sure which direction the road would go. The only one with a vague sense of vision and confidence was Peter, but neither he nor anyone else knew where it was leading. He spoke very little, but when he did, his words seemed more profound than the busy chatter of the rest, and people stopped their activities to listen to him discuss astrology, human frailty, spiritual growth, people's personalities, and the certain destruction the earth was headed for if people continued in their selfish and isolated ways. Everyone agreed that, in effect, Peter was their "guru," though he never stepped in actively to lead anyone or direct their behavior. The Buddhist appreciated him because he was interested in spiritual matters, while the confused ex-SDS radical "followed him around like a dog" because he seemed so sure of himself. The two other couples related well to him and Candy because they represented proof of stability and permanence in sexual relationships. Extroverted Jesse and Yale respected him, for he seemed to evince some depth they perhaps felt lacking in themselves.

As the winter progressed, little by little, facades were lowered and some pretensions dropped, as they must when people live in constant proximity to one another. This process was further accelerated by three factors: drugs, games, and purposive discussion. Through the disorientation of mescaline and LSD in particular, old certainties could not be taken for granted, with everything and everyone becoming subject to new scrutiny. Potential threats to psychic and even physical survival could become more apparent, and paranoia could set in; the so-called "bad trip." Yet in this friendly and supportive environment, the opportunity for reliance on and empathetic communication with others was increased to where a generalized feeling of trust could build up through drug use. Although not uniformly and equally so with all individuals, no one person appeared threatening to anyone else when tripping together. The energy released also permitted them to share intense emotional experiences. Hence, strong feelings of various sorts developed for one another.

Games took on great significance. They placed people in situations where everyone had to conform to the common behavioral frameworks that games presented. In games like "Thumper," they sat around in a circle, each having a non-verbal identification symbol (such as clapping twice) that the others would have to recognize. Each person was then supposed to do his own symbol followed by someone else's; that other person, in turn, repeated the process until someone made a mistake. At this point, the erring person had to take a gulp of wine. Inevitably the game ended with everyone drunk and gleeful. Another game was more theater than play. Having no specific rules, people played different roles for fun, pretending they were other people they knew, being funny, but also "trying on" other people's personalities and behaviors. These games not only introduced new realities, put a common set of rules on people, and forced them to interact, but did so in a way that emphasized non-verbal communication, change in states of consciousness, and shifting identities. All these attributes were crucial in accelerating personal change as well as group process.

It was during the course of a certain game that the Dobson house people coalesced into a tightly knit group. Everyone there recalled this experience as the pivotal event in the evolution toward a commune.

One evening, a group of traveling strangers needing a place to stay showed up at the house. They and some of the Dobson people played an assortment of games, Peter eventually recalling the game "power," which Ken Kesey had taught him. The rules were simple. Everyone had turns at taking complete command of the group for short periods of time. Everyone had to do exactly as the leader said, so long as there was no physical injury involved. This game had fascinated Peter, for it freed people to experiment not just with each individual's power, but with group power; the kind of tremendous energy that is generated when all the people in a group put all their unwavering efforts into one activity. It was also a way of breaking down people's usual resistance toward working selflessly with others.

Yale was the first to lead the group. What does one do when one has complete control over a group of people? He was paralyzed with indecision. Finally, he suggested that a conga line form with him as leader. Holding onto each other's waists, the people formed a line that wound from room to room, went out doors, slithered into the barn, and wound up collapsing in the hayloft. Next, it was Peter's turn. Back inside the house, he got everyone in a circle and commanded them to chant a mantra. The idea didn't go over too well with the participants, but the chant continued. Peter was fascinated by the power generated merely through vocal utterances in unison. As he led the chant, he thought how fantastic it would be if such concerted group action could be put to use for "higher purposes."

By the time it came time for one of the group of strangers to take power, everyone in the house had gathered to participate in the game; about 20 people in all. The stranger commanded everyone to take their clothes off, giving no further instructions. This was the first time Dobson people had been naked together. They were very uneasy, nervously twitching, and looking away from one another.

Then it was Jesse's turn. Walking into the center of the circle, he stood there not knowing what to do. In the heavy silence he perceived a sharp distinction between people who lived in the house and those who didn't. Without looking, he could almost feel the physical presence of Peter, Candy, Mary, Yale, Bill, and the others. It was a strange sensation, for he previously thought that notions of vibrational communication "were a lot of hippie bullshit." On the other hand, he felt hostility toward the strangers, believing they had plotted what would amount to gang rape. The scene was all set and ready to go; all it needed was someone to make the first move toward orgy. Jesse felt an overwhelming sense of identification with his comrades as they all realized simultaneously that they were "being taken." Other members of the group later corroborated Jesse's intuitions; they too felt the presence of their friends in the room, sensing an intense but unexplainable empathy and trust in one another.

Lying down with his back to the floor, Jesse simply declared by virtue of his power that the entire game was over (thereby preserving group honor and chastity). Everyone was silent and motionless until Candy, with a rush of feeling for Jesse, walked over and laid down on top of him. Immediately afterward, all the others spontaneously and quietly laid down on them, creating a pile of naked bodies. Jesse's arms were stretched upward through the mass of bodies, and though he couldn't see, he perceived where his friends were. There was no groping, but a quivering sensation as many Dobson people were crying. Yale, the formally mannered, jovial Ivy Leaguer, who professed to take nothing seriously, was silently sobbing. Jesse, at the bottom of the pile, clasped hands with Peter at the top, who slowly started pulling him up. Jesse was amazed, for despite the weight of the bodies, he felt such a charge of energy through Peter's hands that he seemed to rise through the mound effortlessly, people gently falling away as he moved upward.

Everyone, shaken and confused, quietly put their clothes back on. The strangers began to laugh nervously, made small talk, and without being asked, withdrew to the barn for the night. The Dobson House people could not explain what had happened to themselves or why, but they emerged with an ineffable sense of cohesion. For the first time, they felt that they really belonged to one another; that they simply didn't need anyone else. Although the event itself was not overtly sexual, the undercurrent was, and beginning that night, sexual activity in the house escalated. Peter, who was trying to work out some form of sexual relationship that went beyond just two people, urged Candy to sleep with Jesse. She agreed to, she said, as an act of charity, knowing that Jesse didn't have a woman, and that he must be terribly horny. They slept together only one night, both feeling embarrassed later. But others, not in a firm couple relationship, openly slept around with one another until they moved out of the house a couple of months later.

For Peter, sex was primarily a form of communication and social bonding between people. For Candy, sex was almost meaningless. By her account, she lost her virginity when she was twelve years old at the progressive school when the 40 year old school master, after discovering she and a boy engaging in sex play, volunteered to teach her how to have sexual intercourse. Because her school life was largely a steady stream of passionless sex after that, she attached no special significance to it; she could take it or leave it. Thus, for her, the usual sexual barriers between people easily could be put aside. Peter's overriding urge was to share intense energy through human communication and bring people together. At first he thought drugs could be the vehicle, but after a lot of drug taking at the Dobson House and living in close proximity with other people, he became aware of the more primal, more social importance of sex. In addition to recognizing the sex urge as a sensual need, he also saw it more than ever as a way of establishing close relationships with many people.

But Peter was cautious. He realized that haphazard sex was meaningless and often destructive to relationships. He wanted to bring someone else into his and Candy's life in a way that would not disturb the uneasy peace between them. If only one person was brought in, the balance would be destroyed, for one of them was bound to be the odd person out. He therefore sought other couples. After the ice-breaking "power" game incident, the possibility of forming a quadruple was openly discussed and Peter approached the couple who operated the head shop. Although the woman was open to the idea, the man was not, for this was, he said, the first time he had ever been deeply in love. He was admittedly jealous. Peter was disappointed, but kept trying to break down resistance through discussion. He wanted very much to live with people who would not reject one another's needs at any level, including sex. Although the quadruple idea had not yet worked out, he was nevertheless glad to see most of the unattached people sleeping with each other.

As winter began to fade, discussions, drugs, and games continued. The Buddhist, when at the Poor People's March on Washington in 1967, met an archetypal flower-child hippie whom he liked very much. Two years later, he ran into the same hippie and two other friends, and invited them to visit Wilfred. Shortly thereafter, the three new people arrived at the house, bringing with them the latest Bay Area assortment of games, frivolity, spontaneity, laughter, heavy drinking, and drug taking. The new arrivals came from working-class backgrounds, and were not really as carefree as they tried to be. One in particular advocated "fun at any cost," and though entertaining to live with, gave definite signs that he was constantly getting high in order to escape a less pleasant internal reality. He was a full blooded Menominee Indian whose hated alcoholic father was a president of the American Legion post in his home town.

Along with the new gaiety and the warmer weather came discussions of buying land. Many at that point considered themselves a communal group, and Peter in particular began to think of directions it should take. Sitting in a rented house doing drugs was not exactly conducive to personal growth, and in its place he suggested they get into a natural environment so that they could more easily explore natural relationships that would "organically" flow from their new life together. They would design and build a house, plant a garden, and eat good food together. Although some declared they would never move to any piece of land, most agreed it might be a good idea. Some thought so because they, too, were evolving a dream of community in which people would work for their material and emotional livelihoods, giving to others, while relying on them for help in return. Others were interested because the only tangible thing they had was this group of friends, regardless of what it did or where it went. The question was, who was willing to financially commit themselves to the purchase of land? The Buddhist was willing to spend his auto accident insurance money on it instead of going to India, but the amount involved would not pay for anything worthwhile. Everyone looked to Peter, who not only seemed to have the most articulate ideas on community, but also promised to provide the rest of the money it would take. His mother had already lent $30,000 to his brother to start one commune, and she would no doubt lend Peter some money to supplement his inheritance in this case.

Through a real estate agent, they found an isolated 120 acre tract of land for sale in Wilfred The price was reasonable because, despite its great beauty, it was virtually inaccessible by car. After seeing it once, Peter decided this was the parcel for him and made a down payment (one day before Harvey from the Parson's Crossing Karass, who later began Grasshopper Farm, made a similar offer). But leaving the Dobson house led to some complications. Upon inspection, the owner of the house declared that the residents had destroyed it. Jesse countered that it was not destroyed, "just well lived in." Nevertheless, the owner sued them; putting a lien on the land they had just purchased. A lawyer was finally hired, and the case was settled out of court a year later. Each of the residents agreed to pay from two to four hundred dollars for damage.

The land was visited frequently during warm days. Only when people thought it would be sufficiently warm at night did they make preparations to move. Not everyone was excited; particularly the women. They were hesitant about the prospect of struggling against the elements for purposes not quite clear to them. Candy now had a baby to look after, as did Mary who had two children, and this caused doubts in their minds. Still, the women were by their own admission, so meek and retiring and the men so set on the idea, that they went along with it.

A festival was scheduled at Knowland College the day they planned to move. The Dobson House people were included because one of them boasted to the sponsors that they were great musicians. Although few knew how to play anything, they collected old bottles, washboards, cracked guitars, and one concertina, calling themselves the "Jackson Meadows Jug Band." Tripping on acid, they sang and banged, yelled and danced their way through the audience who responded with cheers and applause. Thus, before even technically residing at Jackson's Meadows, they had already established its reputation as a repository for bizarre eccentrics; Centerville's own Merry Pranksters.

Peter recalls that evening as one of the most mystical of his life. He led the concertina and was dressed like a Gypsy, and despite all the noise and confusion, he slowly began to feel he was drifting out of touch with everyone else and the surroundings. Sliding into another dimension of time and place, he felt he had become a real Gypsy. Trying to tell his housemates what he was experiencing was like trying to talk across centuries and oceans, because for him, he was clearly experiencing another lifetime. He experienced living in a wagon camped in the European countryside; Candy and his child with him. For the first time, the full implications of his being a father, a family man, and a member of a clan hit him. While others packed their belongings in a truck, he foolishly decided to walk to the Meadows, finally sitting by the road in the darkness contemplating how he could manage commitment to both his family and his clan. His friends, in turn, were put off by his introspective, almost autistic behavior. Thus, the first night on the land, divisions were present that were later to plague the fledging commune.

Random Drifting, Coalescence, and Fusion

At this juncture, it will be helpful to get some kind of larger view. The events at George Grayson College and the Dobson House set the stage for a future dynamic that is reasonably illustrative of much in the communal and CC movements of the region, as well indicative of JM's prospects. Further, they point to the influences brought in from previous circumstances and more distant phenomena in the society at large, so as to provide a glimpse into the precise ways and reasons these movements began. But the events in themselves, of course, only reveal so much. In order to start to get a handle on a greater understanding of the goings-on there, a closer, deeper look is required. Consequently, supplementary information and interpretation beyond accounts of events and participants' thoughts is important.

By asking certain concrete, empirically answerable questions relevant to the larger process, it is possible to get firm answers that provide better insights into that process. For example, what varieties of people participated in the initiation of this commune? What kinds of experiences had they shared that enabled them to embark upon such a joint venture? What dynamics brought the commune into existence, and what was its place in the broader social order of the area?

With respect to the first question, of the fourteen people who moved from the Dobson House to JM, only eleven could be considered Dobson House veterans, as the last three joined the group shortly before the move. Only three were females, two of these joining the commune as members of couples, largely at the urging of their mates. The third woman had two children with her for whom she sought some kind of substitute family. Thus the commune came into being largely through the efforts and expectations of the males.

JM's founders were not adolescent runaways or "teeny boppers," but averaged 21 years or more. All had lived and worked away from their parents before coming to Wilfred and had already experienced sides of life that many older people hadn't. In many ways, they were older than their chronological age. Except for Candy, only three late joiners were in their teens, and even these people had seen and done much for their age. More than half were from Eastern European backgrounds; a proportion higher than one might expect to find in the society at large. In addition to the Amerindian, one was half Alterian. In light of the popular assumption at the time that youthful dissent largely stemmed from suburban upbringing, it is interesting that youth from the suburbs represented a minority, and small town backgrounds were adequately represented.

JM's founders came from class backgrounds quite representative of the American population: a small minority upper class, a bulky middle class, and a working class that fell somewhere in between. This fact plus the distribution from upper to lower within each class indicated that as far as JM was concerned, the CC was not the purely middle-upper middle class phenomenon it had often been reported as being. What appears to be a better indicator than class background for dropping out of the SS into the CC in this study, was the rapid change of status within the classes during childhood upbringing. A significant majority experienced one kind of child rearing approach and family lifestyle in early childhood and a quite different one later in adolescence. This does not indicate that non-CC youth hadn't experienced this kind of fluctuation in social mobility, but it might suggest that a disproportionate number of such youth joined or formed communal groups like JM. It is also interesting that more than half the founders did not come from white collar business or knowledge sector occupations. This, too, contradicted popular stereotypes of youthful social dissenters' parents generally being professional, management, or sales people.

Half of JM's founders came from broken homes. There is evidence that relationships with both parents in general could have been somewhat more distant than usual with the exception of a few very close ties to mothers. That many had consulted psychiatrists so often, certainly suggests emotional instability of some kind, though perhaps not so severe as the figures indicate. Of the four from the six who consulted psychiatrists, two did so solely to escape the military draft. Significantly, most of them remember being very lonely during childhood and adolescence. Although two thirds had the basic confidence to believe they were their parents' favorite child, most felt alone and estranged from the world of their peers.

There was significant diversity in educational background, similar to the society at large. Members ranged from college graduate to high school dropout. The level of academic achievement, with a couple of exceptions, was not very high. Most, through lack of ability or effort, had experienced failure in an educational setting. Most admitted either being virtually alone and withdrawn in school, or the opposite, having too many superficial friends and meaningless activities. Some individuals appeared to have excellent, even if erratic, social skills, while others communicated little or did little outside of what they narrowly considered to be of crucial importance to their personal lives. The first JM generation appeared to have a fair share of the social and intellectual skills one might expect, but the way they were distributed and manifested was at best uneven, with self-admitted latent hustlers clustering at one end of the spectrum and brooding philosophers at the other.

Lacking most were employable skills, which is understandable for a group so young. Yet age is no explanation or excuse, because among other youth their age, with comparable class background but no college background, one might expect a modicum of employable skills to be present. The "spoiled" or "lazy" explanations popular then did not hold up because all had had jobs; some from high school on up. The kind of jobs held, however, were very unrewarding, low paying positions characteristic of unskilled labor. What is more interesting is the lack of a relationship between employment potential and years of schooling. Those who had gone to school more had worked less, picking up skills in English literature or botany instead of carpentry or retailing, where jobs were far more available. It appears that those who had entered college did so with great expectations, only to find the experience either more difficult or irrelevant than anticipated. Similarly, the prospects for work outside college was by comparison even worse than going to college. This then discouraged them from obtaining lower level skills. Opportunities for obtaining those skills that might have been available with a completed higher education had been closed off due to failure or disinterest. Accordingly, those who were concerned with such matters at this time in their lives searched for alternative skills, such as astrology.

All had become freaks before they reached Wilfred, but they were still in transition while at the Dobson House. All males had avoided the draft, most people had been arrested for victimless crimes, and a few had been jailed for political activities. Nearly all had demonstrated against the Vietnam War, though some admitted they did it more for entertainment than from a sense of conviction. All had smoked marijuana, with some going on to more potent drugs, such as amphetamines and psychedelics. One even sampled heroin. None had tried cocaine, which was neither widely available nor in vogue then. For most, however, the introduction to and the use of psychedelics occurred only after reaching the Dobson House.

Half the people specifically mentioned drugs as precipitating pivotal events in their lives that resulted in important, conscious changes of behavior. Half of these viewed their critical drug experiences as opening up thrilling and positive new vistas, while the other half cited those experiences as triggering severe reaction against certain of their own behaviors that they became aware of during "bad trips." But there were other critical experiences besides drugs, also. One had been exposed to and recoiled from the big time underworld, and others had had religious experiences and glimpses of other realities that are scoffed at in the day-to-day world. One woman had been affected by unfortunate sexual experiences while another was still recovering from a bad marriage. One rebounded from coming a hair's breadth away from death to rethink what was really important in life, and what was not. For another, a parent's death was the trigger for change. Personal and ideological influence by other people and ideas also entered the mix, one having been directly inspired by CC celebrity-heroes, and another being caught up in the political upheavals in Paris in May and Prague in August of 1968.

What had happened to these people after turning hippie-radical-freak? Most were in the process of rebounding like pinballs from situations they had gotten into after bidding farewell to the straight life: unhappy college experiences, terrible jobs, isolation, broken love affairs, or abuse of certain drugs. In the search for meaning and the reasons for the misfortunes that had befallen them, major shifts in intellectual and emotional orientation were occurring. Two ex-radicals, after finding that political revolutions were not completed after a semester or two, and after discovering that being mauled by the police was outright traumatic, were in the process of moving away from radical politics, though they retained their conviction that the quality of life in America was terrible. Another was in the process of building the very political perspective the other two had abandoned. Yet another was moving from an interpersonal psychiatric orientation toward outright mysticism. The remaining people did not know which way to move. All this is not to say that the Dobson House was total confusion and despair. Many were enjoying their free floating status, being only mildly concerned about lack of direction, while others, though repulsed by certain past experiences, were eagerly attempting to discover new possibilities.

Everyone who eventually joined JM was in a liminal state; that is, they were attached to no fixed ideology and no fixed institutions. Those people who were not attached to one another through couple relationships were more erratic and open to greater change than those who were. After having relatively carefree and indulgent childhoods and relatively unrewarding recent pasts, they faced an even more uncertain if not ominous future. Unlike most people in society who theoretically were more dependent on family, school, career, or some form of ideology for direction in life, these people had little to rely on outside themselves. They were figuratively, if not literally, suspended in psychosocial space/time. Peter obviously had more direction than most others. The few who were working toward possible careers or goals elsewhere expressed little interest in the idea of a commune. The others were searching, open to alternatives, and were in a state highly susceptible to suggestion. The heavy use of psychedelic substances undoubtedly lowered the threshold of suggestibility, further breaking down old entrenched cognitive structures while providing glimpses of possible new ones. On top of cognitive destructing and reconstructing was the intense impact of integrated peak experience.

Associated with drugs either as cause, effect, or both, was psychological and even physiological stress. Not only were people concerned about the Vietnam War, insensitive America, and their loves in the future, but many were aware that at a deeper psychological level there was constant tension. There was a clash between what their parents had expected of them and what they had actually done; between their values and those apparently dominant in the society; between wanting to do and be things and not being able to. Physical fatigue also set in with overindulgence of psychoactive substances, but also was precipitated by such things as long periods of little sleep due to a constant flow of visitors, crowded conditions, and frequent partying.

In short, Peter entered a situation that was pregnant with potential for the radical relearning and alteration of behavior by all concerned. It contained all the necessary ingredients for what used to be called brainwashing, except that there was no deliberate manipulation of conditions to foster such changes. Because Peter seemed to have some answers and appeared quietly self-assured, some people began to model their behavior after him, while others listened critically but attentively to his ideas. Unlike other stressful situations where individual competition or conflict was often built in, this one had the potential for social bonding. The people were close, outwardly friendly, generally supportive, and shared many views and behaviors. Thus, given Peter's previous intentions and the situation in the house, the move toward closer interpersonal relations and eventual communalism was not surprising.

But Peter neither was, nor wanted to be, the only focal point through which all the individuals would relate to one another. Such an organizational form certainly would not be truly communal. How was a collection of individuals, some of whom were willing to follow Peter's lead and some of whom were quite independent, to be transformed into a coherent group with each member relating directly to all the others?

The critical factor here was the occasional and precipitous dismantling of interpersonal barriers among Dobson House members, first to the point of physical and mental nakedness, and then to contact. At the least, such experiences resulted in no sense of invasion of one person by another, and at most, involved an exhilarating synergetic sense of fusion. It is by no means coincidental that all the members cited the night of the power game as the virtually ecstatic moment when the collection of individuals became a communal group. They became a kind of living social organism with an awareness common to all members, yet perhaps with a greater, an ineffable, independent awareness and power of its own, beyond the grasp of each person individually. Within the group, a sense of absolute trust manifested itself, even if momentarily, and was reinforced, at least the night of the power game, by a kind of alliance against a quasi-hostile out-group. On top of this was the sexuality that was latent in the moment and overt afterwards. Sex bore the same emotionally forceful integrative message at the physical level that was perceived at the intellectual level.

After being briefly exposed to such experiences, some of the people were motivated to explore them further; to search them through to see what intensity they could add to life and what direction they could give. Like those who experience fleeting union with God, nature, or beautiful music, and thereafter seek or create situations so as to repeat or perpetuate them, some of the Dobson House people wanted to do the same with respect to people; their people. Their goal was to create an environment where intense interpersonal experiences could be repeated and heightened. Instead of regarding people as inconveniences or as instruments to be employed in the attainment of certain ends, people and relationships in and of themselves would become the focal goal. Who needed a future when the present could be timeless? Why did they need to be dependent on the larger society's institutions when they could create their own?

Thus, the idea of a commune became increasingly appealing. Not only would it allow them to create new lives deliberately for each and new relationships for all, but a large commune located on open land would serve as a refuge for others wishing to experience the same thing; to experience what the established social order was apparently either afraid of or incapable of providing. In addition to giving its members something tangible and whole upon which to pin their identities, living in a commune would also give them vision and purpose. Many would feel a distinct sense of pride at being freaks who were at a new social frontier, carving out a new way of life. They began to see themselves not just as mere individuals or as a single commune, but as part of a larger social and historical process. They began to feel they shared a special destiny with other communards, such as the people at Parson's Crossing, who had undergone a similar collective euphoria at its inception that was still going strong one year later. So why couldn't they?

Not everyone, however, held to these ideas with equal enthusiasm. Some agreed to go along with the idea only because there were no other alternatives. Even among those who professed commitment, there were deep but vague fears of failure and of losing more than they could gain. Finally, there were competing commitments. Some joined the venture because of loyalties to individuals in the group, others to the group as a whole, and still others to an ideal.

3. Expansion: Summer Excitement on the Land

When Peter bought the land, snow was still on the ground. The day the deal was closed, Peter, Yale, and Bill dropped some acid and went to the land to survey their new domain, taking an ax in case they wanted to mark anything off. Parking the car on the town road, they had to walk in on an abandoned road for a mile in order to reach the meadow. On the way down the road, "acid consciousness" began to take over as the three of them simultaneously became concerned about who was carrying the ax. Stopping, they laughed to discover each was worrying about his own safety. Despite the humorous honesty, they all commented that it was uncomfortably strange for the same thought to cross one another's minds at the same time. When they reached the land, they found a huge tree that had fallen over the fence. Yale slammed the ax into the dead trunk where it was forgotten that day, but consciously not removed for six months afterward. As an afterthought, they realized the symbolic significance of burying any potential hatchet.

After the gesture of peace, they split up, each wandering over the land, running through the woods, following streams, watching clouds drift by, and marveling at the crooked shadows the tree skeletons cast across the snow. Peter eventually found himself at the top of the steep hill that overlooked the meadow below. As he looked out over the distant mountains and valleys, a strange feeling came over him. It was as if an energy force drove him to start briskly walking a broad circle in the clearing atop the hill. Circling for what must have been three hours, the radius finally narrowed to where he was in the center, spinning around. In exhaustion, he finally fell to the ground, looking up through tree branches at the clear blue sky.

Peter began to feel a great surge of emotion for the land. At the same time, he felt that he was breaking out of the last layers of the shell that was his learning, his society, his civilization, even his life. He was no longer himself but an Indian, not governed by American social convention, but by the land and nature. He also felt Indian hatred for him; the white man, the intruder. Suddenly, a certain large tree called to him, somehow communicating that it was the source of all life on the land, a great nurturant being; strong, silent, and giving. It became apparent to him that the being was female, specifically a great mother to the life on the land. In his experience he drew closer to it, merged with it, and suddenly found himself making love to the tree. Later, Yale and Bill eventually found their way to Peter where all three sat side by side looking out over the valley. Enmeshed in their own thoughts and emotions, Peter finally broke the silence by communicating what he was seeing before his eyes. Slowly and quietly, he said, "Blood, the land is covered with blood." The other two were startled by this, and as Peter continued by saying that death was coming to the land, they got up to leave.

On warm spring days, the Dobson House people spent afternoons on the land. Tripping and naked, they ran through the fresh spring grass, waded in the stream, and made love in the privacy of little clearings that dotted the hills next to the meadows. The first time Jesse visited the Meadows, he wandered naked onto the same hill Peter had been on earlier, and there he found a clothed young woman he had never seen before. She was from Parson's Crossing, whose house one could make out across the valley before the trees fully blossomed with leaves. She explained that the people from her house often took walks here because it was such a beautiful piece of land. Not only were the views breathtaking, but the land itself was extraordinary, having a fascinating mix of rock outcrops, open fields, and dark forest. For generations, local farmers had been using it for pasture land, providing a steady assortment of grazing animals that had kept the grass well mowed and the encroaching woods in check.

The first full day on the land, a campsite was prepared by the stream next to the meadow. Tall saplings were cut for poles to construct a frame around which polyethylene plastic sheeting was tacked. All the kitchen materials were kept inside this tent. In the center of the clearing, they constructed an open fireplace. Later a brick oven was constructed nearby, the bricks having been removed from an abandoned and collapsed farmhouse on the road about half way between the Meadows and Parson's Crossings. The stream, which bubbled up from a spring in the north meadow, was the source of drinking, cooking, washing, and bathing water. Sapling pole and plastic tents were constructed up the side of Eagle Claw Mountain, out of view, but within a few minutes walk from the central area. Stones were set in place, forming a dam across the stream. The small pond it created was deep enough to completely submerge a number of sweaty bodies when the day's work was done. In the center of the south meadow, a two acre garden site was chosen. After the back-breaking labor of hauling boulders and innumerable smaller stones from within the perimeter, Parson's Crossing was prevailed upon to plow it with their tractor. Finally, a large pole and plastic teepee was constructed at the kitchen area.

The physical work was very strenuous, requiring brute physical strength for lifting, hauling, chopping, and pushing. The women found they could do very little of this work. Almost from the very first day, a division between the sexes developed that had not existed when they lived in the Dobson House. Males were working together, running into town after materials and information, and discussing problems while the women hung around the camp building fires, cooking, watching the children, and expressing their displeasure. But as the women became more disgruntled, the men grew more confident and assertive. There was hard work by daylight and hard drinking by fire light, with the women feeling out of place in both contexts. Filled with a sense of self-importance that their new roles gave them, some males became actively domineering. This was particularly true of the Menominee Indian, who, though well liked by the other men, aggressively articulated a home-spun philosophy asserting that the only thing women could do well was bitch, divide men from each other, and destroy "good times."

The spring and early summer was so filled with activity that few people took the time to sit and quietly probe each other's psyches. In the words of Jesse, "We were so preoccupied with our own immediate work needs that we didn't think about going beyond. We built things to physically justify our existence there, rather than constructing anything emotionally or socially." The men didn't think about what was happening because at that stage they were quite happy with their new found activities. The women said little, not knowing how to change things and having to face a strong male dominance faction that would ridicule their complaints. No one there, at that time, had ever heard of women's liberation.

Toward mid-summer, much of the initial heavy work had been done. Gardening became predominant, dulling the edge of male bravado to some degree, while giving the women a role outside cooking and child tending. Working in the garden now required the tedious labors of hoeing, weeding, bug killing, mulching, and pruning. Candy had a run-in with the Menominee Indian that began with her complaining about his drinking and his criticizing her for sharing some of the fruits of his work with visitors without asking him first. As a male, he believed he had the right to veto and control her actions, while she would not stand for his interference in so much of her life. Finally, alluding to her living with Peter, the primary owner and architect of JM, she told him that if he didn't like it there on the land, he could leave. This was the first time that anyone had ever brought up, even if indirectly, the latent issues of expulsions and special privileges in this new, open, and free social experiment. While the incident shocked some of the males, the females never had sufficient nerve or status to confront the men this way themselves.

The only firm link between the sexes were the couples, and even these relationships came under severe stress. Candy, for example, at only 19, was taking on a mother role as people began to look to her for nurturance and restrictions, just as they looked to Peter for leadership. She was advising and admonishing people five years her senior. They had resented her meddling when they didn't ask for it, however, "just like children," according to Candy. She resented being thrust into this role, not having the freedom to be happy-go-lucky and carefree because she had a child and was Peter's woman. Peter, too, came to expect her to be very adult and responsible, chastising her for being immature in her attempts at control while supporting others for being spontaneous and having fun. She became angry with Peter, who usually spent evenings down at the campsite singing and banging drums by the fire, while she fearfully remained with the baby. Other males criticized her behavior as hysterical, one saying that all she did was "complain about ghosts and run around accusing people of having and spreading staph infections."

Other couples were having their problems as well. The couple that Peter and Candy wanted a quadruple relationship with was still fragile due to the different partners' responses. Bill and Mary broke up, each going his and her own way; Bill rather independent and Mary still fearful and insecure. She took up with the Menominee Indian, but he was too demanding even for her. Her primary concern was that she didn't know how to raise children by herself. She sought out any situation in which there were many people present, hoping for help in taking care of her children. But though they enjoyed her children, none of the men took any responsibility, and she increasingly became dissatisfied.

After moving to the land, sexual activity diminished, for there was growing tension between the sexes while at the same time the opportunity for it decreased. Working all day and everyone sleeping by the fire or in the teepee at night, couples had to make a special effort to get off by themselves. In some ways the desire for sex decreased as physical activity and integrative emotional experiences, not that unrelated to the sex experience itself, partly displaced overt sexual activity. Moreover, Peter had largely lost interest in sex as a way of establishing social bonds, discovering something more powerful and more fascinating: energy bonds.

Every night, usually high on alcohol or drugs, they sat around the camp fire playing drums, clapping their hands rhythmically, watching the dancing shadows on the trees, and dancing themselves. No longer singing popular songs, musical structure broke down, with individuals making up their own repeating melodic phrases in throbbing rhythm very much like chanting. People became so involved in the moment that they rapturously danced around oblivious to the others, sometimes "speaking in tongues." Claiming not to try to put on "back to the natives" acts consciously, many said that at times they blanked out or found sounds coming from their mouths that made no sense, yet felt appropriate, seeming to have an independence of their own. During such moments of intense involvement, Peter could perceive bands of energy connecting all the people involved. By concentrating, he claimed he could alter the bands, making them stronger and projecting them where he wanted. Later admitting to becoming intoxicated with his new found powers, he imagined himself forming groups of energy-bound people under his leadership. At the time, however, he thought of it in terms of the good deeds that could be accomplished by many individuals working together so closely.

Nearly everyone was becoming more mystically oriented. Only the politically inclined people like Jesse and frustrated academicians such as Yale resisted. People swore they felt the presence of Indian spirits on the land, and in themselves. The Indian spirits were assumed to be the source of the strange tongues. Often people went naked, or wore breech clouts. Yale and a few others, instead of undergoing cultural regression to the clothing of primitive tribes, acted out a psychological developmental one by wearing large diapers on a number of occasions. People even took on Indian names, such as Red Fox and Blue Owl, and though crediting the Menominee Indian to some extent, insisted that most of these behavior forms spontaneously emerged because of the land, the elements, and the life conditions there. Some people claimed to have caught glimpses of spirits on the land. Candy, for instance, was certain that spirits caused her temporary blindness, that voices spoke to her, and that a giant man had come out of the bushes toward her. Once she was startled to look down from her tent to see a man hanging by his neck from a tree limb (at this time she never drank or did drugs).

On his visits to Parson's Crossing, Yale learned of Ebenezer King. This "colored man," according to a book about the history of Wilfred, had bought his own freedom from slavery, married a black published authoress, and moved to the area. He borrowed money for land, becoming one of the first black men in America to own a farm, which according to the description included part of Jackson's Meadows. At first, little attention was paid to Ebenezer by local residents, and he and his family kept to themselves. Eventually, hostility toward the family grew to the point where local ruffians used to ride by shooting at the house, with Ebenezer returning the fire. After sending his wife and children away for their safety, his house and barn were set ablaze and he was killed.

With Yale flavoring the account around the JM campfire, everyone came to assume that Jackson's Meadows was Ebenezer's farm, that he vowed revenge on all white people before he died, that he was buried on the land somewhere in a secret grave, and that local people claimed to have seen his ghost. Even superrational Yale claimed to have momentarily seen a black figure going up a side path at dusk, whom he chased but could not find. Others said that they also got strange feelings at that particular and other spots in the road. Someone else had heard the Parson's Crossing people speak of Mother Remington, a woman who generations ago was accused of being a witch and leading a coven. Thus, mysterious bits of information, dug out of dusty volumes by the scholars and literati of Parson's Crossings, took on an ominous reality by the time they passed through Jackson's Meadows. Most were convinced that the spirits definitely existed, and that as blacks, witches, and even Indians, they hated the land's living residents for being part of the very civilization that had oppressed and destroyed them.

Stories of evil doings and impending catastrophe were also spread by visitors, who, instead of being referred to the Dobson House by the street scene, were now sent to the Meadows. They arrived from cities in droves telling of muggings, rape, secret concentration camps set up by the government, potential race wars, rising CO_2 in the atmosphere and melting ice caps, imminent floods, nuclear testing, and earthquake forecasts. Such gossip was the major source of information regarding the outside world, for none of the group read newspapers, and there was not one radio on the land. If they accidentally heard a broadcast or saw a headline, they didn't believe it anyway, after all the lies they believed they had been previously spoon-fed by the media and teachers. Longhairs came and stayed from days to weeks, setting up their own plastic tents all over the land. Peter welcomed them, subscribing to the apocalyptic assumption that the world was on the verge of catastrophic upheavals, while at the same time proclaiming the dawning of the Aquarian Age. People could come to the land to escape the coastal tidal waves and metropolitan infernos and to establish new relationships between people and things and between one another. Because no individuals could really "own" pieces of the earth, anyone was free to live on the land. With the increasing number of visitors, Jackson's Meadows was referred to by hip residents in the area as a societal refugee camp.

The little country lane Parson's Crossing had hoped would lead to idyllic serenity became a busy highway to the New Age, jostling with dust clouds from vehicles ranging from a VW bus with a plastic bubble and wings made to look like a World War II fighter plane, to psychedelic school buses; from motorcycles to pick-up trucks with built-on "A" frame cabins sporting God's eyes swaying from the eaves. Some of the arrivees were cool-headed revolutionaries who had come to check out this latest manifestation of the CC. Then there was "Crazy Fred" who wore nothing but jockey shorts and a red bandanna to cover his bald head. He carried a little notebook in his hand in which he constantly made entries that no one else could understand. There was the fellow who sat cross-legged all day under the big tree up on the hill eating nothing but pure honey and tabs of LSD until he disappeared one day. There was also the "incredibly up-tight guy" who followed everyone around snapping questions at them, such as "Why did you sit down?" when someone sat down, or when someone was holding an ax, "Is that an ax you're holding?"

Since sex between members was declining after the initial period of exploration, visitors became the chief source of erotic gratification. Members of Parson's Crossing, having already gone into their own "monastic" phase, although unhappy to see such a frantic scene so close by, sometimes visited the Meadows in search of partners of either sex. Local high school and street freaks also visited with more than one set of parents becoming irate over what they believed their daughters were engaging in while there. A few young girls, obviously runaways, went from bedroll to bedroll; in the end refraining from all sexual activity feeling that, since they meant very little to anyone in particular, they were being taken, again and again. At one point, someone was rumored to have gonorrhea. People sat around calculating their chances of having contracted it by mapping out coital chains containing information on who had slept with whom over the past weeks.

During the first part of the summer, there was an immense amount of drug taking. Most of the drugs were brought by visitors. Almost everyone was either wandering around in drug induced worlds of their own, or worrying about hustling some dope from the new arrivees. Peter's first visit to the spiritual group, the Krishna Brethren, and his talks with its leader convinced him he should stop using drugs. The Brethren's leader found it impossible to develop complete commitment to a group enterprise if drugs were around to deflect people's efforts. "If you want to develop a true community," he said, "you must get rid of drugs."

Frustrated with a lack of accomplishment at JM, this advice instantaneously struck a resonant strain with Peter. He returned to declare that he was no longer doing drugs, and others, especially the women, took up the cry, urging everyone else to quit. Mary, who by now was fed up with what she considered the non-direction and hedonistic stagnation around her, suggested that a no-drug rule be adopted. Those in favor of it spoke out (which happened to be much of what at the time could be considered leadership), and those opposed said nothing, with the result that during the next few days, carloads of people left because of the apparent new rule. The evacuees included some old core members such as the Menominee Indian, while the couple who owned the headshop and who also did some dealing in town also decided to leave.

Some time later, the Brethren leader, James, visited JM, asking if his group could move there, apparently feeling there was little possibility for expansion if they were to remain isolated where they were. Since JM was a center of great activity, the possibility of finding new members was no doubt a consideration. Peter agreed, indicating an interest in learning more of James' ideas. Although all the remaining people at JM experienced a sense of relief after the drug crowd left, many were dubious about another group arriving. By this time the Brethren numbered 16 or 17, having few females (all the original 9 were males). Finally, it was agreed that the two groups would remain separate on the same land, living in two different encampments, yet free to mingle if they wished.

The Brethren built one large odd shaped tent out of poles and plastic in which everyone slept and all belongings were kept. Later a tree house was built. A special cabin where auras could be read was constructed off the ground on stilts so that the earth energy currents wouldn't disturb the readings. Because of the compact living conditions and the bad weather that kept everyone inside that summer, interaction between the Brethren members grew quite intense. Discipline was severe and all energies went into realizing James' dreams of a group that could act as one, marked by respect and dedication by each individual for each other, to the point where they pledged their willingness "to die for each other." Complete loyalty was demanded as a means of concentrating energies; each person being in phase with and amplifying the other.

Drugs, alcohol, and "promiscuity" were forbidden, and, on occasion, James expelled members for violating the rules. He could often sense that transgressions had been made, confronting certain individuals who would then admit their misdeeds. Constantly on display to other Brethren, his interpersonal skills and perceptions were being tested all the time. Sure that James was no charlatan, those who lived with him the longest and who knew him best became the most convinced of his special powers. Although it is doubtful that any Brethren had been exposed to psychological encounter techniques, they constantly confronted one another, demanding honesty, openness, and the destruction of all psychological defenses. Of course, James did most of the confronting; forcing behavioral and attitudinal shifts in the others who were too confused and weak to resist. Among other things, this method was intended to destroy hesitation and uncertainty; those aspects of the human psyche which prevented the full release of intrinsic, boundless energy.

There were physical feats that people were required to perform in order to rid themselves of fear. One, for example, was to jump from a high stone ledge into a gorge in the bottom which there was a pool of water. People were also urged to let their actions be guided by the intensity of feeling, not by cautious and constricting intellectual concepts. Only by feeling the rush of energy in the course of commitment and action could one be complete and free from misfortune. Proof was offered. Didn't so-and-so get into a terrific wreck with a car and walk away without a scratch? Didn't they sit around the campfire one night with all their money gone and nothing to eat but a few turnips for them all, and someone showed up the next day with a whole load of food? For those who felt trapped, paralyzed, inferior, incompetent, and directionless, the message was clear. Whatever you do, do it fully and don't worry about it. Uninhibited action will integrate you completely with the forces that control the outcome.

The outlook of the Brethren was apocalyptic in the literal sense of the word. War, disease, riots, and natural disasters were bound to befall man and there was no way to prevent them, James said. As the world rushed toward and passed through the Picean holocaust, it would then enter into the Aquarian age of human togetherness and spirituality. Instead of trying to topple governments or change social structures, the Brethren went directly to what it regarded as the source. Instead of dealing on levels of materiality, it saw itself as tapping pure cosmic energy so that new sensibility could be molded for the crisis to come. By wiping out the negative and replacing it with the positive, a social force could be created that would carry mankind across the abyss to the other side. The Brethren were learning to be this social force. As individuals, they would eventually go out into the world to teach others and to lead the fearless survivors into the New World after the powerful have destroyed themselves. According to one of their songs, the meek were inevitably going to inherit the earth.

While the Brethren grew more cohesive and purposeful with each passing day, the JM group did not appear to be evolving in any particular direction. People still came and went, drank and did drugs off and on, slept around, and generally did "their own thing." Peter wanted to make a cohesive community out of his group, but wasn't sure how. He, more than anyone else there, visited the Brethren's camp; talking and listening. In many ways his world view (cosmic energies, apocalypse, and all) was not too different from the Brethren's, though he could not subscribe to the strident tone and group-think he saw developing. Those at JM who had spiritual leanings admired the Brethren in a way, yet had similar reservations.

The rationalist faction was openly derisive of the Brethren, being quick to point out their contradictions. For example, the leader and a few of his top "lieutenants" were the only ones who could ride vehicles while everyone else had to walk. With all their talk of love, they had alienated the townspeople by the way they wildly careened around the country roads in their vehicles. By emphasizing spirit, they were neglecting the material side by dumping garbage all over the land, running motorcycles up and down the hills next to the meadow, and defecating on the ground next to the road. Above all, JMers objected to the proselytizing by Brethren members, who, when they did come in contact with JM people, were usually talking about the superiority of their own group.

Conversely, the Brethren looked upon the JM people as uncommitted hippies reveling in carnal material pleasure. Mary agreed, and she and her two children left her old group to join the Brethren. The situation never really deteriorated into open competition or hostility, however, except perhaps the time the Brethren leader was away and a lieutenant took over, leading the members on a wild shouting and running spree through the woods, singing "our leader is better than your leader."

In an effort to convince JM's Peter and others to join the Brethren, James quietly visited the JM campsite, sitting and minding his own business, but gladly talking if others struck up a conversation with him. He also offered to read people's auras. But when Peter declined to join, and it was apparent that other JM members were not going to change their ways of living, James had a vision. He said that a terrible disaster would befall JM; he had seen a great fire. When JM members found out about this prognostication, they were angered to think that James self-righteously viewed their lives as so misdirected, some of them interpreting his vision as an attempt at psychic coercion. But despite what others thought, Peter's experience with the Brethren had a profound effect on him.

Despite talk of the cosmos and primal social forces, JM Peter was still faced with the dilemmas presented by day-to-day affairs inside his own group. Some of the greatest problems were caused not by strangers, but by friends of members. Certain individuals at JM were plugged into other networks; many of whose members would descend on the Meadows "like a cloud of locusts." These people were particularly hard to deal with because feelings could easily be hurt. One such network was the alumni of the progressive school in which Peter and Candy met. They brought preconceived, sometimes "arrogant" notions of how the place should be operated. Although they didn't have children of their own, they advised Candy that she was rearing her baby incorrectly. Moreover, after they had come to view Peter as a kind of guardian at the school, they consequently expected him to pick up after them on the land. Four of the progressive school people remained at the Meadows; two of whom (a couple) were staff members at the school.

The Buddhist, who had previously introduced the male dominance oriented drinkie-druggie hippies from San Francisco, also brought his old girlfriend from Chisholm College and her new boyfriend. Although considering themselves full-fledged members of the commune, they did what they wanted, when they wanted, irrespective of everyone else. The man also had formal training in group therapy and in encounter techniques, skills that led to difficulties later that autumn. When the specter of a cold, uncomfortable winter raised its head, people became concerned with building year-round shelters and earning money to last them till the next summer. Meetings were instituted to organize work, but this fellow turned them into encounter sessions. While some visitors liked the sessions, being more interested in psychodynamics than survival, Peter and the other core members, who worried about starving and freezing, obviously didn't like them. Peter claimed that the frustrated therapist enjoyed the idea of leading people, and by turning the meetings into encounter sessions, became the leader, giving him an importance he otherwise didn't have. Others noted that the sessions succeeded in reducing cooperation by tearing the group apart. The screaming, accusations, ganging up on certain individuals, and "who-are-we-going-to-pick-on-tonight" meetings finally came to an end when most people just stopped going. The couple drifted off by themselves, building their own cabin at the edge of the land.

Another network was introduced by Elliot (later known as Red Fox), the ex-SDS leader, who came to be regarded as a "pain in the ass" by some. Drifting in and out, he was often not there when people needed him, returning to disrupt the delicate equilibrium established during his absence. Moreover, he told many people he met to go visit Jackson's Meadows: "his commune." Individuals arrived indicating that Elliot said they could stay; people ranging from down-and-out street freaks to sociology instructors and researchers. Nearly every weekend, a group of his student friends showed up with grocery bags brimming with food and beer, waved hello, and disappeared into the hills. Not only did they blissfully walk past the campsite full of hungry people who often had nothing more than a bag of brown rice for the next meal, but left tin cans and garbage strewn over the land. This irked the members to the point where they actually called a meeting to deal with the visitor problem. People complained that Elliot's friends' behavior was symptomatic of an attitude that many others had; that the Meadows was nothing but a summer resort vacation retreat rather than a serious effort to build a new way of life. Finally, it was resolved to give them the deliberate, hostile, icy shoulder treatment when they next came, rather than directly asking them to leave, The strategy worked, for they never returned again.

With this instance of collective decision making and communal cooperation, those previously discouraged regained hope for something constructive to come of the summer. The no-drug rule also was an encouraging sign, but it, too, reflected people's hesitation to communicate what they really felt. Actually, many people had mixed feelings on the subjects of visitors and drugs. Some visiting strangers were welcome and some were not, and the only way to find out which were desirable was to admit everyone. Although some didn't speak out in favor of drugs, perhaps agreeing at one level that they shouldn't be done, at another level they really wanted the freedom to indulge and visitors were a good source of supply. On the other hand, if they did exercise full power to exclude outsiders, who knows what good people they would turn away; hard workers, entertaining personalities, talented artists, creative thinkers?

This general visitor problem was dealt with in two ways; both of which were aimed at screening out those not seriously willing to commit and contribute. First, a large sign was posted listing all the prohibitions supposedly enforced on the land. "No drugs, no staying overnight without a parent's permission if you are under 18, no shitting in the land except in the latrine, no pets, no use of soap in the stream." None of these posted regulations were strictly enforced (except perhaps soap in the stream), but it was hoped that they would discourage visitors while pleasing the townspeople at the same time. The selective enforcement did not work however, because it was inconsistent.

The second solution was the development of a cold shoulder treatment toward all strangers. Becoming tired of being nice to new people and answering unlimited questions from them, the core people constructed new plastic tents and teepees way up in the hills, "grooving on the land," sometimes not coming down to the kitchen area for days at a time. When they did, they were often gruff and uncommunicative with those still living in the valley. Food supplies were low, with some core people beginning to stash their own supplies in their tents, while the core women usually got stuck with the burdensome task of cooking for the motley mob of hangers-on. Coming to rely on one another so much that they felt they just didn't need outsiders, the core people communicated more by nuance than explicit exchange, each assuming they already knew "where the other's head was at." As the summer wore on, some people, particularly Yale and Bill, became aggressive and arbitrary with outsiders, thinking that their orders and insults were contributing to the order of the place.

A steady stream of so-called straights also made their way to the land, some to complain about the freaks who banged on their doors in the middle of the night asking directions to the Meadows. The Meadows people were conscious of the necessity for maintaining good relations with the local straight people and went out of their way to invite them to visit. A little missionary spirit was also involved, as the Meadows people felt that those leading the hopelessly tedious and oppressive straight life would learn something from their new, free style. Local farmers, impressed with the communards' attempts to make farming a way of life, came giving advice where they could. Church pastors and preachers came to investigate their spirituality and perhaps win a few more souls for Jesus. Voyeurs came; husbands, wives, and small kids, leaving their cars and gawking and giggling while eating their picnic lunches at the edge of the Meadows. Carloads of beer drinking, lower working class men spilled onto the Meadow, and while occasionally belligerent and looking for a fight, at least weren't afraid to get near the hippies and talk to them. By the time the beer drinkers left, everyone was usually drunk and on good terms. Saturday afternoons took on the atmosphere of cultural exchange functions, people cautiously feeling each other out, eager to find a shred of commonality they could rejoice in, while all the time knowing they lived in different worlds. Of course, the most hostile townspeople never visited.

Specific events were set up whereby the two worlds could ceremonially get together. The Meadows people held a large picnic at which a number of straights appeared. To earn some money, Meadows people worked for a local extended farm family. One Sunday they organized a softball game which was billed as "Hippies vs. Townspeople." Even a hippie wedding was held for the benefit of the town. Discovering that Yale had sent away for a document legally making him a pastor, a newly arrived Meadows couple decided to get married. In their finest lace and with flowers in their hair, the people stood in a large circle in the middle of the Meadow holding hands, dancing and singing around the couple.

Going to Centerville for supplies, Meadows people, often tripping, would pour out of bizarre vehicles in outlandish outfits, singing and playing musical instruments, once meandering down Main Street to extend their greetings. Sufficiently disculturated so that most inhibitions regarding public behavior were gone, they simply didn't care how they acted. Having their own reference group and microsociety, they could no longer be ostracized from that societal context. Although they really did not wish to offend, they liked to shock. Emulating the behavior of Yippies and Parson's Crossing's most famous founder, they enjoyed the attention they attracted through their antics. The blowing-people's- minds brand of spontaneous theatrics was there too; performing unpredictable acts in order to elicit unpredictable responses. The response was entertaining to the JMers; just as their performance entertained some of the townspeople.

By midsummer, just about everyone in the area knew of Jackson's Meadows, and inevitably contradictory reactions set in. The standard rumors of sexual debauchery and perversion were generated and circulated largely by local women. Many were sure that the Meadows had become the main source of drugs in the region; the obvious cause of the drug use explosion at the local high school. Some even claimed that the property values in Wilfred would go down. Local people became especially upset after the Brethren moved to the land. They accused the Brethren of reckless speeding down country roads, endangering life and limb. Because it was difficult to ticket them on these back roads, farmers wanted to take matters into their own hands. At one point, they considered cutting a tree down across the road around a sharp curve, hopefully causing one of their vehicles to crash. Although they never did it, feelings ran high, and few locals distinguished between the two longhair groups. As far as most were concerned, they all lived at the Meadows and a hippie was a hippie.

Others had a strange fascination for the place. Pickup trucks and four wheel drive vehicles appeared on the road that hadn't seen through vehicular traffic since horse and buggy days, slowing down to a crawl where the road bordered the meadow. The communards often worked and played with no clothes on, and the occupants of some of these surprise vehicles undoubtedly caught glimpses of young breasts and pubic regions. Some drove into the meadow ostensibly to ask directions, often incoherent, as their eyes wandered over to the naked women working in the garden. Just before he stopped taking drugs, Peter was tripping and felt an overpowering compulsion to climb to the very top of Eagle Claw. With an awesome feeling of energy, he ran to the top to shout out over the valley at the top of his lungs. A little man who evidently was hiding behind a tree was startled and fell backward over a rock. Getting up and backing away, he indignantly mumbled something about "crazy hippies."

Other townspeople in official capacities began to keep a watchful eye on the Meadows. A county conservation agent was discovered by the stream that in mid-summer barely had enough water to keep a frog wet; claiming he was checking if anyone was fishing without a license. The town health official also visited the commune making sure that there was proper waste disposal and a water supply fit for drinking. The health inspector, a local medical practitioner, admitted he was under pressure from certain factions of townspeople to enforce the only codes the town had at the time. But sympathizing with the communards, he only made recommendations, gave warnings, and was generally helpful. The councilmen also visited the land, advising against building any inferior structures to get them through the winter in the "unlikely" event they were thinking of staying. The police came out twice during the summer, having no particular business, saying they were on patrol.

With another segment of the local population, the Jackson's Meadows commune was quite acceptable and even admired. People went out of their way to speak to the Meadows people in town, some even being a little unsure of themselves, as if they were talking to celebrities. Certain individuals offered them help, gave old tools they no longer needed, or granted them discounts on food and supplies. Of course, no Meadow people refused favors when in need, and acts of charity from local residents encouraged some Meadows people to exploit their generosity. Sometimes straight people would go out of their way to talk to them to get things off their chest. Many admitted they wished they had the nerve to just take off and do what they wanted, but they were trapped by spouse, kids, and payments on the car. Others spoke of their utter confusion with the war in Vietnam, the ghetto riots, their own kids thinking so differently, the cost of living going up, and everything changing so fast. Some broke down and cried, while pouring out their personal troubles. Often Meadows people didn't know how to deal with their unexpected confessional role, mumbling words of encouragement in their embarrassment. Evidently, because hippies were outside the straight world, people could communicate their misgivings to hippies without having to suffer the repercussions such confessions would surely bring on in their own milieu.

The oldest local farm families treated the Meadow people as they would any other homestead, having many of the same concerns, interests, and respect for the processes of nature. The newest straight residents, too, felt an identification with the commune. Having moved to the area from the cities themselves within the last five years or so, they still felt like outsiders; not fully accepted by most of the natives. For example, one of the Meadows' best straight friends was a man engaged in a struggle with the town fathers over what he thought was a flagrantly discriminatory high tax assessment. In short, those in the town who were marginal to the local social and political structure, often those who had been around the longest or shortest periods of time, were sympathetic to the commune.

On the other hand, those who lived there before the mass exodus from urban areas began in the 1960s or those who worked in businesses and small industry rather than agriculture had little or no sympathy for the communards. Potentially marginal people, who were consequently socially insecure, such as unskilled laborers and clerks, were the most resentful. Even those whose feelings were somewhat neutral eventually passed into cool noninvolvement with the commune for fear of being ostracized by their neighbors. A number of local citizens indicated to the Meadows people that although everyone else in town didn't care for the hippies, they thought they were okay. Thus many people blamed others than themselves for the hostile feelings. Even the general store had to acquiesce, confidentially admitting they were cautious about being too friendly with the new longhaired residents for fear of losing business from their regular customers.

At the time, many of the communards really didn't care what the townspeople thought about them anyway. Only Yale and Bill made any consistent effort to reach out to specific local people, partly for public relations reasons and partly because they enjoyed it. Being "ambassadors" (and they were) gave them a feeling of importance, and Yale in particular enjoyed and excelled at cracker barrel talk, having grown up in a small town where his father was the political big shot.

Most of the other communards at JM however, were too involved in getting themselves and the commune together to be concerned about the town. Each day required working, building, and planning to keep them busy, and they didn't need any outsiders to entertain them daily because they had one another. Some were deliberately defiant, flaunting their contempt for straight social conventions by using profanity within earshot of some, or laughing at the "uptight" behavior of others. But most Meadows people just didn't consider the consequences of talking in a crowded store about a couple "balling each other in the bushes," or swimming naked at the nearby public pond.

Most JMers didn't feel the need to be cautious or diplomatic. Many felt confident for the first time in their lives. Just about everyone on the land had a heady sense of the hand of destiny on their shoulders, for they fully believed their lifestyle was the certain way of the future, and it was just too bad for those who didn't realize it. Their view that the world was beating a path to the commune's door was supported by the fact that so many people came to visit them, including the journalists and students writing papers for college. Even Parson's Crossing evidently was passé, receding into the shadows as the spotlight shifted to Jackson's Meadows. What the Meadows people didn't know at the time, however, was that Parson's Crossing was sending all the crazies, weirdoes, bikers, and newspaper people who showed up at their door down the road to the new hippie commune.

Despite the excitement and activity, the most responsible Meadows people felt there was no discernible progress in the building of a solid communal group. When the Brethren moved onto the land, a mirror was held up to the original group. Having the two communes side by side, it was easy to see little change among the Meadows people while day by day the Brethren welded itself into a progressively tighter group with an increasingly consuming sense of purpose. Some JMers were envious, but most were glad they were not living under such tight regimentation. Peter, having seen his sex bond plan fail and his energy bond approach not work either, now looked toward the Brethren as a possible model. While James was a great influence on him, the authoritarian approach of forcing bonds through subservience to a higher order still put him off.

It didn't, however, put off Mary, who lost patience with Peter. After waiting for him to take some decisive action, in the end she found him only equivocating. James was specifically wooing Mary and paying great attention to her children. His approach possibly appealed to Mary, first, because a decisive, dominant spiritual leader was making a fuss over her, and second (perhaps more important) she felt she would be in a context where her children would be cared for and raised with a consistent set of principles. James was also becoming aware of the significance of children in perpetuating communities and beliefs. Mary and her children left the Meadows group to join the Brethren, having traveled to Wilfred in a desperate search for a greater cause and brighter future that they did not find in the Meadows group but observed in the Brethren.

Indirectly, the Brethren also caused the Buddhist to leave the Meadows. Closely allied with Peter at first because of their religious orientation, he could not accept Peter's growing mysticism. Because Buddhism is founded on day to day and sometimes mundane empiricism, his kind of religiosity was not recognized by the land's highest religious and mystic authorities: James and Peter. On the other hand, his world view wasn't recognized by the non-spiritual faction either. Finding himself alone and lacking influence despite his being the only other member financially contributing to the land, he began to phase himself out. After arranging to have lumber donated to the Meadows to build a house, he returned from a trip to find a permanent cookshack built from the lumber without his consultation. Later, his father went to the trouble to bring a truck that was in working order that required only four decent tires to allow it to pass inspection. But what little available money there was was "frittered away on ice cream during trips to town" instead of buying tires. Fed up, he gave up, joining a circle of visitors to form a small, idle socializing clique. Finally, when a truckload of people assembled as the "Jackson Meadow Jug Band" on its way to the Woodstock rock festival, he joined them. Impressed with the real Aquarian spirit he found there, he boarded one of the famed Hog Farm commune's buses and headed for points unknown, eventually joining a Tibetan Buddhist monastery in England.

When at Woodstock, he ran into Jesse, who had also left the Meadows earlier. Not very committed from the beginning, Jesse came and went often. Many complained that he was all ideas and little work, getting everyone excited about a project, but shortly afterwards disappearing. From his viewpoint, the Meadows wasn't going in the right direction anyway. He, more than anyone else, harbored a sociopolitical critique of society, and had no one at the Meadows with whom he could share his views. Once he decided that JM was a dead end, within days, he was in the city where he led a frantic existence holding down three acting jobs at one time. Deciding that this, too, was leading nowhere, he returned to Centerville several months later approaching Red Rose Collective. After much internal discussion there about unreliable hippie types and a security check throughout the underground network, he was admitted. He later became quite close to Charles, and was very active in terms of relating to other freaks in the area. Initially through JM, he had found that there was at least a potential for a milieu in which he would not be considered a "dropout" or an "outlaw." Accordingly, his move to Red Rose was intended not only to bring him into a group with firm direction, but to teach him a set of skills he could use in helping to bring about a society with different conventions and rules that would not exclude him as the SS had.

Elliot, although he never severed ties with the Meadows, for all intents and purposes dropped out. He traveled in midsummer to Berkeley to undergo the Electric Kool Aid Acid Test, stayed with the Hog Farm at Glacier National Park, and visited a number of famous communes, from anarchist Tolstoy Farm to the hard-work-and-earn-money commune begun by Peter's brother. On his travels he met and lived with a mysterious young woman. She seemed very ethereal, appearing to be tied down by no earthly concerns except her baby. The person she had previously been living with was keeping the baby as a hostage to make her come back to him. She said the fellow keeping her baby was literally the Devil incarnate, and because Elliot "gave Jesus vibrations" to her, she pleaded with Elliot to go with her to rescue her baby. She finally left without him to rescue the child herself. The next time he saw her was months later on the front page of a newspaper. He then discovered she was one of the Charles Manson family, Linda Kasabian, the one who was testifying against Manson in the murder trial. Of all his previous escapades (drugs, student revolt, Paris and Prague, Jackson's Meadows) this was the most explosive and decisive. He saw how easily "Satan became Jesus and vice versa," how almost identical was the nature of good and evil, and how the more one wielded power in the name of aid and benefit, the more likely one was to wield it for purposes of exploitation and destruction. The only way to avoid being taken in by something or someone was to increase one's own personal power and understanding so that the misguided and unscrupulous could be resisted. He reenrolled to finish college and embarked on a disciplined study of yoga at an Ashram, where he was eventually joined by his SDS friend who had originally been so smitten with Peter.

Although only six Dobson House members remained, by autumn others had replaced those who left. The original people formed a nucleus, with certain others forming a core group around it. The core, between ten and fifteen members, were deferred to with respect to use of space and facilities. For a person who was visiting the commune for a short while, however, this distinction between core and non-core people would not be clear to see, for some of the other passers-through were also loud and demanding, knowing they would be leaving soon regardless of other people's reaction to them. Those outside the core generally stayed at the campsite if they didn't have tents or vans of their own, or remained scattered about the Meadow. Moving into the inner circle meant moving onto Eagle Claw and the other hills.

Other categories of visitors were those who came to see what a commune was like, find out about the CC institutions elsewhere in Provincia, or look for excitement in the form of fresh air, drugs, booze, sex, and good conversation. Since there were never formal votes to admit people or to expel them from the group, people imperceptibly moved into the core by taking on some important function without unduly agitating anyone else, and by always being around the other core members. One had, in fact, become a "member" when the other members began to notice when the person wasn't around. Some moved into the core more on the basis of their work skills, while others didn't contribute much materially, but were pleasant and entertaining. The quickest way to break in, however, was to become a core member's mate first.

Moving out of the core was approximately the reverse of the moving in process, except that there was a certain status attached to once having been a core member that kept them somewhat participatory until the abrupt end, when they would leave. This status was supported by their experience in dealing with old problems and by the fact that they were sure of themselves (compared to the new members). One would no longer be considered a core member if he or she increasingly left the land for long periods of time, and if his or her absence wasn't commented on one way or the other. Some people, for example the Buddhist, resented the subtle pressure to remain on the land, which implied that only people with second rate loyalty and dedication were the ones who periodically left.

The phenomenon of constant turnover had much to do with the paralysis the nucleus talked about. As people with slightly divergent orientations dropped out, the possibility for more unified action became possible; but, as new people joined, new divergent orientations were presented. For example, in losing Jesse the radical, they gained the amateur therapist. JM veterans also came to abandon the naive assumptions with which they came to the land, but when they tried to apply their new knowledge and perspectives they were usually opposed by newer people not yet exposed to at least a few inevitably disillusioning experiences. A common point of contention, for yet another example, was represented by the planning faction vs. the "organic" growth people; the latter, usually new people, contending that a correct consciousness and natural process alone "would make it all come together." But neither "structure freaks" nor "go with the flow" people had full reign; thus suspending growth (and/or collapse).

Those who had sat dozens of times through the same kinds of discussions and arguments that never achieved resolution were the ones most likely to drop out. On the other hand, many of those who appeared to be innovative visitors looking for a situation where their ideas could be put to the test confided that they were turned off by the paralysis and the autocracy of the nuclear members. People who were most comfortable in a structured situation floundered and withdrew from the amorphous and subtle process of becoming a member: no sets of rules, no formal statuses, or no prescribed tasks to accomplish was more than they could psychologically cope with. But those who were comfortable in it were also inhibited by the arbitrary behavior of those who had the sense of casual confidence that seniority brings. Although they intimidated many guests, senior core members were modeling their behavior on the Brethren lieutenants who seemed to have great success with it. One visitor said he left the Meadows solely because of one person (Yale) "who was always yelling at everyone to get out of his way."

In short, all potential factors for change in one direction or another seemed balanced off and neutralized by one another. Further compounding this situation, thereby further making what potential leadership there was even more unhappy, was the fact that the system specifically encouraged two kinds of people to increase their numbers: those who were most insistent on getting in, regardless of orientation and purpose, and those least likely to have articulated ideas and directions to apply to the situation. The articulate either didn't want to join because of the paralysis, or if they did, were the first to lose interest after not being able to get anything done.

The only one with sufficient power, material and interpersonal, to force a change, was Peter, and he did not act decisively. Candy and some of the other women on three separate occasions went so far as to urge that the commune be dissolved, thereby allowing people to go off to discover new paths and permitting the nucleus people to keep the land perhaps to try again, provided they found the right people. But because this decision like any other had to be made by consensus, the proposal was not acted upon.

What human leadership couldn't do, falling temperatures and shorter days did. With the first signs of winter approaching, a great settling out process began with van loads of fair weather hippies packing up, heading for warmer climates. Conversely, those with no apparent alternatives began to get serious about settling in. Because no common work or project policy could be agreed upon, knots of individuals got together to work on their own, some attempting to donate their efforts to the entire community, others fending for themselves. Peter and Yale decided to build a communal house next to the road in the strip of woods that separated the two meadows. After the foundation was dug, they sat around the hole not knowing what to do with it. Yale wanted a simple design, Peter wanted a seven sided house because the number seven had magical qualities, and neither had extensive building experience. Looking at the immense hole, they became discouraged at the prospects of finishing it before winter, especially since they had very little money. Peter suggested they abandon the project, which they did.

By this time, Peter and the ex-SDS activist were the only ones seriously considering what to do. Some people were drinking every day; others were out collecting botanical specimens. Most were not yet really concerned about winter, with the first full freeze over two months away. Peter and the activist began work on a temporary house that would at least get everyone through this first winter. It was situated at the edge of the meadow close to the stream so that carrying water into the house would not be such a struggle. When it appeared that there would not be enough scrap materials to complete it, Peter began to think of the need for money beyond the hand to mouth amounts they were living on that summer.

Money in small amounts came from a number of different sources: haying for farmers, odd jobs, checks from home, and a couple of low paying jobs for Yale. There were also food stamps that Peter and Candy at first applied for and received. They later expanded their "family" to include other core members of the commune, and because there were no policies to cover this phenomenon at the time, the local welfare office acquiesced. Most of the cash came from Peter (really from his mother), Yale, Bill, and Bill's new "old lady," Gracey, who came to the Meadows late in the summer. The Brethren had just earned money picking apples, and this gave Peter the idea of a contingent going to pick grapes not far from his home town. Although it was distant from Provincia, most of the core people agreed to go.

While picking grapes, the group lived in Peter's mother's summer cottage nearby. Not having the therapist and Yale along, "there were no fights," and the core group recoalesced into a cohesive unit during that period.

When they returned to Wilfred, work on the house began in earnest. Some new people joined (one whose helpful father was a carpenter), and others found old barns to rip down for free lumber. They bought a good second hand truck which they used to haul materials. In the meantime, however, Peter had dropped out of the building project to start his own structure. Up to this time, he was torn by his divided loyalties to Candy and the baby on one side and the commune on the other. Now, after many disappointments with the commune, he finally decided to fend for his family first. He had given up struggling with the therapist, with the result that the meetings ended (and with them the therapist's power base). Those who wanted to, worked on the big house while both Peter and the therapist drifted off to build their own houses; the therapist "conning visitors and new people into helping him" and Peter buying new materials with more money his mother lent him. Unlike all the other buildings (the therapist's cabin, the communal house, the cook and storage shack, and the small structure the Brethren left in the north meadow), Peter chose a spot on the far side of the stream part way up Eagle Claw to build his small A-frame.

The women collected as many vegetables from the garden as possible, spending days on end canning, while a root cellar was dug that when emptied by spring would serve as the hole for a new outhouse. The Meadows people obtained Centerville library cards and made a run on "how to" books all that fall.

Analysis

The impending onset of winter and the changing circumstances it would necessarily bring also created an important juncture from which the first spasms of genuine communal living could be more clearly viewed. While most members had no time or inclination for an in-depth assessment, it was evident that the fledgling commune's initial spontaneous cohesion devolved to a social simplification or deculturization process, which in turn, slid into a disintegrative spiral. Attempts to halt it through imposition of order through rearticulated tasks, roles, and external contacts had saved it from possible early demise. This arrested progression can be seem simultaneously at individual, institutional and community levels.

With respect to individuals, an incredibly diverse mix of people passed through JM that summer, ranging from the extremely able and ambitious who were frustrated by the limitations placed on them by the SS, to the extremely emotionally disabled and incompetent who were attempting to escape the paralyzing demands placed on them by the SS. Some of these people ended up in mental institutions after their summer sojourn in JM, while others moved on; one, for example, to develop highly employable skills in auto-mechanics after dropping out of Chisholm College. One former core member even went on to become a "top executive" in one of the largest health food wholesaling houses in the nation.

The original Dobson House people began to manifest characteristic behaviors which correlated with key themes in their life histories. Those who had experienced close and rewarding relationships with both parents, such as Elliot, and had been most active in grammar school and high school, later becoming most politically active in college (Keniston: 1968). They had close friends, took the initiative in decision making situations, and actively pursued personal and social goals. Yet viewed over time, particular commitments were neither limitless nor long-lasting. Elliot for example, led the SDS in college, but left there to participate in JM, and then left JM to participate in a religious organization. Jesse, though not so close to his parents and far more unsure of himself than Elliot, first committed himself to JM, yet was one of the first to leave, and to become a committed revolutionary at Red Rose Collective.

Peter, on the other hand, appeared to be an archetypal hippie at first. Having a particularly warm and indulgent relationship with his mother that tended to exclude his father, he manifested a somewhat passive, uninvolved, and erratic stance toward people and society. He never participated in school activities and had few friends. Attracted by altered states of consciousness attained through psychedelic drugs and absorbed in self-related concerns, he sought personal salvation. Yet he developed an intense commitment to an ideal that began with the Summer of Love, evolved through the Dobson House period, and became even stronger as the summer wore on. While he initiated the idea of a commune, in the end, he was plagued with indecision and lacked the necessary interpersonal confidence and initiative to carry out his dream.

Since there were no males who had close relationships with their fathers to the exclusion of their mothers, no behavioral patterns connected with such people were available for observation. Females, on the other hand, did have close father relationships, but no clear pattern was discernible at that time, except possibly a high degree of emotional independence. Those females having close relations with their mothers, unlike the males who demanded indulgence, exuded nurturance, and were the prototypical "mother earth" figures.

A growing and common theme in the backgrounds of many who came to live at JM was a poor and distant relationship with both mother and father. These people neither articulated ways to demand nurturance nor to give it. Though they needed close personal contact, they found it most difficult to obtain. They also lacked self-confidence, making little or no effort to control their environments. These people needed a tolerant, supportive milieu the most, but took a minimal role in creating it, leaving that for the others to do.

So far, individuals' psychosocial backgrounds have been related to behavior in a communal context, indicating how life history patterns carry over into, mold, and define new situations in particular ways through the actions of the people involved. This suggests the idea that most patterns of behavior are set early in life. Yet it is abundantly clear that in radically new situations like the Dobson House experience, pivotal changes in attitudes and behavior occurred. Such conditions were carried over to JM and extended, further escalating the rate of individual change. There was continued drug experience, conversation, literal and figurative nakedness, and physical fatigue to help accomplish this. Although there was probably less sex between the original members, there were spasmodic episodes with visitors and other people who had just arrived. Complex games had turned to less involved rituals, but they still brought people together under emotionally intense circumstances.

A very similar, though differently structured environment existed in the Brethren camp. While sex and drugs were minimized, other stress-producing and social bonding mechanisms were present, creating at least as intense an atmosphere as that in JM. Periods of literal starvation, strenuous work details, deliberately induced fear in the performance of potentially dangerous physical feats, and games necessitating absolute trust between participants created this atmosphere. Similar to JM people, but even more pronounced, was the psychic tension already present in the individuals who joined. Many Brethren were lost souls; so psychologically tormented that they sought dependency on a strong charismatic leader with a total religious ideology.

In their initial stages of development, JM and the Brethren were not just characterized by a coincidental combination of factors that merely happened to create an environment conducive to radical behavior change. In their fusion phases, where emotional intensity and direct unencumbered communication was specifically encouraged, the environment for change was intentionally created and its catalytic factors deliberately escalated. Instead of individuals being affected by a constant set of external conditions characteristic of normal circumstances, there was a snowballing effect in the communal internal dynamic whereby the initial behavior alterations in each individual brought about further modifications in the behavior of all the others, which in turn precipitated yet additional changes. Such an accelerated dynamic was made possible by the removal of communicational barriers and behavioral buffers that under most circumstances exist between people to modulate relationships, thereby heightening interaction and changing mutual responses.

In short, communal living was not only supportive of individual change, but virtually made it necessary. This change was not aimless or haphazard. These communes acted like crucibles, picking up individuals who were drifting randomly, and fusing them into a contiguous whole that was internally cohesive yet highly fluid, ready to take any shape. Thus, it would appear that the communal form of social organization might be more than just a curious by-product of broader changes within the society; it can serve to accelerate changes while providing a substrate from which specific new forms can grow.

What new forms were evolving? And if the transformations were non-random, what were the organizing principles that were at work? Both JM and the Brethren concentrated at first on dismantling old structures, on destroying old patterns of behavior and ways of maintaining relationships learned at home and at school in the SS. Before new forms could be taken up, old ones had to be discarded. With the Brethren, when one pattern was about to slip away, another was forcefully pushed in to take its place. James not only had a well-articulated ideology that provided ready substitutes, but his manner of accomplishing the task was extremely effective. At crucial moments, James was dramatically present, buttressed by the group's belief in his parapsychological powers, to urge an alternative. Most cognitive and behavioral structures were replaced as they collapsed, thereby maintaining some continuity and overall rubric. Because the ideological rubric was simple and generalized, tending to overlook the usual contradictions and complications of everyday life, and because the emphasis was on social interdependence (most specifically dependence on James), the group functioned as an extremely cohesive unit.

In contrast, JM's "unlearning" process continued past the point where the Brethren's had stopped. But as old behaviors broke down, there was no articulate replacement procedure, and often there were no replacements at all; hence a regressive syndrome. For JM people, complex life in a technological society turned to a simple agrarian one, then to a primitive one, and in some cases to a primeval existence. It was not by accident that loin cloths and diapers were worn, that tribal tongues were mimicked, and even sub-languages with little or no symbolic content invented. Neither was it coincidence that regulations for complex and diverse behavior forms fell away to where simple repetition became the rule, nor that music, song, and dance often became throbbing, grunting, and writhing. For many, disculturation was so thorough that what social process remained often appeared to be governed by biological rhythms instead of conscious decision.

At first there was a conscious effort to cast away all constraints placed on behavior by etiquette and procedures required for achieving goals in straight society's institutions. But this process took on a momentum of its own, reaching a point where few, if any, socially prescribed behaviors remained. The steps required as means to obtain ends decreased to the point where there were often none, with many objectives being dropped or the procedures themselves becoming the objectives. One didn't need to earn recognition from colleges, parents, or employers because it was immediately obtainable in their commune. One didn't need socially defined rewards if one could have physiologically based "highs" and orgasms. And nobody seemed able to offer a rational explanation as to why deferred gratification was morally superior to instantaneous gratification. Material possessions were regarded as tickets to entrapment, requiring a loss of personal freedom in order to earn money to purchase, then to protect, the possessions. In moments of romantic rapture, the earth was seen by some as their foundation that furnished food, and the sky was viewed as their roof, providing nurturant light and moisture. Only the most fundamental tasks seemed worthy of effort with so much else bountifully available. And for others, physical labor on those immediate tasks was intrinsically rewarding, providing a sense of physical involvement and concrete accomplishment that no white collar job could offer.

Accompanying the development of these simplified behavior forms supported by mystical and romantic beliefs, were self defeating and destructive attitudes often at the root of much of the communard's behavior. A kind of sociocultural guilt was expressed by the beliefs of many that the spirits, witches, Indians, black ghosts, and people encountered in past lives were hostile to them as individuals, as Caucasians, and as representatives from a violent society. It is also probable that feelings of insignificance and powerlessness were behind the bizarre hippie behavior designed both to attract the attention of SS and to ridicule it at the same time. Lack of competence and fear of failure was certainly behind much of the move to terminate attempts at developing complex social, intellectual, and economic skills. On the other hand, attempts by JMers to relate themselves to historical, prehistorical, or even mythical figures was a necessary step in articulating new roots in time. Provocative behavior also could have been attempted in order to demonstrate genuine irreverence and independence. And although the extent to which complex behaviors and structure in social situations were broken down could be criticized, many people inside the CC and out agreed that life in America needed a certain amount of simplification.

In the communal context, countervailing tendencies toward both negation and affirmation were magnified out of proportion, as the evils of society and the innate goodness of people were blown up to visions of impending apocalypse and ultimate salvation. Simple explanations for some events and inadequate ones for others grew into contagious concepts of fatalism and mysticism. Those most predisposed to such orientations had experienced a series of personal holocausts in their pasts, along with helplessness and the arbitrariness of events. Death and divorce of parents, failure in school, unfulfilled expectations, and serious accidents dominated many of their backgrounds. Added to unfortunate past experiences were situational factors. The natural environment of the

Meadows was omnipresent and pervasive; forcing on its population its own inevitable pace, seemingly independent of those who lived there. Understandably, its mysteries attracted great interest. Starry skies that urban and suburban dwellers seldom saw and glowing campfires in the night combined to lend an atmosphere of infinite expanse and timelessness; a juxtaposition to human limitations.

In addition, people arrived at the Meadows daily with stories of impending calamity in the outside world, some of it true, but much of it unfounded rumor. The isolation, lack of evidence to the contrary, and involved communication patterns at JM served to amplify these incoming messages to the point where what was normally unbelievable became entirely possible. Pronouncements of an individual who suffered from psychotic hallucinations were just as valid as anyone else's insights, becoming part of JM's social reality. Indeed, cosmic energies, epochal transformations, and mysterious forces provided explanations preferable to physical or social causality, for they at least went beyond the human, and therefore rationally based, capriciousness and unpredictability they experienced.

The situation did not evolve into complete otherworldliness, total do-your-own-thingism, and social paralysis, however. As summer faded and colder weather approached, attempts to reverse or at least control the spiral that had set in became more frequent. Many had found that beyond sex, drugs, and trance was a dark, empty abyss. If present trends continued, there would be no place else to go except into an existential black hole of psychic or even physical death. Among those who had reached this state of mind were some who had pushed the limits of sensual endurance the furthest. In patterns of reversal, James forecast holocaust if things did not change, and Peter attempted to ban drugs on the land. Jesse and the Buddhist began to lose interest, while Yale and Bill attempted to control the influx of people. And the women who had children and had been wary from the start, began to act.

Almost forgotten was the vision of community for its own sake. Instead of becoming more cooperative and interdependent, and working together to create a better environment for others, people increasingly wandered off into worlds of their own, preoccupied with themselves in their altered states of consciousness, building little except physical structures, which anyone could do. True, they had experienced great moments, but it became apparent to many that these could not be goals in themselves. There apparently had to be a greater purpose to go along with the design for life they felt they had discovered. And even those moments of joy were becoming rare. Behavior had to be mobilized, and despite the supposed coming of the post-scarcity society, money had to be obtained. The pressures of seasonal changes eventually appeared beneficial. Work, rather than play, seemed to reverse a disintegrative trend, creating some sense of unity, even if it was achieved at what some regarded as being a superficial level.

Of course, social organizational forms and institutions varied as a reflection of the variations in environments and people. Because most people are born and socialized into a society that has pre-existing institutions, few people are faced with the task of virtually creating their own from the start. However, not having any institutions to modify, and rejecting those in the SS that they could have used for models, members concerned about the original communal vision and the survival of the group set about the task of creating what they believed were new forms. The approach was haphazard, creating ad hoc organization to deal with problems as they arose. There was little planning for eventualities not foreseeable in the immediate future and no one suggested organization for organization's sake to have it ready in case of need. By their pattern of response to problems, most did not realize that they could or should be laying the groundwork for eventual institutional forms. In fact, organization and institution were the very things about the SS that nearly everyone disliked the most, and lack of constraint and freedom from rules was nearly worshipped as a faith in the CC. Those people who attempted to organize others for specific tasks either suffered ridicule or apologized for being "structure freaks." But despite the anti-institutional ideology, organization did evolve.

Couples coming to the land presented the most obvious foundation for social organization because of bonds already established. But there was great strain on the couples, some breaking up and others going through much turmoil. This was due primarily to the close proximity and availability of other partners. But the primary reasons, though sex-based, were not sexual. Two other modes of bonding gained prominence, causing divided loyalties among those who found themselves in one or the other of these growing sub-forms. The first was the mother-child unit and the second was same-sex cohort groups, both of which have greater prominence in nonindustrial societies. Just as biological rhythms seemed to increasingly govern behavior as social forms were stripped away, so did biology seem to be at the root of these shifts in relationships that came into prominence when a complex technological society was left behind at the Dobson House.

Of course, sex was the basis of, if not the dominant factor in, hetero and homosexual relationships. But it was also the basis of the mother-child bond. Despite hopes and protestations by some about fatherhood being equally as important and time consuming as motherhood, it did not become very apparent at JM. What made the mother-child relationship more important was the fact that mother and child had to be together most of the time. The men were more mobile, often visiting, going to town, and working around the land, while the women remained in only a few places because carrying children around was more of an inconvenience. Even if given to the men for short periods, infants were promptly returned for breast feeding and breast-sucking pacification. Older children had to be looked after and could not crawl or wander untended in the areas where the men were doing heavy work. Because child care largely involved food preparation and sleep, the mothers were often confined to their home tents or the kitchen area. This resulted in even more cooking and cleaning tasks for women, which further freed the men for non-domestic activities. Thus there was progressively less contact between children and fathers or father substitutes.

Moreover, there were additional conflicts that intensified as the summer progressed. Whereas the men fantasized about rugged, stimulating environments, mothers wanted comfortable, quiet ones for their children. Whereas the men partied and sought immediate gratification with little concern for the future or practiced spiritual asceticism with grand cosmic schemes in the distant future, the mothers worried about the foreseeable, concrete future. How could the children have good medical attention and healthy diets? How would they manage in the very cold months ahead? Would they be safe from accident with all these unstable, drunk, tripping strangers around?

In part, same-sex cohort bonds stemmed from the special mother-child bond. The mothers, who really constituted a small common interest group, formed the stable nucleus of a larger group of women who shared many skills and attitudes. Though more mobile than the mothers, the other woman found they had many similar experiences to discuss, and frequenting the same areas as the mothers at JM, also fell into cooking-cleaning roles. The major factor separating men from women in general, however, was the type of work involved. The women found they were not only unskilled, but physically incapable of much of the heavy work being done at the beginning. This meant that the men spent even more time together than previously, developing a sense of camaraderie derived from common challenge and experience. Intensifying this, however, was a virtual ideology of male superiority introduced by those usually from the working class, whose backgrounds indicated they had very poor and distant relations with their fathers, spending most of their time around women regarded as inferior. The situation at JM made the ideology seem quite tenable to some. Not only were the males the ones providing ideological leadership for the social experiment, but also the most noticeable, the most exciting, and to some, the most important work.

Along with sex-based work conflicts was a developing political hierarchy, despite an ideology espousing absolute equality and full participation. In actuality, some people had better decision-making skills than others, and some were more interested in participating than others. In this instance, skills derived from individuals' SS pasts played an important role in the creation of a collective future. But just as important were extenuating circumstances at the Meadows, which were not defined by social concerns, rules, or institutions, but were instead molded by fundamental factors of time, space, and ecological conditions.

Time spent at JM and the sequence of arrival was initially quite significant. Unless particularly aggressive or self-confident, people came through the Meadows. Newer people deferred to those already present when they arrived. Often one person arrived only one day sooner than another person, but that other person did not know it, assuming the person already there to be an important cog in the social wheel. Because people were constantly coming and going, reckoning this was difficult as well as important. But if a newcomer remained long enough, through inquiry and observation, he or she could determine core people. This meant that deferential treatment was then shifted to them only. The respect and attention that was accorded them paid off in knowledge as well as favors returned. The core people knew where all materials, places, and people were. They knew better how the Meadows functioned, had an air of confidence that seniority and familiarity bring, and spouted wisdom gained from their previous even if limited experience in communal living.

The core people also had access to private space. Being on the land earlier and feeling some kind of priority associated with Peter and the Buddhist, they felt free to choose and build campsites on the more secluded spots. The core people sought out each other's company more often, and when visitors or recent arrivees wandered into their camp area, the intruders were often frozen out of conversation, causing them much discomfort. Eye gaze was not even directed toward outsiders, and because it made them feel as if they did not exist, they would leave. This spatial differentiation even took on permanent geographical proportions; the core people and more aggressive newcomers claiming the hills as quasi-inviolate, while outsiders gathered in the open-access meadows.

Deferential treatment was also accorded to those who did the most constructive work, even if those work freaks were simultaneously resented. So, too, were those who contributed the most money and goods. Guilt related to the ethic of not taking what one doesn't earn probably played a minor part, for the post-scarcity ideology maintained that wealth needed only for survival should be there for the taking. Most people availed themselves quite easily of others' tents, food, and clothes. Some even complained that the core people were being selfish and counter-revolutionary by not deliberately sharing equally all time, space, services, and goods. But beneath the self-justifying ideologies were more mercenary interests. Those who produced little or none of the goods were careful not to offend regular providers. And those who invested more time, effort, and money struggled harder to obtain their way and insisted that their opinions be listened to. Self-confidence, participatory initiative, intellectual ability, social skills, and productive capacity tended to cluster in the same individuals.

Finally, a critical factor was ownership of the land. Peter provided three fourths of the money to purchase the land. Openly professing that in the Aquarian Age the land belonged to everyone, and never forcing anyone to leave, Peter's power to evict was in other people's minds even if not in his. The potential was shockingly exposed when Candy in her fight with the Menominee Indian, asserted that by virtue of her relationship to Peter, if anyone had to leave the land, it certainly would not be she.

Thus there developed a distinct leadership within the core. Where no offices or formal procedures were set up to choose and ensconce them, combinations of the above mentioned criteria did. Leadership then, was not defined by an agreement among individuals in the system, but by the system itself. As the system became clearer and grew by increasing differentiation, leadership status increased for those most qualified and productive in the greatest number of areas. For example, Peter exercised the most influence, though lacking organizing skills and decisiveness, because he owned most of the land, provided most of the money, was a hard worker, fit in well with the male cohort faction, and was a member of a couple relationship with a child. Bill and Gracey (the new woman who replaced Mary in a relationship with Bill), for another example, were first of all a couple. They worked hard, had organizing skills, and contributed some money. As two individuals, they probably exercised more influence than any others outside Peter. In short, the strength of such factors as couple status, parent status, physical work, organizing skills, property ownership, and financial input, taken as a composite, manifested actual leadership, even if undeclared or unrecognized.

Thus in this fledging, barely organized social system, there were specializations and divisions of labor that many ideologically pure anarchists would have abhorred. But along with these lateral divisions were also vertical ones that certainly would have dismayed any good Marxist. Not emanating from ideas in people's heads (in fact, most were contrary to the ideas expressed), they arose largely from the interaction between human biology and the physical environment. This was particularly true as autumn advanced, as the specter of hunger and cold precipitated some unusual changes in behavior by some people toward others. But it would be incorrect to attribute all the developments to environmental factors alone. The skills and ideas people brought with them to JM certainly helped articulate this fundamental interaction in particular ways. And to be fair to the role of the intellect in human affairs, the ideological position of those involved undoubtedly modified the advance toward organizational differentiation and stratification that would have occurred under ordinary circumstances. Nevertheless, overall response to evolving conditions around JM, more than learned skills carried with them from their earlier lives in the SS, determined what leadership emerged.

External influences, or lack of them, had as much significance as internal individual behavior and institutional dynamics. The internal redistribution of outside information undoubtedly helped to keep the communal vision together. The thought of returning to urban, corporate, technocratic "Amerika" was repugnant after hearing more of the stories of societal collapse that drove them into the commune in the first place. Information about JM trickled out from visitors passing through, and word of the existence of JM as a New Age community had quite literally spread across the nation from coast to coast through hip networks. What knowledge the townspeople gained about JM was at first accomplished through the cultural exchange events and through the gossip of uninvited guests and voyeurs. Many townspeople were curious about JM. What couldn't be discovered was apparently invented, as unfounded belief in JM's demonic excesses in drugs, sex, and barbaric living modes was widespread. Beliefs and fears, some legitimate and others not, formed the basis of discriminatory behavior toward JM practiced by a majority of the townspeople. In short, the highly selective admission of limited information into the Meadows initially increased the likelihood of its survival in terms of internal dynamics, but the limited information that leaked out to the SS also served to create more of an external threat.

While it was hoped JM might eventually become self-supporting, far more material resources entered JM than left. Gifts, welfare, savings, social security checks, inheritances, and loans formed the bulk of JM's cash; all of it earned through participation in the SS. Some money was earned by performing odd jobs for the local farmers who preferred hippie labor because it was inexpensive. Food produced by commercial firms and goods produced in factories were used despite JM efforts at producing more and consuming less. Although the Meadows was far from self-sufficient, its members' dependency on straight institutions was, indeed, greatly reduced. But instead, many services were performed for JM by others in the growing CC. Parson's Crossings, for example, plowed the garden, and exchange between JM and Parson's Crossings was frequent, with JM doing most of the receiving.

An extremely large number of longhairs passed on and off the land during the summer. Nearly 1,000 stayed a couple of days at a time or longer. Not being members, they helped to disrupt any coordinated activities the members planned. These transients contributed to the unintended degree of JM's disorganization. Because there was no formal internal organization, and therefore no fixed boundaries, membership was an informal process and status. There were only degrees of membership, and only those people anarchically inclined, or those insistent, desperate, or enthusiastic enough to push their way into the center could do so. By the same token, loss of actual or potential members was also not haphazard, though it, too, was informal, involving degrees of leaving. Those with less of a stake who were disturbed by the entropic tendencies, apparent stagnation, and lack of visible progress toward anything, gradually drifted out and away.

In short, the system tended to attract the competent, ambitious people who would then quickly become disillusioned from the lack of organization, and leave. At the other extreme, the system also attracted the unskilled, passive, and good-time-Charlies who exploited JM while being supported by it. They tended to remain longer and in greater numbers than the very ambitious people, despite the periodic pressure on them to work, because they could not see many alternatives. Those who pressed for more organization were soon discouraged by their inability to organize those who didn't want to be organized, so they eventually turned their energies elsewhere. The resulting inactivity led to tendencies toward immediate gratification, and simple behavior patterns tended to increase. Those people with greater demands were simply worn down to a state of frustrated resignation. They were defeated not by opposition, but by indifference.

Thus JM had a built-in "winding down" mechanism that if left unchecked, would have ended the system, leaving its remnants to be dispersed into the outside world. If not reversed, money would stop coming in, food would cease to be produced, and buildings would not get built. But this state was never reached, as spasmodic attempts to wind it up again were made. Moreover, those who refused to give up generally had the biggest ideological, financial, and personal stake in the outcome. They fought running battles with those who had articulated beliefs, convictions, predispositions, and preferences, but who didn't really have to face the consequences if things didn't work out. If conditions got too unpleasant, those people would simply leave.

Also with respect to the outside world, JM's early existence served two important functions in the creation of a wider Provincian CC. First it provided an arena in which people escaping from the cities or from unpleasant personal circumstances elsewhere could relax. They could commune with nature, if not necessarily with other people, while being exposed to wandering hard core freaks who proselytized against the evils of society and for the ecstasies of the hip life. Although some visitors were repulsed by it all, many others underwent changes in attitude and behavior during their sojourn there that drew them further into the CC lifestyle.

Secondly, JM was pivotal in the recruitment of people into the nascent CC forms developing elsewhere in Provincia. Because it was widely publicized in underground circles and known as an "open" anyone-welcome commune, JM was the first stop for many people eager to explore Provincia and communal life. Even if they did not remain at JM, they obtained information about other communes in the region, and instruction as to how to find them. Although the exact figure can't be calculated, a considerable number of people who later settled into communes and other alternative institutions in Provincia first entered the regional CC through JM.

Thus, JM's first few months of existence showed mixed results. While it performed a valuable recruitment function for the regional CC, and was increasingly seen as a threat by the SS for this very reason, it struggled through some difficult internal situations. Certain paradoxes appeared that either defied resolution or were denied. If totally new environments would give people the opportunity to develop entirely freely in new directions, why did levels of collective competence and confidence often coincide with events in the life histories of the membership? How could the land be open to everyone if visitors and turnover in membership created paralysis? Why, in a new society, where distinctions between people were purposely eradicated, did new roles and specializations emerge? If the materialism of bourgeois society was rejected as superficial, why did the perpetuation of this microsociety seem to hinge on mobilization for work and earning money? Was the force of human consciousness and will really as powerful as everyone thought, if physiological rhythm and the seasonal changes could so easily dominate behavior? Why did an egalitarian organization totter on the edge of dissolution until authority began to emerge? The sense of euphoric union experienced at the Dobson House became increasingly difficult to replicate, and as people drifted away from one another, communal survival dictated the creation of primitive informal structures that would hold them together.

4. Dissipation: Winter Disillusionment and Death

A celebration was held on the traditional Thanksgiving holiday. All the houses were complete, food was stored, a huge wood stove was installed in the communal building, and some firewood was already stored. All the overlapping networks were invited, including the progressive school crowd, but not the college related people, who were no longer affiliated with the Meadows. Two new networks were present. One consisted of hometown friends of Peter and his sister, most of them of high school age and a middle class, who were awed by the scene they were witnessing. The other network consisted of street people: veterans of Telegraph Avenue in Berkeley, Haight-Ashbury, and New York's Lower East Side.

The communal house was called "the long house." It was a two story affair approximately 60 by 25 feet, constructed of old barn and unfinished boards that gave it the appearance of "a giant orange crate." Posts set six feet into the ground and protruding two feet above it, served as the foundation. There was no interior finishing, but drapes, tapestries, and wall hangings served just as well. Guitars, drums, and flutes also hung on the walls, and a donated piano sat in the corner. The kitchen area was at one end with a wood stove and a sink with a drain, and in the center stood a pot belly stove. Up a narrow spiral stairway was one long communal room with no partitions. Sleeping bags and mattresses lay lined up against opposite walls and, depending on mood, fashion, and sexual involvement, were sometimes separated by blankets hanging from the ceiling.

There were forty to fifty people in the house the night of the party, including Peter's mother, helping to test the soundness of the house's construction. The dancing and the music were so boisterous that the house literally rocked back and forth, with the pot belly stove eventually sliding off its stone base. Peter, though he no longer did drugs, still drank wine, and was dancing wildly about the house almost oblivious to what else was happening.

Everyone was drinking hard that night, and one of the visiting street people was so drunk even before he got there that he passed out and slept all night outdoors in the driveway of the closest straight neighbor's house. The drinking and the dog fights that night were omens of things to come.

The issue of dogs emerged as one of the most divisive in the history of the commune. A couple of the street people who had two German shepherds were asked by some to join the commune. They were happy to do so, but other members, including Peter and Candy, put their feet down, refusing to have any more dogs. The street people chose to leave rather than give up their dogs.

The anti-dog argument was clear. Dogs cost money to feed, license, and get shots for; money that really couldn't be spared. Moreover, they disturbed the peace and the wildlife, and were dangerous in winter according to Parson's Crossings, because they ran down and killed deer in the snow, raising the ire of the local residents. The previous year, Parson's Crossings' favorite dog was shot by a local resident because of such activities. Also, dogs were particularly bothersome in a tight living space. The pro-dog faction contended that most criticisms were minor compared to the fact that people needed their dog's companionship and love, and that if members of couples had each other, or if Candy had a baby, then they should have their dogs. Hip culture was full of wandering individuals with dogs tagging along whom they felt closer to than they did to most people.

What made such an apparently inconsequential issue important was that the central protagonists and antagonists were from the leadership. Peter, Candy, Bill, and Gracey were against, and Yale and the therapist were in favor (each having his own dog). The dogs of other people were slowly whittled away until the therapist's "old lady" contracted hepatitis and the both of them left temporarily. Peter then moved to get rid of the therapist's dog, asking the commune to agree, which it did. When the therapist returned before the dog was actually removed, he cried, saying he couldn't stay there without his dog, whereupon the commune reversed its decision. The dog episode had "blown Peter's image." Previously known as good, benevolent, and accepting of all, Peter had now proven to have personal desires and manipulative strategies like everyone else. By taking a stand, he became a fallen idol, appearing to contradict the Aquarian ethic while exposing his human fallibilities.

Peter became fed up with the commune. Many of its members, he felt, were weak people who didn't know how to say "no" for fear of offending someone else. Seldom conveying (or articulating?) their own feelings, they would agree with whomever happened to be forcing the issue at a particular time. Incapable of making communal decisions and enforcing them, Peter increasingly felt Jackson's Meadows was a lost cause.

After the dog episode, most of the dominant people spread out physically and mentally, leaving distances of varying lengths between one another. The therapist, despite his tears, soon left with his dog, giving his cabin to a street people couple who were beginning to exercise strong leadership. Peter lived in his A-frame with his family until Candy went to his mother's house while he went to live with the Krishna Brethren for a couple of weeks. He was considering joining them. Shortly afterward, he too contracted hepatitis and returned to his mother's house to spend the winter recuperating. Bill and Gracey built a little cabin on the back of the truck the Buddhist's father had donated. Disillusioned with Peter, the ex-SDSer left to study yoga with his friend Elliot. The couple that was married in the Meadow usurped public space by making over the second floor of the cookshack for their private use, and after being criticized, decided to leave. They had wanted to join the Hog Farm Caravan anyway, they said. Yale, not involved in a relationship, remained in the communal house. As the winter set in, only two of the original nucleus remained in the commune. The strongest couples had set aside private quarters to which they could retreat for privacy when things in the long house got too hectic. Once again, the place had very little articulate leadership.

Life at the Meadows contracted into a kind of isolated closeness that a hostile outside environment enforces. People had to face each other every day, and in one way achieved a new level of intimacy. Sitting all day, day after day, in the same house, people learned about each others' pasts, opinions, and proclivities. Many of the younger teenagers regarded the winter as one of the most important events in their lives because "it taught (them) so much about people that (they) never knew before." Enforced interaction produced a kind of cohesion that the scattered summer activities wouldn't allow, leading people to grow dependent on one another for company, conversation, and chores, while the interpersonal tolerance threshold went up. The irksome behaviors of individuals were tolerated by viewing the offensive people as "total human beings," and exaggerating their redeeming qualities. Where compensating factors were not enough to cover particular flaws, people often held back their most personal feelings, while claiming honesty and openness. Thus the communards learned to put up with events and episodes that would drive most other people up the wall. Unlike the Dobson House people who had developed friendships before moving to the Meadows, the later JM generations were thrown together by travel and circumstance. They had to make the best of it, for many simply had no other alternatives.

Sex, as in other communes, was a problem. A number of unattached men had difficulty with females anyway, and the Meadows provided a degree of personal anonymity which allowed them to be comfortable. They could relate to women, joke, and make innuendoes without having to come across for them, because there were always others around who could. Still, they got very "horny" hearing couples make love at night in the dark across the room. Eventually, "you just learn not to let it bother you." Others in search for religious meaning found that sex only diverted their efforts at "getting themselves together." One male accused his woman of not understanding the nature of spiritual quest, as she cried, pleading with him to have sex with her.

The public line taken was that sex was no more or less important than eliminating one's wastes, eating, or breathing. Some humor was used to control it, as when one noisy couple was loudly reprimanded by a chorus of voices complaining of being kept awake. Outright sexual humor, however, was absent, with no allusions, no grinning remarks, nor anything resembling locker room jokes; even when no members of the opposite sex were around. For those couples living in the long house, lovemaking was unquestionably inhibited by the cold, even if not by the crowd. Despite assertions that there was little of special significance about sex, it was usually reserved for after the lights went out or for when no one else was around. Sometimes people would unobtrusively sneak off in a corner when others were in a different part of the house. One couple was discovered making love under a blanket in a corner when people noticed that the house was shaking and fanned out indoors and out to find the cause! In sum, though there was sex, there was little mystery and eroticism.

Of the 25 members that winter, 16 were involved in eight couple relationships. Of the remaining nine individuals, seven were males, with one of the two females having just left a "miserable" relationship with her husband. Three of the couples had formed at the commune; the other five having started elsewhere. There was little playing around, as couples were firmly identified as such and were off-limits to other couples and singles. In only one case did a triangle develop, but it was done in the open. In such a tight living situation, a secret affair would have been impossible anyway. For horny male visitors, the situation was confusing, for it took a while to find out who was unattached. And if one approached an attached female, he risked becoming persona non grata. In contrast, visiting females would get the simultaneous rush by three or four unattached males, each politely trying to out-maneuver the other. Accordingly, few women went to bed alone unless they really wanted to. Given the sexual scarcity, impersonality did exist, despite the stated ethic of getting to know and like someone before sleeping with them.

Living in such close quarters, intimacy in all areas simply could not be maintained. A school busload of people arrived including past members of the Living Theater. Desiring to live communally, they visited the Meadows to see how it was done, and when they unintentionally got snowed in, they decided to stay for the winter. But after a week they couldn't stand it anymore, and left trudging through the snow, returning for their bus the next spring. Meadows people commented that the bus people wanted to "go too far with this together thing," while the bus people and other visitors noted that the Meadows people had a very noncommunal quality of holding back. They accused JMers of being inarticulate; not aware of human potential, not being honest with one another, and curiously removed from what was going on around them. Perhaps the Meadows people knew what they were doing. Less concerned with personal honesty and communal ideals, they were more interested in keeping the survival enterprise going than in confronting one another or in having to deal with abstract intellectual issues.

Drinking was the foremost escape mechanism. As the winter progressed, the volume of alcohol consumption and number of people indulging increased. The more the men drank, however, the more the women refrained. Although drinking permitted a superficial conviviality, it undoubtedly inhibited sensory input and interpretation, thereby decreasing communication and contact with pressing environments. Presumably, herein was its escape value. While alcoholic escapes were not sought by everyone, the constant flux of visitors with wine was tempting. Moreover, the street people and their friends had a history of hard drinking, creating a receptive environment for alcohol. Finally, alcohol was more easily obtainable, cheaper, and less legally risky than marijuana and other drugs. Accordingly, fewer drugs were done, although everyone smoked marijuana when it was around.

Another distancing factor was the constant flow of visitors. Although fewer than in the summer, the confines of the house favored heightened interaction with visitors, who provided diversion. Some brought news of events in the cities, the whereabouts of friends, and the situation at other communes, while others brought musical instruments, astrological skills, stories and myths, and half-truths conforming to the Aquarian ideals. Someone mentioned that the word "lunatic" comes from the Latin word for moon. During full moons he claimed everyone was subject to aggressive and animal-like influences like werewolves, citing higher murder rates as evidence. Many communards agreed, talking of times they really felt weird on such occasions, and using it to explain bizarre behavior in themselves and friends. Another story concerned Nova Scotia, where many freaks were buying land because of low cost, with its eight month growing season and palm trees, and no political repression of longhairs. Some communards were eager to believe these exaggerations and were disappointed when others claimed knowledge of snow cover at least eight months of the year. A nearby commune was rumored to be keeping uncaged lions and tigers in order to prove that man and beast can live together harmoniously. That commune, Secret Ponds, was actually keeping regular game animals in pens for sale and exhibition. No doubt, part of the distancing process involved believing in perfect solutions to be found in distant utopias. Subscribing to fantasy apparently helped remove people from present reality.

Another distancing mechanism was to leave the commune temporarily. Visitors and residents were constantly arriving and departing. Feeling the need to leave as soon as possible, some people walked 12 miles or hitched to Centerville through windy and icy weather to buy one food item that a visitor with a car could have gotten the next day. Others would leave for the cities to see if their cats, given away earlier, were all right, or because they had a dream indicating they should leave. Unable to admit they wanted to find a sex partner or to just get away, many felt guilty about leaving. Nevertheless, in mid-winter, Yale, Bill, and Gracey took off across the country to visit some old and famous hip enclaves they hadn't before seen. Such trips provided an escape from the deadening boredom and pressure of constant, repetitive personal interaction at the Meadows.

There was also emotional distancing from the physical environment. If someone smashed a thumb between two rocks, he would pay no attention to the blood oozing from under his purple nail, while others would chop wood in shirt-sleeves in sub-zero weather. Band-Aids, insulated shoes, and yelps of pain were considered throwbacks to the soft SS life they had left behind. Some were preparing for survival once all societal institutions collapsed, as they were bound to do. Others found meeting and conquering physical hardships an exhilarating and purifying experience. There also was social pressure not to complain, and some tried to outdo others in their selective asceticism. But the overriding reality was that life at the Meadows was undeniably hard, necessitating hardened defenses and some insensitivity to a difficult and encroaching environment.

Not all the communards were hale and hearty. Every communal group had its hypochondriacs who spent an inordinate amount of time in bed, but if there were any in the Meadows, they were difficult to spot. Many people stayed in bed because there was often no reason to get up, and it was warmer under the covers than elsewhere. A greater incidence of communicable illness was often found in communes with large populations or high person per unit space densities, stemming perhaps from the crowded, unsanitary living conditions and numerous visitors. Improper diet (including extreme natural food regimens) and general stress from constant turmoil and rest-inhibiting noise also contributed. One JMer recognized the deteriorating health conditions, claiming that LSD inhibited antibody formation, thereby increasing the likelihood of lingering illness among people who did too much acid. Thus communal living was absolved of the blame. Another resident commented that living at JM was like living in the Middle Ages. At times it was as if the plague had struck, coughing and hacking being audible from all different parts of the house. At other times it was beautiful in its simplicity, with the sweet smell of wood smoke, the muffled plunking of a stringed instrument, and the swish of colorful embroidered clothes passing through slanting yellow rays streaming from the windows.

Interspersed with quiet suffering, drunken parties, and idyllic moments, were times of crisis. The situation took a turn for the worse when the defacto leadership: Yale, Bill, and Gracey, left, and virtually anyone who showed up was allowed to stay. Some were speed freaks from the city who sought out the Meadows as a halfway house to unscramble their broken speech patterns, pull their lives back together again, gain interpersonal confidence, and live in a less threatening environment than the city. Others who showed up were too far gone for others to help. One fellow sat in the corner next to the stove for days on end saying nothing, only to suddenly scream out that "they" were coming to get him, and that "they" were already in the room, pleading for someone to save him from "them."

The case that caused the most turmoil was Randy. A recently arrived woman met a "very lonely fellow" on a trip to the city. Because "he didn't have any friends," she brought him to JM. After the leadership left, he grew increasingly aggressive and quarrelsome. He often stared into space or looked menacingly at people, shook them down for money, and threatened them with a large hunting knife he always carried. Moreover, he kept the woman who brought him there a virtual prisoner. On occasion, he beat her, and toward the end, forbade her to talk to anyone else in the house. If visitors so much as looked at her, he would casually pull out his knife warning them to keep away from his woman. He almost never let her out of his sight. Because no one person had the authority or brute power to throw him out, a unanimous decision was necessary, but many refused to commit themselves to his expulsion. After all, what right did people have to throw out someone whose home it was just as much as theirs? No one was there who was with the commune when it started, only one of them helped build the house they were living in, and none owned the land under their feet.

Some were used to living with people like Randy and others were afraid of him. Some claimed expulsion ran counter to the principles of a free society, and others argued that he should remain for therapeutic reasons. But probably underlying the paralysis was lack of confidence in their own perceptions, and a loneliness and an unwillingness to offend anyone, even Randy. Meetings were held in which people said they would give him just one more chance. Each time he broke down with tears in his eyes, swearing he would never threaten anyone again, but his promises were always broken.

Unable to mobilize themselves to get rid of Randy, some did arrange for the woman to escape. While Randy was diverted on an errand, she walked out of the Meadows and hitched a ride to freedom, still fearful he would find her and kill her. Contrary to JM hopes, Randy did not pursue her, leaving only periodically in attempts to trace her whereabouts. After Yale returned from his travels and sat through meetings rehashing the same issues concerning Randy without settling anything, he finally phoned Peter for clearance to throw Randy out. Yale returned bringing "tidings from the chief," and the power to throw anyone out or take any action necessary to straighten the place out. After much cajoling and anger at Yale's autocratic pronouncements, $10 was taken from the communal funds to tide Randy over, and Yale, with everyone's backing, led him to the door.

A fundamental paradox of hip culture had been solved in an unsatisfactory way. In the Aquarian Age, everyone was to be accepted as a person; not a thing, a role, or a status. That included the downtrodden, the confused, and the troubled, gathering together to create the new world. But how to deal with the chronically disruptive person who lived off, but did not believe in, the human community? Where did individual freedom end and social responsibility begin in the community? Should the group save the disruptive person or itself when it came down to a clear choice between the two? Despite all the talk of community responsibility, many avoided it, and some even felt that if Randy wanted to beat his girl, that was his affair. Others had neither the confidence nor the social skills to end Randy's oppression. The Aquarian ideology of openness, mutual care, and social collectiveness had opened JM to anyone and anything; attracting those who needed care more than they could give it, and fostered collections (not collectives) of lost individuals. Unfortunately for the dream, it took individual authoritarian action based on property rights to solve this particular problem.

Relations with the townspeople were also disintegrating. Most area residents were aware of the liberals' protests against the war and the power plant, got wind of Red Rose's blossoming political activities, knew of the Brethren's fanatical proselytizing, and began to perceive anyone male with hair over his collar as a threat and any female with a patch on her jeans as a nymphomaniac. To some extent, ill feelings toward the Meadows was a byproduct of the animosity toward all freaks in the area, particularly the politically oriented ones. Moreover, Jackson's Meadows didn't meddle in affairs outside its own, for its members had come there to avoid entanglements with the straight world, and there were enough problems on the land to absorb most of their time and energy. Yet by conforming to hippie stereotypes, they fanned the flames of hostility. Bathing was very difficult because of cold temperatures inside the house, no running (let alone hot) water, and dozens of people milling about. Sometimes they managed to get to the dormitories at Alpine College where they luxuriated in soap and water, but most of the time they really were dirty and somewhat smelly. This offended straights more than longhairs because longhairs regarded anything the body produced as natural, not dirty. Charcoal smudges from the stoves made them look even grayer than they were. Furthermore, JMers were often seen drunk or stoned in public, occasionally baiting the townspeople. Largely because of their appearance and accelerated flamboyant and provocative public behavior, Jackson's Meadows people were recognized apart from other freaks and resented even more.

One night, a band of snowmobilers raided the land, circling the house for hours in their anonymous outfits, masks, and goggles, one yelling that the residents better be out of there by spring or they'd live to regret it. Even former friends became hostile, and for good reason. The family who lived near the entrance road to the Meadows had allowed visitors to park in their driveway and let Meadows people use their phone. But eventually visitors and newer members began abusing the privilege, barging in at all hours without knocking, making long distance phone calls without paying for them, and taking food from the refrigerator. The husband awoke one morning to find his driveway blocked. Finally managing to get out and get to work, he furiously stormed down the road to the longhouse late in the day after drinking. Meeting one of the women outside, he challenged hippie masculinity by declaring he was going to fight it out "with a man, if there are any around here?" Bursting into the house, he found only more women at that time and a little curly headed fellow with thick eyeglasses who cheerily asked him if there was anything he could help him with. In utter frustration the neighbor left, but thereafter his house and driveway were closed to the Meadows people.

While local functionaries were discussing what to do about Jackson's Meadows and other hippies in the Centerville area, a group of local men got together, and after many cans of beer, vowed to rid Wilfred of its communes. The library indicated it would no longer honor cards of people from JM until dozens of the overdue books were returned. Not being sure who belonged to JM and who didn't, the librarian asked all the most disheveled looking hippies at the check-out where they lived. Also, the local welfare office got in touch with the state office about a food stamp policy toward communes. With the increasing incidence of shoplifting, alarmed merchants followed any long-haired customer about their stores with eagle eyes. Even if they were only partly responsible, they were a visible target. There was also a pile of unpaid hospital bills attributed to Jackson's Meadows with names on them no one at the Meadows recognized. The Meadows people asserted that not they, but visitors had been going to the hospital and billing the commune without their knowledge. Even the town clerk was apparently after them, and someone warned them to keep their property and school tax receipts as proof of payment.

The Wilfred town council began to act on state zoning guidelines, hastily drawing up a set of interim regulations forbidding the construction of any domicile beyond two family capacity without specific town council approval in accordance with "public health, safety, and welfare." "Family" was defined in terms of marriage and blood relations. Neither could existing facilities be remodeled for purposes of "a change in the use or character" of those facilities without approval. Thus, in addition to business enterprises, all hotels, dormitories, resorts, extended farm families, and communes had to gain prior approval from the council (and there were no hotels, dormitories, resorts, and extended families coming to little Wilfred in the foreseeable future). No limitations of power had been placed on the council except legal appeals procedures and the possibility of voting the interim regulations down two years later. Moreover, what constituted public health, safety, and welfare was not at all defined.

Peter, through visitors, letters, and phone calls, was keeping posted on the latest developments. Even the town fathers contacted him and his mother, communicating their displeasure at what was going on at the Meadows. Candy was again urging him to throw everyone out. His mother countered by saying that the immature residents would outgrow it, and Peter's principles wouldn't allow him to deprive people of a home. Yet he replied to his mother that the commune was never intended to be a kindergarten. He had foreboding dreams of impending danger at the Meadows that bothered him to such an extent that he wrote a letter warning people against drugs and drinking, and particularly fire. He recalled James' vision that a fiery holocaust would sweep the Meadows if it kept following its unspiritual ways. But the return of Yale, Bill, and Gracey, and the evolution into leadership positions of two newer people, Zach and Janet, indicated things might take a turn for the better as spring approached. Yet problems remained. Some people were resentful that Gracey and Janet had come to assume almost all the power at JM. They kept the money Yale donated from his sawmill job, compiled the food stamp lists, collected the stamps, kept them and spent them, did the shopping, organized meals, controlled the use of the commune's only remaining vehicle, and reprimanded people who were not regarded as doing their full share of the dirty work, such as washing the dishes. Yale, Bill and Zach still exercised a spasmodic overt leadership, but it was these women who set the fundamental daily tone and pace. People complained mostly about Gracey for her constant nagging and depressions. But Gracey and others claimed that most people sat around waiting for her and Janet to cook.

Moreover, the other people professed ignorance of the intricacies of welfare, expected to be taken care of, and would let the place collapse completely if left up to them alone. This was a problem situation potentially for all kinds of households, but particularly troublesome for communes.

In early April, a rapprochement was made between the dissident factions and individuals. Spring was on its way and there would be the garden to plant, plans to fulfill, and warm weather pleasures to indulge in. They realized, as painful as it was, that the turnover problem had something to do with the problems they were having. Although nearly all were new people themselves at one time, they decided finally to close the Meadows to new people, regardless of how Peter felt. They felt that they had finally achieved an understanding and equilibrium that must not be disturbed if the place was to develop constructively. Visitors would be welcome, as they provided diversion and material luxuries, but they could not remain long or become members. Hopefully, unlike other communal decisions, this one would be upheld.

One day, as the moon approached fullness, some visitors no one had ever seen before showed up with a couple of gallon jugs of wine and some dope. Everyone was in good spirits and some people started drinking in the afternoon, especially the younger kids from Peter's home town. One woman commented that they were in for a "heavy night" with the drinking starting so early. Zach later came back from town with a bottle of scotch that he had mysteriously obtained there. As the evening approached and wore on into the night, some of the people became very intoxicated, crawling into sleeping bags to go to sleep, while those unattached males who were still ambulatory were busy trying to win the sexual favor of a girl who had been visiting there a few days. Even some of the women had been drinking heavier than usual. Yale had not come home from the sawmill, going instead to have a few beers at a honky-tonk bar in Centerville, and the divorced Alterian woman was up at Alpine College staying with a student activist whom she had met on one of her trips there to take a shower. Annoyed at Zach for having drunk so much, Janet, who was pregnant with Zach's baby, retired to their cabin alone, while Bill and Gracey went to sleep in their truck very high on dope. The couple interested in yoga bedded down in the cook shack where they often went to escape the partying. As the house settled into quiet, a candle in a saucer by a mattress flickered as the only source of light.

Suddenly, someone awoke to the acrid smell of smoke. The upstairs was filled with it. People began coughing as someone shouted that there was a fire. Because a red glow emanated from the direction of the stairway, the person closest to the window at the opposite end of the house kicked open the window, in some cases rousing the people next to them out of bed. Stepping and tripping over Zach who was in a sleeping bag by the window, whom they thought certainly must have been awakened, they jumped to the snow and broken glass below. Hearing the racket, people who were downstairs ran up the stairs to see only flames and feel a wall of heat. The fire could be seen moving across the walls and along the floor, and within a minute or two, the entire house was engulfed in flames. Because they all slept with no clothing on, some stood dazed in the snow with nothing but blankets wrapped around them while others were naked. The fire generated such intense heat, they were forced to back away and silently stand and stare from a distance.

The people from the outbuildings gathered with them hopelessly to watch the house burn to the very ground. Virtually everything in the house was flammable. It was over in minutes. Some cried. One girl sat in the snowbank to play the guitar she obtained from the cookshack, and Gracey asked everyone to hold hands in the night silence. People looked into each other's faces with the aid of the fire glow for reassurance, but there was none. Four faces were missing: Zach, the two boys from Peter's hometown, and a girl visitor. While the others were immersed in shock and perhaps denial, a member known as Pepsi Joe had run down the mile long icy road to the nearest neighbor's house that had the telephone. He burst through the door naked with burned flesh hanging from his back, to ask them to use the phone to call for fire trucks and ambulances. Although later he didn't remember how he got there, he vividly recalled the husband phoning and the wife trying to wrap him in a blanket while asking her young son to help her. The son, perhaps four years younger than Pepsi Joe, couldn't keep his mind on what he was doing as he kept trying to watch television at the same time.

Analysis

The holocaust had struck, not through the SS as all imagined it would, but through JM instead. People had come to JM to escape death in Vietnam, violence in their homes, television addicts' lack of concern for real people rather than electronic images, and in short, the decaying sense of humanity and disintegration of institutions all around them. But the very conditions they sought to escape seemed to be recreated at JM on a smaller but more lethal scale. Both James' visions and Peter's dreams had been laughed off by many people as just further manifestations of their mystical hocus-pocus and moralistic overstatement to get people to conform to their own private wishes. Did visions and dreams really foretell the future, or worse, create it? Were the stars or hidden planetary forces to blame? Did the spirits of the land finally exercise their karmic rights? While in the world of JM's mystical ideologies these were legitimate questions, the more socially and politically oriented people had other concerns. Was partying and getting stoned intrinsically bad after all? Was unnecessary hard work and compulsive organization ultimately rewarding? Would people, if freed from the control of authority, destroy themselves?

Although the aftermath of the fire and the possible explanations for it will be explored presently, it must be acknowledged that the calamity also marked the end of another fundamental communal phase. In more closely examining this phase, another level of explanation will be engaged that focuses on the new people that created a different membership mix, the means and methods of recruitment, the changing environmental circumstance, and the internal social dynamic. Putting aside the surface explanations of chance, accident, or use of too much drugs and alcohol that night, through examination of the above processes alone, it will be possible to see how the stage for probable failure and tragedy was set, awaiting any number of possible triggers.

There was a significant difference between the generation that settled in for the winter on the land compared with that which first moved to it. Overall, there were more people involved, at first glance seeming to constitute a rather large group. In reality, however, with continual coming and going, there were usually between 10 and 15 on the land at any one time. This winter generation had more women than the original group, and all but one was involved in a couple relationship; a possible indication of greater stability. But one was a captive, while another was involved in a menage a trois. This generation was considerably younger, with almost as many people in their teens as in their twenties. There were fewer eastern European Jews and more Alterians and other minorities. The number of Protestants declined, while the Catholic representation shot up. Moves during childhood increased in this group, indicating possible instability, while those coming from suburban environments rose sharply.

Class backgrounds shifted significantly toward the lower end of the traditional spectrum. Instead of predominantly upwardly mobile parents as before, a majority here either showed no change or indicated decline. Regarding parental occupations, the technical industrial sector representation, vis-a-vis the knowledge and professional sector, grew somewhat, while the proportion of Bohemian parents rose significantly. Thus, the picture so far presented for this group clashes sharply with the stereotypical image of the hippie emerging from a middle class, non-Catholic, non-minority, parentally indulged, and experientially naive background.

Other more psychologically oriented facts reinforce this conclusion. The proportion of those people coming from broken homes was even greater than the initial generation, and the high proportion of adopted children is quite significant. An inordinate number indicated alienation from both mother and father. The same people were also far more hostile toward their parents than the initial generation. The winter generation, in addition, completed fewer years of school, had a lower academic performance, and never participated in extracurricular activities, resulting in a much higher percentage of high school dropouts.

A higher proportion of the winter generation had few friends, and felt great loneliness in childhood and adolescence compared to the founders. None believed that they were their parents' favorite child. While one consulted a psychiatrist for reasons of avoiding the draft, two had been in mental hospitals, indicating severity of disturbance, and though emotional instability may or may not be higher in the lower socioeconomic classes, it is usually treated less. In actuality, the level of emotional turbulence and confusion in this group was quite high. While this may be attributed as a significant casual factor in the decline of JM over the winter, it is also an effect of SS events preceding their arrival at JM. This winter generation life histories are marked by severe beatings by parents, incest, parental wife-swapping, extremely large families, children being taken from the mother by the state, and institutional experiences. Thus, violent and disintegrative processes began for these people long before JM was ever conceived. It was the hope of finding family, a sense of belonging, and peace that drew them to JM in the first place.

This second generation generally led a difficult existence after leaving home, too. Compared to the first generation, far more of these people had to work while in and after school, taking unskilled factory, dish washing, waitressing, and other lowest paying jobs with no future. One had been a big time drug dealer who got roughed up by the Mafia, saying he was tired and scared of "the whole guns and knives thing," and another was a street prostitute. These were not the spoiled kids that longhairs were so often accused of being. Indeed, more than half had been in jail before coming to JM; some incarcerations admittedly being justified with respect to laws broken. But a high proportion of these jailings stemmed from outright harassment and abuse of the law by police. The arrest rate in this generation was significantly higher, and none resulted from political activities. They were vulnerable to the police because of their hippie appearance and constant travel. One second generation JMer was being sought by the FBI for draft evasion.

Drug use was common to all, but unlike the first generation that had largely confined itself to marijuana and psychedelics, the second generation had placed more emphasis on speed, with a significant number going on to barbiturates and opiates. Some were in fact ex-heroin addicts who deliberately sought out JM as a place where they could hopefully remain free from the habit. Perhaps the most serious problem was alcoholism. Although some came to JM specifically to "kick," the drinking went on. And in the end, alcohol was the immediate cause of the fire. Significantly, nearly all of those who proceeded on the common route from marijuana and psychedelics, beyond speed, to "downs" (barbiturates and opiates) were from a working class origin. Regardless of class background, however, the end of the drug cycle was alcohol for all those who did not stop the use of psychoactive substances altogether.

Only two from this generation had attended any politically motivated demonstrations. Moreover, none regarded themselves as having a political orientation toward social change. Instead of altering complex situations, they found it easier to change their own psychic orientation as large numbers with a spiritual orientation indicate. But again, the spirituality varied with class background. Whereas those from working class backgrounds tended to face their problems by consuming alcohol, those with similar troubles from the middle class tended to shift to a spiritual orientation. Those with working class backgrounds felt less loneliness than those from the middle class, functioning satisfactorily even if peripherally in SS institutions. By contrast, most of the middle class spiritually-oriented people had been cut off from social intercourse in the past, feeling relatively powerless to influence human affairs or change the course of events. Those with working class backgrounds, though also feeling powerless to control institutions and larger social phenomena, could perceive at least some influence over and response from their small circle of friends or acquaintances.

Pivotal experiences in their evolution from straight to hip were in certain ways also different from the initial generation. For some, it was a natural progression from Bohemian parents and households. But most were particularly hardened veterans from Haight-Ashbury and the Lower East Side, or runaways, or divorced women rebounding from bad marriages. Political action consisted of window smashing instead of peaceful demonstration. Death had also become a reality to more people in this group. Not only were dead parents represented, but the former husband of one of the women committed suicide. As with the first generation, one was a refugee from the criminal underground.

LSD experiences were critical among the middle class, better educated members. One blamed the dissolution of her friendship network on acid because its members' deepest, threatening secrets were revealed when they tripped together. Left alone afterward, she turned to JM. Another, on his first LSD experience, was converted to the street scene after "realizing" that he was worthless as a human being in the cosmic scheme of things, and in the course of his last trip, he quite literally saw himself die and be reborn as a new person (this particular trip took place after the fire). A few others, although already confirmed freaks, had gained some glimpse of communal vision at Woodstock. And another was personally influenced by spending time with the famous beat poet and hippie guru, Allen Ginsberg. But for many, the CC was simply a refuge where no exclusive criteria for membership was in effect. One many year veteran of mental hospitals deliberately sought out hip culture because people would accept certain behaviors of his that the SS would not tolerate. Another working class individual who had been trying to function in a cultured upper middle class milieu, gave up, dropping into hip culture. And the hip lifestyle and JM in particular appealed to one working class woman "because it was more casual and no one demanded anything of you. You were accepted for yourself, and not for your money, clothes, etc."

In short, the hip ghettoes in various urban centers became free zones where fixed behavioral codes were held in suspension. Due to the deteriorating conditions there, many sought a new refuge from the original urban refuge. The new retreat became rural areas, where ills blamed on the general urban environment supposedly could not spread. JM was only one of these new rural enclaves, and many of the same problems that earlier enveloped the urban hip ghettoes eventually did make their way to rural areas.

Beyond the individual life history influence on events, were the inevitable social interactive determinants. One way to better understand what led people to join a rural commune, is to trace and describe the nature of feeder networks. While some people wandered to JM with no previous contacts, a majority of the membership came to JM at the invitation of friends already there. Of the twenty members to become JMers over the winter, twelve came in by way of various networks. One came by way of Elliot's college contacts, two from Peter's home town, and three from Peter's former progressive school. The progressive school people in turn also had contacts in urban hip ghettoes, which led to the introduction of two other related networks. Three people came from the street scene directly, and three more arrived by way of the IBM family.

Each network had its own character, and by noting how many members each contributed, it was possible to get a sense of the kind of transformation that had occurred at JM. For example, the Chisholm College network was not represented at all, and only one arrived by way of Elliot's college friends, indicating that the level of education attainment would probably be low. The people coming from Peter's home town were confused suburban adolescents tasting the thrills of life away from parents for the first time. The progressive school people were passive and mystically oriented. Finally, there were the street people and IBMs who were generally working class with a mix of competent and erratic individuals. Thus, floating networks to JM served as conduits for people, material wealth, and ideas from college, urban, and even suburban CC enclaves elsewhere.

But even though communes served as points of intersection between individuals and networks, they had an internal dynamic of their own. JM was influenced by the personalities of those who joined the group. Also interfering were the inevitable dogs and visitors. Besides the mix of life histories and alcohol that created the potential for catastrophe, the holocaust was immediately catalyzed by visitors who appeared early in the day with a supply of wine. The deteriorating situation was further exacerbated by those who left the group. Permanent dropouts from JM have already been mentioned, but temporary or quasi-withdrawal from the commune perhaps created an even greater problem. Gracey, Bill, and Yale were absent for significant periods of time, and Peter and Candy left early in the winter, not to return until after the fire. Unlike the former triumvirate who left with the intention of returning. Peter and Candy had finally given up on JM.

Peter's withdrawal had not put an end to JM, for he refused to take the final step and demand that everyone leave his land. Instead, a greater leadership vacuum was created that encouraged a further group decline that was only kept in check by a number of other factors. Many of the JM people had no other place to go, forcing them to make a go of it, and the winter environment that drove people indoors in a way contributed to the group's cohesion. Although it caused some people to want to get away more, it also forced those who remained to interact. Relationships of some depth did develop despite the periods of bickering and contagious depression. In the end, a new leadership was emerging, only to be snuffed out by the fire and ensuing events.

But there is a more of a social psychological explanation that lends supplemental insight into the disintegrative process that occurred over the winter. Referred to here as distancing, this appeared to be a phenomenon common to most of the communes. It involved a process in which individuals backed away from one another after an initial period of near ecstatic communion. The initial fusion phase usually involved more open sex, clusters of individuals working together, great enthusiasm, spontaneous display of interpersonal affection, and an emphasis on honesty and the communication of innermost feelings. After just a few months, sex within the groups diminished sharply, people worked in smaller combinations, a noticeable decline in optimism and expectation occurred, more interpersonal reserve was evident, and a shift in communication away from personal concerns toward instrumental tasks was recognizable.

There were a number of reasons for the interpersonal distancing phenomenon, that if not checked, could lead to the early dissolution of the commune. The most obvious was the fact that, as time passed, despite highest hopes, individuals found that others were not always what they first believed them to be. Only later did it become evident that some had some serious problems or created serious problems for others. Also obvious was the inevitability, despite pledges of ever-lasting commitments, that people changed their beliefs and behaviors as they gained new experiences with different situations. This kind of change was accelerated by the intense nature of the communal context.

There are more subtle reasons for distancing, as well. After the ecstatic beginnings or initial introductions, during which people exposed their innermost selves as they came to trust their partners implicitly, individuals became vulnerable to the slightest perceived undermining of that trust by others. Mostly unintentionally, others threw sensitive personal information back in their faces in frustration over some unrelated issue, or made later statements that seemed to contradict what they might have mistakenly interpreted initially as a fundamental understanding, or demonstrated inconsistencies between words and deeds; a process understandable for the hated SS, but shocking when encountered in the CC.

Beyond the contents of these kinds of communication patterns were the forms that they took. Unlike a couple or nuclear family, whose members can exercise considerable control over the evaluation of a relationship, group affairs could spin out of the control of any and all of its members. Events could occur in the group that affected every individual, yet they directly concerned only one or two people. Feelings could build up or decline between certain individuals that could also reshuffle ties among the others. Whereas there was only one relationship between two people or three among three, among five people there were ten relationships, among ten people there were forty-five, and among fifteen people, there were one hundred five relationships that constituted the social context and which could change as a result (Moore: 1963). Unless there was an organizational shift toward specialization of roles and simplified channeling of communications, and clear authority such as developed by the Brethren, the larger the size of the group, the less likely the degree of cohesion.

Material concerns, in addition to recruitment and turnover, brought about changes after the fusion phase. After the initial period of spiritual, interpersonal, and even political preoccupation, housing, food, money, equipment, clothing, and heat gained in importance to the point where they became priorities. Those insisting on psychic intimacy often neglected matters of material support, accusing those who chose to focus on the more concrete and pressing concerns of abandoning the reason for forming the commune in the first place. And those concerned about the encroaching winter and group survival increasingly regarded the interpersonal relations freaks as short-sighted, unrealistic, or even lazy.

Both accusations were correct to a certain extent. The ecological and economic conditions created real needs and new priorities which if left up to the social philosophers, would have ended the commune. Furthermore, the fire would not have been the disaster it was if it were not for the cheap and shoddy construction, or if people were working all day instead of talking and drinking. On the other hand, people who avoided confronting painful interpersonal issues, which if left to fester could also destroy the group, did seize upon survival as a convenient avoidance issue. If the social situation was going to deteriorate to where it offered even less of an alternative than SS institutions, what indeed was the point of survival as a group? It was undeniable that physical survival for the group was achieved over the winter only to be undone in the spring largely by psychological and social problems.

A counter argument to both these positions is that both aspects are necessary to group survival in the long run. Not only can exclusive focus on interpersonal encounter precipitate the collapse of material support through lack of attention, but it can also lead to inordinate psychological demands on all the members such that heightened conflict results, and the commune can blow apart regardless of material conditions. Boredom, too, can have the same effect, with each learning more than they care to about the other. With no external focus on changing conditions and events, interpersonal stagnation can set in also. Yet an exclusive work/survival focus can lead increasingly to an individualistic ("me first") orientation contributing to the drifting apart of members and thoughtless behavior concerning group welfare. A combination of both orientations seemed to lead to both group and individual survival as well as to psychic reward, as certain more stable communes, such as Parson's Crossing, demonstrate. This was true where instrumental work was a major concern of the group, if it required some degree of cooperative organizational effort and served as a constant stimulus and source of experiential content around which interpersonal relationships could further develop.

Another form of internal differentiation and distancing concerned interpersonal power in the context of relationships. Fusion, complete honesty, and interpersonal orientation foster conditions under which people can penetrate each other's consciousness to an inordinate degree. So long as the exchange of information and interpenetration of consciousness is equal, everyone's sense of belonging, common purpose, and infusion of life from others is heightened. But each person has a different background with different skills and relative abilities. Thus, in circumstances where intense exchange occurs, some people receive more than they give. Through certain situational factors, planned strategy, and personality factors built into the situation, some individuals lead others into situations more favorable to themselves, and consciously or unconsciously, used information received from others to manipulate them into certain behaviors through selective psychic reward and punishment. Although this process is universal, it was potentially more acute in communal situations where safeguards against dissemination of personal information and institutional guarantees in favor of a balanced flow of that information were virtually non-existent. So-called charismatic personalities flourished in such situations, where their spontaneous interpersonal skills allowed them to invade and saturate the psychic space of others. Most notable in this study were the reluctant leader of Red Rose Collective and the not so reluctant efforts of the Brethren's James.

Inevitably, there were individuals who came to understand what was happening, due in large part to their not being swept along by a charismatic leader such as James, who told them how to interpret events. They often reached the conclusion that they were getting the smaller return in exchange. Whether justified in their belief or not, the only way they could halt the process was to withdraw partly or completely from the exchange. While some continued to seek security by developing a dependency on the more charismatic individuals, others rebuilt the barriers that were so carefully torn down during the fusion phase. The feeling of getting psychically "ripped off" and losing status and prestige in the group while feeding the rise to power of others, caused a defensive posture that created distance between the individuals concerned. Or, it led people to gain competence in certain other special skills to attract some attention and earn some approval for themselves.

In sum, through the various processes outlined above, JM went through a period in which communion broke down. Individuals grew more distant, even as they got to know one another better. In those groups that disbanded, distancing was complete. In those that survived, such as JM, the limited distancing occurred in two basic forms. The first was one of continued involvement with the invasive persons, in which defensive postures were balanced off by felt needs for interaction and joint task performance. The second consisted of breaking direct engagement, building growing intermediary ties instead, and increasing mutual reliance between different individuals due to growing specialization of skills and tasks. Both trends were at work at JM simultaneously, as the simplification and disintegration process of the first summer led toward dissolution until checked by environmental pressures and deliberate attempts at coordinated collective action. The winter represented a period in which each process more or less kept the other in check, with an overall disintegrative trend slowly making itself apparent until just before the fire.

It could be said that the fire resulted suddenly from the cumulative stressful effects of this prolonged stalemate of forces in the communal system. On the other hand, less skilled, knowledgeable, and emotionally stable people, and all the behaviors associated with them, rushed in to fill the vacuum left by more articulate people, and group amorphousness through lack of screening, shared objectives, and decision-making mechanisms exacerbated the situation. On the other hand, strong abstract ideals of acceptance, equality, and freedom to do as needs dictated, and the realities of the strength of group identification, the apparently successful struggle for survival, and lack of alternatives for many, kept the enterprise going until something had to break. The break was more disastrous than most dared contemplate, and in many ways should have brought the social experiment to an abrupt close. Instead, drastic changes resulted that set JM off in another direction.

5. Stabilization: Transition After the Dream Ends

Subsequent to the tragedy of the fire, any changes, survival or collapse, or new direction, were not at all certain for an unexpectedly lengthy period of time. This was so despite the fact that four were dead and four were in the hospital. The house was gone and with it virtually everything anyone owned, from sculpture and artwork they created, to logs and diaries they kept, to false IDs that had taken years to put together. Individual memories were the only links with the past for all concerned. Some survivors, because they lost their IDs, didn't even exist from a legal standpoint. One set of parents came to get their daughter while all those communards not in the hospital moved into the cookshack. Cleaning out the second floor storage area, they busily went about the business of survival, resolving not to give up; to make the social experiment work so that the victims shall not have died in vain. Those at home, at friends' houses, and in the hospital, silently wondered what the fire meant, why it had happened, and if they should go back.

Repercussions in the area from the fire were mixed. One large city newspaper made headlines out of it, while in another nearby city, no word of it was disseminated. One folk-rock singer on a listener-sponsored FM radio station composed an impromptu song eulogizing the dead. Local newspaper reporters and town officials came out to survey the scene and pick through the ashes for human remains and scraps of evidence. Some of the townspeople are known to have said they were glad it happened, and that the communards deserved it, while others worried about the reputation of the town, feeling partly responsible for not enforcing zoning laws earlier. Some went to JM just to look at the disaster scene, but many went instead to offer their condolences and what help they could. Old clothing, food, tools, blankets, and mattresses were stacked near the cookshack along with junk they could never use, such as broken lawn furniture, three-legged tables, and galoshes with holes in them. The General

Store set up a carton for donations from the local people, too. Even four beer drinking rednecks who volunteered to drive some supplies in over the quagmired roads in their jeep said on the way out, "You guys ain't so bad. It's those people at the MacDonald House that are causing all the trouble."

Elliot, hearing of the fire, arrived with sacks of organic food ripped off from the macrobiotic restaurant he frequented. Jesse, now at the MacDonald House, volunteered his help, and the entire Moore Commune walked in carrying bags of groceries. Jesse directly reprimanded Parson's Crossings for doing little to help out, thereby precipitating strained relations between that commune and the Red Rose Collective. Parson's Crossing rarely visited the Meadows any more, but they welcomed and comforted Meadows people when they went to Parson's Crossings, thereby not deserving all of Jesse's ire.

The influx of well-wishers only added to the confusion. There was barely space on the cookshack floor as commune members had to struggle to find a place to sleep among the visitors. Elliot was still resented for his numerous friends, some of whom brought dope. While the embers of the long house were still smoldering, people passed joints around the cookshack, gossiping and telling jokes, and commenting on the full moon. The gravity of the situation it seemed, had not yet hit the residents, while some visitors were insensitive to what the others had been through. Absolutely no one in the commune talked about what had happened. It was almost as if there never had been a fire.

Meanwhile, Janet was due to have her dead lover's baby in a month and a half. After some pressure from her parents to stay home, she resolved to return to the land to have her baby. Pepsi Joe, who was seriously burned, remained in the hospital for weeks, and then went to his stepfather's house near Chisholm College. One injured woman consulted a medium after leaving the hospital, and another borrowed Parson's Corner's book to throw the I Ching. When neither received a strong indication they should leave the Meadows, they returned to give it another try. They were nevertheless convinced that disasters like the fire "just don't happen. It was done to teach us something. We have to find out what." While the most obvious reason was drinking, others insisted it went deeper than that. Why was everyone drinking? Why did it happen just after a new cohesion and good feelings had developed among them? Was there a curse on the land? The dead will be reborn to begin to work out their karma anew, but what about the living? What directions should be taken this lifetime?

Peter was informed of the tragedy by phone. Because Peter's mother knew the mother of one of the dead boys and felt partly responsible, she went to inform her, and her daughter's boyfriend informed the parents of the other. Both parents took the news well. Curiously (or maybe not so curiously given the troubled relationships many JMers had with their parents), neither Zach's nor the visiting girl's parents contacted anyone connected with the Meadows. The dead were quietly laid to rest with no lawsuits or recriminations. After agonizing a few weeks, Peter, Candy and the baby returned to the Meadows to reoccupy their A-frame. Meanwhile, unable to face what had happened, most of the Meadows people rushed headlong into making plans for the summer; plowing and planting the garden. Some, however, felt a discomfort and uneasiness, but kept silent, fearing to face the group's wrath if they expressed their doubts.

The situation came to a head one evening when everyone was gathered to eat in the cookshack. Peter, who was there with Candy, was critical of the fact that only one person volunteered to cook the meal, and upset that there were so many new people. He hardly recognized anyone, and noted that six of the people who should have been there, weren't. A few weeks earlier, he had mentioned selling the land to someone else interested in being a patron to a social experiment. Bill finally asked Peter if he still wanted to sell the land. By this time the cookshack was stone silent. Fourteen pairs of ears honed in on the conversation between Peter and Bill.

Peter replied that he did want to sell, and when Bill asked him why, after a long pause, answered, "Because the land doesn't want us here." Peter went on to say that the spirits on the land had been telling them all along to get off, only the Meadows people had been so insensitive that they hadn't perceived the spirits' communications. Peter claimed he was in contact with them day and night since returning to the land and he understood their message. But even before, there had been definite signs anyone could have recognized had they been aware: ax heads flying off the handles, a few people almost setting their hair on fire while leaning over kerosene chimneys, and the previous week the door to the cookshack came off in Yale's hands. The spirits had been forced to escalate their communication, causing the big fire and taking some of the members' lives so that the others might be saved. While away during the winter, Peter had visions and dreams of the house on fire and, to prevent injury, even considered traveling to the Meadows to burn the house down himself when no one was in it. Moreover, Peter reminded everyone that the place had been the last stronghold of the Indians fighting the hated White Man, that Ebenezer King's ghost still walked the land seeking revenge against the whites, and that witches used to dance on the crest of Eagle Claw under the full moon. Now there were four more unhappy spirits walking the land.

No one questioned Peter's contention that there were spirits on the land. Some of the people backed him up; one claimed to see little people peering from behind trees. Another spoke of a strange force which almost caused her to leap from James' old tree house. Others commented on their frequent nightmares. Candy reacted fearfully, telling of strange figures hovering about their A-frame, refusing to tell her horrible dreams because the telling might make them come true. She said she could only wrap her baby in her own and no one else's blanket because she didn't know what destructive forces were in the strange blankets. The final evidence was the eerie darkness in the cookshack; no shadows were cast even when the sun shone through the windows. Candy was unabashedly afraid to stay on the land. Others, particularly those recently arrived and also the youngest people, reacted to all the negative talk with dismay, breaking down and sobbing, thinking they had found a home and a family only to find it disappearing.

Bill, Gracey, and Janet formed an opposition to Peter and Candy very cautiously. They respectfully protested that they had not perceived bad omens or hostile vibrations from the spirits. If given the chance, they wanted to resist the spirits' hostile energies and eventually win their friendship by performing deeds and exercising sensibilities sympathetic with theirs. Peter countered that it was too late. The spirits had spoken and were adamant. If Bill tried to resist or outdo the spirits, he would be drained, leaving him with a vacuum inside that would be disastrous for him. Peter claimed to know the immense strength of these energies, for he and no one else had been in direct contact with them. Gracey intimated that with all the members working on it, their energy had to be stronger than the spirits' to which Peter vehemently replied that love, not strength, was needed in order to be compassionate and understand the position of the spirits.

Apparently resigned to her new fate, Gracey asked who Peter would sell the land to: a developer, a speculator, or someone else who would live on it? Wouldn't whoever bought the land come into conflict with the spirits too? No, Peter replied, because only those who are open to the perception of the spirits can be affected by them. Then the question was raised as to whether or not there were non-believing materialists in their group who scoffed at the idea of spirits, thereby remaining immune. Yale, of course, believed in nothing, and Peter admitted he could own the land and survive. Bill asked if they could all stay after helping to raise money for Yale to buy it. Peter said that was circumventing the issue, while Yale caustically remarked he would give eviction notices to everyone there if he owned the land. Yale clearly wanted the land, but had by now become disillusioned with the idea of a commune.

With this, Gracey made one last plea to the entire group. Wasn't the energy of love between people stronger than spirit energy? Even if the land was sold, wouldn't they move somewhere together? She passionately asked for people to speak up, saying they should at least stay together. The answer was a long silence. Finally, Gracey resorted to asking people to commit themselves to a position, one by one around the room. Roamer, the ex-mental patient who was "freaked out" by cities, Clara, the runaway who had no place to go, and Janet, who needed a home for her baby, were the only ones beside Bill and Gracey who wanted to remain on the land and stay together. Yale wanted to stay on the land alone, if possible. All the others made qualified remarks rationalizing the group splitting up. Those most open to spiritual orientation were scared by Peter's arguments. Others insisted that one doesn't have to live with people in order to love them. It was possible to love people thousands of miles away.

In short, despite behavior to the contrary, no one was willing to admit they didn't love one another, thereby allowing themselves to conform to the Aquarian ethic verbally. Gracey perceived the contradiction, bitterly declaring that she had been living with a group of people who didn't really feel what they talked about. In their largely young and loveless lives, they had not yet come to realize there was more to the emotion than they had so far known, and that it involved far more than the uses they found for the word they brandished so facilely. She accused them of not being prepared to make commitments to other people, through good and bad. To them, love had essentially only meant sharing fleeting enjoyable experiences

The discussion of love and commitment inevitably got down to those who had died. Peter finally blurted out the fact that since the fire, no one dared probe the meaning of the fact that four human beings whom they supposedly loved had perished. Why hadn't they discussed it among themselves? Why couldn't they face it? If they loved them so much, why didn't they show any emotion, remorse, or sorrow? What could the death of their commune mates teach them about the direction and meaning of their own lives? One member protested that her dead communal brothers and sisters were happy when they died, and that was all one could expect. But Peter contradicted her, saying they were miserable, and that's why they drank so much. She countered that it was at least an honorable death, and that she had thought of the commune's continuation as a memorial to them. Peter insisted that dying dead drunk was not honorable, despite what others believed, and what the people at JM wanted to believe themselves.

The evening had been a cathartic explosion, with the shrapnel of guilt, sobs, anger, and soul searching hitting everyone. All grappled with the meanings of social responsibility and death itself, even if they did conceptualize them in terms of spirits and energy forces. After a year and a half, the social experiment was apparently over. Some, especially the older and original people, were melancholy to see their dream dashed. Resigning themselves, some sighed and talked about going to Alteria, because with escalated government repression, it probably wasn't safe to stay in America anyway. Others just didn't know what to do, except that they were certain they wouldn't return home, to school, or to their former straight lives. For each one of those disappointed, there were those who appeared relieved, as if a huge burden had been lifted from their backs. Hardly able to contain their enthusiasm to leave (also mixed with discomfort at remaining to face those who felt sabotaged by their intended exodus), some made plans to leave the very next morning. Peter and Candy were sad to see it end, but they knew it had to, and were happy to be free of the responsibility. Peter would give each person as much time as was needed to find a new home before he would sell. But before the gathering broke up, Bill asked Peter one last time if he would be willing to stay or let the others stay on, despite the spirits, "if we all did get together," agreeing upon a goal, and making the firm commitment to continue. Peter said he would, if everyone wanted it that way.

For the next three months, the Meadows hung in suspended animation. Some of the people half-heartedly worked to keep the place going (Bill, Yale, Gracey, and Janet: the old leadership), and others marked time until some alternative turned up. In truth, few had any place to go or anything else to do, as most were displaced persons who had originally come to the Meadows because other options which were either closed off or rejected as intolerable. Those who left after the meeting to explore new opportunities had returned within a couple of week's time, apparently finding the outside world as inhospitable as before. As could be expected, those who were youngest, least educated, and from the lower socioeconomic class backgrounds were hardest hit.

What kinds of alternatives were considered? Returning to parents or step-parents was an option for some. Annette, the black woman, went home with the Alterian divorcee, but did not remain there long because her step-parents refused to support them and because they could not tolerate the restrictions on their freedom that living there placed on them. After a week of staying with friends in intolerably overcrowded conditions, they returned to the Meadows. Janet, who went home after the fire and the death of her unborn baby's father, also found she could no longer live with her parents' constant reprovals and isolation from hip age mates. She returned to the Meadows to have her baby.

Others thought about obtaining their own farms. Bill and Gracey had some money saved and talked of traveling to Alteria to look for some land. They later bought a cheap farmstead there, but when they applied for a permanent residence visa they were refused, pending a hearing on Bill's arrest and drug use record, and on his proving he had skills sufficient to earn his own living. They kept the farm, but decided to live in Provincia, slowly making moves to secure their entrance to Alteria, including getting legally married. Annette, who was also pregnant, and her mate tried to enter Alteria, but were hauled off the bus. Asked by the border guard how much money they had, they were told it was insufficient to be admitted even as tourists, and were refused entry to the country. When their bus fare was not refunded, they had to hitch all the way back to the Meadows.

The third alternative was travel. Some hadn't hitched around the country since the previous summer and had itchy thumbs, while a few had never seen the country at all. Some people questioned whether or not travel was more of an escape than a genuine alternative. After much wondering and searching, wouldn't they have to settle somewhere and work to create a solid basis for a rewarding alternative life? Others countered that they were not prepared to settle into anything yet. The world was still there to be explored, and they didn't want to get trapped in a rut like their parents. Others argued that life was so unpredictable that it was useless to make plans and try to fulfill them. They would rather drift around until they fell into a situation they liked.

Still others looked into possibilities of joining other communes in the region. A macrobiotic-diet-and-yoga enthusiast struck up a friendship with the two Red Rose women who themselves had similar dietary and physical disciplinary interests. Although he was not in the least politically inclined, he began to think of yoga and diet as community building and rallying points for the CC as well as an individual pursuit. Still not quite sure how he would integrate his old persona with new revolutionary interests, he was invited to join Red Rose. But like Jesse before him, he was admitted after much reluctance on the part of the veteran radicals. The women argued that a balanced revolutionary community had to contain all elements of the CC, and that Red Rose must attempt to reach and politicize the hippies.

Others hopped around. Two young women visited Secret Ponds only to reject the idea of moving there after they found out they wouldn't be living with lions and tigers, and that the men there were older than their own fathers. Another two went to Last Ditch Farm where they did nothing but hard work, eventually participating in a rebellion against the landowner and leader. One, the Alterian divorcee, finally returned to Last Ditch, having found a rewarding relationship with one of the men.

Peter went to the Krishna Brethren which had grown significantly in membership since leaving JM the previous fall. After being there only a short time, he was perceived as a person with special spiritual status, and immediately collected a band of followers within the Brethren. When it came time for him to become a member formally, he openly stated before a grand meeting that while he would like to join, he would maintain his complete independence, refusing to obey orders unless he concurred with them, and reserving the right to take leave whenever his intuition or spirit forces dictated. Despite this heretical and potentially disruptive position, he was admitted. James acknowledged Peter's special spiritual powers and the Karmic problems between them had to be worked out, but said that in the long run the Brethren would benefit more from Peter's presence than his absence.

Of the twenty people who left the Meadows early that summer, twelve joined other communes; ten of them within the Provincia. Five went to Walnut Hill. Because there were no couples there when JM was breaking up, and because the most influential Walnut Hill woman regarded couples as a stabilizing influence, Bill and Gracey (whom she met though Parson's Crossing) were invited to join. However, when Bill and Gracey finally moved in, they took Janet and her baby with them. Later, another former JM couple returned to Provincia, and finding their closest friends at Walnut Hill, visited them, slowly becoming considered part of that membership. Annette and her mate went to Moore Commune where they stretched an invitation for a short visit into a permanent stay. One woman joined Last Ditch and another eventually went to a commune at the opposite end of Provincia whose members she first met at a regional commune meeting arranged in part by Red Rose Collective. Yale, the last of the originals to leave, finally let go of the Meadows when he was invited to help get the Rainbow Farm commune under way. Thus, the communal network, which people had been only vaguely aware of, became a strong presence in the minds of most. The network was strengthened by virtue of many JMers traveling it and sometimes joining other groups.

Even if members of JM slowly drifted away over the summer, the Meadows as a commune did not come to an end. Some who stayed hoped that the old people could reconstitute themselves into a communal group, revitalize themselves, and prove to Peter that they could live on the land harmoniously. Before he left, Yale went to work daily at the sawmill, turning much of his salary over to the communal bank account. Food stamp lists were still made out with different people taking turns as official head of the family. Bill, Gracey, and others worked hard on the garden, for at least they could harvest the crops to take to their new home. After the backbreaking work of pulling out rocks and sticks, spreading compost, raking, and planting seeds, Bill circled the acre patch of furrowed land at dusk, playing his flute and listening to its echo in the valley, hoping it soothed and nurtured the seeds as well as the people gathered around the cookshack.

The site where the longhouse had been was cleared of all debris, encircled with a little stone wall, and respectfully planted with pumpkins, flowers, and herbs. In this smaller garden stood the only reminder of what once was: a single post that had been part of the foundation into the top of which was driven some nails which had partially melted together forming a shape of four fused crosses. Someone had found the metal object in the rubble after the fire, and everyone marveled at the way fate or the spirits had caused the fire to melt the nails to make one cross for each of the people who perished.

The previous summer, Bill had kept a guest book that anyone who stayed overnight was asked to sign, and when it was finally destroyed in the fire, it contained well over a thousand names. This summer would bring even more visitors, but unlike the previous year when there was no visitor policy, this year one forbidding visitors was set up, only to disintegrate shortly afterward. No one knew if Jackson's Meadows was going to be in existence for ten days or ten years, and whether or not pre-fire policies were still in effect. No meetings were held because as far as many were concerned, JM was no longer a commune, but a piece of land to live on until something better came along.

Accordingly, visitors asking to stay received different answers. Roamer, Bill, and Gracey told people that the commune was closed, and that if it were going to pick itself up out of the ashes, it must do so as a tightly knit group. They turned many people away. But others invited anyone to stay on, particularly those visitors who contributed food or had connections that could lead them to new situations. Most were able to stay if they were insistent, because no one had the authority, the will, or the backing of the group to throw them out. Thus, the same processes at work the previous summer were operating again, though the circumstances were different. Nearly any tenacious person could join, but everyone was told that it would be temporary; that the owner was probably going to sell the land.

The vacuum created by the lack of leadership and the exit of the old membership, drew in a large and unlikely mix of people. Summer had begun, and with it came a marked increase in the circulation of voyeurs, lost souls, social theorists, and urban cultural revolutionaries. No attempt was made by these early joiners to control the numbers of the later arrivees, because as new people themselves, they felt they had no prerogative to organize anyone or anything on the land. Furthermore, like the older members, they believed that the commune would collapse at any moment. Some of the new people moved in to experience the thrills of communal life, while others had been on the move for a while, hoping to find a home somewhere in Provincia.

This all led to a curious combination of individuals with very different backgrounds, and who had very little in common except for the earth they stood on. A look at the feeder networks and some of the stated reasons for coming to JM are instructive at this point. There were thirty-six new people who became members throughout the summer; thirty-two of whom joined through acquaintances who were already there, only four having no previous connections. Some stayed on for only a few weeks, and others longer. Of the thirty-two connected people, seven came through the IBM-Mother Humper network, eight came from Peter's home town, eight came directly or indirectly through Elliot (who was still telling people about his commune), five were from the urban street scene network, and two came from another commune. Thus, a few were friendless drifters and some came from tough, hard drinking, and sometimes violent environments. Some were young suburban kids eager to learn the ways of hip life, some were highly educated people who were searching for sociocultural alternatives, some were flower children grown older and wiser, and a few had found the more regimented communal life elsewhere unrewarding.

What the feeder networks didn't indicate, however, was the wide diversity in age and educational background. Age of independent adults ranged from thirteen to near forty, and the five children attached to parents ranged from less than one year to ten. Some were illiterate tenth grade dropouts, while others were highly trained professionals with various academic degrees. Among the professionals were a published poet, a movie actor, an artist, a high school teacher, a psychotherapist, college instructors in psychology and sociology, and the author of this study. Among the others were ex-marines and Vietnam veterans, groupies, runaways, and political activists who had taken part in such events as the Chicago riots in 1968. All cautiously entered JM, gradually finding out who the others were and where they came from. Although half did not intend to make JM their full-time home, even if given the opportunity, they all wanted to establish permanent ties to the commune if it survived. Only two temporarily joined for the sake of experience, all the while intending to move on.

By mid-June, the original people had drifted away, most of the new people drifted in, and whether or not JM would continue as a commune was still unresolved. People just hung around, doing only enough work to survive from day to day. New people, eager to be accepted, would attempt to prove their worth by working in the garden, carrying water up from the stream, chopping wood, or washing dishes. But after noticing that few people were doing much work, they too slowed down, laid out in the sun, and took pleasant strolls over the land. Each new arrivee, learning that the lackadaisical attitude was the modus operandi, eventually slid into the slow pace of life.

Peter returned to the Meadows after his stay at the Brethren, bringing with him Roy, one of the top Brethren lieutenants. They had come to announce that Peter was selling the land to the Brethren. Peter explained that while he had received no indication from the JM people that they were committed to continue, he didn't want to sell it to a real estate developer. He had read once that there were seven holy men who took stones with spiritual energy in them to plant in various parts of the world, and he thought one of them was planted here. Both he and the Brethren sensed great spiritual energy on the land and agreed that it had great potential for those capable of using it, though it might destroy those people characterized by "negativity." After getting no reaction, he said that fifty Brethren would arrive the next week to re-occupy the land they lived on the previous summer. They would be coming to experience the spiritual intensity the older members of the Brethren had experienced the previous summer, but which was impossible to achieve with all the visitors and commotion where they were now living. Since the Brethren were to re-occupy only part of the land, the general understanding was that the JM group could remain.

Bill, who pointed out Peter's change in position regarding people living on the land, commented that, paradoxically, things had come full circle; that after all his and Gracey's efforts to remain on the land, now that they had the chance to remain, they had already made plans to leave and there was no turning back. Others expressed their doubts; one declaring that the Brethren didn't care for the land itself, having left garbage all over it when they moved out the previous summer. Peter responded by agreeing, adding that with the Brethren's emphasis on spirituality, they neglected the material basis of things, and that was where JM could help the Brethren balance themselves. But by the same token, it was true that JM neglected spirituality, and the Brethren would help JM in this area. Also, while the Brethren confronted and probed one another's motives and thoughts, JM people hardly ever communicated serious concerns to each other. The nonverbal, intuitive approach to living together was good up to a point, according to Peter, but if carried too far, even intuitive communication would cease, leaving only superficial relationships. Thus, by living together on the land, Peter concluded, the two communes could compensate for each other's weaknesses and aid each other in their growth.

But JM veterans recalled the Brethren's missionary zeal and heavy-handed way of dealing with people. One declared she didn't "want a lot of people following me around telling me my ways are wrong and trying to convert me." She asked if Roy was moving in with the other Brethren. Peter replied that Roy would be the group "overseer." Speaking directly to Roy this time, she point-blank asked him, "Are you going to be our overseer, too? You people have a strong way of controlling people." Roy replied that there was a lot of misunderstanding regarding the Brethren, and that "We are not here to tell you how to do things or how to live; that's your business." Roy would come instead to share his spiritual insights with others. He would be no "boss," but as people learned the lessons he had learned, they would go along with the flow, having faith in him and his knowing what to do.

Reactions to this new development were varied. The old leadership and the few left at JM who knew the Brethren from before, went ahead with plans to leave the Meadows. The down-and-out people, mostly spiritually oriented and with no place else to go, didn't mind the idea, thinking they would check out the Brethren and perhaps join. Even Janet considered joining, because her friend was already a member and because she was looking for the best home for her baby. The over-30s took a wait-and-see attitude, while the young people from Peter's home town apparently didn't care. It was only the toughened street people who clearly opposed the Brethren moving in, being wary about having any form of authority around. They warned that despite Peter's assurances, it was inevitable "that JM couldn't stay intact." The Brethren would get rid of JM because the only tillable land was the land JM people live on, or the Brethren would get themselves and JM thrown out by the town for polluting the streams, for not following the health codes, and because the local straight people didn't like them.

The Brethren were soon forgotten as new visitors continued to arrive. Bill and Gracey packed tools and utensils to take with them, while often two or three nights would go by before Yale would return to the cookshack from work. Yale's interests had shifted away from the Meadows to the town of Wilfred, where he worked. He knew many people (straight and freak), and decided to run for the elective office of state senator. An alternative political party of old radicals and regional students had asked him to run against a Democrat and a Republican as the best known and most affable hippie in the district. The rest of the Meadows people largely followed individual pursuits on the land. Some played badminton, others lay in the grass, some played darts against one side of the cookshack, and others sat in the meadows in little circles chatting and sewing patches on their disintegrating clothes. Although the place had the appearance of a CC country club, not all was pleasant, as Hank and Zeke, for example, were withdrawing from their physical dependence on alcohol, and others, such as Clara and Roamer fearfully wondered what was going to happen to them with no place to call home.

Although Gracey was leaving shortly, she still managed the group's affairs. While often trying to get out of cooking for everyone, she was competent and enjoyed the responsibility to some extent. As July rolled around, she orchestrated her last monthly communal rejuvenation ritual by again drawing up a list of names for food stamps. By establishing who was definitely in the commune and who was not, who was officially "head of the family" and who would carry the food stamp cards with their signatures, the commune was legitimized by the SS. Moreover, the Welfare office reaffirmed it for the communards, as well, in that everyone had to state clearly their intentions to remain and take responsibility for obtaining food. With the drawing up of the list, at least two over-30s, Norman and Patrick, who had been in a state of limbo regarding their status as members, breathed a sigh of relief as they were asked whether or not they wanted to be included. The new list also served to bring previously peripheral members into the center of the group. Because the old leadership no longer intended to stay, other people had to replace them, and some were reticent about accepting the responsibility.

New people began to think of JM as their home and consider what it would take to survive the frigid weather that lay beyond the lazy and bountiful days of summer. Finally, one evening after rumors had circulated all day that "the women are planning something," Boop, Cindy, and Janet from the IBMs and Mother Humpers, called the first meeting since Peter announced he was thinking of selling the land. Boop started by saying the place was "like a fucking summer resort." If this was going to be their home, she said, and if they were going to live together, things couldn't go on the way they had for the last month or so. The cookshack was a mess, not having been cleaned in weeks, with rotting food lying under the counter. Dishes getting washed, meals getting cooked, and even firewood getting chopped for fires to heat the food and dishwater, depended on individual whim. People were stashing their own food supplies away and not sharing it. The weeds in the garden had become so large and numerous that it was difficult to find the plants among them. Also, they would have to have a new house built if they were going to stay the winter and people should start thinking about it, even though it was still early summer.

The response was mixed. The old-timers just excluded themselves, saying they were too busy preparing their own moves to get reinvolved, and some of the street males got up to play badminton (among them was Boop's old man, Zeke). An original member noted that the meeting was an exact replica of hundreds he had sat through since the previous summer. "If I had taped one, then we could have played it at all the other meetings, saving us a lot of time and effort," he added. Someone commented that no one wanted to work because they thought the place was going to split up, but Janet, who had just had her baby and was breast feeding it at the meeting, countered that that excuse was no longer valid. Hank suggested dividing up the work along the lines of "chicks and cats," but there was strong objection to this rigid sex work role definition, not because of an articulated radical feminist response, but because Roamer said his favorite work was kitchen work and under no circumstances would he give it up.

But when Janet suggested that a list of jobs be posted and people be assigned to them, a roar of protest rose from those still sitting around. Among the most vociferous were people who had bad institutional experiences in the past, and cited them: school, the Marines, mental hospitals. Roamer pointed out how mental hospitals were supposed to help people recover, and did up to a certain point, but after that they taught obedience and dependency. The only work he enjoyed in the hospital were projects patients had initiated. After his admonition, it was proposed that all work be left to individual initiative. But all those with communal experience guffawed at this, saying that that approach would never work, for if it had, this very meeting wouldn't be necessary.

Finally, it was resolved that all would get up for breakfast together and decide who would do what chores. Patrick was to blow the horn in his VW camper when, because there were no clocks at JM, he saw the sun's morning rays reach the cookshack door. Cindy reminded everyone that material survival was not the only concern; that if they wanted to stay on the land after the Brethren moved on to it, they had better be a cohesive, purposeful, vibrant group so the Brethren would want them as neighbors. To this Hank replied that it didn't make any difference to him what the Brethren thought because he certainly didn't want the Brethren as neighbors.

The women and Roamer were right. The material and economic outlook for JM was bleak. Peter, who had bailed the commune out in the past, would no longer be a part of it. Yale was the only person holding down a regular job, but as he felt less commitment to the place and he contributed progressively less money, time, and effort. Patrick had little money to contribute, but volunteered his minibus for transportation. Norman contributed cash ($600 over the summer), but eventually came to consider himself a patsy and sugar daddy for some people at the Meadows. Visitors were an unpredictable source of food, with some expecting to be fed while contributing nothing.

Actually, the food situation was not that bad. There were cartons of bruised but mostly useable vegetables and fruits that the supermarket gave JM for fifty cents. The Food Stamp people were not cracking down as they had been doing in some other communal CC regions, and the twenty-five dollars that JM paid into the program provided enough stamps to feed twenty people for a month. There was also the garden, which could potentially produce enough food to feed everybody over the summer, except for grains and meat, thereby helping to save food stamps for other storable items. It could also provide enough food for canning to last them through the winter. The forest was full of dead trees for wood for heat and cooking, and shelter could be provided by materials from demolished buildings in town or local torn down barns.

There were individual sources of income that inconsistently contributed to communal projects. Roamer received a social security payment because he was declared unemployable due to his mental health record. Allen, the political activist, and his friend from high school days were also drawing social security checks because each had one dead parent and they were technically still in school. Some old Haight-Ashbury-East Village veterans were adept at panhandling, obtaining enough to buy beer, candy, and ice cream. Some sporadically received checks from parents as birthday presents or enticements to return home.

Despite many people having been dope dealers in their urban pasts, dealing being a major part of the underground economy, none engaged in it now. One returned home to harvest a field of marijuana he planted, only to find that one of his "friends" had beat him to it, keeping all the money. Some, from lower class or street backgrounds, engaged in shoplifting, limiting it primarily to expensive food items such as steaks, and to chain stores so that local proprietors wouldn't be hurt. This practice, however, was criticized so much, not for moral reasons, but for fear of bad relations with the town, that nearly all shoplifting ceased.

With the advent of pregnant women and new mothers at the Meadows, welfare became an important economic factor. Three already had young children and three more were pregnant, expanding JM's reputation as "the Baby Farm." Some were new to the welfare game, and for them, particularly Janet, there was no other alternative. But for the IBM's and Mother Humpers, it was a challenge to outsmart some contemptible bureaucracy, though the monetary need was still very real. Regardless of whether or not people were rationalizing their actions as a way to destroy the government's welfare system, maximizing benefits was the way to go. It required some misrepresentation, especially in a communal context. The visit of a welfare worker to the Meadows serves as an example.

Cindy had just applied for welfare, and her social worker asked if she could come out and see what the living situation was like. JM people immediately interpreted this as an excuse to satisfy her prurient and voyeuristic inclinations through the use of her position (to come see the hippies free of charge by official visit). Because welfare regulations were based on biological family relations, they had a built-in anti-communal bias. Although this particular office was not yet challenging the communally declared family concept as being equivalent to a family based on blood relations, it did insist that a welfare recipient maintain a bona fide separate residence (a permanent structure with a stove). Thus, if Cindy lived with other people whom she claimed were her "family," they, and not welfare, were liable for her support. Candy temporarily moved out of the A-frame on the day of the scheduled visit and Cindy moved in, setting up a Sterno stove. Janet already had her cabin, but she was prepared to lie when said she cooked on her own heating stove. JM was more fortunate in its ability to misrepresent the facts than more tightly knit communes because it did have separate buildings for people to claim as their own.

The young woman showed up in jeans, barefoot and braless, and indicated in word and in manner her sympathetic position for people who followed the hip lifestyle. Yet she acknowledged that she had "a job to do." While expressing an interest in visiting JM again to go swimming with the hippies, she also asked very personal questions required of her job. She inquired why Gracey just urinated in the grass instead of in the outhouse. (Answer: Because "the outhouse smelled too bad.") Why did Cindy's old man leave her? (Answer: Because "he was not into the father trip.") The social worker politely begged forgiveness for asking these personal questions, and in response Cindy politely lied, saying they understood the position she was in.

The women lied about a number of things throughout the interview. Gracey urinated in the grass primarily because it was closer than the outhouse way across the field. Cindy's old man was hiding in the woods until the worker left. Question: "Were you on welfare in the Bay area? Answer: "Yes, first in San Francisco, then Berkeley." Truth: She was on welfare in both places simultaneously; drawing payments from both places while traveling back and forth between them. Question: "What did you do for money before that?" Answer: "Panhandle." Truth: Deal dope, shoplift, and panhandle. Question: "Is this your only child?" Answer "Yes." Truth: It was her only child, but it had drawn four AFDC payments in the Bay Area because three other women had borrowed the baby to go down to the welfare office, each claiming it to be hers. Question: "How did you get to Provincia?" Answer: "Hitched here with Zeke and Boop." Truth: Flew with Zeke, Boop and Hank on Boop's father's credit card.

But Cindy wasn't lying when she said she was broke. Even if Boop paid for Cindy's air fare, she was not supporting her from day to day. Likewise, it was true that she couldn't work, that food stamps alone couldn't support a baby, and that the baby hadn't had anything healthful to eat in days. Cindy was essentially in a desperate position and the only person who could at all be considered responsible for her was Hank. But his shoplifting and dealing skills were no longer operational in Provincia. Being a high school dropout and an ex-Marine with a dishonorable discharge, his chance of landing a job was out of the question. When asked if he could get any job he replied by waving his long pony-tail at the questioner, adding that, "Few people will hire longhairs, and when they do, you can be sure it is for the lousiest, menial work at the lowest pay."

Hank went on to explain his strategy for ripping-off welfare. Even though his long hair was a real reason for not getting work, he said, welfare would not accept such social excuses. Cutting off his hair was out of the question because it would be cutting off his identity, his potential friends, his culture, and his basic human right to be free so long as he wasn't hurting anyone else. He got medical excuses exempting him from work in some large cities from doctors at the Free Clinics there. The more people who rip off welfare, he said, the more tax money goes into supporting it, the poorer everyone gets, the more people get on welfare, the more dissatisfied with the capitalist state they become, the sooner they will turn to revolution and socialism.

But welfare did not become a way of life at JM. Some were opposed to it on altruistic grounds, others had other sources of money and didn't need it, and others were afraid to apply because they were in hiding from bureaucratic record keeping "Amerika" as runaways, draft evaders, and "criminals." Nevertheless, JM was to become a poverty pocket, welfare or no welfare. Even if people obtained money, there was either little likelihood of using it constructively for the commune or of holding on to it for individual purposes. If a person didn't lend money when he had it, he was considered selfish by many and counterrevolutionary by others, and was treated coolly by the rest of the group. This would result in his losing touch with his closest reference group, the people who affirmed his role and identity as a person and a member of a society. On the other hand, if he lent it out, it was almost certain he would never get it back.

Even if a person had some money hidden away, there were few ways he could spend it without the others knowing. If he bought an object to use or wear, people would see it. If he just wanted a delicacy to eat, and others were around (as they usually were), he either would have to forego it or buy some for everyone. More than once, individuals were "caught" leaving the group under pretext of having some important business to conduct in town, only to be discovered in a Centerville restaurant eating a greasy cheeseburger. Although they grinned sheepishly when discovered, and the others said nothing, each one knew what the other was thinking. Thus, guilt about one's own dedication to the New Age ethics of "sharing with the brothers and sisters," and fear of ostracism from the group usually made the retention or accumulation of money nearly impossible.

Some people were at first willing to sink their meager resources into communal expenses, but soon found that practice unrewarding because most of it was consumed (1) in survival instead of growth and constructive development (for example, food instead of building materials); (2) in covering other people's mistakes (paying for traffic tickets); (3) in supporting inverted priorities (sinking

$57.50 into dog licenses and rabies shots instead of buying tires for the truck); (4) in condoning carelessness (spending money to replace rusty saw blades that wouldn't have to be replaced if people hadn't left the saw in the rain); (5) in excusing other people's irresponsibility toward the commune (donating money for communal expenses that others would otherwise have to donate if they hadn't already spent it on beer or candy).

In short, JM was like a sponge, always able to absorb the limited available money, but never becoming saturated enough to spill over into anything else. Anyone who entered the system soon found that if he wanted to stay, his funds would quickly be depleted. Thus intracommunal equality was achieved to a marked degree, even if it meant that everyone became equally deprived.

Burdened with the propensity for disorganization (or blessed, depending on one's viewpoint), JM struggled over the next few weeks to devise ways of getting dishes washed, children fed, the garden weeded, and wood chopped. Plans would work for a few days, then collapse. Progressively fewer people got up in the morning with the car horn because they "couldn't get to sleep last night," were "hung over from drinking a jug of wine a visitor brought," or "didn't hear it up the hill." Those who were annoyed most by the chaos, usually the hardest workers, complained and called meetings at which the same mundane issues were rehashed, resulting in a new plan, or no resolution at all. But eventually, some of the problems began to resolve themselves. People slowly discovered specific chores they didn't mind doing a little at a time. As more people became involved, the emergency demand declined, and as the work load was spread, it became lighter for each.

Problems were never completely resolved, necessitating periodic struggles, sometimes leading to momentary crises. Roamer, for example, took kitchen-related work quite seriously, and at one point, took out his frustration over the lack of participation in cooking and cleaning chores by others by attacking an underfed dog who kept stealing food and who belonged to one of the people he was annoyed with. Seeing him smash the dog on the head with a large wooden bowl, many were frightened by the violent display, indicating later that it was a wonder he hadn't killed the dog. "Better the dog than the owner," someone else remarked. But even with such episodes, the younger people new to the CC and to communes (particularly from Peter's home town) largely remained oblivious to work necessities. Instead they took mescaline, looked at a leaf closely for the first time, lost their virginity on a hidden grassy knoll, listened open-mouthed to the experiences of more experienced freaks, or wrote torrents of love poetry to Pepsi Joe's thirteen-year-old sister. One of them, when finally forced into dragging water buckets up from the stream, loudly and cryptically paraphrased the army's recruitment slogan at the time, "Join a commune! Learn a trade!"

The commune picked up most after all the old leadership left. Most people had come to expect the original veterans to perform the important tasks. The newer people felt inhibited by Bill, who often treated them as if they weren't there, and by Gracey's periods of depression and complaining. It happened that Bill, Gracey, Janet, and her baby all left the same day, leaving only four pre-fire people plus the new recruits. As people embraced and good-byes were said, there was a feeling of trepidation among those remaining behind as it dawned on them they didn't know how to apply for food stamps, what they were supposed to do to the outhouse so it would pass inspection by the health people, who they were to ask for a permit to build a new house, and if there was any money left in the communal bank account. While the engine of the car that was waiting to carry Gracey away idled, she walked quickly through the garden, pushing aside the weeds to explain to people what was planted where, and what was supposed to be done to them (sticks in the ground for string beans and tomatoes, snip off the buds on lettuce and spinach, watch out for red bugs on potatoes, don't let the corn get too ripe before you pick it).

Later that day, a minibus-load of remaining JM people returned from a shopping trip exuberantly talking of plans for the Meadows. Initial fear of responsibility for running the place had now shifted to elation. Now they could operate the Meadows the way they saw fit, for there was no one or nothing to prevent them. After living at the Meadows for five months and never once going food shopping, Clara organized the expedition to the supermarket, deciding what was needed after consulting everyone else, and measuring that off against the amount of food stamps they had. She proudly proclaimed that "this was the first time I've ever done anything like this. I didn't think I could do it. Now I know why Gracey complained about all the work involved in shopping."

Pepsi Joe spoke of going to the library to get a book on how to build a root cellar so they would have fresh vegetables all winter. Roamer wanted books on canning, and someone else would start designing a new house. Everyone fantasized about Thanksgiving, still five months away, in which steaming dishes would be placed on rough-hewn tables, pumpkins piled on the window sills, and corn stalks bunched in the field. They would invite all the neighbors, straight or freak, to a great feast, so they all could see that JM didn't contain such a bunch of losers, incapable of fending for themselves. "Why wait till Thanksgiving?" it was asked. "let's have it at harvest time!"

The euphoria of momentary revitalization subsided in the next couple of days. Those who weren't in the minibus making plans for the future were getting drunk with a carload of greasers who arrived with a case of beer. When the minibus returned, those who had been drinking were in no mood to hear about work plans and projects, and this served to dampen the spirits of the planners. By the sunlight of the next morning, the cookshack was in shambles. Food dropped on the floor, garbage was spilled, and dirty dishes were strewn around. Some wondered if it wouldn't still be a continuation of the same old problems. Nevertheless, they were still excited and looked forward to the new communal undertaking.

In their excitement, most remained remotely mindful that the Brethren were going to move on to the land at some point soon, and that served to make it even more imperative that they get their own house in order quickly. Looking back over the period between the fire and this new beginning, it was also time to take stock of what had happened and assess the group's resources for the days and months that lay ahead.

Analysis

Aside from taking four lives, the fire brought JM to the brink of extinction. But because the old structure and vision broke down, a new effort could be made with new people. Hopefully, the string of old cycles that edged the communal enterprise ever closer to disintegration had been spectacularly, even if tragically, broken, and the way was now clear for renewal. What shape would this revitalization take? Would the same processes be repeated or would lessons be learned from the past? And what were the implications for the CC outside JM, if any?

The reaction to the fire brought JM's external relations into clearer relief. While townspeople felt both sympathy and hostility, the town could no longer leave affairs at JM to take their own course. Much of the initial fascination with the fear of the hippie movement had dissipated with the fire, and most outsiders were prepared to take longer and harder looks at the goings-on. And what's more, they would probably take action.

The disaster demonstrated that contact between JM and other CC groups could be helpful to all concerned in times of need. Moreover, it also exposed a potential for linkage that might serve more general beneficial ends. Parson's Crossing, though quite removed from JM in attitudes and interests, was sympathetic, and the MacDonald House people took time off from their political organizing activities to express concern and offer aid. Even a previously unknown commune appeared after reading of the disaster in the newspaper. And most significant, those people who left JM did not return to the cities or a straight life, but migrated to other communes, and visited JM regularly, establishing links between groups that casual contacts could never rival.

It was almost as though the commune was beginning again, with important exceptions, however. Those most unskilled and least socially competent from the winter group were the ones who could not or did not relocate. They returned, with the result that many of the pre-fire behaviors and attitudes returned also. Furthermore, there was not a repetition of the euphoria fusion phase that had originally occurred at the Dobson House. Though there was sporadic communing between various combinations of people, it never involved the group as a whole. The newcomers had entered a vacuous situation created by others before them; most had never known each other before, let alone reached an agreement to initiate a radical social experiment together. Finally, the same feeder networks that had provided membership in the past were still at work. Thus the commune's death and rebirth was not complete. Vestiges of the old remained while the moment of spontaneous creation was missing.

Even if the renewal was not complete, what other alternatives were there if the commune was to survive? One option was to establish a complex set of rules that would force work, accumulation of capital, leadership initiative, and coordinate action on everyone. The backgrounds of many individuals and the dominant ideology made this impossible, however. Another was to rely on support from the outside in the form of welfare, gifts or grants. But this, too, was impossible to accomplish or maintain because of JM's minimal reciprocity potential in terms of paying taxes on income, making purchases, or demonstrating competence in any enterprise. Still another was to become largely self-sufficient, relying on the natural environment to dictate necessary behaviors and provide support. Yet the mere existence of an external society precluded any possibility of closing off JM's boundaries completely. All its members originally came from the outside and were not versed in self-sufficiency skills, and the temptation to return to the outside world was great when the going got rough. Also, even if support from the outside was not enough to allow JM to maintain an equilibrium or to prosper in the long run, it permitted shorter term survival without causing mobilization of necessary behaviors for eventual self-support. If JM was slowly running down, heading for eventual stagnation and disintegration, then the best alternative was to rewind the entire original mechanism and begin the cycle anew, attempting to modify it as it progressed so as not to repeat old mistakes.

One of the ways to begin again was to have a sudden and significant turnover in membership. The older membership having been accounted for, the backgrounds of the newer members bear closer examination. The feeder networks more than ever contributed very characteristic kinds of persons with wide-ranging differences in background. Thus, although the overall figures indicate something, those for the various networks mean more. Rather than commenting on each separately, they are lumped into (1) young people from suburban backgrounds plus Peter's home town and others who arrived independently; (2) the street people of the IBM or hippie variety; (3) Elliot's contacts with college-oriented people.

The average age of this new group was 21.9, the oldest so far of the three major groups of recruits, with the founding group being 21.4 and the second 19.2. But suburban youth in this newest group averaged 17.1 years, while the street wing averaged 21.7, and the college crowd, 28.4. Protestant representation climbed slightly while Jewish declined, with nearly all Jews being related to the college network. The 2.3 average number of homes lived in with parents, the lowest so far, indicated the young age of the suburban segment and the relative stability of some of the older people. There was, of course, a rise in suburban background with this generation, and all those with a college background either came from urban areas or small towns. The continued small representation from upper class background, and relatively large representation from the blue collar class may be typical of the distribution for American society as a whole, but quite surprising as far as communal and CC stereotypes are concerned. Rapid upward mobility was once again characteristic of the young suburban people's families, but not at all characteristic of most of the others. Again, a large proportion of parents' occupations were from the technical or unskilled sector, and little from the business and professional. The continued representation of Bohemians from past decades remained significant.

For the first time, unbroken homes narrowly out-numbered broken homes, but there were still signs of family disintegration. Two whose parents were still married claimed distant relations with their parents because of the large number of children in their families. Death of a parent as a cause for family break-up rivaled divorce. Adoption on the one hand, and on the other, virtual abandonment by parents was also present in this generation. Death in general was a key factor. The untimely death of siblings or close friends constituted significant turning points in the lives of many. At least twenty-three out of thirty-four had parents, close family, and very close friends and lovers die within five or six years prior to their coming to JM. The modes of death particularly were informative about the society at large with accident, violence, or premature stress related diseases taking the greatest toll. The emotional impact on age mates and young adult children of the deceased, it appeared, was quite serious.

This generation was not so withdrawn, non-participatory, lacking in skills, or low in self-esteem as the previous ones, though the various feeder networks differed widely on this. The street people again ranked low in this area while college people ranked high. The percent receiving psychiatric treatment, or having been jailed or arrested, was essentially unchanged though certainly higher than one might expect for an average sample of the American population. Unlike the second generation and more like the original one, the reasons for psychiatric consultation did not completely stem from emotional instability, and some of the arrests resulted from politically motivated actions. The older people had long employment records indicating they were not "spoiled or lazy." Those people who didn't, were for the most part very young and still in school until this point. There was definitely a strong representation of political concern, especially among the college related people. The spiritual orientation so evident in the first and second generations was somewhat weaker here. Some, however, had been through phases of serious dedication to both spiritual and political concerns, on the whole, shifting in orientation from salvation by individual means to salvation through social action. About the only significant difference in this generation from the others was the effect of the military draft. It was no problem for most; either being too old, too young, or veterans. And for those whose problem it still was, outright evasion was the dominant solution.

The wide differences in age and background in this generation requires further comment. Whereas the nucleus for JM in 1968 consisted of people around the same age, the early 20s, by 1970 the recruitment in terms of age range was spreading out in both directions. Both younger and older people were being pulled in until what was essentially a youth phenomenon also came to include not only children and adolescents, but over-30s as well. A similar pattern was also developing in other area communes. These newer recruits of varied ages tended to lack the same ecstatic sense of significance, of timelessness, of fate, or of all-encompassing commitment to ideals that characterized participants who initiated communal enterprises.

The under-20s did not for the most part come to JM for purposes of creating a new order in the world or to find eternal truths. Neither did they gather to develop a new lifestyle. The tone and environment was already set, and they came to try out a going operation. To some, political revolt, which they had only experienced through the media, was no longer in vogue. Others had participated in window smashing demonstrations and high school revolts for reasons they admitted they little understood, and were now on the rebound from such kinds of commitments. And others, particularly those with poor situations and emotional difficulties, were only trying to escape the social demands of parents and school.

The over-30s came for another set of reasons. For the most part mavericks, they had toyed with the beatnik lifestyle and campus socialist organizations in late 50s and early 60s. Having come to an uneasy peace with their society by the late 60s, they found the doors of apparent social change once again flung open, this time wider than ever before. Unable to throw all caution to the winds as the radicals and freaks in their twenties had done, they moved slowly and cautiously into the breach to see what was happening. The over-30s shared many attitudes and experiences that made it difficult for them to fit into the modern technocratic, specialization orientation of society. In the early part of their lives, they had parental love and support. They had confidence and the desire to achieve drilled into them, and were quite successful and happy in a small and familiar milieu. On moving into more impersonal and fiercely competitive situations, they were sensitive to the strain, and were somewhat justified in their criticism and contempt for the large institutions that fostered insensitivity and aggressiveness in men. Their early indulgence and competence not only gave them the confidence to be creative at an early age, but also led them to expect more from the "real" outside world than that world was able or willing to provide. They were non-conformists from an early age, and set themselves apart from most of their peers. But as they tested and pushed institutions to fulfill their individual demands, institutions pushed back, sometimes with devastating effects on them.

Thus, their idealism often turned to cynicism as their previous hoped for roles as social catalysts turned to real non-roles in social periphery, and their previous drive to be successful shifted to an exploration of new ways to change the world. Believing that institutions were unmovable, each sought to change his personal world, through travel, art, and sometimes, drugs. Not conforming, they often did not want, or were not permitted, to get on the usual university-based social mobility escalator for good jobs and rewarding positions in the worlds of industry and commerce. Finding that if they had not gone to graduate school they would probably have better jobs was a bitter pill to swallow, especially after their horizons regarding human potential were widened through that education. Switching careers and continuing their learning in the hope of getting somewhere, they sought to grapple with society and explore their options while trying to maintain some creative independence. Thus, they remained marginal to the institutions they worked in, talented and full of promise, but seldom fulfilled. In the late 60s, finally, they could explore the possibility of breaking free into a milieu that would not only tolerate, but perhaps would appreciate their talents.

The over-30s brought a stabilizing potential to JM, quickly perceiving its inconsistencies and contradictions. How was it, they asked, that so many could claim total commitment and love for one another and yet leave JM whenever they had the chance? Despite the love rhetoric, many people obviously felt trapped at JM, taking advantage of any major excuse to leave. The search for community had evidently led some to the realization that many close relationships can be restricting as well as liberating. Also, they asked, how was it that so many seeking community, self-realization, and recognition used the "crowd effect" of communal life to shrink away from responsibility and accountability? Many under-30s, it seemed, despite their rhetoric, clearly had sought out JM so they could hide behind others when it came time to demonstrate certain skills and acts necessary for survival.

But what worried the over-30s the most was JM's state of economic affairs, as they observed a dynamic that made the accumulation of wealth for capital investment in the enterprise impossible. For what JM clearly lacked was an enterprise that would have enabled the communards to create needed resources for themselves, rather than relying so heartily on the outside generosity that was bound to cease at some point. Though the over-30s were by no stretch of the imagination materially oriented, often accused of being economically naive by their SS colleagues, they began to question the moral purity supposedly gained through voluntary poverty in the effort to achieve a greater good, and the assumption that voluntary poverty was completely voluntary. If a viable sociocultural alternative to the SS was going to be created instead of the mere destruction of the SS that some of the younger people claimed as their goal, it appeared that the thinking and behavior represented at JM would not be up to the task unless changed by the new lease on communal life given by the sale of the land to the Brethren.

6. Organization: Mobilization for Adaptation

On the Fourth of July, a strange black car pulled into the Meadows and stopped. Two longhairs got out and without consulting anyone, went up the path to Eagle's Claw. Coming down an hour or so later, one of them turned out to be the Brethren leader, James, who approached the JM group loudly asking, "Which one of you people, if any, consider yourselves permanent residents here?" His aggressive manner surprised and put everyone on the defensive, but after a few seconds Zeke managed to say "I do." James then announced to him that "Everyone has until August 31 to decide whether or not you want to join the Brethren. Those who don't will have to leave the land." As he went on talking, Zeke, who was getting visibly disturbed, protested that Peter had said JM people could stay as long as they liked, separate from the Brethren, if they preferred. James brushed the question aside, saying he had the right to set any policy he wanted because he now owned the land as well as everything else in the Brethren. "The Brethren trust my decision as to what to do with this land, just as I trust them in anything they do. We have a tight thing going. We know what we want. We are here to get into each other's heads and to deepen our spiritual understanding, and to do this we have to have complete harmony. If you want to stay, you have to be with us in this."

Zeke persisted and others joined in. "Suppose you don't believe in the same spiritual thing but you understand the feel of the land, you care for it, and it cares for you. This means we have more right to the land than someone who just plunks money down to buy it. I'll have to wait to see the real attitudes of the Brethren people before I can decide whether or not I join." When someone finally quipped, "Belief can't have a deadline on it," James answered by saying, "Believe by August 31, or get out." He then launched into a complex metaphysical description of the Brethren cosmology involving vibrations, energy forces, and levels of growth that supposedly explained why his policy was necessary. When at the end he rhetorically asked "You understand?" he was somewhat jolted by Zeke who proclaimed, "No." Not bothering to re-explain, James went on to say, "I realize that a lot of people think I come on too strong. Maybe I do, but that's the way I am, and that's the way I operate." He pointed out how his method of operation made the Brethren as successful as it was, growing to 100 members since last summer, with new people joining all the time. It was expanding, setting up new branches, and organizing a federation of communes. He further asserted that they did have respect for the material as well as the spiritual, citing as proof the fact that they now "have the media in this country": a rock band to earn them money while spreading the message. Evidently realizing that further conversation was useless, he abruptly left, saying he was "full."

Zeke and other street people ranted about James' manner. "Him and his college-type intellectual ten dollar words. He probably didn't understand them himself. There's only one way to deal with them smart types and that's to force them to talk about real things everyone can see and understand." Someone else compared James to a general arriving in his field car to plot strategy, only to rush off to plan another battle. Another referred to him as a fine example of a business executive and top management in freakdom. The conversation shifted to strategy in dealing with the Brethren. Some people were sick of being on the road and floating from place to place. This was their home and they were going to defend it. They wanted to go to the Brethren the very next day to have it out with them. "Do the rest of the Brethren know what's going on? They are supposed to be our brothers in the age of love, sharing, and peace, and they're throwing us out of our homes?" Hank, half joking and half serious, suggested a pitched battle as a solution to the problem. The people at the MacDonald House in Sutton (Red Rose Collective) might particularly be interested in helping out, he added.

Norman, Patrick, Pepsi Joe, and other older, or intellectually oriented people became disturbed at the turn the conversation was taking. Incensed by James' attitude also, they advised a wait-and- see attitude, exploring other options before resorting to violence. JM couldn't prevent the Brethren from arriving, but they could try to communicate with the membership, who would hopefully see James' folly and convince him to let JM remain. After all, the land was big enough to hold hundreds of people. Another weapon that might be employed was the threat of unfavorable publicity for their action, as the media was so important to them. In the long run, however, the Brethren would have legal recourse, and if JM failed to convince the Brethren, there would in the end be no fight between the two groups, but between JM and the police. Thus, hasty, thoughtless action was to be avoided and all attempts made to reach out to the Brethren.

Roamer, Clara, and others in the macrobiotic, spiritually-oriented hippie wing expressed disgust at both the street people and the intellectuals for thinking in terms of conflict before the Brethren even got to the land. JM should hope for peace and harmony and realize that whatever came of it, things would certainly turn out for the best. Everyone should sit back, let events take their course, and not interfere with anything by negative thinking.

While the intellectuals quietly reflected on the possible merits of their position, the street people laughingly suggested building a stone fort in the Meadows and launching an invasion up the sides of Eagle Claw. In view of their no smoking, no drugs, no alcohol, no promiscuity rules, one even suggested sending all the JM women up to the hill with cigarettes, LSD, booze, and "an invitation to fuck." Thus, the internal divisions that were to characterize JM the rest of the summer were apparent the first time the group openly dealt with the Brethren problem. The street people wanted to bring it to a head quickly, the intellectuals wanted to talk it and think it away, and the hippies wanted to pretend it didn't exist.

What shape would the conflict take if outside SS authority and regulations were to be called in only as a last resort? How could JM's small, disorganized rabble stand up to the Brethren's large, tightly organized, and highly motivated membership? Would other communes allow themselves to get drawn into a struggle between a group of religious fanatics and a band of people often perceived as inept, beer drinking refugees from urban life?

On the morning of July 6th, a convoy pulled into the Meadows, consisting of a huge ten wheel truck loaded with old barn timbers, and three vans packed with the Brethren members. A few JM people went out to greet them, and point out the old lumbering road that circled up behind Eagle's Claw. While the vans ferried people from the Brethren center to the Meadows throughout the day, the truck struggled to get across the stream and up the wood road while people scurried about, repairing the road as it made its way up the hill. The road, which was the only access to the hills behind the Meadows that the Brethren intended to occupy, ran through the middle of JM's settlement between the cookshack and the abandoned truck Roamer lived in. The day before, the road had been rutted grass. The midday sounds were the hum of insects and the rustle of leaves. But now, clouds of dust billowed up from the gravel that had been exposed by vehicular traffic, while shouts, commands, and cheers echoed across the valley. What had once been a retreat from the frenetic pace of urban industrial life, overnight had become electrified with the "creative energy" of fifty excited, highly motivated, and committed Krishna Brethren.

Amazed, many JMers sat in the grass and watched as overseers marched at the head of singing columns of Brethren across the meadows, while twenty people struggled to lift half-ton beams by hand up the steep sides of Eagle's Claw. A steady stream of people carried jugs of water from the stream to the crest of the mountain, as polyethylene lean-tos and tents sprang up over the hillsides. Some JMers expressed envy at the level of constructive activity the Brethren could maintain, and all acknowledged that the Brethren was certainly a "together group." Nevertheless, many were simultaneously appalled at the regimentation and the power of the overseers who demanded and received almost superhuman effort from the regular members. For days orders rang out from the hills. "Jerry, where are you? Get your lazy ass over here!. OK, everybody in Rodney's group, back to work! Leon! Leon!" (shouted in unison by a band of voices). One JMer likened Eagle's Claw to a giant anthill, while another remarked that he felt like he was witnessing the construction of the pyramids. Brethren activity extended well into the night as motorcycles and vans passed in and out at all hours. Bursts of laughter and occasional screams of terror rolled across the dark meadow from flickering campfires in the hills.

The previous summer, the Brethren were guests of JM and lived on a small part of the land. This summer, the JMers were the guests of the Brethren, and lived on a small portion of the land, in and near the south meadow. While no boundaries were declared, unofficial territorial lines became clear from the outset. East of the stream, except for a knoll the A-frame was situated on, was JM, and west of it was Krishna Brethren. Two access routes were recognized as "public" rights of way, one being the road through the south meadow and the other, a foot path near the house on stilts through the north meadow. The Brethren territory was in turn divided into three separate settlements, each of which had two overseers. One was located on the crest of the south hill, another behind (west of) Eagle's Claw, and the third on the summit of Eagle's Claw looking over the Meadows.

These settlements were planned before members left the Brethren Center. James said that from past experience the Brethren had learned that groups larger than fifteen people did not work well, and because forty-five to fifty people had come to the Meadows, three was the optimum number of fifteen-member groups. The move to the Meadows was in part an attempt to decentralize the center while building up a regional federation of fifteen-person communal groups. But the membership was not ordered to belong to any particular group, nor were allotments set up. James selected seven overseers (one of whom was Mary, one of JM's founders): two for each group and an overall overseer (Roy) attached to one group but in charge of the entire operation. In a meeting at the Brethren Center, it was suddenly announced that the Brethren had acquired the land, and that anyone who wanted to could live on it. The identities of the overseers were announced and the membership then freely chose the overseer they felt most comfortable with. By coincidence, the number in the groups were almost evenly balanced on the basis of this choice.

Except for the noise, bustle, and confusion brought by the Brethren, life in the JM group went on with the usual ambivalence and indecision. Plans were made to settle in, but were not enthusiastically pursued because of the somber shadow of the August 31st eviction deadline. Both communes were distantly polite to one another; individuals pleasantly nodding good day if they passed each other on a path. At first the Brethren were too hard at work setting up their facilities to bother much with JM at the policy level. Conversations occurred, however, between JMers and specific Brethren people. Those who felt they needed a break from the torrid pace on the mountain and who clearly were not as enthusiastic about the spiritual orientation as other Brethren talked with JMers of everyday experiences, secretly asked for cigarettes, and on occasion tripped on LSD and had sexual liaisons.

As facilities went up and Brethren people had more spare time, they invited JMers to visit them on the hill and think about joining. Most JMers accepted the invitation at least once; the hippie wing going most often. Yet everyone agreed they could not consider joining. The leadership was too autocratic, and many members seemed to be walking around in a daze. They appeared unable to relax or let go to enjoy themselves in ordinary ways. All they talked about was the Krishna force, saving themselves from despair, and turning the world on to their way of life. The street people were annoyed or bored by all the abstract talk, and while the intellectuals were fascinated up to a point, they soon became exhausted and exasperated with circular discussions that in their view had no relation to the real world.

Most JMers thought there was something "scary" about the Brethren, too. For example, Black Jack, a black fellow and professed poet, claimed he was being sought by the police for permanently paralyzing two patrolmen with Karate chops. Constantly and aggressively talking, he nervously brandished some object he had with him, once repeatedly throwing his machete into the ground while he spoke. Another was Floyd with dark, recessed eyes who sinisterly peered at anyone who spoke to him without responding. Once when a blood-curdling scream came from where the road crossed the stream, about five JMers ran down to help whoever had been hurt, only to discover Madelaine, a recently released mental patient, explaining to the gathering crowd that the overseer had told her to express her anguish fully by screaming so that she could "get it all out."

While the Brethren approach to psychotherapy might have had its merits, its approach to physical therapy was questionable. When people complained of illness or injury, they were told to disregard their symptoms as only material concerns, and to concentrate their mental energies and faith so that the physical afflictions would pass away. Many did disappear with time, but some didn't. There was a fellow with infected toes whose feet swelled up so badly that his father had to come to get him after fellow members carried him down the hill. There was also a woman with vaginal hemorrhaging who demanded medical care for a week until she left the Brethren to seek help on her own. Nevertheless, many were convinced that, given enough effort, mind could control matter in any human situation.

Although officially denied by the leadership, some members believed that their JM settlement was a kind of boot camp for future spiritual warfare. This was revealed when Jesse and Jake, former JM members and now part of Red Rose Collective, came to visit the Brethren as part of their political work to keep tabs on local communes. After a trip up the hill, they returned to their car shaking their heads in disbelief. Someone told them the Brethren had come to Eagle's Claw Mountain because life on earth as they all knew it was about to cease. Race riots would envelope the cities and spread through the countryside, but the Brethren's isolated position would permit them to defend themselves. When the oceans rose and the land sank in the inevitable world cataclysm, Eagle's Claw would be high enough to keep them above sea level. They would build a citadel on the mountain and train people to deal with the aftermath of the holocaust. After the calamitous events ceased, they would go into the world to teach the survivors while struggling against those who preached false doctrines.

The Red Rose Collective was also told that the Brethren would play no part in the Free Provincia movement it was organizing. Although they shared Red

Rose's views on the evils of American society, uniting to build alternative societies at this time was useless for the Brethren, in view of impending world destruction. The efforts of mere humans at remodeling social and political institutions was insignificant when it came to the unleashing of cosmic forces, they said. Free Provincia and the Brethren could work together where their aims were parallel, but beyond that, the Brethren would pursue its own goals. Red Rose was appalled that longhairs could believe such simple-minded, superstitious "bullshit." This commune they concluded, was so mystically fascist in its obedience to and worship of James, it was almost Hitlerian. After this experience, Red Rose never seriously tried to include the Brethren in their movement, which was supposed to be aimed at all CC types.

Parson's Crossing was alarmed by the sudden reappearance of the Brethren in Wilfred. To begin with, all Brethren traffic passed by their house, shattering the idyllic world they were trying to create. Also, they had already been visited by a group from the Brethren, giving them a quiet and friendly but fanatic "rap" about the collapse of society and salvation through joining the Brethren. They also mentioned something about obtaining more land in Wilfred, and some Parson's Crossing people feared that the Brethren were after their farm. Lastly, they had gotten word that the Wilfred residents were up in arms over this most recent hippie invasion, along with talk of a vigilante group possibly attacking all "the hippies up there." Parson's Crossing had finally established peace and anonymity among its straight neighbors after two years, and now they feared the Brethren's noisy presence might rekindle old animosities toward them.

The Brethren's "noisy presence" was dramatically felt when, without permit or prior approval from town authorities, they hired two local ex-convicts to dynamite some rocks for them. In order to build a solid foundation for the large building they were constructing and to obtain a water source on the mountain, they began blasting late one afternoon. The booming sound was heard in all corners of Wilfred. Angry local farmers, councilmen, and the peace officer arrived the next morning. After complaining that the cows weren't giving milk and expressing concern that the water table might be permanently altered, they discovered that construction was underway on a structure for which the Brethren had obtained no building permit. The town officials immediately halted the dynamiting and construction pending an appeal at a special hearing. Because the possession of dynamite was legal, however, the Brethren kept the explosives.

With work on the main project forcibly halted, Brethren attention shifted increasingly to the Jackson's Meadows Commune. After weeks of gentle and benign treatment, the Brethren realized that JM was no closer to joining them or leaving the land than when James first spoke to them. Even those JMers most sympathetic to the Brethren were appalled by the dynamiting and devastation of the land. Moreover, the Brethren leadership had discovered that some Brethren were being lured down to the Meadows to escape from work and indulge themselves in sensual pleasures. A shift in policy occurred, designed to keep the two groups separate and to escalate pressure on JM either to join or get out. When members of both groups were seen talking to each other at the stream, one overseer yelled to the Brethren people, "Cut all the bullshit. You're either with them, or with us. Come here and get to work." In another incident, Roy led a group of Brethren down the road past the cookshack, all of them facing the JM group and loudly singing, "You better change your evil ways." Later, a JMer asked an overseer why JM couldn't remain on a small part of the land separate from the Brethren. She answered, "You can't let pigs through the gates of heaven."

Conflict burst into open hostility when Roy visited the cookshack to announce policies regarding the land. Previously, he had come to convince, cajole, and manipulate people into joining the Brethren. On those occasions, some JMers felt that they were being "hypnotized" by his technique of intensely staring people in the eyes, talking in dramatic, soft monotones, and telling them to put aside all concepts so that they could be open to his simple truth. This time he came to lay down the rules. There was to be no drinking, no drugs, no promiscuity, and no visitors during weekdays. Then angry JMers immediately responded that he had no right to direct their lives; that he could not boss them around like the robots he had in the Brethren. By virtue of Peter's word, they could remain separate if they wished. Furthermore, they made it clear that they considered Roy personally offensive, inept, and tactless in the way he related to all people: Brethren, JM, or otherwise. Roy became particularly angered when informed that half of his own people thought the idea of kicking fellow freaks off the land was morally wrong, and that he didn't even take into consideration the opinions of his own membership. Flatly told that JM would neither join the Brethren nor leave the Meadows, shaking with anger, Roy replied that JM would not be around by August 31st and that "absolutely any means" would be used to get them out by then.

Everyone in the cookshack interpreted that statement as an open-ended threat that could lead to anything. The Brethren perceived a radically different reality from most JM people, and with all their talk of death and rebirth, and the meaninglessness of the physical body as only a fleeting form manifested by spirit, some JMers became concerned for their own physical safety. People began to consider the apparently real dangers they faced and personal alternatives, while trying to decide whether or not and to what extent they were willing to struggle with the Brethren. The intellectuals concluded that to give in to the Brethren demands was to capitulate to fascism. If the CC was to offer an alternative to the abrogation of individual rights so often seen in the SS, they argued, then the Brethren must either be stopped or taught a lesson. For others, particularly the street people, JM was their one and only home and it had to be defended. The hippies, however, could see merit in the Brethren argument, though they could not for the most part agree, and began to see themselves as mediators between the "militants" on either side.

When Peter returned from his trip to look for new land, he found to his chagrin that the troublesome situation he thought he had resolved by selling the land had worsened to potentially disastrous proportions. Hoping to make both groups happy, he had unintentionally created a situation whereby the past human suffering at the Meadows that he hoped to atone for might in fact be repeated. Having made promises to both communes, he found himself caught squarely in the middle. On the one hand he realized the Brethren was heavy-handed and insensitive in its demands, yet he believed the continued existence of JM would benefit no one.

One evening while Peter and other JMers sat around the campfire near the cookshack, Patrick rambled on about the ascetic, self-flagellating nature of the Brethren and how restrictive and self-righteous its tenants were. He likened their charge that JM had "evil ways" to witch hunting, and then referred to them as the new Puritans. Peter belittled Patrick's verbal analysis replying that "categorizing and labeling them doesn't mean a thing. The question remains, how are we going to resolve the conflict?" In this instance, the hippie approach proved far more convincing than academic intellectualizing.

But minutes later inside the cookshack, Pepsi Joe tore the conceptual rug out from underneath Peter. Peter suggested that the JM people leave because there was lots of land elsewhere. Men could not be free, Peter said, if they remained obstinately attached to material concerns. With a brilliant flash of improvisational theatrical insight, Pepsi Joe interrupted Peter, asking him to move so that he could sit where Peter had been sitting. After an embarrassed silence, Peter moved to another spot in the cookshack with Pepsi Joe taking his former place. As Peter began to speak again about the ease with which people could find a new place to live, Pepsi Joe again asked Peter to move so he could have his new seat. Pepsi Joe's street-wise point had been clearly made, ending hours of conversation.

But why did the Brethren want JM off the land eventually; and why did they wish to control JM's behavior while they were still on the land? It was not, they claimed, because they wanted the houses and land all to themselves, nor were they hostile to non-believers. According to their ideology, it was because JM was (1) unclean and polluting; (2) the center of negative energy on the land; and (3) a source of evil.

With respect to pollution, the cookshack was indeed dirty most of the time. JM was not sufficiently organized to keep it clean on a regular basis. Flies abounded, and rotting food could almost always be found somewhere in the kitchen area. The physical appearance of many JM people was disheveled; the IBM's especially taking pride in their ragged, slept-in, loved-in, and all around lived-in clothing. Vermin and disease were also connected with the accusation. The Brethren claimed that JM had always been unclean, pointing out the hepatitis a few people came down with the previous winter. They also cited the current staph infections. The most telling evidence, however, was lice. JM had always had a problem with lice, though they came and went in cycles, and even when effectively disposed of, invariably someone returning from the city would reintroduce them. Unfortunately, getting rid of lice required a degree of social organization, coordination, and cohesion that JM normally didn't have, thereby lending credence to the idea that dirt and vermin were symptomatic of "untogetherness" and social decay.

One night, when visitors took up all the sleeping space in the cookshack, Clara slept at Janet's. She didn't know she had lice, but spread them to another building. With easier bathing, better facilities, and a control on visitors, this could have been avoided. But as a result of this incident, midway through the summer JM did get rid of its lice by having all of its members sleep outdoors for a week, throwing away an old stuffed couch, leaving mattresses outside, washing all clothes and blankets, and having a communal hair wash with a special louse killing shampoo. It took days to convince all the JM people to join in the effort, for just one holdout could have made the entire exercise useless.

Because of their organization and demand for obedience, the Brethren dealt more effectively with the problem. When DT was reported missing from his camp one night, he was confronted the next morning. "Did you spend the night with the Meadows people and did you sleep with any of their women?" Admitting doing both, he was publicly reprimanded, inspected for lice (which were found), and immediately forced to soak his hair in kerosene. An enforced cleanliness came to all Brethren with mandatory daily swims in the river two miles beyond Eagle's Claw, requiring a grueling hike over difficult terrain. When a girl refused to go one day, claiming illness, she was expelled from the Brethren for insubordination. Despite questionable methods for enforcement of cleanliness and orderliness, most Brethren felt superior to their JM counterparts. Reminiscent of societies with severe class or caste distinctions, symbols and behaviors related to inferiority and pollution arose. The symbolism of the Brethren being located high on the mountain and JM living low in the valley was evident, and certain Brethren members reported actually becoming nauseated when being physically near the cookshack.

JM argued that it was the Brethren who were polluting the stream with soap, the land with scrap materials, the air with exhaust fumes from their vehicles, and themselves with the chemical preservatives from the canned surplus food they ate. Although some people on either side recognized the merit in each other's position, the two largely bypassed each other in the heat of argument.

JM's supposed "negative energy" was blamed as the reason for the Brethren not being able to concentrate on their work, for their difficulties in achieving spiritual development, and even for their troubles with the town. The Brethren claimed that sitting on top of Eagle's Claw they could actually perceive a magnetic field emanating from the Meadows below that sucked their creative energy from them. At times, they felt drained of enthusiasm, ambition, and concentration, and the Meadows was the only explanation for it. Having a special spiritual mission, their task was to collect as much positive creative energy from the cosmos as possible. But having a focal point for the parallel collection of negative energy so close to them was making their task impossible. JMers, who clearly perceived that they were being scapegoated, asked Brethren for specific examples of negative energy. In response the Brethren connected JM's negative energy with its overt conflicts, drugs and alcohol, uncontrolled sex, and visitors.

Brethren rules strengthened identity and cohesion while controlling conflict. Loss of control and expression of anger in particular was considered threatening to collective identity in their communal group. Many Brethren with psychiatric histories of violence had sought spiritual salvation in the Brethren as a way of dealing with their own unexplained rage. To see rage expressed before them again retriggered confused emotions and supported their conviction that JM was a querulous, collapsing group that did not deserve to remain on the land. Moreover, Brethren were afraid of certain JMers in the context of escalating conflict. How did they know, for example, that JM's potential violence wouldn't be turned on the Brethren?

JM violence came to the Brethren's attention through a series of incidents. One was Roamer's propensity for "flipping out" under stress, demonstrated the time he hit the dog over the head, chased the Brethren's pet pig with an ax, and threw food and utensils at the cookshack. Also, when some visitors tried to convince Clara to sleep with them all and she refused, one became enraged, causing her to fear for her physical safety. And Randy (with the knife) returned. Everyone present welcomed him, not knowing his previous history. Yale appeared later, and spotting Randy, ran over to him, shouting that he (Randy) had been thrown out once before, and demanded that he get out now. At this, Randy pulled out his knife ostensibly to whittle a piece of wood, but Hank approached Randy with a sharp wooden pole he happened to be carrying, and poked it in his stomach, firmly saying, "Drop that knife or I swear I'll run you through with this." Randy then joined the Brethren "for life," only to be expelled by them after less than a week. Another event occurred when, after drinking malt liquor together, Zeke started a fight with Hank which Patrick had to break up. Hank left the Meadows the next day loudly complaining, "How the hell am I supposed to get my head together in this place with so many fucked up people around me?"

JM admitted its shortcomings in the area of violence, claiming it was trying to change. Roamer sat in remorse for days after each time he flipped out, castigating himself for not being able to control his anger. Even Zeke, after his fight with Hank sat drunk and sobbing, asking himself out loud why he always ended up attacking his closest friends. But JM also pointed out the violence in the Brethren that they tried to pretend wasn't there. The Brethren people were asked about the fist fight Roy and Black Jack had on top of Eagle's Claw. The Brethren answered that it was only a threshold in the growth of a relationship they had to go through in order to reach greater love. After Roy and Black Jack "got all their negativity out," they supposedly became the best of friends. Then the Brethren were asked about the screams of terror they heard one recent night. This was excused as coming from a girl who had a fear of heights whom they were forcing to walk across a beam they had positioned between two posts high off the ground. They believed they had to force her to get rid of her fears so that she could let her creative energy in. "Even though she freaked out," they claimed, "she's better off now." Finally the JM people asked, "How about Madeleine jumping out of the tree house to the rocks below?" Madeleine responded that she didn't jump; she walked off it attempting to levitate herself after hearing a talk by Roy on the power of the Krishna force once people learned to tap it. The Brethren had an answer for everything.

The second brand of negativity was the use of psychoactive substances. The Brethren at this point were legally responsible for what happened on the land, as promised to Peter, and potential injuries, ODs, and arrests for disorderly conduct, or possession of drugs became their concern. Furthermore, a reputation for illegal or immoral goings-on at the land would rub off on the Brethren, and they were having enough troubles with the town as it was. But more important, the presence of alcohol and drugs at JM was a source of temptation for a number of "weaker" Brethren members. Not only was the use of drugs and alcohol considered to be negative behavior, but it also demonstrated that Brethren ideals and rules could be broken.

But why were drugs and alcohol taboo in the first place? The Brethren believed that wherever there was extensive use of drugs and alcohol, inevitable suffering, frustration, crime, violence, lack of concern for other human beings, and an inability for people to help themselves followed. They saw it at home with alcoholic parents, they saw it in the transformation of Haight-Ashbury and the East Village, and now they saw it in JM. Above all, many of them saw it in their own past. Some had experienced psychotic episodes on drugs, ending up in mental hospitals, others had become involved in petty crime through drugs, others had become addicted, and still others had hit rock bottom, ending up on the street, divorced, friendless, and hungry. Although most Brethren credit psychedelics with giving them their first glimpse at other realities, the lack of discipline that followed was worse.

Thus, in order to construct a new way of life, constant effort with no diversion or crutch was necessary. Having gone to the extremes of abuse, they reacted from the depths of despair by going to the opposite extreme of abstinence. Moreover, the schedule, regimen, and total effort required by the tight Brethren organization meant that deviation even by a few would interfere with others' efforts. Finally, according to the Brethren ideology, psychoactive substances were unimportant compared to the rewards creative energy had to offer, and the "high" substances provided was inferior to that achieved through commitment, faith, and work that allowed cosmic forces to enter and direct them.

Was JM really paralyzed by booze and dope as the Brethren claimed? Strong drugs were done sparingly, because they were difficult to come by. Marijuana wasn't smoked that often because the supply depended on the generosity of visitors. It apparently didn't interfere with the simple kinds of work tasks at JM. However, those people most interested in obtaining psychoactive substances did seem to work and participate in decision making less than those who were less interested, even when they weren't high. Thus it was probably not the dope but the dope seekers who could be blamed for any lack of industry. On the other hand, alcohol interfered with work and the accumulation of monetary resources. Work usually ceased when there was drinking, if for no other reason than the fact that physical coordination was affected, making it difficult or dangerous. Also, nearly all the incidences of violence at the Meadows were connected in some way with it. Alcohol, being legal, was too easy to obtain, could be purchased with a minimum of money, and could be imbibed in any situation.

The third area of negativity was indiscriminate sex. Many of the arguments given against drugs and alcohol also applied to sex. Moderation, however, and not abstinence, was the Brethren ideal as their "no promiscuity" rule indicated. Frivolous and indiscriminate sex had been a part of many of the members' past experiences. Like drugs, they contended its "high" was a poor substitute for spiritual highs, often being an escape more than a search, something to occupy and physically gratify oneself instead of thinking about and working toward spiritual fulfillment. If undertaken thoughtlessly and frequently, sexual relations carried individuals from person to person with little chance for commitment to any one person, group, situation, or state of consciousness to develop. Instead, the Brethren ideology insisted that an intimate physical relationship should only follow and supplement an already existing psychic one. In this manner, something solid and reliable in the way of social relations could be built. On this basis, James and some overseers had the power to determine who could sleep with whom, and when.

The Brethren apparently found that in their efforts to construct a stable social organization, stable heterosexual dyads were the soundest building unit. Potentially impersonal physical sex was played down with the relationship, and more spiritual (psychic) aspects played up. Psychic orientations (for example, "getting into each others' heads") were more person-specific, leading toward commitment to particular individuals. But the spiritual emphasis of the commune also allowed for spiritual energies exchanged in dyadic relationships to be channeled to benefit the entire commune. Thus, keeping relationships on a spiritual plane meant keeping people committed to the Brethren. And finally, stable heterosexual couples were more likely to yield children: the guarantee of perpetuity for any society.

But Brethren objections to supposed promiscuity at JM did not just reflect prejudices in favor of their own standards and experiences. Sexually transmitted disease and vermin (for example, lice) in their crowded living conditions, had to be avoided. Also, it drew visitors to JM, and the Brethren wanted to limit the number of visitors. Furthermore, the supposed availability of sex in the Meadows was an ever-present temptation, threatening to lure some people away from the Brethren, particularly those who were leading celibate lives against their wills. Participation by some members could demonstrate that sacred regulations were violable. Most threatening, however, sexual liaisons could lead to close personal ties between JM people and Brethren members and the loss of Brethren members to JM. The slower, easier pace at JM was appealing to the "weaker" members of the Brethren. How could the Brethren convince JM to join the Brethren if Brethren members were joining JM?

Although sex was freer at JM than in the Brethren, it was no more so than it was in conventional SS. Despite loose talk and lack of formal rules, there were built-in controls. Nearly all the women were members of couples. Because it was almost impossible to keep illicit affairs secret in such tight circumstances, there was little adulterous behavior. The only significant exceptions were the one last failing effort by Peter to establish a quadruple with another couple, and street males who occasionally indulged while on drinking sprees out of town where they hoped word wouldn't get back to their women. Many male visitors who were expecting something else, quickly left when monogamy became apparent. Unattached JM males for the most part either had to leave the Meadows to fulfill their needs, (mostly street people), or remain, struggling to control or deny their desires (mostly middle class hippies). In either case, most did not have adequate courting skills in a milieu where there were no convenient traditions such as dating. Despite talk of being free, most women remained passive, waiting to be approached by males.

The fourth aspect of negativity concerned the disorganizational influences of outside contacts. There is no question that visitors interfered with JM's constant efforts to organize itself, but visitors were a source of concern for the Brethren too. The constant partying going on down in the Meadows, so tempting to overworked, tired Brethren, was largely attributable to visitors. Upon discovering the Brethren were there, visitors wandered up the hill to see what was going on. Although the Brethren always welcomed the opportunity to proselytize, in this situation visitors interfered with work and meetings. Most disturbing was their fear that the continuing flux of visitors provided a pool from which JM constantly picked up new members. Every day that passed that JM increased in size made it only that much more difficult to liquidate.

The information visitors brought with them and took away was a special problem, exacerbating Brethren difficulties in convincing JM it should quietly disband or join up. Reporters not only came from the underground media, but the mainstream as well. None were hospitably received by JM, wanting to minimize exposure because of the shady pasts of members as well as the desire for stability. The one exception for JM was a local reporter who it was felt could help JM in its struggle with the Brethren. The Brethren, however, craved publicity, hoping to add to its membership. But at the land, all reported unfavorably about the Brethren's fanaticism and attempts to evict JM. Religious views competing with those of the Brethren also arrived with visitors. Many carried their own private brands of astrological cosmology by which they sought to interpret their and others' experiences in a milieu where other forms of explanation simply didn't seem to hold up. Many Buddhist converts, particularly Zen Buddhists, wandered into the Meadows, revealing their beliefs in the course of conversation, as did a number of Christian ministers, who came to preach the gospel and give away Bibles and other printed matter. Exhausting and mind-bending discussions probing every corner of the psyche and the cosmos were not unusual. A particularly convoluted one occurred spontaneously between a Christian missionary, Roy (a Brethren missionary), an astrologer, and two Zen Buddhists. The atmosphere was similar to that portrayed in historical accounts of the last days of the Roman Empire, of feudal Japan, of the demise of the tribes of Israel, or of Medieval Europe after the plague had struck, in which self-appointed sages and holy men wandered through the rabble of confusion attempting to spread to others the light they had found for themselves.

The proverbial quiet strangers appeared from nowhere to lend a hand in creating a little order out of chaos, only to leave again shortly, like the Lone Ranger or selfless Samurai. They appeared in all shapes and sizes, and always alone. One was Neptune, who was naked except for a pair of tattered shorts and who had an immense tangled head of hair and beard. Walking everywhere barefoot and sleeping in bramble patches, his path to salvation lay in asceticism. Another was Maureen, who actually became a member of JM for a month or so. When she arrived, an inner voice told her of the conflict between the groups and that Roamer should become the instrument for its resolution. Accordingly, she and Roamer spent hours each night in conversation and instruction, she the master and he the disciple, all aimed at him gaining self-confidence, and acting in the commune in an assertive and constructive way.

Talk of revolution also filtered into the Meadows. Visitors told of their bone chilling experiences that both encouraged JM with hope of dramatic change for the better, and scared them with visions of total societal collapse. Two fellows came through, for example, who had participated weeks earlier in the rioting and firebombing of the Bank of America at Isla Vista. Even the revolutionary counterpart of Neptune came trudging into the Meadows: Marvin, the bushy bearded radical who left his mark on every major Movement event from the Pentagon demonstrations (where he became a celebrity by urinating on the Pentagon steps in defiance of hundreds of gleaming bayonets), to Columbia, to Chicago.

Visitors also brought sobering reminders of the real outside world in Vietnam, despite the fact that many JMers had grown weary of years of anti-war activity. One was a local veteran, smartly dressed with close-cropped hair. The veteran was drunk, sitting by the fire saying how nice it would be to kill and roast a deer, to which somebody promptly responded that JM people didn't believe in killing anything. The visitor became angry at this, aggressively asking if anyone had seen death. Before anyone could answer, he yelled that he had seen plenty of it in "Nam." He had seen hundreds slaughtered and felt joy when he saw American planes drop napalm on villages, adding that people had to kill to survive, and that "you people will have to kill too. They (the military and police authorities) won't let you alone." Nearly in tears, he moaned that the communards just didn't know what it was like "out there" (meaning the real world), painfully exclaiming that he was a murderer and that he not only hated "them" for turning him into a murderer, but hated himself as well. Eventually "they" would come to the Meadows and force the people there to either kill or be killed.

Very soon, the prophecy seemed to come true. A couple of evenings later, some people panicked and ran when they looked up to see a column of olive drab figures dressed in military gear entering the Meadow. After the confusion, about a dozen soldiers explained they were members of the National Guard on summer maneuvers a few miles away down the abandoned town road. Really pipe fitters, insurance agents, and clothing store salesmen, they sneaked out of camp to visit JM when someone told them there was a commune down the road.

Thus the flow of visitors kept JM in touch with other world views, making its people aware of different ways of seeing things. Visitors and outside contacts were above all needed to affirm their perception of the situation and their determination to struggle with the Brethren. It was with relief than that most JM people received words of support from visitors. One woman visitor came down off the hill laughing, saying it was impossible to talk to the Brethren. They had their own distinct way of explaining things that was not at all "open to common sense and experience." When she asked them for proofs they deferred to "God" or said, "We know it to be true," or insisted "You shall be shown some day," or admonished, "You must have faith in order to open yourselves to the truth." When she tried to argue concepts with them, "they contradicted themselves, claiming that words and concepts are only bullshit," yet according to her, they had plenty of words and concepts of their own. She wished the JM members good luck in their dispute and left as quickly as she could.

Beyond Brethren charges of pollution and negative energy, was an implied, though never directly stated feeling that JM was evil. For JM to be mistaken, ignorant, wretched, and misled was one thing, but to be obstructionistic, deliberately defiant, plotting, and disrespectfully satirical was another. Where there was so much obvious good within the Brethren they thought, then only something equally as powerful and other worldly could account for the JMers' successful resistance to and rejection of that good. The other power had to be evil.

The Brethren assumed the JM people knew that by joining the Brethren they would be bettering their own lives while helping to salvage the world. Much of the discussion revolved around JM saying it wanted the freedom to decide what to do without being forced into any action, while the Brethren argued that self-determination was irrelevant when the outcome was a foregone conclusion. They likened JM's behavior to an obstinate child refusing to do what he is told even though he knows it must be done for his own good. But when a JMer said that living in JM was more beneficial to self and society than mindlessly conforming and being exploited by living in the Brethren, they could not believe that individual was serious.

A very serious event in Brethren eyes was the defection of DT to JM. Like defectors everywhere, he particularly was regarded as a criminal; lazy, breaking rules, and too weak to resist sensual diversions. Conversely, he was welcomed by JM as a hero; intelligent to see the faults of his former system, and brave to leave it. To most everybody's joy, DT subsequently reaffirmed many of JM's assessments of the Brethren. He described how people were trapped there because the Brethren took all their belongings when they first entered and then fostered group dependency. Any other nearby commune (JM) was the only reasonable escape route. Also, he said Roy was a despot who deliberately played on people's weaknesses so he could control them. He further claimed that people were afraid of Roy, believing that he not only had special powers, but evil powers at that. DT also revealed the existence of an occult black magic clique within the Brethren, having been a curious dabbler in it himself.

Roy in return, demanded that JM banish DT from the land, which of course JM refused to do. Although a defector is always a thorn in the side of a belligerent in struggle because of information revealed, morale boosted for the other side, and precedents set, these factors alone did not account for the intensity of Brethren concern over DT. The answer lay in the fact that many Brethren believed DT to be a witch. For all they knew there could be more witches among the people at JM. In some Brethren minds, all of JM was tarnished by evil, as evidenced by the testimony of one of their six year old children who, when asked what he thought of JM, matter-of-factly replied, "We are white magic and you guys are black magic." Thus an entirely new dimension had entered into the conflict, making the situation even more volatile. Added to the possibility of police intervention and physical violence, and the present realities of anger, frustration, argument, and threat, was the fear of witchcraft.

The situation was ripe for the use of witchcraft, and the possibility was frightening to both sides. Sorcery had historically been the last line of defense for the homeless, the persecuted, the roleless, and the propertyless, with its incidence being most widespread in those societies having the greatest proportion of marginal people. Many of the people at both JM and the Brethren were cut off from society's usual institutions and thrust into a search for new ways to interpret events in their lives and to act on them. While the street people tended to react immediately to concrete stimuli, and the intellectuals struggled to interpret experience with rational concepts thereby hoping to plan their behavior in accordance with institutional realities, the hippie and spiritual wing at JM chose to rely neither on strict empiricism nor on rational constructs. Instead they chose to magnify elements of non-ordinary reality and intense experience along with simple logical constructs that bore little relation to the common sense laws of the physical universe. Unlike the Brethren, the spiritually oriented people were neither a majority at JM nor were there clear notions of alternate reality agreed upon by the group. Many at JM were still in the process of search.

The Brethren, however, were in the process of elaborating an alternate reality that had already been found. As individuals at various levels of "spiritual development," they were attempting to impose spiritual interpretations on their past experience as an explanatory tool, and on their future experience as a guide to action. But despite this coherent new reality presented by the leadership, many others were open to the idea of malevolent forces. Thus the Brethren, far more than JM, was not only subject to threat by evil because of its supposed good, and to disruption because of its structure, but also by witchcraft, due to its mystical world view.

DT knew that some members of the underground black magic faction in the Brethren could and would perform satanic rituals directed against JM. And everyone knew that the overground white magic techniques, such as group concentration on a certain desired outcome in order to make it happen through collective mental energy (called a "thought force") would be used in trying to influence JM's actions. But because most of JM didn't fully believe in the efficacy of such techniques, they were not concerned by their practice, often referring to them as a big joke. In the Brethren, however, significant numbers of people did believe in the validity of such practices, with the result that they were gravely concerned if they had any indication that sorcery was being directed against them.

One night, JM engaged in a two hour long chant with wailing voices and rhythms beat out on logs and pans. Begun by Peter, it had no special significance beyond letting off steam for most JMers, though it might have had some for Peter. The Brethren, however, reacted with great concern, some coming down the hill to see what was happening, others mentioning it the next day, wanting to know why it was done. DT knew of their vulnerability and enjoyed the sense of power he had over people who thought he might be practicing witchcraft; people who had power over him until he defected. DT dabbled in simple rituals, even carrying around a book on witchcraft, and wondered whether it could actually accomplish what it was supposed to. But he never publicly admitted his doubts, preferring to let the Brethren think what they wanted to think about him, which was the worst.

Patrick even joked about making voodoo dolls and hex symbols and placing them in the woods where the Brethren were sure to find them, but he knew that could possibly lead to such a fearful and panicked reaction on their part that it might be disastrous for everyone concerned. The fact was, JM people were fearful of the extremes to which the Brethren might go in enforcing the leadership's will. Because their message was directly from "on high," would the Brethren do anything to enforce "His" will, all the while assuming they could act with divine impunity? If the body is only temporary and inconsequential because the spirit is eternal, might they not injure or destroy other people's bodies if they felt the need was great enough? Because they emphasized absolute faith in the group and in the leadership, couldn't they act as a mob out of control, or worse, as an instrument of a leader's command? Although the Brethren never read newspapers and were hardly aware of him, Charles Manson and what he represented loomed in the fearful imagination of some JM people.

Analysis

These two groups, although appearing in some ways to have so much in common, such as certain CC ideals, work for a new society, and communalism, were drastically different in many other ways. Occupying the Meadows together, both were forced to interact, and did so with very little peace, love, and brotherhood. As the conflict was about to spill over into open hostilities at any moment, it was clear that certain positions had been established and goals articulated through their involuntary relationship that made each more sharply defined.

The individuals who eventually joined both groups came essentially from the same pool. They were, generally speaking, people who were not confident or optimistic when it came to dealing with an array of social institutions. They preferred the limited, more responsive milieu that they thought secluded communes could provide. About 75% of the members of each group were in some kind of "trouble": with alcohol and drugs, their families, the law, their own emotional backgrounds, schools, the armed forces, and/or the employment market. The other 25% were extremely capable, being able to engage very constructively in social environments of a wide range, from extreme order or disorder, that could paralyze most others. The membership of both groups was similar in age range, and with regard to social class backgrounds, exhibited the normal distribution that could be found in the larger society.

The obvious distinction between the two groups seemed to reside in the content of their belief systems: one appearing strident and totalistic and the other confused and spontaneous. But the ideological content was actually not that different. Most shared some kind of other-worldly view coupled with a propensity for direct action in this world, along with a healthy sprinkling of skepticism that was more openly expressed by JM than by the Brethren. Both welcomed, yet feared, the inevitable apocalypse, though it was not conceived of in exactly the same ways. Indeed, belief systems were very similar in the way they obfuscated rather than revealed basic motivations and behaviors. In both groups, they were commonly invoked to mask more mundane egocentric interests that could not be openly acknowledged.

Where the belief systems really differed was in the way they were applied through organizational form. James had regular visions and out-of-body experiences which, with some instructional help, he increasingly interpreted in terms of astral travel and passage through various planes of existence, past, present, and future. Those around James were convinced of the validity of his experiences, and they in turn passed the word on to others. As his original small entourage of blue collar followers grew rapidly through the influx of lost middle class people who were eager to believe in something that transcended their frustrating lives, James also grew in confidence and leadership ability. The willing followership and the able leadership fed on one another until membership subservience and regimentation evolved with full-blown charismatic and autocratic power for James.

By contrast, JM's possible charismatic and autocratic leader had stepped to the sidelines, leaving a vacuum at JM that was filled on an ad hoc basis as emergencies arose. JM members had sufficient previous group identities (street gangs, academia, home town networks) such that they already had subloyalties within the commune, not requiring monolithic allegiance to keep it going. Most of the growing waves of Brethren recruits were picked up as individuals who really had little previous CC identification, and as such, were more vulnerable.

The Brethren membership was, therefore, susceptible to the excesses that a threatened monolithic social system can go to when there are few in-group checks and balances. The mix of belief system, organizational format, and external challenge condoned group-think and extreme moralistic self-righteousness, which in turn, under further duress became deeply embedded psychologically. This, then, became fertile ground for xenophobic responses, such as repugnance at perceived human pollution, fear of assumed evil, and the practice of sorcery. Without external this-worldly tools to achieve their ends, for instance SS laws, economic sanctions, or outright physical force, they turned to more esoteric means to deal with what had come to be seen as the enemy.

While it might be tempting to look at each group separately in the search for internal forces that caused the Brethren and JM to develop their clearer structures, identities, and goals over the summer, not much would be revealed. Each, in the end, gained more shape and texture largely as a result of the conflict between the two. Seen as a relationship, even if as an increasingly hostile one, the responses that one generated in the other was the essential driving force in vitalizing one and revitalizing the other. Through this unpleasant process, not only they, but also other communal groups in the area, came into higher relief as social entities, as they all were slowly drawn into the JM-Brethren issue and responded in various ways. Thus, the tension acted as a kind of leveraging force to make it even clearer that many communal groups existed, each with its own interests, and when taken together, constituted a genuine milieu substantially separate from the SS. Everyone became more aware of a regional CC, not only as reasonably well-shared states of mind and lifestyles, but as a complex sociocultural system as well.

Although the competition and conflict might be the means by which the regional CC was further solidified and expanded, the cause of the process, the real JM-Brethren issue, remained essentially unaddressed. While people internal to the struggle saw it as involving abstract principles of fate, salvation, and new age freedom, and people external to it viewed it as hippie craziness, religious fascism, or inexplicable non-sense, the fundamental issue was the human use of limited space and the resources that space provided or fostered. Despite all religious, political, and pop-psychological rhetoric, one group simply wanted the other group out, whether by evacuation or dismemberment, so as to enhance its own perceived position. The other simply wanted to stay to protect its own perceived position.

7. Proliferation: Conflict, Growth, and Development of a Counter Society

After JM stated its refusal to leave as a response to Roy's ultimatum, a meeting was held: a rare event at JM up to that point. A state of war existed after Roy threatened to use any means necessary to get rid of JM. Many people agreed with the Brethren's assessment of the quality of life at JM. But rather than disband, or join the Brethren and have them succeed with their "bulldozer tactics," they said that this time JM really had to change. Thus, for the first time, people seriously considered what would be necessary to pull themselves together as a group. Roamer stepped into the lead by making numerous suggestions.

First, people had to care for one another, otherwise the whole effort would be a waste. People couldn't abandon the commune by thoughtlessly going into town drinking, doing drugs, and behaving in ways that would give the group a worse reputation than it already had. Second, by getting itself together, JM might convince Peter not to sell all the land to the Brethren or it might be able to prove to the Brethren that JM would not be a disruptive influence. Third, the visitor problem had to be tackled. Each person, rather than leaving it up to someone else, had to take the responsibility to enforce the prefire rule by informing visitors the commune was closed. Fourth, work details had to begin in earnest. Wood and building materials had to be gathered, the garden cared for, and town zoning and health officials courted. Roamer emphasized that they should not let the conflict with the Brethren overly distract them from the work ahead. Finally, in the event they had to leave, JM should look into the possibility of finding a small piece of cheap land elsewhere or of opening some kind of store in Centerville so they would serve the community while unifying themselves and earning money.

It was understood that none of the over-30s would remain full time over the winter because they had commitments elsewhere. They therefore would neither assume the burden of making key decisions nor help steer JM off in a direction it would not otherwise go. While younger people knew the older ones had more experience and a few were on guard against losing their autonomy, the over-30s were equally on guard against assuming dominant roles. It was agreed that the older people would only make suggestions and help out where their skills were recognized as vital to the commune's survival.

It was through chance contact with the over-30s that the Red Rose and Liberation Farm Collectives were drawn into the JM-Brethren conflict. The day after JM's meeting, Jesse and Bill MacDonald arrived leaving word with Patrick regarding the cancellation of the area-wide men's meeting that had been announced earlier at gatherings of all the local freaks at Liberation Farm. Jesse happened to ask what was happening at the Meadows and Patrick told him of the escalating conflict. Jesse's immediate reaction was critical of JM, since he had once lived there and left. He agreed with the Brethren in its claim that JM was an "untogether" collection of individuals with no common interest who were thrown together by chance because they had no other options. JM, he said, never looked deeply inside itself to really see if it was worth perpetuating itself. Communal living meant deep commitment to the people one lives with, and constant effort and attention had to be given to working out problems. "Do you really want to be together? Are you real friends? You must first decide on this before you decide to fight the Brethren. And only your commitment to each other will make the struggle worth while or winnable." Did JM have a planned contingency strategy? Was it armed for self-defense? Suppose fifty Brethren came down off the hill and literally carried away Janet's little cabin; what would JM do? Also, Jesse complained that JM had no interest in anything outside itself. There were more important things to do than lie in the shade and smoke dope or run naked through the grass. Although JM came to Liberation Farm gatherings, it was only to take free food and beer, rather than to contribute. Why didn't JM help weed the Liberation Farm garden? Why didn't JM come to the Vital Victuals Restaurant and Liberation Garage? In short, why didn't JM actively work for revolutionary change in Provincia?

Patrick responded by saying that JM was a different commune than the one Jesse knew only two months previously. Nearly all the old people were gone and the new people were working out new relationships. They were now beginning to hold meetings to work out answers to the very questions Jesse posed. JM might still become involved in the Free Provincia movement, but it would take time. Moreover, Red Rose didn't appreciate the time and effort that the fight for literal survival entailed. "When protecting the very land you stand and sleep on, and finding enough food to eat to ward off hunger are your concerns, then participation in political rallies and community projects becomes a frivolous activity." Jesse listened carefully, and despite agreeing that the Brethren was misdirected in its aims and procedures, still indicated no significant moral or material support for JM. Opportunities for closer ties between JM and Free Provincia were left open, however, when Jesse suggested they meet in the future to discuss the struggle and invited JM men to visit the Liberation Farm men that evening in Sutton in lieu of an area-wide men's meeting.

While many JM women attended their first women's meeting that evening, five men from JM (including two over-30s) visited the Liberation Farm collective where the discussion quickly shifted to JM's problems with the Brethren. Unlike Red Rose, the Liberation Farm Collective enthusiastically supported JM. Allen, a former JMer, still felt a visceral dislike for the Brethren that, in turn, infected the others. The Brethren should be resisted not only because they were fascists with long hair, but because they were seeking to use and strengthen the very SS institutions used in the oppression of the masses. The Brethren would eventually use police power, support legalism, continue to accumulate pieces of green paper (money) to control people's lives, and claim the earth (or pieces of it) as their own to do with whatever they pleased. "The earth belongs to all of us!" one shouted.

In combating the Brethren, they urged JM to use any means to survive, too, even those provided by the SS if necessary, since the Brethren would. Because the Brethren were in reality part of the "system," one shouldn't worry about using one part of the system to resist another. JM should attempt to reach out to the local straight community. "We can't make revolution for the people if we don't go to them to show them what we are, and to explain why we are." Also, for the first time, they consciously toyed with the idea that through the struggle, a more permanent federation of communes and freak farms could be established. The struggle could be a vehicle for building a coordinated alternative subsociety in the area. With these assumptions in mind, a plan of action was outlined.

First, the Liberation Farm people knew a friendly reporter at the Centerville newspaper who would only be too glad to do an exclusive story on the Wilfred communes. The story should distinguish between the two communes at the Meadows, and be sympathetic to JM. Second, someone should check out zoning regulations, property transfer procedures, and so forth in hopes of preventing the sale of the land from going through, or preventing the Brethren from remaining if the sale did go through. Even if the zoning regulations were drawn up to exclude all longhairs from the town, they might be selectively used against the Brethren. Third, JM should have a large cookout at the Meadows and invite all the other communes and alternative institutions in the area. Perhaps allies could be found while the Brethren, from their vantage point on Eagle's Claw, would see the people and might believe JM had general CC support. Fourth, they should talk to councilmen, health inspectors, and zoning officers to explain JM's position and explore how JM might better please the town. Fifth, everyone should strive to keep communication links with the Brethren open, thereby preventing any further solidification of the notion that JM people were evil quasi-humans against whom any action would seem justified. Finally, everyone should try to expose leadership lies and exaggerations, thereby keeping dissension in the Brethren ranks alive.

Shortly thereafter, the Brethren established a rule that none of its members could come down to the Meadows alone. Any member would to be accompanied by someone else who would keep his or her companion under a watchful eye, thereby discouraging anyone from seriously considering JM's position or speaking his or her mind. JM tried to counteract this by going up the hill to initiate conversations, but this policy failed because most JMers hated the thought of going through the circular arguments most discussions turned into.

Still, JM people discovered that many of the Brethren were grossly misinformed by their leadership. Many Brethren refused to believe Roy's threat to use "any means" to get rid of JM, saying instead that Roy couldn't have any malice in his heart. He was really, they claimed, pursuing the struggle with JM's best interests at heart. Wasn't JM now having regular meetings, doing work, cleaning up, and considering outside projects? For the Brethren members, that was proof that Roy had planned to go this way all along. He was a saint, they said, and JM just wasn't open to perceiving that fact. The Brethren also didn't know the real reason the Brethren moved so much of its membership from its center to the Meadows. By speaking over the phone to councilmen in the town where the Brethren center was, JM discovered the town threatened to evict them if they didn't either get more toilets or fewer residents. Toilets, it seems, were more expensive than relocation. The Brethren also believed that a voice had come to Roy "from the highest" proclaiming the August 31st deadline. To their shock, they later learned that the date was originally casually mentioned by Peter, who earlier thought that all JM people would probably be gone by then. Furthermore, Brethren rank and file believed the Brethren had already bought and paid for the land. Meanwhile, JM had every reason to believe the deal had not gone through because the Buddhist part-owner from the original group was still in India and had not yet been contacted.

The notion that the Brethren leadership should be accountable for its actions to the rank and file was invariably countered with statements such as "the Brethren is based on absolute faith and unity, and we cannot have faith or unity if we keep going around questioning James' and Roy's every move." Still, certain Brethren were indeed questioning the leadership, with indications of serious internal divisions coming to light in the heat of an argument in which an overseer proclaimed, "We are prepared to lose half our people if we have to, but we will have our way." Some JM people, letting their fear get the better of them, thought he was referring to casualties in a pitched battle, but a later conversation Norman had with a dissident member clarified the statement. The Brethren leadership feared that half the membership would quit the Brethren in the course of the struggle.

The fellow Norman spoke with, a mid-twenties university graduate, was deeply disturbed by what was going on. He was concerned not only with JM's imminent eviction, but with the autocratic manner in which Roy operated and the foolish brinkmanship policies he followed. The troubled dissident, a yoga enthusiast who had been searching for a community in which he could socially express his spiritual goals, was initially elated at finding the Brethren. But the experiment was going sour, he said, and he had to do something to stop it. He was determined to remain with the Brethren and reform it by challenging its leadership, thereby salvaging the purity of Brethren ideals. He and others would go to the Brethren center to talk to the leader, James, and to bring the matter up at a grand meeting. There was a chance for success, he figured, because there were others who also had doubts about Roy, including the middle aged local spiritual medium who was a kind of spiritual teacher for the Brethren at the time.

Thus, the divisions within the Brethren also followed the same lines as the divisions in JM. Those Brethren who corresponded to the street people and the older intellectuals in JM were opposed to the dominant hippie type leadership, and like JM, these two allied forces reacted in characteristic ways. Whereas the street type people entertained no thought of being able to change the Brethren and drifted toward JM, the Brethren intellectual dissidents were repulsed by the lack of vision and confusion in JM. Having confidence in their ability to change the Brethren, they chose to challenge the Brethren leadership instead. Moreover, there was interesting interplay between the divisions in each commune that cut across communal boundaries. Street people in both communes enjoyed doing drugs and drinking together, feeling comfortable with the unpretentious way they related to one another. The intellectuals of both camps basically agreed about what was happening, and enjoyed communicating with one another. These two quasi-alliances leaned in favor of JM in the struggle if anything. The hippies also found it easier to communicate with one another and found it difficult to take a committed stand of their own one way or the other unless forced to. Some Brethren hippies were involved with JM in peace making activities. Only those of higher hierarchical rank and those of the black magic subcult in the Brethren avoided friendly contact. Those hippies most open to interpersonal attachments across communal boundaries, refusing to let group loyalty or allegiance to abstract mystical principles stand in their way, were also those with records of past mental disturbance and bizarre psychohistories. On the one hand, they could be viewed as paralyzed by equivocation in the face of generalized commitment, but on the other hand, being more psychologically defensive, they could be seen as more aware of potential threats to individual survival in social situations. Because they were "abnormal," they could more easily see the excesses of commitment to group than the "normal," conforming, emotionally stable people could.

One incident serves as an illustration. As a gesture of friendship (and as a move to woo him away from JM) one of the Brethren members asked Roamer to go swimming "with the rest of the Brethren." Roamer refused, saying that if he had been asked to go swimming with that individual as an individual, he would have gone, but because he was asked to swim with a group, he wouldn't. The other fellow persisted in a patronizing way, until Roamer blew up, screaming "cut all this group bullshit. It's all getting me fuckin' up-tight, see. I'm an individual first, and then a member of something." At that point the fellow told Roamer he loved him. His apparent hypocrisy infuriated Roamer even more, to the point where, in a rage, Roamer physically struck out at him. Despite his political and social non-violence stand, Roamer was becoming psychologically violent by being forced into a group context. Seeing the situation deteriorating, Clara ran up and grabbed the Brethren fellow, pulling him away, whining something to the effect that fighting would solve nothing. Though she and

Roamer were in the same peace faction within JM, her way of dealing with the situation was to try to be a member of both groups rather than pretending to be a member of no group. Whenever she witnessed arguments or group strategy sessions, so much anxiety was generated in her that she almost broke down and cried, and such signs of conflict always resulted in her physically removing herself from the event. She said she spent much time up on the hill trying to be a peacemaker, but always had to withdraw when the Brethren tried to convince her to join them.

The atmosphere in the Meadows was extremely tense, The struggle weighed heavily on everyone's mind. No one knew what would happen next. One night, heavy traffic up and down Eagle's Claw began about midnight, with Brethren people loudly yelling to one another. Something was up, but fearing the worst, no one in JM left his or her bed to see what was happening. Eventually, some Brethren came down the hill and built a huge bonfire by the road not too far from the cookshack. This was the first time the Brethren had invaded JM's territory other than to pass through it. As the Brethren gathered around the fire, Roy spoke in a Hollywood version of an American Indian accent, while people painted each other's bodies like savages going on the warpath. Everyone started chanting, breaking into a dance around the fire that slowly built up to a frantic pace. A mob of silhouettes jumped, danced, and whirled around the fire, crying out in strange pseudo-Indian tongues as JM had done the previous summer. JMers fearfully contemplated what all this was leading up to. But as the frenzy reached a peak, the Brethren piled into the waiting vehicles which then roared out of the Meadows into the darkness.

Relieved and safe, everyone went back to sleep, although still disturbed by Brethren's use of their space. The next day it was revealed that the Brethren had "raided" the Brethren Center, running and screaming through their house, pulling people out of their beds, banging pots and pans, and setting off a stick of dynamite on the lawn outside. The townspeople had called out their only policeman to see what was happening. When he arrived, his car was surrounded by fifty screaming "Indians" who started rocking it back and forth. Scared and helpless, he sat in the car until they lost interest. The Brethren later described the incident as one of their greatest collective experiences. But JM people were very disturbed about the Brethren using the dynamite. The Brethren discounted JM's fears, saying that by going to such extremes, great spiritual growth was achieved. The hill contingent had learned the ecstatic joy of group commitment in action, and those at the center "had their minds blown," learning never to take any situation for granted.

A day later, the Centerville reporter that Liberation Farm had contacted, showed up at the Meadows dressed in a business suit. After spending a few hours on the hill with the Brethren, he returned to JM to get a balanced picture of the struggle. A few days later, a front page article appeared that very clearly distinguished the two groups, and contained every accusation JM could think up regarding the Brethren, including their impression that they were like the Charles Manson Family. Although the Brethren point of view was outlined later in the article on a back page, this was over-shadowed by a third perspective from surrounding straight farms and the Parson's Crossing Commune, favorable to JM for minding its own business and unfavorable to the Brethren for its Messianic zeal. The chief impression the article created, however, was that of a massive influx of wild new hippies into Wilfred.

The Brethren leadership realized that they came off looking quite bad, and were clearly unhappy. After growing positive press coverage about their center, this was the first time an article about the Brethren had been critical. Red Rose Collective indicated, to both JM's and Liberation Farm's surprise, their disapproval of having an SS reporter brought into the fray. Even if the Brethren were a "bunch of fascists" they said, what good was it to cause them grief if by calling in the straight press, everyone was caused grief? All the article would do was panic Wilfred residents into wanting to get rid of all longhairs. A revolutionary perspective was needed, they said. One doesn't create an alternative society by using, and thereby strengthening, SS institutions such as newspapers; one shouldn't expect a full and complex treatment by any journalist who spends only a few hours in any situation; one doesn't achieve a public impression of CC solidarity and vitality by airing dirty linen in public.

Roy, following his own parallel strategy of making overtures to town officials, visited the police station in Centerville where he claimed the police said they would be glad to help the Brethren get rid of JM. What Roy didn't tell JM, however, was that the conditions necessary for that to happen would be extremely difficult to bring about. The Brethren first had to legally establish their own presence on the land.

The feelings of the town were publicly aired a couple of days later when a special town meeting was called to sample Wilfred opinion before the town council decided whether or not to issue the Brethren a building permit. It was a crucially important meeting for the Brethren, for if a permit were not issued, plans for the winter would have to be drastically altered. A huge crowd filled the school auditorium. One resident claimed it was the best attended meeting he had ever seen in Wilfred. In addition to five people from JM and seven from the Brethren, there were two from Rainbow Farm and also Bill, who was now living at Walnut Hill Farm.

The meeting started by someone asking the Brethren overseers what the Brethren were all about. Roy gave his standard speech about purity, trust, faith, closeness, and love that was so strong they would die for each other. They had come to Wilfred not to "take over the town," but to serve it and to share with it their unique answer to the world's woes. Someone interrupted to ask whether or not they were a "family." Instead of saying they were a family, realizing the difficulty of proving that according to Wilfred's regulations, Roy replied that they were going to apply to the state for religious institutional status. With this change of strategy and Roy's apparent inability to answer questions directly, some people became annoyed. One fellow asked a question and then angrily yelled at Roy to "shut up" before he had a chance to answer it. When in response Roy lost his cool also, someone chided him, "temper, temper," obviously referring to the contrast between his anger and earlier talk of love. Roy shouted back that his "temper, temper" was "love, love." A woman asked about their filthy habits, swimming naked in the public pond and having so many visitors coming to live with them. Roy replied that this was JM, and not the Brethren. In fact, the Brethren would evict JM if allowed to stay, he said. The woman replied, "Well, at least that's some bit of good news." A lawyer finally stood up saying that all personal recriminations were beside the point, and demanded to know if the Brethren were in violation of any laws.

The Brethren intended to build a three story wooden structure with electricity, running water, and flush toilets that would house seventy five people over the winter. Asked where they were going to get the money for this, the Brethren countered that if one lives in harmony with self and others, things just naturally come; that material concerns need never be a worry. But questioners insisted on knowing specific monetary sources. After finding the sources irregular and unpredictable (donations, acquisitions from new members, and projected earnings from their rock band), townspeople declared that the Brethren would never raise enough for structurally sound buildings. Someone indignantly wondered how they could spend all this money and still receive food stamps. Questions turned to ownership of the land, the Brethren replying that they didn't yet own it, but that they had signed a lease with an option to buy. When one of the councilmen asked them to produce a document to prove it, they said that they didn't have it with them, but the piece of paper was "around somewhere." Finally, townspeople wanted to know if the Brethren had broken any laws, which it turned out they had. One in particular involved their continued construction on the building after being told to stop.

At this, one irate citizen demanded to know why he had to pay a fine for such infractions, and these hippies didn't. How could the Brethren expect the town to be helpful to them if they disregarded its laws whenever they pleased? Roy answered that the Brethren followed a "higher law" than the town. At this, the audience groaned. In disbelief, someone asserted that if the Brethren wanted to live in this town with "us mere humans," they would have to follow the same rules everyone else lived by. Another particularly hostile recent migrant to Wilfred asserted that the hippies were ruining this quiet, beautiful community, and that something had to be done about it. Seeing the meeting about to disintegrate, the chairman concluded that a permit could not be issued until the Brethren proved ownership of the land, and that construction requirements for a public building with dormitory space would be carefully researched.

After the meeting, private conversations broke out throughout the hall. The town's newer residents expressed the most hostile feelings toward the longhair influx. Some women were angry that such young and inexperienced people should imply that the townspeople weren't living their lives correctly. A man commented that under no circumstances should a permit be granted because the town already had the death of four young people on its conscience. One fellow walked up to the councilman insisting that it was not necessary to conform to present laws saying, "it would be better to pass a bunch of new laws." The Brethren stood around telling people that while the townspeople's shallow interests were opposed to the Brethren living in Wilfred, their souls were not, and that if people would only open themselves up, they would realize that their hidden spirit forces really wanted the Brethren to stay. How did they know this, some townspeople asked? Roy replied that they saw a white light in the room indicating the presence of pure spiritual energy.

Some longhairs concluded that while they had no love for the Brethren, what they witnessed that night had grave implications for the evolution of the CC. One commented that towns all across the country were relying on similar tactics of enforcing code technicalities that were the antithesis of conservation, cost reduction, and simplification values espoused by the CC. Wasteful codes were not only used to prop up capitalist interests in towns and discriminate against the poor, but also as a tool of repression against longhairs. Others nevertheless agreed that the Brethren could not remain completely outside the social rules of those people with whom they came in contact. Only a potential threat to the town, the Brethren posed an immediate threat to JM's existence. While the Brethren had to be controlled in some manner, being forced to conform to laws that they neither made, supported, nor found helpful was not the way to do it. There had to be a middle ground between repressive uniformity and aggressive free will. It remained to be seen, however, how the middle ground would be established and who would enforce compliance with it.

For JM's intellectuals, the question was: How could the smaller, looser system avoid being gobbled up by the bigger, tighter ones? The town was out to get the Brethren and the Brethren was out to get JM. But the problem didn't just apply to these antagonists in a growing three-cornered dispute. After the meeting, Yale (who was now a member of Rainbow Farm) approached the JM people making some cryptic remarks to the effect that all three parties, and particularly what now called itself JM, had no right to be involved in an uproar over the land. He sarcastically remarked that the social scientists at JM "probably staged the whole thing" so they'd have something exciting to study. Yale had openly stated that he would take charge of the land after JM and the Brethren had exhausted each other or driven each other out. Yale felt that JM should rightfully be his because of past association with Peter. It was possible that if Yale wanted the land badly enough, he might indeed end up with it. He was the only longhair accepted by most of the townspeople, meaning he had access to their legal and political machinery.

And what about Red Rose, Liberation Farm, and the whole Free Provincia movement? Should JM begin to affiliate itself with that as a means for obtaining allies and a back-up network of its own? Many members didn't like Free Provincia's "heavy raps about revolution and guns," and didn't want to get drawn into something they would be sorry for later. They felt there was also a danger in being swallowed up by the expanding revolutionary movement, as well. An absurd picture of a political "food chain" presented itself in which Yale was pursued by JM, which was pursued by the Brethren, which was pursued by the straight institutions, which were pursued by Free Provincia. Because alliances could be formed in all combinations, the situation seemed hopelessly confusing. Pepsi Joe asked, paraphrasing a famous line on an old television program, "Will the real enemy (The Brethren, the town, Yale, or Free Provincia) please stand up?"

In this survival struggle, JM's space and materials were shrinking day by day. The Brethren picked vegetables from JM's garden, and never returned tools they borrowed. They siphoned gas out of visitors' vehicles, and parked many of their own vehicles near the cookshack. Moreover, sovereignty over JM's buildings and belongings was being contested. Cindy was asleep in the loft of the A-frame when the door opened and three Brethren walked in, proceeding to rifle through her belongings before she surprised them by asking what they were doing. When they replied that they had come to take a few blankets, she replied that she needed them and asked them to leave, which they did. She reported $60 in welfare money missing from the A-frame a week later. Boop was in her cabin when two Brethren entered saying they were "going to move a piano in here so that one of our members can practice every day." JM informed the Brethren that if it was going to move into Boop's cabin, the group would have to use physical force to do it.

Jesse again visited the Meadows, but was still hesitant about taking sides. He saw no value in getting embroiled in a conflict that could absorb much of Free Provincia's time and effort, especially for the sake of saving a group most of whose members seemed to care little about working for fundamental social change. JM people asked if Red Rose could at least intervene in some kind of mediational role. In order to act as a mediator, Jesse protested, both sides had to accept the credibility of the mediator, and he was sure the Brethren wouldn't recognize Free Provincia in that capacity. JM counterargued that it was worth a try to find out; to give the Brethren Free Provincia's opinion even if unasked for. Minimally, it would demonstrate that the Brethren couldn't run all over JM without being held accountable by some other quarter of the CC. Jesse left, promising to have some people from Red Rose and Liberation Farm show up at a cookout JM was planning, so they could talk with the Brethren.

Late on the appointed afternoon, a carload of people from Liberation Farm arrived. About a dozen JM and Liberation Farm people made their way up the hill where they found Roy in the midst of a lecture-demonstration to a silent gathering of over fifty Brethren. Speaking in his Indian accent, he ordered "two squaws and two braves" from the crowd to surround a girl he had been chastising for some rule infraction. Holding hands in a circle around her, the people chanted and rocked back and forth. At first thinking it a joke, the girl tried to break out of the circle. Failing to do that, she laughed nervously for a while, eventually breaking into tears and, in a state of panic charged Roy that he was "crazy." Finally telling them to all sit down, Roy explained this episode demonstrated that many things could be learned through the body, without words, for the body had a liberating function. He had discovered that his body had almost let his spirit leave it a number of times.

Roy's chief rival, the one who was going to challenge him at an all-membership meeting, came over and introduced himself. As others came over, it was not long before serious discussion began. One of the Liberation Farm women explained that her collective was working to help everyone in society by struggling to win back freedoms that corporate America had usurped. The Brethren answered that they too were helping by aiding local farmers harvest their crops, and by bringing bus loads of black kids from urban ghettoes to the country. "When the shit hits the fan," a Brethren member said, "we will be here to help." The Liberation Farmers asserted that such an attitude would offer too little, too late, and that the Brethren should go out and actively try to prevent the shit from hitting the fan in the first place. Then, almost as if the confrontation was staged for dramatic effect, Jesse, the political heavy, joined the JM-Liberation Farm collective group on one side, and the spiritual heavy, James, joined the rest of the Brethren, making his first visit to the land since the day he told JM to either join up or get out. The atmosphere was extremely tense as the two individuals took each other on directly.

For his citadel to exist, James stated, it was necessary for there to be no other groups on the land, because the citadel was there to enable the Brethren to teach "oneness" to people who could then go out and spread the message after the cataclysms. "I know this to be true because I have experienced other planes of existence with other entities, but you are limited to material forms." Norman interjected that James was "full of shit," and that his fantasies were creating a severe emotional strain for everyone. Jesse, on the other hand, told James that he couldn't arbitrarily set deadlines and decrees. The way to proceed was to assess the situation as it is, and with everyone involved, work out solutions that fit evolving situations. Jesse suggested that everyone talk and have dinner together. James was too busy, he shot back, adding "We are going to come before the world and the world will know! Everyone here (pointing to the Brethren) has faith in me and they will teach the rest of the world." "If they are going to teach," retorted Jesse, "why are you doing all the talking?"

After a stunned silence, Mary stepped forward claiming that the Brethren didn't have to bother with negotiations or worry about ultimatums because JM needed "a good kick in the ass." "We know it to be true because God is on our side." There was another silence. To hear her parrot this slogan so often used by hated SS conservatives was tragicomical, eventually causing everyone to laugh. But James brought everything back to a somber mood by saying he had seen into the future and divined that JM would be better off if forced to leave. Finally exasperated, he terminated the conversation, declaring, "I own the land. I want the JM people off. It's as simple as that."

At this, Clara blurted out information just discovered by JM through a phone call to Peter's mother. "We know you don't own the land and you haven't leased it. All you have done is signed an agreement releasing Peter and his mother from legal responsibility for what goes on here." James faltered, saying he had a lease on a piece of paper somewhere and he would find it. Pepsi Joe interrupted to insist that JM knew there wasn't any such piece of paper. "If you stay on the land, instead of you teaching us, we have some things to offer and teach the Brethren." He went on to explain how life at the Meadows had helped rehabilitate ex-speed freaks like himself and people with emotional problems by giving them self-responsibility. James then cut Pepsi Joe short, menacingly declaring he would drop all pretenses and politeness at that point. Visibly angry, he stated, "We're just gonna move in and take over all the land."

At that, people started to turn away, convinced the battle lines had been drawn. Norman and Patrick, hoping to talk James out of any rash actions, pressed him to decide if he really wanted JM out at any cost. When James asserted that Peter had told them from the outset that JM would have to leave, they countered that Peter said they could stay. James then backed down saying that if there were drastic changes in JM, maybe they could stay beyond August 31st. But who would judge them, JM asked, James? Did he know what was really happening here while he was away at the Brethren Center? James replied that he knew what was happening at the Meadows even though he wasn't there. He could feel the "negative vibrations." "Give us some examples of what you mean," a JMer insisted. There was no answer.

The Meadows people trudged back down the hill to eat dinner and talk strategy. Although Free Provincia had tried to maintain neutrality in the confrontation atop Eagle's Claw, they now admitted their great antipathy toward James and the Brethren. JM people felt elated and quite proud of the way they handled themselves; some of the usually fence-sitting hippie wing even having joined in the verbal battle. But others reminded the group that JM had to examine itself more closely. "Would we be so together tonight if the Brethren weren't here?" one asked. Others replied that they would be even more together because all their energies wouldn't be absorbed in fending off the Brethren.

After a while, the Free Provincia people excused themselves, saying there was a town meeting up in Alpine that night concerning the distribution of Red Rose's newspaper called "Free Provincia." Despite no laws to back them up, the police had stopped two freaks from giving it away, and the rest of the Free Provincia people had gone up early to round up longhair support for the meeting. Most JMers decided to go to Alpine ostensibly as an act of reciprocity and to demonstrate an interest in community affairs. The gesture was significant. Drawing Free Provincia into the Meadows meant drawing JM into the growing Free Provincia network.

Meanwhile on Eagle's Claw, the Brethren leadership was also having a strategy meeting. James was visibly shaken by the confrontation. Some members remarked that they had never before seen him without his air of impenetrable confidence. James was sick, he said, of having JM look a gift horse in the mouth by not joining the Brethren. The Brethren would have to move immediately to oust them. The Brethren also realized they could no longer expect help from the town or the police. On the other hand, the appearance of political revolutionaries in the Meadows gave the appearance they were allied with JM, and they might even back JM with physical force if the situation deteriorated. Moreover, it became clear there would be no third party arbitrator to appeal to or a set of rules for the struggle that either side could rely on. The Brethren could only act directly on JM, yet hopefully in a way that would minimize the possibility of violence.

The next morning, twenty-five Brethren came down the hill carrying tents, belongings, and gear. The Brethren were simply going to directly invade and saturate JM's space and time. While tents were pitched close to the JM structures, Roy announced that the Brethren were moving in; that they would sleep in the cookshack among JM people if they felt like it, use their stove and other facilities, and invite themselves to dinner. In raw anger, JMers told Roy that no one had better eat their food or sleep in their beds if they didn't want a fight on their hands. Later in the day some fights nearly did break out. In reaction, JM called a meeting in order to arrive at some agreed upon way to handle this new crisis, but they couldn't manage even this, as Brethren members poured into the meeting in numbers greater than JM itself. What was the sense of talking strategy if the "enemy" was helping to make it?

While the Brethren were jubilant at the end of the first day of the invasion, JM was demoralized; even despondent. People had come to expect some new crisis each day, either from the town, the Brethren, or from within JM itself, but they had somehow managed to cope with it. This situation, however was too much. Brethren followed JM people around everywhere, attempting to cajole them into joining the Brethren and/or changing their lives, forcing involved metaphysical discussions, and claiming they were hounding JM only because they wanted to help JM "find itself." Everywhere one looked, there was a smiling but insistent Brethren member returning the glance. By bedtime everyone was completely exhausted. The only relief was that the Brethren hadn't yet moved into the cookshack or eaten their food.

Nevertheless, about half the JM membership had somehow managed to get together privately to discuss what to do. Suggestions ranged from physical assault (some mentioned the fact that if Hank were there he would have literally killed someone by now), to embarking seriously on a campaign of open drink, drugs, and sex. JM could not retaliate in a fashion similar to that of the Brethren because the Brethren had far greater members than JM. JM's great advantage now as that it occupied the land's only buildings, and if its members left them unoccupied to harass the Brethren's main camp up on Eagle's Claw, the lower Brethren camp simply would move in, thereby allowing the Brethren to stay the winter even if they didn't get a permit for the new building. Someone commented that the situation wasn't all that unusual, citing the times they were flooded with visitors, and remarking that JM was normally so disorganized that there was very little of anything the Brethren could really disrupt. It was laughingly concluded that JM's "untogetherness" was really its primary strength in this situation, and that if everyone could hold out, the Brethren would give up before they did. After all, it was the Brethren members, and not JM, who had to keep the pressure on, and they couldn't go to all their meetings, listen to their lectures, and work on their projects if they spent all their time harassing JM.

Hope turned to confidence within a few days as JM people noticed the Brethren were around the cookshack less often. After Roy's big announcement, he had hardly been seen since. When Brethren members were asked where he was, and they replied that he was busy with all the other work he had to do, JM members laughed, saying Roy had really skipped out on his followers, leaving them to do the dirty work. Within a week, an entire day would go by that the Brethren wouldn't be seen. Perhaps they were switching to a different tactic after finding out that this latest one was too much for them to handle; that it was more of a drain on them than it was on JM.

Regardless of the Brethren strategy change, JM kept to its basic approach. It would permit the Brethren strikes at JM to pass as harmlessly as possible through the gaps created by its disorganization, and encourage area longhairs to demonstrate support for JM. About a week later another feast was held, this time incorporating people outside Free Provincia, including members of the Parsons Crossing-Walnut Hill Karass who loathed virtually everything Free Provincia was doing. The occasion was Yale's birthday, and despite the fact that he had designs on the land and everyone knew it, all suspicions were put aside as jugs of wine were passed. Fifty three people partook in the merriment, later to be joined by thirty Brethren who, after the leadership had left to go to the Brethren Center, were curious to know what the gathering portended. Thus, in its struggle with the Brethren, JM had extended its newly evolving outer directedness toward another major segment of the area CC: the Parson's Crossing Karass.

While establishing far better relations with the outside world, tension-ridden contact with the Brethren continued. Fear and tempers ran high as rumors and true stories circulated on either side. One night after the Brethren returned to their nearby tents, an argument ensued in which people hurled accusations at each other. When Zeke, who had been drinking, yelled, "You're not going to burn my house down with me in it!" others from JM ran to break up any fight that might start. Black Jack then stood up to reprimand both Brethren and JM. "What's all this talk about machetes, and burning, and shit like that man?"

There was a factual basis for fear of violence and, although Roy never admitted it as Brethren policy, he probably used the threat of violence to bring further psychological pressure on JM, hoping they would give up in the face of possible bloodshed. Peter later said that he believed that Roy was deliberately trying to scare JM while unifying the Brethren through fear. Two rumors circulated among the Brethren, one asserting that JM had talked the Free Provincia revolutionaries into launching an armed attack on the Brethren. The other held that after the permit went through and the citadel was built, JM would simply burn it down, and though everyone would suspect arson, there would be no proof.

JMers had reason to fear for their safety too, for Roy had openly stated that the cookshack was the center of all negative energy on the land and that it would have to be destroyed. Everyone knew the Brethren were still keeping their dynamite sticks. JMers had also concluded that, in the end, the Brethren members would do anything Roy told them to do. This was particularly alarming because Roy was literally out of his mind as far as JMers were concerned. JM members reasoned that his credibility and position within the Brethren was on the line because he was totally responsible for the success of the Brethren venture at the Meadows. Thus, it was not unreasonable to assume that the destruction of the JM commune for Roy had become a personal obsession.

Reports from people leaving the Brethren indicated that Roy strove for total obedience by constantly questioning the members' faith. The faith that he demanded was not in doctrine or principles, but in him and his judgment. Not to have faith in him meant that one was inhibiting the ecstasy of "oneness" and the unity the rest of the group could experience, thereby bringing social pressure as well as guilt on anyone who held back in expressing faith. "I am willing to die for you, are you willing to die for me?" he asked on a number of occasions. Once, he tested them by saying, "If I saw fit to burn down a house down the road, would you have the faith to follow me and do it?" Everyone agreed that they would. Even Black Jack, who was constantly at odds with the Brethren leadership, often seeking out JM people to tell his troubles to, admitted, "I need them, man. I'd crawl on my knees and eat shit if they told me to. I'd die if they threw me out."

Brethren cosmology, as well as interpersonal dependency and self-abnegation, contributed to JM fears that in a final act of desperation, the Brethren were capable of any behavior. Many Brethren had absolutely no doubt that they were right in trying to get rid of JM, and not to act on what God had told them to do was far closer to sin than throwing people out of their homes. What they were doing with regard to JM, they rationalized, they were doing for JM's own good. Among the Brethren, JM was likened to "a child sitting on a railroad track with a train speeding toward it." Rather than reason with the child or ask it to get off the tracks, one runs and removes the child against its will. Moreover, the rescuer in the onrushing train analogy could risk his or her life because getting killed in the service of good through selfless compassion was an elevating and liberating act. In the Karmic cycle, in order for the soul to be permanently liberated from imprisonment on the plane of earthly existence, past wrongs had to be righted through good deeds. Physical death was not only tolerable but preferable if one knew one's act was on the side of ultimate good. It meant that entry into the cosmos as spirit energy could be achieved or at least brought that much closer. One Brethren member remarked that her life was unimportant; that the significance of her existence was only as an instrument for the Krishna Force to accomplish what it must on the earthly plane. Would the Brethren literally sacrifice themselves in ultimate struggle, taking JMers with them, JMers asked?

The taut stalemate finally broke the following Sunday when all but four members of JM and two visitors went to Liberation Farm. Roy and the entire Brethren swept down off the hill and literally surrounded those who stayed behind. While the Brethren quietly sat down in a large circle, Roy angrily demanded that there be no visitors except on weekends; no smoking, drinking, dope, etc., and that no more than eight people at a time could gather around the firepit outside the cookshack. Roy then pointed out why none of the JMers there should remain with JM, urging them to either leave or join the Brethren. Clara wavered and was almost convinced to join the Brethren by Roy's forcefulness.

When the rest returned, they were furious at having the Brethren come down to "terrorize" small groups with this new "hit and run" strategy. Because Roy supposedly would be down to restate the rules the next morning, a number of JM people got up early to meet him head on, but neither he nor any of the Brethren showed up until the next day. Even their tents by the cookshack had not been slept in. It was decided that someone would talk to the lawyer handling the sale of the land to see how far it had gone and if he knew where Peter was, so JM could contact him about selling the whole parcel to them instead of the

Brethren. Pepsi Joe had a $2,000 trust fund for his education, but he could wrangle a way to use it for the land, and Norman had been saving money for land anyway. Also, people would contact other communes to determine the extent of their support and to ask them to show up at the Meadows en masse if the Brethren made any more mass moves. While Red Rose was still noncommittal, Liberation Farm was all for the idea, one even saying they would be glad to come and "bust some heads." Even Parson's Crossing indicated that there were a number of individuals who would come if help were needed.

Roy and some Brethren barged into the cookshack the next morning and started to lay down the rules. JM people disregarded him, then accused him of being a pathological liar who specialized in manipulating helpless people. As other Brethren walked in, JM verbally pushed Roy to the wall, citing point after point where he had lied, particularly the bit about the Brethren owning the land. To the amazement of the Brethren members, Roy finally admitted they didn't own the land, "but we will soon." Trying to change the subject as though nothing had happened, he went into another rap about people having to trust him, even when he admitted he had lied about land ownership.

Roy then demanded a meeting with all of JM so he could make his announcements. Roy was told that if he wanted a meeting with everyone in JM, it was up to him to round them up. When he finally settled on informing only those present, no one paid any attention to him; talking and laughing among themselves. In a fit of anger, he finally gave up and left the cookshack. But some Brethren stayed on to talk. One, a new face, apparently had refused to join a work detail and got away with it. He apologized for Roy's approach, saying that other members would work out an amenable relationship with JM. JM people responded that there had been no sign yet (with one exception) that people were willing to bypass Roy's authority, and that if someone were going to do it they had better do it soon before something calamitous happened.

Then began a forty hour non-stop marathon argument, threat, and confrontation, that had some wondering if they would emerge alive. Later that afternoon, Brethren started concentrating their proselytizing efforts on Roamer, probably because they felt that he was most understanding of their viewpoint and had come to assume an important leadership role within JM. But again, Roamer lost control after some hours of harassment . He thrust a knife he was peeling vegetables with in the direction of one of the Brethren. This got back to Roy, who became very disturbed over the incident. Finding Roamer in his truck where he usually withdrew after such episodes, Roy pleaded with him to establish some kind of self-control. In return, Roamer made Roy promise not to pursue policies of division, animosity, and narrow group loyalty.

Throughout the day, those JM people who could still stand to keep up the arguing began driving home the point that Roy wasn't competent to lead the Brethren, and though he had more confidence and charisma than they, he would lead them down the road to folly. The Brethren membership, JMers argued, had given up on themselves by putting control of their lives in someone else's hands. "Fight back," "use your own judgment," "govern your own lives!" were some of the statements heard during the arguments. Brethren responded that they couldn't disregard Roy's wishes because it would be a selfish thing to do, and further, it would disrupt their "beautiful unity." Moreover, Roy was on a higher plane of understanding than they, and because of that, he was better able to lead, even if the followers couldn't comprehend his reasons.

After the most exhausting day yet of constant dead end argument, JMers were about to turn in when Norman's voice was heard rolling across the moonlit meadow. "What do you people want? Us to turn into robots like you? I'm my own man. Why don't you people get out of here and leave us alone?" Norman was sitting with some Brethren around their campfire, his loud protestations drawing the attention of more people, Brethren and JM, who also gathered around the fire. The arguing escalated as point and counterpoint shot through the flames to opposite sides of the circle as the JMers pushed the Brethren to explain why the Brethren couldn't function without Roy, why they were letting themselves be used by egomaniacs, why when presented with undeniable facts they chose to disregard them, preferring to go with "feelings," "vibrations," and spiritual leaders' perceptions instead.

Most answers were half apologetic, but one short-haired member who looked more like a fullback than a flower child, glared menacingly at Patrick as he spoke. "Are you willing to die for what you believe in?" Patrick replied that he probably would in certain worthwhile circumstances, but that the Meadows was not one of them. Coolly but intensely the fullback continued, "I am willing to die and I am willing to kill. That's how much faith I have in Roy and James. James asked me once before if I would go into town and kill ten people if he told me to, and I said I would. I would do it now, too." At first dumbstruck by his statement, JMers pressed him to see if he really meant what he said; to see if their worse suspicions about the Manson-like character of the Brethren were true. "You'd do it even if Roy said so?" they asked. "Yes," was the answer.

At that point, someone wondered aloud where Roy was. A Brethren member answered, alluding to Roy's telepathic omnipotence, "He's probably listening to everything going on here." The remark proved astoundingly correct as Roy stepped out of the darkness into the firelight. He took the offensive for the Brethren, repeating the same old accusations. With this, previously apologetic Brethren aggressively backed him up, one fellow saying JM was unfriendly because the first day he approached the cookshack, two people who were outside, went into it. He was asked if they saw him coming or if someone inside the shack had called them to enter the shack. How did he know the two people were purposely avoiding him? "I could feel it," he replied with emphasis. A JMer replied, "Feelings don't tell you everything that's going on; you have to balance them off with facts to get a more complete story, and none of you like to deal with facts."

With this, Roy shifted to sarcasm. "Oh, is that so," he retorted in mock surprise with a wailing voice that other Brethren people began to imitate. After that, Roy began laughing in a distinctly forced and phony manner. One by one, others joined in until all the Brethren were making laugh-like noises that to JM people sounded hideously demonic. For about five minutes, any questions or statements by JM people elicited the same response, with Roy making cryptic remarks and others following with "yeahs."

The JMers were tempted to get up and walk away, as the entire spectacle had an eerie quality of total absurdity. But they persisted, as leaving would resolve nothing. For the first time there was a clear cut, conceptualizable, polarized clash between two very distinct realities; each attempting to force the other to rearrange itself into its own pattern. In this case, argument might lead somewhere. All the JM people closest to the fire were over-30s. Up to this point in the summer they had stood back, letting the other JMers do most of the talking. Here, they could no longer be bystanders because the events of the last few weeks had completely governed, and now even threatened, their lives. It was an all out battle, using the weapons they knew best: words. Although the hippie and street people heard all the ruckus, many weren't interested enough to come over to see what was going on. Instead, teachers, psychotherapists, poets, and social scientists passionately bayoneted the Brethren with what they regarded as the cold steel of logic and empiricism. But at the same time, the over-30s people felt strange in their championing of pure rationalism and objectivity, having previously prided themselves in their emotionally antiseptic professional worlds as aesthetes and humanists.

Could another reality be touched, let alone impaled? Roy's diabolical laughing episode had evidently been undertaken to demonstrate that it couldn't. The questions of evidence and proof were mundane and limited compared with the realms and dimensions with which he was dealing. So, too, were individuals' mere words compared with the escalation of emotions achieved when person after person threw their feelings onto a communal heap. Roy momentarily stopped the uproar around the campfire to tell the intellectuals they were "not listening or looking behind events or words." Norman's poet friend shot back, "I guess everything you do around here isn't what it seems." "Yes, that's exactly right," replied Roy with the entire group resuming its I-know-something-you-don't-know laughter. Roy again stopped the laughter to say that JM was limited in its perceptions because it saw only material forms. But Patrick cut him short, "I've had enough of your abstract bullshit: positively, negativity, spirituality, materialism, and all that. I want to pin you down to something we can both talk about and understand. Just what the hell do you mean by material and spiritual?" Roy gave no answer and then again began laughing, again joined by the other Brethren members. Patrick waited until the laughter died down and repeated the same question. Roy's response was to start singing the Brethren's theme song about temporary flesh and permanent spirit. He was dutifully joined by the others.

Then Roy led everyone in loud Indian-like whooping, after which he began to speak in his grade B movie "redskin" accent. When Norman in disgust called him an "incredible buffoon," Roy glared and grinned at him saying "Me Indian brave. (Laughter.) It about time me take-um some scalp. (Laughter and oohs and aahs in recognition of Roy's upping the level of verbal threats.) Me go find enemy and cut out heart." (More nervous laughter.) The poet broke in exasperatedly proclaiming, "I can't believe this. This is just like Lord of the Flies." Only one Brethren member knew what he was referring to. Roy then shifted into a lecture format, shouting his standard rap. In return, the JMers kept interrupting him, telling him that his monologue had nothing whatsoever to do with solving a specific, real problem covering specific, real people on a specific, real piece of land.

Roamer and Madelaine (the troubled girl who previously believed Roy so much that she injured herself trying to levitate herself from the treehouse) had joined the crowd now, and Roy finally stopped as Madelaine screamed at him between her sobs. "God Damn it Roy, they are fucking trying to tell you something! You're always so fucking busy doing things, you don't know how to listen!" After a shocked momentary silence, Brethren shouted her down as Roy resumed his monologue. Then Roamer yelled out from the edge of the crowd, "Roy, you are going back on what you told me in the truck. This is not working toward integration. She is a member of the Brethren, man, and you've at least got to listen to her." Roy then answered, questioning her loyalty while threatening her status, "I don't know, Madelaine, are you a member of the Brethren?" "If you don't like the Brethren, why don't you split?" another voice chided. Roamer angrily shouted back, "Is that compassion? Someone standing here pleading for understanding and help in understanding what's going on, and you tell her to split?"

Another Brethren woman commented that Madelaine was always wrong because she did not "follow orders." Obviously embarrassed by this comment, most of the other Brethren pounced on her, telling her to "shut up." Patrick loudly commented he had never seen any group of people treat one another so harshly in the name of love. "Is this the way real brethren act toward each other?" At this, Roy began howling and whooping, the others joining, jumping up and down in their places. He then ran off hopping, jumping, and skipping down the road, across the stream, and up the hill followed by every Brethren except one who remained seated. Norman yelled after them, "That's it, Roy, run away and everyone will follow you like a fuckin' bunch of sheep!"

The fellow who remained spoke up for the first time that evening, saying that not all of them were sheep. Though this fellow claimed that the Brethren couldn't be understood through "mere" words and concepts, he tried to explain that Roy went into his Indian whooping routine when he felt the negative energy around him to be so great that he and the Brethren were getting drained. The jumping and hollering was intended to recharge their positive energy and carry them away from the negative energy source. A van with more people from the Brethren Center pulled up, and the course of the evening's argument was outlined for them, in a quiet, rational way. JM people asked them questions that made the discussion sound more like a seminar on electrochemistry or quantum mechanics than a fight for survival. Some JM people insisted that matter and energy were only alternative forms of the same process, one not being able to exist without the other, while the new Brethren people at the campfire argued that energy could exist without matter and that the spirit plane was pure energy. Why was it that negative energy could drain positive energy, but not vice versa, a JMer asked. The Brethren were stumped by that question.

By now it was 3 A.M., and more exhausted than before, people made their way to tents, vans, and shacks to get some sleep. The JM stragglers still sitting by the fire commented on the absurdity of the situation. The only way it could be resolved was for Peter to be forced to take sides. It was feared, however, that before anyone could find Peter, someone could get killed. At that juncture, another car pulled into the Meadows, and Patrick, reflecting on the bizarre events of the evening in which the commonly understood casual laws of the physical universe no longer seemed to be working, sardonically remarked, "This is probably Peter now." Incredibly, Peter, who was not even supposed to be in the US at the time, stepped out of the vehicle. He joined the few people left around the fire where he was told of the latest events at the Meadows, including the opinion that Roy was mad, and that anything could happen. Norman summed up, "Tonight is like a Greek tragedy, with plots, mistaken assumptions, and central characters entering the stage together for the grand and final tragic act, except that all this is real."

Peter sat mumbling to himself in riddles and metaphors, "Karma, Karma, good Karma, bad Karma, your Karma, my Karma." When told that he had to take an active role in resolving it, he spoke as if there was little he could do. "It has to be this way. Karma is being worked out." A JMer insisted that Peter could not escape the consequences; that regardless of what happened he would be caught in the cross-fire. Peter responded, "I know that. This is why I have returned. I have come back to be killed." When a shocked JMer interjected, saying Peter couldn't be serious and was probably stoned on the rocks in the mountains and the stars in the sky, Peter replied, "What's the difference? Life or Death? Whether we are rocks or distant stars? It is all ordained for us."

The next morning, the younger people and some of the street people said they wanted to go hear a rock band in Alpine that evening. The intellectual wing thought it was an irresponsible thing to do. After all, Peter was here and they should settle the question of the land once and for all. Roamer sympathized with those who wanted to leave, indicating he realized that the last weeks had been a terrible strain on everybody, but that leaving at this crucial point was not the way to handle it. With this, everyone agreed to stay. When Peter was spied sitting on a log in the Meadow, everyone went over and small-talked with him in a very cautious and deferential manner, until someone popped the big question. Would Peter sell a piece of the land to JM? Peter quietly replied that he couldn't break his promise to the Brethren. Furthermore things had not changed. JM was together over material forms such as land, but not in the important areas of individual growth and group development. There were always other pieces of land, and if JM really had purpose and demonstrated it from the beginning, they could probably have remained at the Meadows. As it was now, the Brethren, who demonstrated such purpose from the outset, should not be asked to change the terms of the original agreement.

The intellectual wing challenged him on every point. The street people did not say much of anything and the hippie wing, including Roamer, was somewhat shocked and disturbed to see Peter, JM's founder and former guru, under attack. It was pointed out to him that JM had no legal leg to stand on if the Brethren owned all the land and could kick JM off if it wished. Also, they said, Peter grossly underestimated the importance of material concerns on everyone's lives. No matter how much they loved and needed one another, who could survive if their living space, their means of obtaining food, their place in the overall community, and an environment to which they had become very attached, were taken away from them? Moreover, if purpose and unity were any criteria for determining a group's right to exist, Peter should have been at the Meadows this past week to see how purpose and unity caused the Brethren not only to be devoid of human compassion, but also to border on insanity. In fact, they said, compared to the Brethren, one of JM's better points was that it lacked an obsessive compulsion to force its bond of love on the world. Finally, Peter was criticized for prolonging and exacerbating the entire situation.

Peter countered that he had no role to play in the situation now; his last act having been his promise to sell the land to the Brethren. Told that material as well as spiritual injury could result if he refused to sell some of the land to JM, his reply was "so be it." When further pressed, he did admit he would not like to see any more deaths on the land, but let it go at that. At last, he admitted that if he sold part of the land to JM, the Brethren would back out, thereby meaning the deal would be off, and the Karmic future of the land would still be left unresolved.

Disgusted and disappointed by the apparent collapse of their last hope, some of the JMers stopped trying to reach Peter through the use of spiritual concepts. One blatantly remarked that if Peter sold some land to JM, it really meant he would not be able to sell the rest of it once the Brethren backed out. No one with money enough to pay for it would want a hippie commune for a neighbor. Thus Peter's real concern could be financial. Shocked by hearing Peter's motives impugned, someone from the hippie wing defended him saying that he had spiritual insight and could see through complicated matters to the simple heart of them. To this someone countered that Peter's simple insight in this case was naiveté, ignorance, and personal gain. The psychotherapist finally gave his professional opinion, "Peter, you are just full of shit."

At that moment, a Free Provincia car pulled into the Meadows with Jesse, accompanied by the Red Rose woman who was a spiritually oriented yoga enthusiast, and Charles, Free Provincia's chief theoretician, inspiration, and architect. They joined the group, listened quietly until the JM people finally gave up, and then began to question Peter. Now another world view swung into action as the same people who had listened to legalistic, social scientific, psychotherapeutic, street type paramilitary, and mystical arguments throughout the conflict now faced the revolutionary interpretation. Jesse started off, but was curiously subdued compared to his usual approach, perhaps finding it difficult to attack his old guru and father figure. When he asked what Peter was going to do about the intolerable situation at the Meadows, and Peter firmly replied "nothing," he said no more.

The Red Rose woman then spoke to Peter in their common language of Karma, talking of rebirth, spirit, and energy, while tying it to compassion, human needs, and the necessity for social responsibility and political action. She blended the political and spiritual perspectives so well that no one else cut in. If anyone could reach Peter, it would be she. While she could understand his position because her own past perceptions were similar, she was "furious" with him because with all his professed concern for people, he was treating them like objects in a cosmic ritual rather than as thinking, feeling human beings. What gall he had to think he had special feelings and insights into human nature that others didn't have. She had been that way herself once, she said, using spiritual abstractions, omens, premonitions, and fatalistic concepts to relate to people because she didn't know how to relate to them in any more personal, spontaneous, and intimate way. In fact, such an orientation could be used as barriers between people. By trying to rise above the whole thing and by being neutral, he was really running away from responsibility. Moreover, his saying he could do "nothing" made her feel he was "arrogant, unfeeling, and extremely self-centered." Finally, his failure to act on behalf of JM in effect put him on the side of the Brethren. Peter said very little, looking down at the ground or peeling bark off the log. When she had finished, he made no attempt to argue back, saying, "O.K. I guess that's the way you feel."

Before uttering a word, Charles passed out copies of a publication instructing people on the use of firearms for self-defense. The mouths of the peace and love hippies there dropped open in shock. Then turning to Peter, he matter-of-factly said, "The way I see it, Peter, you're a fascist pig landlord. You rely on the legal rules and technicalities of the system that was created to exploit people who do not, or find it difficult to, own. And you go away on vacation, traveling about Provincia at will, returning intermittently to keep tabs on the progress of the struggle at JM. All that is, Peter, is the middle and upper middle class luxury of governing people's lives at a distance, and then claiming you aren't connected in any way with the squabbling among the governed, struggling over the little that's left to them. It's obvious that your in this thing for your own interest and profit, and these people here are being exploited because of it. You're just a pig landlord, that's all." Charles rose to leave, indicating that nothing more would be accomplished by prolonging the discussion, and that the Red Rose people had other things to do. They would think the situation over and be in touch.

As the Free Provincia auto left, another car pulled into the Meadows. The reporter from the Centerville paper had come to check out Brethren and JM reaction to his articles. By the time he got to the log, Roy and some Brethren people (who had been watching the previous discussion from their tents) were there talking to Peter. Roy claimed that the first article was unfair and had "caused all the trouble" with the town. He particularly objected to the mention of the Manson cult. He went into his standard rap about the Brethren's role in a collapsing world, concluding that because the Brethren were so different, people would either wholeheartedly support their movement or reject it. Some would see it as "the Devil's work," he said, "just like those who condemned Jesus, the Christ, to death. Others will see infinite good and purity. There isn't necessarily purity everywhere just because it's the Aquarian Age." The reporter argued that issues are seldom as clear as good and evil or black and white. Another Brethren shouted out, "Garbage! I know where I'm at, and that's all that counts in this fucking world. You may be confused by complexity, but I am not!"

As the late afternoon sun spread the shadow of Eagle's Claw across the Meadows, JM people wandered off dejectedly in different directions. JM's last hope for equal legal footing was gone. The strain had been so great that some declared they didn't really care anymore; that having it resolved one way or the other was better than having the battle drag on. At least people could start looking for new situations. Those who were left behind could try to work out some arrangement with the Brethren whereby they could stay on the land in some loose manner after the strongly anti-Brethren people left. Technically, nothing had changed. JM still controlled the structures, the town was still debating whether or not to issue a permit, and the land still belonged to Peter and the traveling Buddhist who had to be contacted before the land could be sold. It seemed only a matter of time before the JM commune would come to an end.

The over-30s members were just as depressed as everyone else, and in some ways more so because of the intense effort they had put in the last few days. They sat together in a corner of the meadow assessing their own roles in the most recent events, and wondering if they had overstepped their bounds by giving the impression they were speaking on behalf of the interests of all of JM when they were only part timers. They finally concluded that they hadn't usurped the leadership of JM, because their chief role had been as critics of the Brethren; a justified action for them to take in any circumstance. After talking about the pleasant things they hadn't had a chance to do in a month, some were so exhausted they fell asleep in the grass.

That evening people chipped in some money for beer, desperately needing release from the continuously mounting tension of the last few days. No one could any longer be bothered arguing with the Brethren because it was pointless, and the Brethren had no reason to push any further. People gathered in the cookshack, many pleasantly high on beer, to joke and talk about anything but the land or the Brethren. Others set the table outside for a late dinner by candlelight. Suddenly, Roy and the fellow who said he would kill ten people if asked to, appeared in the cookshack. Most people paid no attention, while some even gave them a resigned, friendly greeting. Roy announced he had some news for everyone: "There's to be no drinking on the land. You'll have to get rid of all alcohol. No dope either." Some of the younger people laughed ambiguously. The others couldn't believe what was happening. Wouldn't the Brethren let up, even now? Everyone had come to the conclusion the struggle was all over. Why was the Brethren continuing the insanity?

Roy's potential killer accomplice reached over and removed an empty beer can that was sitting in front of Patrick. The idea that "that automaton, that self-appointed spirit goon-policeman" had actually attempted to prohibit an individual's behavior over which he had no prerogative, was more than he could take. Infuriated, Patrick almost involuntarily attacked the marauder, but instead, shaking with anger, he defiantly dared anyone to "try to enforce" any rule. Before Roy and his enforcer could respond, loud shouting and screaming were heard outside the cookshack. Pushing Roy and the other fellow aside, the JM people ran to the aid of whomever was in trouble.

In the midst of his dinner, the psychotherapist had been surrounded by about thirty Brethren. Standing six and a half feet tall and weighing two hundred and fifty pounds, he towered in the moonlight over the sea of shadowy, silent, faceless Brethren. "God Damn you people! Get out of here and go back where you belong! Who the hell are you that you can't even let a person eat a meal in peace? Go on, get the fuck out of here before I throw you out! What kind of people are you that you crawl out of the shadows like mindless insects to surround a few people minding their own business? Go on, get out of here before I break your fucking heads open!" The Brethren remained motionless and speechless until Roy, who had made his way to the center of the mob, spoke to the psychotherapist, in the tone of a clergyman preaching a sermon, "We have to come together," he quietly began. But before he could continue, the psychotherapist thundered back, "If you don't get out of here, you'll come together with the end of my fist!"

Again a high point of tragicomedy was reached. With utter rage, imminent violence, and unconscious humor, the psychotherapist had brought the conflict to the point of no return. Where knuckles touched jaw there would be fusion and unity, but not the kind that everyone wanted. There would be irrefutable proof that the material has a more immediate reality than the spiritual; and that the application of biceps could settle problems more quickly and resolutely than the application of concepts. There were sufficient numbers of incensed people there that a wild melee could have started at that very moment; the outcome of which might have been calamitous. The antagonism could proceed no further without physical destruction and injury, with détente being the only alternative. Time seemed to stand still as everyone remained motionless and speechless waiting for something to happen. The therapist and Roy glared at each other for several deadly seconds. Finally hoping to deflect the confrontation, a JMer asked for a real reason the Brethren had descended on the Meadows this evening.

Pepsi Joe and Zeke, who were off somewhere drunk, heard the commotion and approached the cookshack. Zeke hostile, and Pepsi Joe cheerful, they pushed their way to the table in the center of the crowd. Putting his arms around Roy's shoulder and slurring his words, Pepsi Joe proclaimed that if they were to come together, they would have to work together. Intuitively applying techniques of psychodrama, he caught the belligerents off guard by asking them to act out reversed roles, to the embarrassment of Roy (who agreed to pretend he was Zeke for a few minutes), to the discomfort of Zeke (who imitated Roy), and to the comic relief of the crowd. This went on for about five minutes as people laughed at the absurdity of the exaggerated but accurate portrayals. The tension had been broken and violence averted, but some JMers were still deeply annoyed because nothing had been done about the Brethren's continuing harassment JM. And the previously cautious over-30s intellectuals wanted to have it out right then and there.

Roamer began loudly to chastise both JM and the Brethren. "It was a fucking stupid thing, very inconsiderate, and no good for anybody, to come down here and interfere with what we were doing. It was also stupid and inconsiderate for (the psychotherapist) and others to yell back. This whole scene is insane. We've got to get together, man; it's the only way. I've spent much time in my truck thinking how I can bring us together, and one of my fantasies is to sit in meditation on the (outdoor) oven here and set myself on fire." Some in the crowd shouted out "No, Roamer," for they knew that before Roamer flipped out, he always tipped his hand ahead of time, using fantasy to describe what he would do. Many felt his statement was not a hollow threat. "Well, that's the way I feel, man," he answered, his voice cracking. "My life ain't worth living if I as an individual and we as groups can't live together in peace and harmony." After a quiet pause he started chanting "Om," clasping onto the hands of those next to him, with others following suit until nearly everyone was holding hands in a crowded circle and chanting. The chanting rose in depth and volume until it blended with its own echo in the valley, amplifying the sound even more. After five minutes or so it subsided to a halt, after which Roamer said, "I've got a really great feeling. We can hold it, and see this thing through."

After a momentary silence signaling rapprochement and hope, the poet from JM shouted, "This is a bunch of bullshit! You guys are a bunch of fucking con artists, that's all!" Most of the people in the circle groaned to hear such a discordant note. But the rest of the over-30s and some street people from JM who had not joined the circle, agreed with the poet's pronouncement. As the crowd broke up with reminders that they would all get up at 8 a.m. to work together, the street people and older cynics sat amazed by the faith or naiveté of their communal brothers and sisters. One flatly stated that the real issues had been deflected and predicted that the two communes would not work together the following day. Pepsi Joe's pubescent sister approached him, saying, "Wasn't the chanting wonderful? It really worked and everything will be just fine from now on." Her communal brother, who was old enough to be her father, answered that he believed she was wrong, but hoped she was right. After acknowledging the apparent generation gap within JM, and speculating that perhaps the innocence of younger people could partially dismantle what years of sobering experience had taught older people, she hugged him and told him to cheer up. A Brethren member commented that the reason the cynic could not know that a new start had been made was because, preferring to observe it from the outside, he didn't directly feel the energy generated by the hand holding and chanting. The cynic admitted this was a valid argument by the Brethren on the nature of knowledge. But the next morning his prediction about the two communes not working together nevertheless proved true. They never even came in contact with each other, and one didn't go out of its way to find the other either.

This latest Brethren invasion was not carried out for the stated reasons Roy gave, but as many suspected, stemmed from internal dissensions within the Brethren. The struggle between the two communes had precipitated a series of setbacks for the Brethren outside, and had opened many eyes to weaknesses inside. Roy was under fire for his excessive and incompetent leadership. Harry, the college graduate yoga buff, had openly confronted him at a Brethren meeting. To Harry's surprise, others joined in, some declaring that the Brethren as Roy ran it was a "police state." After saying he would consider what had been said, Roy had come down to make peace with Roamer in his truck, but found himself under attack at the campfire just as he had been earlier on the hill within his own group. Sensing that the focus of the struggle had shifted from one between communes to one between him and everybody else, Roy probably used his largely nonverbal techniques to rally personal support in his own group and deflect rational criticism.

Roy did the same thing on the hill that next evening right before the near brawl with the psychotherapist outside the cookshack. A meeting among the Brethren had gotten underway and even greater support came out for Harry's position in opposition to Roy. But Madelaine had gotten hysterical again, diverting attention from the cool point by point critical attack they were launching. One of Roy's supporters remarked that only the "crazies" and "half whacked out" had objections to Roy and his demands for tight organization and obedience. Just as Madelaine was calming down, a Brethren woman rushed into the meeting to tell Roy that she had seen JM people drinking beer down below. Roy then leaped up whooping like an Indian, and charged down the hill with his supporters close behind, thereby avoiding the imminent attack by his fellow members.

Finding he had considerable support within the Brethren, Harry went over Roy's head to James and the entire Brethren at their center. He had been through the commune network across the country for the last two years and considered himself quite level-headed. Awestruck by the Brethren's potential, he didn't know if his joyous reactions were signs of "ecstasy or of lunacy." Nevertheless he saw the aims of the Brethren as worthwhile and trusted James (though at times he had doubts). Roy, on the other hand, was destroying James' vision. The Brethren had many confused and insecure people in it and Roy took advantage by trying to "capture their weak egos." Unity required that everyone like each other, and though most people didn't like Roy at first, he kept hammering away, asserting they would destroy the unity if they didn't have faith and trust in him. Apparently most new persons found themselves liking Roy against their better judgment. But it was always on Roy's terms, and he ended up demanding total psychic surrender, Harry concluded.

A grand meeting was held at the Brethren center at which Harry raised his objections. According to second-hand information, Harry's challenge was favorably received by some members, and attacked by others. The usual recrimination of "If you don't like the Brethren, why don't you leave?" was heard. And Roy's position as one of the original disciples was in the end unshakable. He would remain as leader of the Wilfred group, but would be expected to follow a much softer approach in the future. Harry concluded that the principles he originally saw in the Brethren had been abandoned, and when his son by a previous marriage came to live with him, he drifted away from the Brethren to more fatherly affairs. Three weeks later he left, and when last heard from, he was running his own yoga institute in another part of the country.

From that time on, the conflict between the two communes de-escalated, partly by design and partly because of newly emerging priorities for the Brethren. Money and economic maintenance became an overriding concern, despite their supposed non-materialistic attitudes. The publicity in the newspapers about the Brethren's big building plans attracted the attention of the welfare people, who cut off nearly $700 in monthly food stamp aid. The Brethren had lost its major source of financial support. Anticipated income from the rock band did not materialize. The time and effort-consuming job of making tape recordings dragged on over the summer without fame and fortune coming their way. Much of the entire commune's monetary resources had gone into equipping the band with sound systems, instruments, a special practice studio, and a large truck to haul the equipment. After the local medium and spiritual guide-father figure broke with the Brethren, the band had become the primary vehicle for channeling group commitment. With all the trouble with the Wilfred venture, it just didn't make sense to pour more resources into the Meadows.

Furthermore, even if the Brethren legally obtained title to the land, realistically, the town would probably not grant a building permit. Finally, the prospect of having to pay for the land loomed increasingly disturbing when viewed in combination with the other financial pressures. Despite having obtained good terms (no money down and 10 years to pay), the burden of a large mortgage became even less appealing when a woman spiritualist friend of the Brethren offered to sell her huge house for half the price of the Meadows.

The Brethren opted to buy the house. The deal for the Brethren to buy the Meadows was never consummated. They remodeled the new house, concentrated on the band, and continued to struggle and eventually win the zoning fight with the town in which their center was located. But this information was kept from Brethren residents in Wilfred, and JM members. Thus, JM spent the rest of the summer in a state of apprehension, not knowing what would happen, still assuming some kind of final struggle or rapprochement with the Brethren would be necessary at some point. But despite the August 31st deadline, life became more tolerable, even pleasant, as Brethren pressure on JM virtually ceased. But so did virtually all contact, except among those in each group who had become good friends. Only one more Brethren member eventually joined JM.

Although JM didn't know it, the Brethren colony was now being maintained on the land in order to earn money. Many Brethren were working at unskilled, low paying jobs in the area, and turning all their earnings in to the commune. Since the Brethren at their main center had already saturated the job market in that area, it was advantageous to stay in Wilfred as long as possible and saturate the Centerville area as well.

August 31st arrived and passed. Although there was a competition between Brethren and JMers in town over jobs, this caused no animosity. Some JMers were actually happy they couldn't find work so they could go back on food stamps.

One night, there was even a joint Brethren-JM sing before the Brethren packed up its tents and moved them back up the hill. JM made assurances it was putting itself together by working more and getting high less, while the Brethren declared it was possible for them both to live on the land. There was no celebration of peace; only a cool détente, with Roy now maintaining that he had used his harsh and bizarre techniques all along to bring about this peace. Nearly everyone guffawed at Roy's attempt to escape blame and take credit. One JM member protested that he was still up to his old tricks by lying to people even now. After that, people on both sides loudly urged Roy to demonstrate that he was not perfect, and that he was still changing and growing, by asking him to admit that he had just lied. To everyone's amazement, he did admit it, and quickly left.

With the deadline safely past and JM Peter having returned from more travels and living with JM instead of the Brethren, a collective sigh of relief was heaved. Although some people sat back enjoying the state of affairs as if a great burden had been taken off their shoulders, others realized that the real battle with an even more formidable adversary was about to begin. Winter. These people busied themselves chopping wood, patching up the interior of the cookshack, and trying to repair an old pickup truck that Parson's Crossing had given JM.

The day after the deadline, Peter walked to the top of Eagle's Claw and sat on the same spot where nearly a year and a half previously he had experienced the presence of Earth Mother, Indians, and blood on the land. Pondering what to do, he was deeply disturbed. This Karmic dispute between himself and James would have to be postponed until another lifetime. He had wanted to see some energetic human effort at spiritual good come to the land, but with the fading of the Brethren from the scene, any chance of that seemed remote. Also, while some people were still involved in drink and drugs, and others were working feverishly preparing for the winter, everyone still seemed to be disregarding the most important reasons for living communally in the first place. There were completely new faces at JM, but it was the same old process. He didn't want to be responsible for the repeat disaster he regarded as sure to come, but conscience would not let him throw the people off the land. Finally, JM had not only prevented the sale of the land to the Brethren, but virtually made it impossible to sell the land to anyone else. Peter was stuck with the whole mess and would not be able to do anything else until he got rid of it.

Rather than see his dilemma in mundane terms, Peter instead looked out over the Meadow and saw a small black cloud move across the clear sky. There it hovered, casting a dark gray shadow over the cookshack, while all around it the grass and trees glistened in the bright sunshine. Not only was this a bad omen, but it was communicating something to Peter: destroy the cookshack before the people it housed destroyed each other. He leaped to his feet and dashed down the mountain, ran up to the cookshack, and grabbed a sledge hammer. After coolly walking past the cooks for the day, climbing the stairs to the second floor and stepping over people still in bed there, he started swinging the sledge hammer at the walls, sending boards flying off in all directions.

The reaction to this new crisis was all too familiar. The hippie wing was either paralyzed by indecision ("Peter must be doing it for a reason, so even if it's my home I guess it's O.K."), or withdrew from it, unable to face what was happening (one, for example, picked up a book and went outside in the grass to read while people were running around screaming and boards were cracking and splintering). The women from the street people faction were outraged, but afraid to go near Peter and his sledgehammer. One stood screaming at the hippie men and the kids from Peter's home town, "Aren't you fuckers going to do something? After all this, after all you've been through this summer, you're going to stand there and let this bastard destroy your home?" The intellectual wing was scattered about the land and at Parson's Corners doing work chores, and had not heard the racket. Finally they were summoned by the women. They arrived and began talking to Peter, demanding he stop.

With two sides of the upstairs section of the cookshack knocked out, Peter stopped, sat down on one of the mattresses, and was quickly surrounded. Asked how long he had been planning this, Peter denied any forethought, explaining how he saw the cloud over the cookshack and JM in a death spin, and sought to prevent it. After much discussion and mutual criticism, Peter decided not to pursue his intention to demolish the cookshack, hoping his attempt had jolted people into an awareness of the destruction path they were on in a way words never would have. Thus, JM survived another crisis.

As the weather got sufficiently cold that the Brethren could no longer live on the hill comfortably in tents, the group which by now had diminished to fifteen packed up and left. Some JM people helped load the last truck out, with Roy not saying a word to them, in contrast to his usual chattering and proselytizing. Some Brethren people warned that Roy saw the Brethren's exit as a personal defeat for him. Not only had he failed in establishing his Wilfred colony, but his base of power within the entire commune was being dismantled. Thus, JM should be wary of Roy in the future.

Afterwards, Brethren reappeared on the land from time to time to cart away trash they had left there. One November day, DT, Zeke, and one of the young people from Peter's home town who was rapidly picking up the IBM lifestyle, were by the cookshack when they heard an inordinate amount of noise coming from the house on stilts. They ran up the road to find Roy and three other Brethren standing on the roof pulling up roofing and boards. The JMers scrambled up to the roof and the young fellow from JM grabbed Roy around the head with his arm and punched him squarely in the face. Roy screamed that he would call in the police, and DT answered that it would be fine with him because Roy would be charged with trespassing. The other Brethren said they had no idea the house was occupied; one going so far as to apologize to DT. Roy had lied to them, saying it was left over from the Brethren occupation, and that it should be dismantled. After threatening to come back with the rest of the Brethren for revenge, Roy and their others left, never to return again.

Analysis

In effect, Jackson's Meadows' inarticulate strategy had succeeded. JM's wine, women, and partying actually did disrupt the Brethren's internal cohesion, though it also escalated the level of conflict. Also significant was DT's defection from the Brethren to JM. The search for allies proved to be very important, too. It was especially disturbing to the Brethren to find that a majority of outside people preferred the dirty, disorganized rabble from the Meadows over the spiritually pure Brethren. Obtaining allies, moreover, established insecurity in the Brethren, creating the fear of potential rather than actual threat. The Brethren's fear of armed revolutionaries made the alliance seem far more important than it really was.

Attracting public attention, which drew the town into the struggle, was eminently successful; so much so that JM also was threatened. Ridding Wilfred of the Brethren gave the town the confidence that it could handle any hippie problem. The revolutionaries blamed the Brethren's demise on their mistakenly thinking that the battle was with JM, rather than with the town. But other freak observers felt that the revolutionaries underestimated JM's threat to the Brethren. This was due, they said, to the radicals' ideological efforts always to place blame on the SS. The divide-and-conquer approach to turn the Brethren against its own leadership worked to some extent. But isolating Roy from his membership also made him desperate, which was potentially dangerous for all concerned.

JM's policy of the free flow of information definitely worked. Researching Brethren legal and financial activities, calling the Brethren's bluff concerning the ownership of the land, and disseminating embarrassing information about the leadership weakened the Brethren internally. Finally, JM's minimal organization and great flexibility, in effect, quickly depleted the Brethren's patience and intelligence, leading them to hasty and counterproductive actions. JM appeared at first to be a vacuum into which the tight knit Brethren could rush with impunity, but instead, JM exerted the pressure that vacuums generate, pulling the Brethren apart. There was such physical and emotional energy expenditure by the Brethren that they lost their will to fight, hence their "negative energy" analogy was not too inaccurate. Not having unlimited resources to pour into the struggle, they eventually had to withdraw and maintain a safe distance.

What was the outcome in terms of cost-benefits? At the institutional level, both the SS and the CC benefited, for both were able to assert influence and maintain a degree of control over an area where they had none before. Many CC people outside the Free Provincia movement, such as Parson's Crossing, regarded the Brethren withdrawal from their community as a blessing. At the group level there were mixed results. While the Brethren lost their Wilfred colony, resources diverted from JM went into other successful enterprises. Some Brethren even claimed they learned some important lessons, finding they could not force their way of life on other people without expecting a backlash. JM survived as an entity, but the seeds had been sown for later troubles.

At the clique level, JM picked up two new drink-and-party people, and the conflict with the Brethren exacerbated already-strained relations between the street people and the hippies. In fact, the unity that often prevailed at JM during the height of the Brethren conflict indeed deteriorated as street people shifted alignment to oppose the hippies and part time intellectual members on the issue of work and preparation for the winter. Changes had also taken place at the individual level. Within days after the last confrontation with the Brethren, approximately three fourths of the people left the land to travel. Upon returning, it was difficult for many to begin preparing for the winter. Some expressed a fear that JM might never settle down. Others gained strength through the struggle, most notably Roamer, who at the beginning of the summer found it emotionally difficult to wash a tub of dishes, and who ended up being chief peacemaker and organizer behind projects to prepare for the winter. Others too, for the first time in their lives, began to realize their actions could positively affect their environments and personal situations.

Also, almost everyone began to expand their horizons socially; realizing that not only could one not escape certain elements of the outside world, but that it was impossible to survive without encouraging contact with it. The conflict taught individuals some important lessons on the nature of the CC. The myth of the CC embodying a unified, joyous world view with which to usher in the New Age was blown. People began to see that all evil, deceit, insensitivity, and insanity weren't limited to the "establishment." They had also experienced the dangers of what Yale called "Commune Chauvinism," being so exclusively concerned with internal communal matters that the crucial task of establishing relations with others suffered. Finally, all had been exposed to the abuses and dangers of charismatic and autocratic leadership.

Above are the more obvious consequences, but what about the more subtle processes at work? Processes described in this chapter laid the groundwork for future social forms and events. The discussion that follows takes up five concerns: 1) the role of conflict in social systemic operation; 2) the fundamental importance and control of the material basis of social systems; 3) the role of ideologies and communications in determining social forms; 4) the significance of entropic vs. negentropic operational modes; 5) the mechanism for growth and development of social systems.

With respect to the first concern, both conflict and equilibrium dynamics seem to be crucial in accounting for this latest stage of JM's development. Each group sought to maintain a certain level of stability, as individuals in both groups who proved too disruptive were ejected. This ejection process was rarely smooth and peaceful, as internal conflicts precipitated the loss of people while bolstering equilibrium. But total equilibrium was never achieved in either group. Thus, though there was a tendency for the system to control the extremes of disruption, the very nature of the systems created disequilibrium and disruption, both internally and externally; particularly when in conflict.

The feedback process (specifically, negative feedback) is often regarded in equilibrium theory as the mechanism by which homeostasis is achieved (Hardin: 1968). Based on the information received, the system can change or continue its actions according to the degree of its successes or failures in achieving certain goals. Conflict, however, is a major source of negative feedback, generating information that can have a homeostatic effect, but more likely one that will create significant change. Because conflict often involves severe threat to the system involved, more resources are mobilized and the stakes in general are higher than in situations where no serious obstacles are met. The outcome is often manifested in radical change in which the system can be destroyed, can have its structure drastically altered in the face of defeat, or can have it significantly rearranged so as to pursue further ends as a result of victory. Or the system can change so thoroughly that it is transformed into a different system altogether. In the case of this study, it was the constant mobilization to meet challenges to the system that kept the system together and gave it its organizational form.

Second is the fundamental role of basic material resources and modes of control over them. Despite all the ideological obfuscation, access to physical support was at the root of the struggle between JM and the Brethren. The survival and growth of both groups was at stake. Though many participants chose not to see it, the most obvious bone of contention was the issue of ownership of material property. Despite talk of the rejection of materialism by both sides, it played a fundamental part in their nonmaterial schemes, and the most critically important material property was, of course, the land. Some attributed great spiritual qualities to it, others found it aesthetically outstanding, and still others were interested in its plant and animal life. But the Brethren also needed it as a place upon which to build their citadel and to provide a buffer between them and the outside world so that internal unity could be achieved. JM people needed the Meadows for shelter and food and as an enclave for activities not permissible elsewhere. In other words, all activities, no matter how exalted or mundane, had to take place on the earth, and as far as forms of property were concerned, none was more valuable than the land. When Peter said that there was land everywhere, implying that there was no need to struggle over one particular piece, he was correct in principle, but in fact he was wrong, for not all people had equal access to, or use of available land. Furthermore, moving from place to place entailed the disruption of the group. Purchasing new land required money which could only be acquired by drastically altering the lifestyles and nature of the group. Thus, land was actually a very scarce resource, particularly when one group wanted complete control over the Meadows.

Those who controlled the Meadows could determine its quality of life by regulating the number and kinds of people who could enter and leave, the times and frequency of entrance or exit, and the variety and amounts of materials and tools people carried with them. They could also dictate the distribution of individuals, their living arrangements, and the kinds of activities they performed. Theoretically, they could even attempt to control thought and consciousness through information regulation by declaring which books, periodicals, or individuals could exist on it, and by limiting the use or ownership of radios, TVs, or drugs. No one, of course, had total control over JM, and this was due largely to a number of other directly and indirectly competing interests in the land, such as certain individuals, other communes, and the town. At the center of the conflict were the Brethren and JM, and the most fundamental issue that separated them with regard to the land was the same one that characterized the operation of each group: a cumulatively manifested self-regulatory system vs. a centrally-controlled system.

JM, with its loose organizational form and no strictly defined leadership, had a loose orientation regarding use of the land. Except for such universally shared values as non-pollution of the stream, non-destruction of live vegetation, and very limited use of machines and motor vehicles, people were essentially free to do as they wished. JM could tolerate the Brethren's presence so long as they didn't attempt to organize JM's activities. JM claimed that use of the land should be determined by individual and collective needs as they arose. They had built up certain minimal routines of land use and there was no reason to interfere with this state of existence.

The Brethren leadership not only wanted to control its own members, but also wanted that control extended to include all people on the land; namely JM. Recognizing that a chain was only as strong as its weakest link, it felt that JM presented a potentially debilitating threat to its organizational tightness. Accordingly, the competing system had to be destroyed, either by dispersing its component people, or preferably by pulling them into itself and reorganizing them according to its own systemic pattern. This way, the Brethren could grow at the same time. Land use would not be determined by individual preferences and mutually self-adjusting patterns, but by direction from an enlightened leadership. This leadership, in turn, was legitimized by divine order, which the leadership had privy to.

The third major interest was Peter, the legal owner, who by virtue of the concept of legality drew in the fourth major interest, the SS. Ownership was a status conferred upon a person by a recognized authority which had the power to enforce that status. But by the same token, no owner had complete control over that land. If degree of control can be interpreted as degree of ownership, then the town, state, and federal governments were in effect part owners. In return for legitimating a degree of control for the owner by issuing a deed, established legal authority reserved some rights of its own. Aside from collecting taxes (a kind of rental charge), having the ability to claim extensive use when it saw fit (right of eminent domain), and enforcing certain behavior codes on it (criminal law), the established authority had control over certain uses of the land itself. These, in the case of Wilfred, included the creation of a water supply, waste disposal, and the construction and location of edifices. Moreover, the town could limit the number of people living in each abode and could define the legal relationship between them to qualify them for residence. These were very extensive rights, almost rivaling those of the Brethren tried to enforce. In return, the town offered legally declared owners the use of roads, schools, fire protection, police protection, and the like.

Established authority could not, however, directly determine what kinds of people lived on the land and how they normally behaved. Control here could only be exercised through the selective use and enforcement of the previously maintained legal rights. Laws ostensibly passed for purposes of safety and welfare could be used to force compliance with extralegal social and ideological norms. If the town or its officials didn't like the people or the lifestyle in communes, through strict law enforcement they could interfere with the commune to the point of paralysis. If it could not be proved that taxes were paid, the land could be confiscated. If it could be proved that laws were broken, people could be arrested and fined. If people did not follow specific codes regarding land use, the use of resources could be forcibly halted and fines levied. This would include finding bacteria in the water supply, flies in the outhouse, buildings in disrepair, people living in the wrong buildings, and too many non-kin living under one roof. Finally, if the legally-declared owner wished to enforce his rights to choose the specific people he wanted on the land, civil authority would be only too happy to enforce criminal trespass law.

In short, governmental authority could impose regulatory influence on the communal system from the outside. The town used its regulatory authority to halt certain Brethren activities, in effect giving them no choice but to leave the land as the seasons changed (climate being a non-social regulatory force). The Brethren wanted to use the same town authority to oust JM so they could use the JM buildings that were built before the enactment of zoning legislation. But they could not do so because they were not recognized as legal owners of the land. Peter and the Buddhist were the legal owners, and neither of them gave their permission for the town to evict JM. The Brethren, therefore, substituted their antinomian divine order and authority for SS sociopolitical order and authority so that JM could be forced out even without civil law. The end result was that the more centrally-controlled social systems, the Brethren and the town, canceled each other out, leaving JM, the more self-regulatory system, surviving and operational, even if significantly changed.

Peter, by virtue of being a legal owner, was a participant in the SS legal system. Yet his ideological orientation held that in the Aquarian Age, land should be open to all and that no one should be forced to move. Thus, while tied to a controlled system, he supported a self-regulatory system. In this way, he canceled himself out, his two opposed partisan positions leaving him in effect neutral. He could have been stronger in his support of JM by permitting them exclusive use of part of the land, but then he would not have been able to sell the rest of the land.

Aside from the four social entities with direct interests in the land, were four with indirect but parallel interests. First was Yale, a potential legal owner who could do nothing but choose to support one or more of the direct participants in the struggle because he had no money to purchase the land himself.

Second, were the other communes who sided with JM. They, too, functioned on a self-regulatory basis, but there was more than an anarchist philosophy that gave them common interests with JM. The other communes feared that the Brethren would attempt to force them to sell their land. Also, they loathed the attention that Brethren activities were bringing to Wilfred. Stricter zoning regulations that would possibly be passed by the town to control the Brethren would certainly affect them as well. Moreover, the traffic on the road past their land created constant disturbance. Finally, the Brethren themselves were a personal hazard as they stopped in occasionally to proselytize.

Third, were the SS townspeople, who, siding neither with JM nor with the Brethren, did favor a controlled system so they could determine events at JM.

Because most citizens were not prepared to take enforcement measures into their own hands, they urged the town government to do so for them. Townspeople feared for their safety on the roads, the local water table level, and for milk production by their cows. They also were upset by nude bathing at public swimming areas. But beyond these were other fears. Would the skyrocketing influx of hippies place a local tax burden on them if their children went to the schools, if they abused town facilities, or if they demanded road improvements into their lands? The townspeople already knew their federal tax dollars were being used for welfare benefits. There was also the probability that the land values would go down. And most frightening was the prospect of eventually losing political control of the town to the growing numbers of hippies who would then make their own land use laws.

Fourth was the Free Provincia Movement who, like government, regarded itself as acting in the interests of a definite constituency even if there existed no electoral structure to select its representatives. And like the town, it was aware that the foundations of human activity, and therefore power, rested on the kinds of access to, and uses of, the land. Unlike the town, however, they championed self-regulatory systems. With the slogan "power to the people," they sought to replace the system of centralized regulatory power that was controlled by particularly powerful interests with a system of their own. Free Provincia had launched a movement to challenge SS authority while attempting to organize the CC into a larger, coordinated, more inclusive, self-regulatory system that could eventually replace it.

Thus, the primary importance of land as the basis for material support of human activities became very apparent. This was so despite ideological assertions that spiritualism or humanism were the only considerations operating. Even after the struggle subsided, both groups had to turn toward pressing economic problems related to land use. The Brethren had to find jobs to earn money to pay off the purchase of the house they obtained in lieu of the land, and JM began preparing for a winter existence on the land and earning money to pay the taxes. Non-material concerns, however, were not unimportant. The ideological assumptions were the factors that sculptured the course of the struggle and molded the nature of the outcome. Words and beliefs, as the most easily noticed aspects of human interaction, achieved significance only in proportion to the value of the material resources that supported the humans involved.

Next, is the crucial role of ideological beliefs in shaping specific social events and outcomes based on material concerns. Ideological stances at JM were certainly not at all unimportant. The importance of the material stakes and the incompatible types of social systems involved were crucial factors in making the struggle so intense. But beyond these were the belief systems by which people sought to make sense of their environment. In the JM-Brethren struggle, the ideological clash served to amplify the conflict beyond the limits it normally should have reached.

A primary factor was the self-contained and the almost universal scope of belief system operating within the Brethren. In a protected environment cut off from the outside world, this Brethren totalistic ideology appeared more empirically verifiable to them than non-spiritual logicoscientific explanation. The Brethren had a well-articulated ideology to go along with their well-organized group. The ideology was expansionist, seeking to include increasing kinds of phenomena into its rubric. To the extent the ideology was not shared, there was also social dissension and cleavage within the group. JM, on the other hand, had a mixed bag of ideologies that varied from person to person. There was, of course, some degree of commonality, otherwise all members wouldn't have struggled to the extent they did. As a belief system, however, it was as entropic as the social organization.

But no matter its coherence and elaborateness, any ideology easily can be held and further developed within a protected environment, such as that provided by a commune. The communal organizational form is particularly conducive to the formulation and expansion of new belief systems (just as it is to embryonic social organizational forms). One evolved at JM emerging with the apocalyptic-spiritual vision of the first summer on the land, and certainly one grew within the Brethren. And so, too, did they develop in all the other communes in the area. As example: a kind of romantic "Waldenism" emerged from the Parson's Crossing Karass, revolutionary socialist anarchism evolved at Red Rose Collective, and radical feminism appeared at Rainbow Farm. General beliefs that vaguely appealed to people who joined turned specific and complex through internal amplification, restricted external feedback, and constant honing due to members pointing out to one another individuals' thought and behavioral inconsistencies. The incubative environment that a commune provided was very important in allowing a coherent world view to form before slowly being whittled away by random exposure to empirical facts evolving from changing circumstances. Given that chance to solidify, however, it could serve as a very strong force in radical social change attempts.

What made ideology particularly important in the Brethren-JM struggle was the spiraling effect it had on the Brethren. When it was tested and found to be lacking vis-a-vis JM, the negative feedback from the testing was disregarded with disbelief. Their belief system had become too strong and rigid. Instead of readjusting their own possible misconceptions, the Brethren leadership, mistaking enthusiasm for accuracy, redoubled its efforts to force events to conform to the design it worked by. Thus, with each episode the intensity escalated. While behavior was becoming more and more extreme as belief was being increasingly and more rigidly invoked, the already serious situation was compounded by the interplay between the two groups. Although JM was not guided by any one coherent belief system, it was motivated by an elevating desire for survival as it was increasingly pressed. Thus, the Brethren had to respond to increasingly intensified resistance.

The final catalyst in the explosive ideological mix, regardless of the content of the belief system, was the fact that the two of them were so completely different from each other in many ways. The spiritual wing of JM believed for a while that it could perform a mediational role. They were wrong, however, for their spiritual beliefs did not have that much in common with the Brethren's;

specifically where the role of material concerns was involved. Not only was there no bridge between the two groups that could serve as a guide for action and the prediction of reaction, but there was virtually no mutually encompassing context within which they were interacting. Neither group acted according to the codes and regulations that bound most SS enemies together. Even though they both consciously considered themselves participants in the CC, there were as yet no pervasive common behavioral rules for both to follow. In short, there was a very real fear that anything could happen, including the worst, and the depth of fear experienced by the people involved should not be underestimated. In the end, however, long range interests and material realities prevailed as the Brethren backed away, got jobs, and moved to new facilities.

Another issue is the organizational modes of control that emerge and their relative efficacies. Given the fundamental importance of material concerns and the ideologies that developed to interpret social and environmental events, a most important consideration yet to be addressed was the way these two systemic aspects manifested themselves together in an ongoing situation. What, indeed, was the systemic nature of the actual organization of events? The key factor in the actual use of the land, for example, seemed to be the overall organizational mode of the people controlling it. At one end of the spectrum of organizational modes was a self-regulatory system (JM), and at the other end was highly purposeful and directed system (the Brethren). Aside from competition for scarce resources, conflict seemed to be generated by the very nature of the difference between the types of systems. The more entropic, slow, easy-going group was particularly upset by demands of the more negentropic hard-driving group, and the latter in turn feared disintegrative influences from the former. This phenomenon (the case between two very different modes of operation) was in fact at the root of many conflicts at all levels of organization, ranging from individuals to coordinated superstructures.

But the severity of organizational form of both groups changed through the process of conflict. The Brethren, despite Roy's escalating efforts to hold it together (or perhaps because of them), developed serious internal divisions, with the end result that the entire organization permanently loosened up to a certain extent. Centralized leadership and planning, though capable of mobilizing activity and creating enormous energy and enthusiasm, could not gather and process all the many more subtle forms of information important for proper guidance of their conduct. Though effective in the short run, it ended in failure because of the inflexibility of the leadership and an inability to adapt sufficiently to new and changing complex situations.

While the Brethren failed to foresee the attitude of the town, the most important factor was the change in JM itself. Just as the Brethren loosened in the confrontation, JM tightened. Under pressure, JM had the choice of falling apart altogether, or mobilizing resources, information, and people to meet its challenge. Regular meetings were organized, work tasks assigned, specialized functions delegated, and the whole pace of activity accelerated. Specialized roles and the interdependence of people could be maintained within a systemic framework by having everyone know how it all fit together. Thus JM's growing negentropization still maintained a self-regulating character. While the Brethren membership essentially served as an action instrument only, virtually everyone in JM became full-fledged participants in the organizing and decision-making. They did so, despite tremendously varying skills, abilities, and interests, because they were forced to. They believed their very lives were being threatened.

In the developmental cycle of communes included in this study, there was first a formative fusion phase followed by a phase involving desocialization and simplification of behaviors. This in turn evolved either into a disintegrative spiral ending in dissolution, or into some organizational form whereby continuity could be achieved. The imposition of regularizing controls was accomplished either by deliberate action of members or by situational factors. External situational factors, such as ecological or economic considerations, and the internal dynamics of interpersonal distancing, combined to create a more or less "defusioned" yet adherent social entity. The adherent effect was achieved by differentiation and exchange between the specialized, interdependent parts; the media of exchange (material resources and information) cementing them together.

The tendency for relatively self-contained systems to run down (entropize) and eventually collapse is well known (Lazlo: 1972). Prolongation or postponement of the process can be achieved not only by stabilizing support systems vis-a-vis various external environments, but by recreating the initial conditions of the internal environment, as well. Thus, the alternative means of communal perpetuation beyond regularization was renewal. Again, either by design or by externally imposed crises, commonality of purpose and camaraderie could temporarily rebind certain people into a new near-fusion state resembling the Dobson House period of JM. It is quite probable that both means occurred simultaneously in varying degrees. Thus, the phase of JM's development discussed in this chapter precipitated by the conflict with the Brethren, led to the extension of both increased regularization and renewal processes, thereby increasing its chances for survival after the immediate threat posed by the Brethren had passed.

Finally is the issue of growth and development of social systems, the ultimate dynamic behind the processes discussed so far. The struggle between JM and the Brethren illustrated some important principles in the expansion and evolution of CC forms specifically, and social systems in general. Although there was some deliberate planning for growth on the part of the Brethren, most other groups opposed the concept, indicating that it smacked of big business and government. But growth occurred despite overall ideological resistance and lack of planning. Even in groups where it was regarded as desirable, it usually occurred in surprising, unanticipated ways.

At the individual level, both demographic and psychological changes contributed to the process. In terms of numbers alone, JM, the Brethren, and most other CC groups were expanding their membership. Many individuals were still dropping out of the SS in order to find more rewarding alternatives in the CC. They could not, however, abstractly join or participate in the CC in a general sense. Because the CC in Provincia was composed of specific people and groups, they had to enter into relationships with these concrete people and groups.

This in turn created unforeseen problems. Greater numbers of people generated a larger demand for resources in terms of living space, food, fuel, and the like. Accordingly, individuals and the groups to which they belonged were forced to adapt to these new circumstances by changing either their tolerance levels (putting up with unexpected hardships in order to realize a greater goal) or their behavior (struggling harder to obtain desired resources). In either case, the character of the social environment that led people to join various groups in the first place changed. Those who had calculated the advantages of the slower paced, cooperative, personally rewarding small group CC life, helped change these very attributes by virtue of joining. Unwittingly, they contributed to conditions that often led to hectic turmoil, competition and conflict, and impersonal relations with the growing numbers of people.

The character of the CC growth process was also significantly determined by the emotional as well as the calculating, rational nature of the people it attracted. Although some saw communes as vehicles for social and personal change, others joined them as a last resort. These people had been unwilling or unable to function in other institutional settings, such as family, school, or place of employment. Yet, while being extremely wary of social or institutional obligations and restrictions, they also complained of loneliness and the need to feel a part of something. The emotionally disturbed found themselves in a particularly unfortunate situation in terms of discomfort. They had greater affiliative needs because of their exclusion from much of normal social intercourse, but because of interpersonal fears and past confinements in their homes, schools, or hospitals, they were deeply upset and distrustful of any commitments to any groups or alternative institutions that could meet these needs.

This general alienation from group or institutional goals permitted some individuals to perceive extremely clearly, from a distance, social processes that others participated and got caught up in, particularly when group aims supported by commitment and loyalty were leading to dangerous excesses and counterproductive results. It was no wonder that in the heat of conflict between JM and the Brethren, the emotionally unstable, in some cases the legally insane, could see the insanity in the struggle that ostensibly normal participants were blind to. Yet because of the "normals'" need for allies and support in the struggle, those who remained aloof or ambivalent were seen as "crazies," apparently continuing the same kind of behavior that originally caused SS institutions to label them as disturbed. Thus, if the drive for individual survival were equated with sanity, it could be argued that many societal contexts, composed of conforming majority members, can be "crazy," while its emotionally tortured, erratic minority malcontents are not.

Yet by the same token, if self-destructive or self-defeating behavior can be regarded as a major factor in poor individual mental health, then from another perspective the societally imposed "crazy" label might be valid. While the alienated and disturbed could perceive serious shortcomings in their social environment, they often were oblivious to the advantages. They often would not struggle to keep or obtain necessary resources to support themselves, preserving tranquillity for the present, while laying the foundation for even greater crises in the future. By refusing to participate in the sometimes unpleasant social processes necessary to obtain and keep land, housing, or friends, they became more vulnerable to the demands of others, reducing their own abilities to create the kinds of environments they desired. Seeking peace and harmony, they constantly found themselves at odds with their human environment.

The advantages of conforming to group pressures had a value beyond making life easier on a day to day basis. By fully belonging and accepting less than perfect conditions as far as each individual was concerned, each shared in the rewards that only the coordinated efforts of more than one person could achieve. While some people on both sides of the JM-Brethren struggle were critical of their own group, they did not want to see the destruction of that group. Their respective communes and fellow communards helped to feed and shelter them, provide companions, and give them a sense of worth and importance by virtue of direct social interaction and task performance. While dissent concerning specific group activities is necessary to avoid serious errors, constant criticism and withdrawal from participation by a sufficient number of people could disrupt all activities, in effect abolishing the group and the services it provided for all members.

Thus, the conflict at the Meadows in many ways could be regarded as a "growing" pain. Growth in membership in the groups led to competition over scarce resources. That in turn forced both groups to seek new members and additional outside resources, thereby escalating the growth that caused the problems in the first place. The alternative to struggle and possible defeat was certain defeat, group mortality, and all that it implies for the individual members of the losing group. If individuals chose to belong to a group, they contributed to its growth, like it or not. If they chose to remain marginal, rather than aiding in an equilibrium or no-growth posture, they often set a destructive spiral in motion.

If the welfare of groups, in this case communes, is considered in addition to that of the individuals in them, then a different but related perspective on growth and development emerges. Many communes reached what appeared to be an upper limit in size, ranging somewhere between 10 to 15 people, often having had more or fewer members at various points in their pasts. As people left to set up their own households or join other groups, they were replaced by new members. Beyond replacement, additional potential members were generally refused. This process was not deliberate or planned, as there was no quota system in operation. Voids in work and social roles were felt and when the "right" person came along, he or she was accepted. If there were no void, visitors who expressed desires to join were often told to start their own communes as the process of formation was an important maturing experience and the admission of any new member might disturb the delicate balance achieved in established groups. Communes which set no limits on numbers either became quite unstable, as was the case with JM, or were forced into making formal internal organizational distinctions such as those developed by the Brethren.

While the Brethren was creating new subgroups within its organization, administered by a central authority, other communes did much the same thing, only in a decentralized way. Hence specific federations of communes evolved, referred to as karasses in this study. The process was deliberate for some, such as the Free Provincia movement, where different groups voluntarily affiliated to achieve a set of sociopolitical goals. New collectives were also set up to colonize additional parts of Provincia. Once established, they were self-governing. On the other hand, the Parson's Crossing Karass evolved with little or no organizational premeditation as people left to establish nearby households, maintaining intricate ties with the original groups and with one another. The only relationship the Brethren established with another commune was the one with JM, and that could hardly be regarded as voluntary. Rather than affiliate, because of scarcity of resources and the authority structure of the Brethren, it instead attempted to absorb JM directly. Thus, in this instance, growth would be achieved by conquest.

Although people constituted the "stuff" from which the Provincian CC arose, communes were the fundamental building blocks that organized them into purposeful activity and periodically catalyzed the formation and maintenance of other types of projects, enterprises, and institutions. The locations of communes, as opposed to individuals or households, were well known, and people flocked to them. Anytime anyone visited them, there was sure to be someone around who could offer some kind of response. Even though any one individual who belonged to a commune might have no resources to pass on to a visitor, as a collective entity, there were indeed extensive resources because they were pooled. If organized aid was needed, requiring a number of individuals, communes could provide the numbers and precoordination.

Communes were attractive also because different ones, varying according to predominant ideology and backgrounds of the membership, could be relied upon to act in rather predictable ways, thereby providing a kind of trustworthy continuity. It was almost understood that if one member would participate, then more than one member would; that if there was any degree of enthusiasm for an action, then there was likely to be more than minimal enthusiasm. In addition, individuals from one commune sought the company and aid of other communards, and non-communal freaks in the area when given the opportunity, largely preferred to visit or participate in communally sponsored activities. Communes and collectives at this stage were the focal points of virtually all noteworthy CC activity in the area. Thus, in a sea of floating individual longhairs, communes stood out as islands; more visible, more solid, and better able to support activity. Being the first unit of any kind having more than two or three members, they became loci which tended to attract even more people.

At the level of social movement which encompassed both individuals and communes, the growth process could also be observed, though with mixed results. In a general sense, as the counterculture movement was still growing, SS people continued to drop out into various CC enclaves as kinds of liberated zones. Although the growth of specific groups was generally discouraged by those already in them, nearly everyone supported the growth of the phenomenon of the CC as a whole and the formation of new groups. The fact that these two objectives could be working against each other, however, was not apparent. Eventually somewhere, space and resources would have to become scarce, forcing some groups to attack others, amounting to a kind of movement auto-cannibalism. This, plus active repression on the part of the SS, led to internal organizational shifts that made surviving groups more efficient with respect to the procurement and use of resources.

To make matters even more complicated, the general movement was attracting more people than it could absorb. Individuals upon arrival in Provincia and Centerville usually had to buy land and housing for their own communes and alternative institutions. This was a very difficult task, given overall lack of funds in the anti-materialistic CC and the difficulties involved in previously unacquainted people getting together to do it. Otherwise, they would settle back into the SS socioeconomy as the only alternative for support, in which case they would not be fully joining in the CC movement. Specific movements, such as the Brethren and Free Provincia, attempted to take them in, but these communal networks operated on only the thinnest margins as far as organization and support base was concerned, had built-in limits with respect to ideological intolerance, and were having all sorts of problems of their own. Because people cannot long remain in a general movement of like-mindedness, requiring instead specific social manifestations to keep them physically, emotionally, and ideologically alive and committed, their Provincian experience eventually disillusioned many newcomers.

The total CC composite of specific movements, communal households, and alternative enterprises, however, did constitute an empirically distinguishable society within a society. It is at this level that many details and variations of growth dynamics came together to create one integrated process. Expansion in population size was necessarily accompanied by growing complexity of organization. In the Provincian CC, as more units were created or added to the social system, they tended to develop characteristics that more clearly set them apart from one another. The process by which these differences appeared, differentiation, not only occurred at the communal level and beyond, but took place within each commune as well. The appearance of these differences actually permitted further growth by making specialization and interdependence between more groups possible, thereby enabling new levels of organization, karass, and subsociety, to develop. It also prevented the destruction of some groups by others because of cross-cutting ties between common interest factions in each.

By way of illustrating this process, it can be said that at the outset, there was a relatively undifferentiated "mass" of individuals sympathetic to CC ideals in Provincia. Each person arrived in Provincia for private reasons, nevertheless reflecting an overall pattern of rootlessness and non-affiliation with straight societal institutions. The mass first became differentiated when specific communal groups appeared, putting various individuals into orbit around them.

Shortly afterward, these communes began to take on special characteristics as each evolved on its own path in the Centerville area, predominantly oriented toward radical politics, messianic spiritualism, art, or back-to-the-land lifestyles.

The communal groups constituted situational arenas where different kinds of people would enter, interact, develop relationships, perform certain kinds of tasks together, and be relatively fixed in specific geographic locations. At the same time, however, each commune differentiated internally as well. Cliques or factions were found in each and usually cut across communal boundaries. Although people in these subgroups often performed certain tasks with one another, they did not necessarily form fully interdependent relationships over those tasks. For example, some liked to read and write poetry together, but they did not need each other for substantive exchange. For substantive exchange, the poets traded humorous lines of verse or money earned for the rent by publishing in return for the food gardeners provided or warmth the wood cutters made possible. These exchanges occurred even if the company of gardeners or wood cutters was not preferred over the company of the fellow poets. This implies that comparable communicative skills and shared attitudes initially formed more of a basis for these kinds of intergroup relationships than material or ecological factors which gradually came into prominence as material needs became more apparent. Eventually these initial kinds of preferences and activities were distributed wherever people existed who shared them, particularly from commune to commune. Hence the growing links between communes.

These links, formed on the basis of a common interest, eventually grew to create a larger coordinated CC system. Initial casual contacts then established channels through which later appeals for assistance could be made in times of material or physical need or emergency. Avoiding the remaining relationships maintained with the SS institutions, into which they were usually pressured and whose behavior codes they were often forced to observe, most communards deliberately sought CC help instead wherever they could. In exchange for this help, recipient communes implicitly or explicitly offered their resources to donor communes, for various future struggles. For example, although JM received more than it gave, a strong reciprocal relationship was evidenced by its physical and to some extent ideological (but not material) support of the Free Provincia Movement. Thus, expanded links were established, tying greater numbers of people, ideas, and places together in a direct manner.

Thus, as communes passed through their honeymoon and other initial developmental phases, eventually negentropizing under pressure from financial demands, political activities, interpersonal difficulties or group conflicts, they, like JM and the Brethren, became able to reach out in some manner. As each commune was internally differentiating, members looked outside to establish more mutually advantageous reciprocal relationships. The process of differentiation that was occurring within each commune simultaneously, in effect, meant that it had to be occurring outside each in all of the others as well. Thus, relationships connecting various parts within each to similar but reciprocal parts of the others outside each could develop. In this way an intercommunal network could and did evolve.

The interconnections between the various parts of the differentiating groups were not random. Factions within each commune became important in the growth process. Intellectuals in each sought out intellectuals in the other, people with leanings toward activism found other activists, artists discussed art, and gardeners traded agricultural information and vegetables. Sexual exchanges were made, romances were begun, and drinkers and druggies drank and drugged together. All this was of course done hesitatingly and sporadically at first, but became easier as time went by. Even in the intense struggle between JM and the Brethren, these relationships were established. This helped to prevent a final break between the two; a final cataclysm, and a final total victory of one over the other.

Through alliances in struggle and conflict, the Centerville area CC that was originally more a state of mind than an empirical fact, developed a solid matrix of reciprocal relationships between partly specialized groups. Individuals formed communes, communes aligned themselves into karasses, and karasses loosely associated to constitute the CC. The closest voluntary ties between individuals were established along factional lines within each commune. Specific links between communes in karasses were articulated on a parallel faction-to-faction basis, which in effect were networks of circulating individuals. In turn, interwoven networks held the CC together, by forming partial alliances between karasses. Where the karasses overlapped significantly and the alliances were strongest, was where the CC was best integrated. Thus, the social strands that tied communes, karasses, and the CC together laterally were respectively factions, networks, and alliances. And this occurred as a self-regulating process despite no broad scale planning by some groups and contrary to grand designs for the CC by other groups.

Consequently, the developmental path of JM (and the other communes) beyond a certain point largely depended upon the surrounding CC context. Contacts between groups permitted new interests to flourish and even presented opportunities for shifts in membership by enabling people to leave some to join others. As the CC grew in size and complexity, the differentiation within it permitted a clear specification of exactly what social units and resources existed, and for the people involved, the articulation of various goals regarding these groups and resources. This process essentially constituted a system of constant responses and adaptations to ever-changing conditions. In this overall self-regulating system, positive feedback loops were operating in the form of cooperative efforts and environmental support that led to a direct but sometimes unsteady unfolding and proliferating phenomenon. Negative feedback loops in the form of conflict and ecological pressures tempered or redirected development in a limited but often more solid manner.

Cooperation and conflict were evident in the episode in JM's development as described in this chapter. The Brethren came away from it a little wiser and more tolerant, while JM emerged stronger and potentially more unified, as well as better integrated into the area CC. The critically important role of material support, even in the context of ideologically directed events, was supremely illustrated, though the full impact of the lessons did not reach many of the individuals involved. Ideological excesses did foster economic and ecological disregard, but did so only until these fundamental concerns became so paramount they could no longer go unrecognized or neglected.

An additional fundamental distinction important to note was that between loose organizational patterns and redundant or erratic individual behavior on the one hand, and more organized social patterns with more rigidly specified or complex individual behavior on the other, there were a variety of possibilities. In general, there are situations where either of these systems, entropic or negentropic, have definite adaptive advantages over the other for survival and growth. Within the overall CC, there were many examples of various combinations in between. The Brethren, of course, represented one extreme, and somewhat less organized was the Free Provincia Movement. Even less organized than Free Provincia, but far more organized than JM, were those groups comprising the Parson's Crossing Karass. Of all the communes, JM unquestionably represented the entropic extreme. Although the fates of all the other groups are equally fascinating, by way of clear focus, JM's continued existence is monitored and examined in the following chapters to illustrate further stages of development in the communal and social movement cycles, and to trace the growing significance of hierarchical (as opposed to lateral) distinctions within them.

8. Disintegration: Decline Through Stress and Stratification

After the Brethren struggle, it became obvious to most JM people that they could not remain isolated from the larger hip community. Because many JMers were new to the area, and others had previously remained isolated, everyone continued the process of discovering other freaks and communes in the area. This process was gradual at first, but accelerated suddenly. Until the spring of 1970, most had assumed they and members of a few other groups were the only ones moving to Provincia.

Throughout the Brethren conflict, JMers were aware of Parson's Crossing, Grasshopper, and Rainbow Farms, but while people from these groups were pleasant during infrequent JM visits, they really had no interest in expanding ties to JM. They were involved in other CC activities and in internal difficulties that absorbed their time. Also, sharing different kinds of experiences, they happened to find little in common with most JMers. JM wasn't aware, however, of the ties developing between the other three communes. One member of Grasshopper had shifted to Rainbow and so had Yale, who by mid-summer had very little to do with JM. Occasional visits were made to JM, but only to keep tabs on the latest bizarre events there. As could be expected, it was the intellectual wing of JM that at first had the closest contacts with these three other communes populated by older, more highly educated people.

JM's first friendly contacts with longhairs in the area besides Centerville street people were with the Free Provincia collectives and alternative institutions. A number of different kinds of contacts developed simultaneously. Some were through the search for help in the Brethren struggle, visits by three former JMers who were now Free Provincia people, and use of the alternative garage and restaurant, while others resulted from the deliberate inclusion of JM in Free Provincia's "revolutionary community" building efforts, and eventually, women's consciousness raising meetings.

Some of these points of contact were more important than others. Liberation Garage and especially Vital Victuals Restaurant fulfilled important needs for JM. The Garage, on occasion, was a significant aid to those JMers too poor and mechanically unknowledgeable to get auto aid elsewhere, and the Restaurant served the very important function of providing a regular meeting place in town. Despite the struggles on the land, much of JM's collective time was spent in town getting food, tools, food stamps, books, and guidance from such agencies as the agricultural extension service. Since no straight establishments in town would permit them to hang out, the only place where members could wait until others were through with their errands was the Restaurant. Although there was seldom enough money among JMers to buy meals, gossip was exchanged, putting JM people in contact with other members of the local freak community who also came to the restaurant.

An important role was played by the two Free Provincia collectives in the conflict at the Meadow who in turn almost drew JM into full participation in the Free Provincia Movement. This cautious alliance between JM and the Free Provincia collectives was not without its strains. Free Provincia people saw many JMers as irresponsible, having more of an interest in partying than in fighting to build a revolutionary society. JM's intellectually oriented members were also viewed with mistrust because, as professionals and academicians who still maintained ties with established institutions, they were considered counter-revolutionary. Free Provincia noted wide differences in age, background, and interests at JM and wondered how the place could ever become a real commune capable of concerted and extended action on any worthwhile project. Finally, they could not understand why JM didn't participate in Centerville's alternative institutions more effectively.

Most of JM also questioned Red Rose and Liberation Farm's intentions and their ways of relating to people. Many JMers wanted nothing to do with the organized violence that some revolutionaries advocated in last line self-defense; this despite the fact that JM had incidences of spontaneous, interpersonal violence the political collectives never had. Other JMers did not want to participate in anything capable of putting them in more physical danger than they already had been with the Brethren. Other younger members recalled that their past violent political activities, which included window smashing and running through the streets shouting "Up the ass of the ruling class!" had accomplished nothing except police repression. Others at JM overgeneralized, not perceiving the community organizing and self defense emphases of Free Provincia as being any different from the bombing and rioting approaches of a few underground groups elsewhere.

Added to this was the mixture of apathetic and apocalyptic thinking that led a majority of JM people to believe there was little if anything they could do to change society anyway, and that even if they could, societal collapse was inevitable, if not preordained. Still others, who were not willing to write off participation in a movement completely, failed to consider the role of social institutions in molding their behavior. They often defensively proclaimed "First I will get myself together, then my commune (or friends), and then the revolution." Only those people with college backgrounds had any sense of confidence in themselves and a belief that through action coordinated at an overall community level and beyond could significant social and individual change come about.

JM did however, participate in a confrontation between Free Provincia and the local SS in which the "revolutionary community" challenged exclusive owner rights of use of private, corporately held land. This challenge precipitated the mobilization and deployment of Provincia's entire tactical police force, and culminated in the deliberate harassment of many longhairs by authorities and physical attack by local SS vigilante groups. The confrontation occurred at Free Provincia's Liberation Farm, where most JM people went on Sundays for food, beer, and talk. When the legal owners of the land the farm was situated on, Knowland College, eventually had the participants declared as trespassers and called in the police to evict them, most JMers initially responded with indignation. Some felt an obligation to help Free Provincia in its time of need, as it had helped JM during its conflict with the Brethren. And revolutionary struggle aside, there was also an element of adventure and excitement that attracted many to the fray.

The College had originally approved the initiation of a student farm amid threats of student rebellion during the national student strike in 1970 after the Cambodian invasion. Demanded by students, its ostensible purposes were to teach "relevant" skills, provide the students with healthy fresh food, and allow the College to contribute to the local community by making more of its resources available to local residents. Although the College temporarily acquiesced by granting the go-ahead so as to avoid serious damage through a student rebellion, it became alarmed again weeks later as it saw increasing numbers of off-campus longhairs getting involved. It decided before the reopening of school in the fall to put an end to it by invoking trespass laws.

Free Provincia people by then had become the driving force behind the farm, as students, who wearied of the physical and tedious work, drifted away over the summer. The remaining and newly involved people were incensed by the College's announced moves. For them, many socially responsible principles were being violated by corporate capitalism, as represented by the College in this case. Among these violations were the denial of community use of privately held underutilized property for purposes of the common good, the deliberate break-up of an open, accessible political forum, and the termination of a crucial demonstration project. That project was designed to demonstrate that people, instead of contributing to the excess profits of agribusiness and the ecological damage associated with it, could produce or obtain their own much healthier and tasty food at minimum cost.

In order to thwart the enforcement of trespass laws that they felt protected the interests of the rich and privileged, Free Provincia decided to resist by calling out as many CC supporters as it could so as to make mass arrests of protesters by the small local police force impossible. Half the JM membership showed up at the next weekly Liberation Farm gatherings, only to find that the local police, indeed, had backed off. The following week, however, after tactical planning by law enforcement agencies, they were met by a large state police force that sealed off access. But some JMers, spontaneously led by Vietnam combat experienced DT, circled through the woods behind it to emerge on the far side of the large field. Dozens of other communards soon followed, charging onto the field carrying banners and a flag for the Free State of Provincia that had been designed and circulated by the Free Provincia movement. A CC crowd of hundreds of supporters cheered from the road as troopers and sheriff's deputies scurried about ineffectually trying to catch the younger, leaner cultural revolutionaries.

Taking the preoccupied police entirely by surprise, the crowd then marched down the road, blocking traffic in its wake, to the College itself, where it proceeded to swarm onto and occupy the main part of the campus. A radio call went out immediately to bring in ambulances, paddy wagons, and a special tactical unit trained in riot control which had been surreptitiously stationed some miles away in case of need. While police photographers busily snapped pictures of the protesters, the angry crowd milled about, shouted threats, and demanded continued use of the farm.

After a very intense and potentially explosive period of speech making and negotiating, a settlement was arrived at in which the "the people" would have use of the farm in exchange for leaving the campus peacefully. The College had been trying to stall any action until the riot squad arrived, but as there had apparently been a breakdown in communications. The mob was growing more restless with the passage of time, so the College gave in. As the jubilant crowd left, the special police finally descended on the campus in full riot gear ready to do battle, but it was too late. Certain violence and bloodshed had been very narrowly avoided. Although too involved to go into here, this confrontation had all the ear-marks of the People's Park battle in Berkeley in which one longhair was killed and others were injured.

But JM people, who were very much caught up in the intensity of the moment and contributed significantly to the events of the day, shortly thereafter began to worry. Some who had arrest records and were currently on probation, realized they were violating probation. Others who were sought by various authorities saw that they were unnecessarily exposing themselves. Still others finally concluded that beyond resisting repressive authority, they really didn't understand the reasons behind the events. In the end, most became frightened and feared for their physical safety as events continued to unfold.

The night after the victorious campus confrontation, local men whom the CC referred to as rednecks raided the farm and destroyed the crops. For the rest of the week, hippies were randomly singled out in the area and beat up by carloads of toughs. In response, Free Provincia mounted armed patrol cars of their own to prevent and intercept any further attacks. A furious war of words was waged in the letters to the editor section of the local newspaper in which a deep hostility toward and ignorance of the CC was clearly revealed in the local SS.

The next scheduled gathering at the now devastated farm attracted only a handful of hard core supporters, including a couple from JM, who nevertheless expressed great trepidation about attending. Their worst fears were realized as pickup truckloads of armed youth and men arrived and a bloody fight broke out, though no shots were fired. Once calm was restored, the Liberation Farm defenders were given a simple ultimatum to get out in an hour, or else. After sending some people off to the hospital, the JM people happily agreeing to take them there in order to get out of the situation fast, armed resistance, of which they were fully capable, was briefly discussed by more militant revolutionaries. As the minutes ticked by, the others became increasingly scared for their lives. Finally, a tactical retreat was agreed upon, and as they left, they could see armed men in battle fatigues moving down the brushy hillside on the other side of the field toward the farm.

This retreat seemed only to embolden the vigilantes even more. That night, after defenses were set up around the Red Rose Collective, shots did ring out as a passing cars fired at their house from the road. Isolated JMers nervously watched their lonely but well-known access road for bands of attacking marauders, but to their great relief none materialized. Throughout the period following the capitulation of the College to CC demands, the police became conspicuous, not by their presence, but by their absence. A conspiracy of coordination between the vigilantes and the police became certain to the Free Provincia people when at least one of the attackers at the farm was confirmed to be an off duty policeman.

When word of this apparent conspiracy reached JM, it only served to reinforce the already growing sentiment among most members that participation in the larger CC community was responsible for their fearful and helpless predicament. Many vowed that they would never again stick their necks out for any movement actions. For its part, Free Provincia people reconsidered their organizing strategies, becoming less involved in specific local issues while shifting to less confrontative efforts on a region-wide basis. Thus, through this turn of events, JM's chances for longer-range social and economic stability as part of an evolving countersociety through integration into an expanding network of alternative institutions were significantly reduced.

At the same time, hostile pressure by the town of Wilfred to isolate and weaken JM further was rising. Having gotten rid of the Brethren, the town then moved on the Meadows by insisting that it conform to every code. But because JM already had residential buildings erected before the zoning ordinance went into effect, the town was powerless to evict them on that basis. The buildings, however, barely provided enough space for living, and despite possible challenges by the town, it was decided to convert the storage shed that was attached to the cookshack into a living area with a floor and a door connecting it to the cookshack. A woodshed was needed in addition to a shelter for a pony that Cindy had purchased with a small amount of saved welfare money. People agreed that the pony was trouble to care for, but if it made Cindy happy, then they were glad to put up with it. Cindy did so much work and had such a stable personality, everyone else knew she would be sorely missed if she left. The building inspector refused to give a building permit for this shelter until he was convinced that it would not be heated and insulated, and that no new people would join the commune because of the new space this building potentially opened up.

Other town officials showed up to check the installation of a stove to be sure there was no fire hazard. Not having enough money to get a well drilled, a spring box was sunk near the stream with a hand pump on it. Failing a strict bacteriological test, the water supply also hung over JM's collective head as a potential excuse for eviction. Also, there was a plot afoot to claim that JM didn't pay taxes for the land.

The town peace officer deliberately harassed JM by issuing three summonses to Zeke. They were given to him while he was driving an old pickup truck, hauling firewood on the abandoned road that bordered JM. Despite Zeke's argument that it was a farm vehicle used on the land, one summons was for having an unlicensed vehicle, another for having an uninspected vehicle, and another for unlicensed operation of the vehicle. Fines levied for these tickets could have wiped out all of JM's financial resources. When Zeke came to trial, he borrowed shoes, a shirt, jacket, and tie and dressed so that his commune mates hardly recognized him. He showed up with Boop to show he was a "family man," and Boop borrowed Cindy's baby to emphasize the point. The judge fined him only $15 for the offenses, which JM raised collectively.

Even if this had not been a deliberate case of harassment, which it certainly was, the issuance of the summonses still served to illustrate to JM people how SS laws worked against the CC and the poor. For example, if JM had had sufficient money, it would have gladly registered the vehicle and got it inspected so it could be used to go to town. Also, Zeke would have had a license if he had not opposed the Vietnam War. He did not have a driver's license because he had changed his identity as a means of evading the draft. In any event, the gradual constriction by the town and JM's resulting increasing inability to respond effectively further undermined its attempts to establish itself as a viable part of a supportive social fabric.

Talk of self-sufficiency, barter, reducing financial needs, and antimaterialistic concerns with human and spiritual values notwithstanding, JM's growing isolation had fundamental economic ramifications that affected nearly everything else. Consuming much of the commune's attention, time, and energy was its constant struggle to obtain money. JM was becoming a rural ghetto with a poverty that was neither voluntary nor ennobling. Unlike the first winter when Peter and some others had some cash reserves to bail the commune out of emergencies, there was no one in a comparable position this winter. All commune money had to come from people earning it, and taxes had to be paid, tools, stoves, and insulation had to be purchased, and grains had to be obtained in sufficient quantities to last through the winter. There was a high rate of unemployment in the Centerville area, few enterprises that could use unskilled labor, and a glut of longhairs in the job market. Many people refused to hire longhairs, some out of a general dislike for them, but others because of their high turnover rate.

JM was in a particularly bad position. Full time members needed money desperately, yet many were unemployable due to mental illness, later stages of pregnancy, single motherhood with dependent young children, and the danger of being jailed if some real identities and social security numbers were known. Those who were employable were young and lacked skills. Available jobs were usually the least desirable, the least rewarding, and the lowest paying, which generated an attitude of disregard and even hatred toward work. Thus a syndrome evolved in which poor job offerings gave rise to poor work attitudes which in turn led to difficulties on the job. These difficulties then often led to firings or quittings, thereby leaving the members' financial situation no better after their efforts. To many JMers, it appeared that work was a useless enterprise.

The only regular salaried jobs that could be obtained were dish-washing for the men and waitressing for the women. After DT and Jean obtained jobs working in the same restaurant, the manager soon made sexual advances toward Jean who rejected him. When she told DT and DT expressed his indignation to the boss, he fired them both. Two other males got jobs washing dishes in another restaurant. They were often picked up after work by other hungry and broke commune members who, in addition to picking food out of the garbage, stole it off the shelves and out of the refrigerator. The manager eventually noticed the missing food and fired them. DT and another follower were later hired by a hospital as orderlies. After sticking it out for months at a pitifully low salary, they began to complain about being stuck with the dirtiest work. The more they complained, the worse the work assigned to them. Eventually they quit, preferring to have free time to live without a salary, surviving on the little money they saved and could hustle.

The careless attitude toward work was not purely an artifact of the unpleasant, dead-end work situations in which they found themselves in Centerville. For a number of JMers, those attitudes and behaviors had built up over a lifetime of dead-end situations at home, school, and previous jobs, leading them to react in predictable ways even when the jobs weren't so distasteful or even when they involved chores helpful to their own survival at the Meadows. For instance, Moore Commune people, after hearing JM needed money, told JM where to apply for a job picking apples with them. But after only a couple of days, the JM people quit because the work was much harder than they had imagined. Antagonizing both the orchard owner and commune which had gone out of its way to help JM, JM members ended up having an apple fight with one another before walking off the job. Later, a couple of older longhaired itinerant entrepreneurs offered JM people a job helping them cart trash and tear down buildings. The job would only last three weeks and earn decent money, and the longhairs would drive all the way out to the Meadows to pick the JMers up and drop them off each day. After a week and a half, even the longhaired bosses got fed up with the JM workers as a result of coming out to pick them up one morning only to find the JM people had been doing drugs the night before and didn't "feel like" going to work.

As far as much of JM's work force was concerned, eventually no monetary need was worth formally working for if the job interfered with their other interests too much. What money was absolutely necessary would be obtained by various hustling schemes, which included borrowing with no intention to pay back, stealing drugs from dealers and dealing it themselves, and engaging in other mysterious activities; the details of which were never divulged even to fellow communards. The ultimate answer to monetary problems was to continue to reduce needs. But the CC operational axiom of consuming less instead of earning more spun out of control at JM. Lack of resources led to conditions whereby the town could harass JM through the imposition of fines or enforced codes requiring store-bought materials. JMers' physical health could be endangered through doctors refusing to treat them, knowing they couldn't pay the bills. Thus, the supposed freedom gained through non-participation in SS economy led JMers to an ever greater loss of freedom in the areas where they were forced to deal with the SS.

Not all people at JM had such ambivalent attitudes toward employment. Yale held a steady job at the sawmill until laid off in what he contemptuously referred to as the "Nixon recession." After collecting unemployment benefits for a while, he took such odd jobs as mending farm fences, haying, working on a surveying team, and tending to animals for a local veterinarian. He later even bought a pair of baby bulls and the machinery from an old sawmill to go into his own pollution-free log hauling business. Pepsi Joe was like Yale, but had far fewer skills, social and manual, and tried diligently to get jobs better than the dishwashing variety. He was a good artist and managed to get small jobs as a cartoonist, but did not earn enough to live on. He decided to leave the Meadows to attempt college; specifically to pick up employable skills. Finding neither employable skills in the curriculum at a liberal arts college nor an imposed work discipline, he dropped out. In desperation, clearly indicating he was tired of drifting around penniless, hustling, imposing on other people's hospitality, and always being at the mercy of the police or other authorities because of his poverty status, he gave up on the CC to join the US Air Force. He was one of the few people in the Centerville area CC over a three year period to drop firmly back into the SS. He joined not out of any great disillusionment with the CC ideals or because of any deep loyalty to America, but because it provided him with money, a home, a place to learn employable skills, and a career if he wanted one.

The older intellectuals had informed commune members from the outset that they had to return to jobs in the fall, and although Norman and Patrick could contribute some money toward the maintenance of the Meadows throughout the winter, most of their earnings had to go into paying off personal debts and expenses. Norman contributed cash, about $100 in addition to the $600 he had dribbled away during the summer. Believing his money would go toward survival necessities, he was chagrined to discover that over $70 was spent on JM dogs for licenses, shots, and setting a broken leg. Instead of contributing cash, Patrick donated useful items such as kerosene lanterns and a chain saw that was well used until it was disassembled once for repairs, parts lost, and never again reassembled.

Money obtained through public assistance continued to generate great difficulties. Periodically, new directives came from the state capitol reinterpreting federal guidelines on food stamps, slowly cutting down on their availability in a piecemeal fashion. When these directives came to JM, the stamps were completely cut off, placing the burden of proof upon the former recipients, rather than on the state, to demonstrate their compliance with the new directives in order to be reinstated in the program. This indirect harassment was apparently specifically aimed at communes, as all of them around Centerville simultaneously received letters announcing cut-offs when most regular non-communal recipients were not asked to comply.

The welfare office evidently mistakenly assumed that food stamps were wanted and needed by all the communes in order to keep them functioning. Although some communes that received food stamps, such as Grasshopper Farm and the Brethren, had vast potentially accessible financial reserves held by certain individuals, JM's situation was one of real, involuntary poverty. But most JMers concluded that they did not want food stamps. Some regarded the constant trips to the office, selecting official heads of family, and keeping track of signed ID cards for certain individuals as a "pain in the ass." Others were concerned that the cushion the stamps provided possibly kept JM from really having to go all out in earning its own way, believing it was morally and economically wrong to depend on the government when the worth of communes as a real alternative to the SS should be gauged on their ability to be self-supporting. Finally, most felt it was psychologically degrading and dehumanizing to have to kowtow to some desk clerks who by virtue of their jobs only, exercised considerable control over JMers' lives.

The other form of public assistance was the AFDC benefits mothers and mother-to-be received. These, too, led to a loss of human dignity as far as the women were concerned. First they were forced to stigmatize themselves and lie to social workers, essentially declaring themselves either sexually promiscuous or abandoned in order to get benefits, forcing them subsequently either to lead mateless lives or to maintain secret and illicit relationships with the fathers of their children or with others.

These benefits also caused antagonistic relations between the women and important people in their lives. Relations with parents were strained when they found out their daughters were on welfare. For example, Jean got drawn into a three-month long battle with her family because, being under 21, she had to get a note from her parents stating that they were not supporting her, which they refused to provide. Another consequence was the trouble it caused with their mates. Because the women now had money and the men didn't, the men made special pleas for some spending money. The women often had to turn them down, however, because they needed the money for the babies instead. Moreover, the women developed a sense of concern for the future security and responsibility for their children that most of the men didn't share. All of this led to constant arguing among mates over spending priorities and questions concerning who really loved whom or what.

By mid-winter, JM evolved to a situation of hard core poverty with patterns of money flow and handling similar to that found in the worst of urban ghettoes. This resulted from a changing membership pattern, a poor employment market, poor education, lack of skills, economic naiveté, and most certainly, community discrimination. The poverty was also involuntary; material conditions being exacerbated by poor planning, careless attitudes, and inverted priorities. This was partly due to the relatively young age of those who stayed throughout the winter, and partly due to near total ignorance of financial responsibility and foresight, whether or not they came from privileged or deprived backgrounds.

As there was progressively less money around, nearly all of what there was went for private expenditures. The pregnant women and mothers contributed some of their welfare money, Roamer spent part of his social security check, and small contributions were made by the over-30s. But few people seriously considered initiating communal projects for anything beyond what was minimally necessary for survival. The ideas of setting up a small storefront business in town, of making craft items on a large scale, and of raising a herd of goats all died by early autumn. One faction claimed that physical survival was the most important priority, while the other asserted that "getting and staying high" was most important because it made all hardships tolerable. Even if there was interest in communal projects, there was no capital available to get the simplest ones requiring the least investment underway. Those who had put sizable amounts of money into the communal kitty in the past only to see it squandered on misguided ventures, soon gave up the practice.

Undeniable divisions and tension quietly grew within JM between the relative "haves" and the "have-nots." The haves resented the have-nots for wanting to freeload off them and the have-nots resented the haves for not communally sharing what they had. The disputes over money concerning welfare mothers and their mates continued, and while some people were actually going hungry, they remarked how Boop had written her father for money for her and Zeke "to eat pork chops while we had nothing but brown rice." There was also a glaring contradiction apparent in the over-30s status of quasi-membership in the commune and the money they had with which to rent apartments and "see movies" in the cities.

Among the street males, a gypsy-like ethic evolved in which one was expected to share everything or be ostracized from the group. One also expected possessions to get stolen by friends from time to time and when pushed, all admitted having secret stashes. Theft, hustling, and fights over resources were becoming acceptable behavioral modes. As in past periods of JM's development, the lowest financial common denominator again became the mean. The more a fellow had, the more he was ostracized, and the more pressure was put on him to share. These JMers did not attempt to accumulate much money and possessions because the more each had, the more each would lose. Unlike past periods, however, the lowest common denominator now was rock bottom; abject penury. Those who insisted on maintaining a higher standard of living could not remain in a commune surrounded by so many people willing to live a materially Spartan life, yet willing to take advantage of the resources of others. Thus those with higher education, better skills, and greater motivation either left the Meadows or kept their relation to it a distant one. This loss of potential monetary contributors further intensified the evolving poverty syndrome.

All these difficulties, largely stemming from political, economic, and psychological factors beyond the awareness of most members in their day to day survival hassles, expressed themselves increasingly in the form of social and interpersonal conflicts and problems within the group. Early on, when it became evident to many that another winter would have to be faced without any prospects for improvement in their situation, a spontaneous purging process was set in motion, and as could be expected, it played itself out along existing factional tensions and fissures. The over-30s who drifted in and out and the full-time hippies expressed the most concern, while the street males claimed there was nothing to worry about. The younger intellectuals and the street females took a vacillating position, verbally agreeing with the worriers, but behaviorally siding with or giving tacit support to the partyers, most of whom were the women's mates.

Autumn was a time of shifts in the entire CC; students returned to school and intellectual sympathizers returned to work. Those hippies with options generally sought out more pleasant environments. Peter and Cindy returned to Peter's mother's house, while his progressive school friends took off for warmer climates. The number and kind of visitors changed too. Those who had no homes to return to began looking in earnest for places to spend the winter. Two young men, Arthur and Claudius, came to JM seeking to make the Meadows their home. Although other visitors asked to remain and were turned down, these two seemed very industrious and friendly, and most of the JM people enjoyed their company and work enthusiasm. Also, couples were deliberately sought because they were always a stabilizing influence on the constantly shifting situation of single people coming and going. Although two couples said at one point they would stay at JM, neither remained when conditions got really rough.

There were people hanging on at the Meadows who contributed little. No one openly questioned their right to remain until a meeting was called by the worriers to discuss the mobilization for winter. It was lamented that in meeting after meeting work projects would be outlined and lazy disinterest would be denounced, yet people were still not working hard and things were still not getting done. Roamer pointed out that general accusations of laziness was not fair to the group as a whole, just as it was not fair for individuals who shirked their responsibilities to hide behind the general anonymity of the group. Accordingly, he suggested that every person take turns explaining the reasons they came to JM and their primary roles and duties if they intended to remain. Everyone else was free to comment on whether or not they thought that person should remain.

The situation was very tense as few people knew what the others were really thinking of them. All the visitors and hangers-on agreed to leave, some of whom had been "visiting" two or three weeks. Even some who joined immediately after the fire were told that their presence was not welcome. Some from Peter's home town came under heavy fire for being in the commune all summer, yet not working or committing themselves to it as their home. Despite their tender age, JM was the real world, and no one else could fend for them as was done by teachers and parents back in their suburban town. Two chose to leave (though they returned a month or so later) and two remained.

The only other people who came in for criticism were the street males. All of them stayed on arguing that if life on communes was to be all work and drudgery, people should live in the SS instead of in communes. They saw their function as making the place a happy place to live. Unstated, however, was the fact that they were attached through couple relationships to women whose roles in maintaining JM was recognized as fundamental. To expel their men would have meant expelling them and perhaps destroying JM. Only men, not women, were challenged throughout the purge. Also, despite the possible destabilizing influence created by the over-30s dropping in and out of JM instead of becoming full-time members, it was agreed to let them remain as welcome members. This was done because when they were around, they did contribute ideas and work.

By the end of the four hour meeting, JM had cut itself down to fifteen full-time people. The oldest were Arthur and Roamer in their twenties. Only two had gotten as far as the first year of college in terms of education. Only five were women. Eight were more or less members of the street faction, four were from the hippie wing, and three represented the vestiges of the intellectual faction.

The issues raised during the purge meeting were grappled with throughout the winter. Work modes was one of them. While most JMers suggested and began work on projects at various times, they were seldom completed. The garden was full of food that could be preserved for winter use and Parson's Crossing and Grasshopper Farm had produce surpluses they were willing to give to JM. All that was required was people collecting the fruits and vegetables and preparing them for storage. There were three major approaches to preservation of foods: canning, freezing, and cold storage. Canning was begun enthusiastically by one person when jars had been assembled through gifts and purchase at a second hand goods store. Midway through the project into which she managed to recruit other people, she disappeared, going to town. The day's work of about a dozen jars was completed without her, but it was never again initiated. One of the Centerville grocery stores rented freezer lockers for a reasonable fee. After looking into the prospect, the idea died, not because the money couldn't be raised, but because no one harvested the food, cut it, and bagged it for transport to town. Cold storage was sufficient for squash, turnips, potatoes, and the like. JM began work on a root cellar next to the cookshack, but after a few days, interest in the project waned. Food from the garden and from other communes was taken only as needed, with none being saved for the winter ahead. To the disbelief of people outside JM, vegetables literally lay in the field and rotted until Roamer and Patrick arranged with a large organic foods concern to salvage what was left of the turnips and squash in order to barter them for grains.

Another problem was vehicles. After the over-30s left with their cars, two new members with vehicles arrived, but one had to sell his soon afterward to obtain money to live on. Arthur's car broke down and he could not manage to get it fixed. The only hope lay in the two idle trucks in need of repair. A pickup given to JM by Parson's Crossing only needed a battery and the brakes repaired. After getting it operating, money was never raised to get it inspected and licensed. It sat in a field until an ex-member came by and asked if he could have it, provided he could get it going again. After about an hour's work, he left with what should have been a much needed vehicle for JM. The other was an old bread truck bought by Arthur, who paid only $50 down, never paying the rest. Although it was ostensibly for work, it ended up serving as a pleasure vehicle, taking people to beer parties in the area and to Knowland College where drugs could easily be obtained. When Zeke ran it into a ditch while returning drunk from a rock concert, the over-30s paid $40 to have it hauled out and repaired. Only a week later, the brakes gave out and it sat on the road in front of Parson's Crossing for more than a week until Boop managed to convince her father to pay for its towing and repair. After once again being put in working order, it failed to start on the first really cold morning. No one was able to start it thereafter, and it remained in that spot, blocking the entranceway.

Projects concerned with immediate comfort, however, were completed. Under Arthur's leadership, the side shed was insulated and converted for winter use. Also, a new woodshed was built to keep firewood dry. Begun by one person who left the next day, the project was completed by others. Firewood gathering was an ongoing project. Progressively cold temperatures served as a daily reminder of how life at the Meadows would be impossible without heat. A sink was installed because the cold made dish washing outdoors inconvenient.

Most projects were completed due to the consistent efforts of Roamer and Walter, who was Jean's brother and Suzie's (Peter's sister) boyfriend. Both of them were from the hippie wing. Walter had been a finger snapping, foot tapping, dope smoking naturally speedy person who couldn't keep his attention on anything for more than a few minutes at a time earlier that year, but who was now assuming the responsibility for the work, permitting his and his commune mates' survival. He put in the spring box and pump for commune use and to satisfy health officials. Roamer made sure that plenty of grains were stocked for the winter, even if vegetables were not. Arthur worked hard at times, but did drugs at other times. None of the work leaders came from the street faction. The women provided the day to day operational foundation of the commune by tending to food, fires, and cooking. But even they evidenced inconsistencies between words and actions. One time after criticizing Pepsi Joe for leaving to visit friends in the city instead of working at the Meadows, the four of them jumped in Norman's car bound for the city, ostensibly to trade vegetables for grain. Despite all the good intentions, JM never evolved a procedure for assigning specific responsibilities for specific projects.

Closely related to the issue of work perseverance was the ongoing conflict over the use of drugs and alcohol. After a period of drug use, the Brethren's James and many other hippies had come to disavow them. Later, after the Brethren conflict, Peter forbade the use of drugs and also got the drinkers to agree not to indulge on the land if he was going to let them stay. These prohibitions ultimately did not succeed, however, as drugs were sometimes done on the sly. The no drinking issue was also raised at a stormy meeting. Other

commteunes, it was argued, did drugs and drink and it had not led to their
ruination, and the drinking majority demanded that their behavior should not be
controlled by the wishes of a minority. This conflict put the street males and
young intellectual wing on one side, with the hippie faction and the women
opposing them. Although all the women had used psychoactive substances at
one time (some heavily), they had come to the conclusion that these substances
were harmful by watching what it did to their mates. The street women called
themselves "wine widows," claiming that alcohol made the men macho, violent,
and irresponsible. Because the men could not control its use, and the women
who were pregnant or were already mothers never indulged, they were for total
abstinence.

The anti-drug-and-drink faction believed it had a good case for prohibition
of drugs and alcohol off the land as well. Indulgence led to the men not feeling
able to make it to jobs or quitting communal work early in order to get high.
After the very purge meeting in which he urged responsibility and commitment
to the land, Arthur took a carload of people to make connections for drugs. Zeke
later ran the truck into a ditch when drunk. Who knows how much was spent on
drugs and booze that should have gone for other purposes?

Just as bad as the material damage was social damage caused by drink and
drugs. Relations with Grasshopper Farm deteriorated when Harvey returned a
dog from JM that had almost killed his puppy, only to find people wandering
around too stoned to know what he was talking about. Red Rose was down on
JM for being more interested in getting high than thinking about political issues.
And the Brethren remained convinced JM was doomed to disaster by their
depraved need for dope and alcohol.

Parson's Crossing tolerated dope seekers who were conversational and
helped with their work, but hated the street people who would enter noisily and
put records on the stereo while the authors there were trying to think and write.
Some became so irked, they asked Yale (who lived there at the time) to make it
known that certain JM people weren't welcome. Even Walnut Hill put JM on its
blacklist after Arthur went there to smoke dope claiming he had no lice when in
fact he did. Thereafter Walnut Hill adopted an unofficial policy of admitting no
JM members into the house regardless of what they said. The women insisted it
was Arthur's driving desire for psychoactive substances that led him to deceive
a sister commune.

Drugs and alcohol were also causing problems with the town. JM members
had been arrested in Centerville for drunkenness and disorderly conduct. Pepsi
Joe got drunk at Knowland College, and while looking for drugs, pulled the fire
alarm and ran through the halls screaming "I'm from Jackson's Meadows and
I'm proud of it!" After the fire alarm debacle, JM people were clearly personae
non grata. Also, tripping on acid in front of the Vital Victuals one night, DT's
friend tried to stop cars in the street, pleading with them (not their occupants) to
stop destroying the world. Led onto a side street by a fellow JMer where he
would be less conspicuous, DT's friend imagined his fellow communard was
trying to kill him. In an effort to escape he jumped off a bridge, landing on the
rocks in icy water 25 feet below. The town rescue squad had to be called and,

considered lucky to have survived, he was admitted to the hospital for two weeks. Town authorities regarded this incident as just one more in a series of irresponsible acts by Jackson's Meadows.

In counter argument, the pro-drug-and-drink faction claimed that indulgence on the land would be much less deleterious than prohibition. Less time would be spent away from the land looking for drugs. Moreover, their habits cost very little since no one was addicted to heroin or other expensive drugs. Knowland College, where they took showers anyway, was a gold mine for free drugs. They admitted certain excesses, such as the time a big acid dealer spent a week vacationing at the Meadows in return for half a jar full of acid tabs, and the time someone left potentially poisonous psychedelic mushrooms on the floor where Cindy's baby crawled about putting them in its mouth. But all in all, they claimed drugs simply were not a material drain on the commune. Drink cost more money in that booze was always available for purchase, but JMers often got away without paying for that too by hustling drinks in working class bars. DT particularly pushed this point, having a fail safe routine of prying money and sympathy from pro-war patrons by virtue of his combat veteran status.

The hard drinking and drugging street people were evolving a hardened attitude toward the world, both SS and CC. They pointed out that everyone was down on them for having the freedom to live their lives the way they wanted, so why should they care how much they disturbed other people? They were all alone in the world anyway, and so long as they had their "brothers" it made no difference what others thought. They were not pretentious and snobbish like Parson's Crossing and Grasshopper Farm, were not crazy religious fanatics like the Brethren, and didn't dangerously manipulate people as calculatedly as the Free Provincia people did. With all the Free Provincia's talk of reaching out to the poor and the working people of the SS, it was JM, not Free Provincia, that had made real friendships among those classes. "To tell the truth," DT added, "I get along better with the rednecks on Irwin Street than I do with most of the so-called freaks in this town." The final favorable argument was that drugs and alcohol helped people to relax, to forget about their worries, to feel better with one another, and to enjoy life. While older people and intellectual types did acid for purposes of enlightenment and sometimes had shattering experiences, many street people had no bad reactions because they had no illusions to be shattered in the first place.

Despite all substances being done, most people at this stage of the commune's development preferred downs in the form of alcohol or barbiturates and on occasion, heroin. DT admitted that downs gave him a sense of confidence he never had when sober with people of a "higher social position." Hank, who had left JM in the summer, returned in late fall, and was, in his own estimation "more mature, having gotten a lot of the shit out of me I had to get out." Starting his sojourn in the CC by smoking dope and working in the Diggers' free store "for the people," he later learned there were no "people," only his friends and drinking buddies. Dope and drugs, he claimed, was "hippie bullshit" that clouded minds to the cold, hard realities of life. Anyone who did any dope had to be naive and stupid. He got along best with realistic hard drinkers. Hank was not only drinking cheap wine now, but whiskey.

The pro-work, anti-drug faction accused the street faction of forgetting that despite all the good vibes that drinking and playing was supposed to create, they got into fights and were having increasing difficulties with their women. They also claimed that the men apparently also had no real basis for communication with each other outside partying and drink, and even that was shallow. Moreover, the street people tended to look upon people not as human beings, but as objects to hustle money or booze from and things to strike out at when they were no longer exploitable. Was reality so unpleasant that they had to get high to face it? Were they like primitive life forms that could only react to simple, sensate stimuli, never planning ahead and initiating anything lasting? By doing just what "feels good" at the moment, didn't they realize they were leaving themselves completely open to capricious events in the future that might not feel so good?

The pro-work anti-drug faction was regarded by the street people as goody-goodies, fooled by a false morality and by self-aggrandizing rationalizations that led them to believe they could build new societies and new individuals. They appeared to the street people as compulsive workers and worriers who from force of habit and earlier learning exhibited the same SS tendencies they were supposed to be changing. With all their talk about communication and meaningful relationships, why was it that the pro-work people were so hung up on work? If the pro-work people were really concerned about people rather than things, they would relax more, join them in partying, and contribute to the good vibes instead of bringing everybody down by nagging about unfinished chores. If communal life was only hard work, they said, then to hell with it, for it was no improvement over the SS.

Moreover, they felt there was hypocrisy among the pro-work people, whereas the street people at least leveled with themselves. Those who complained most about communal work not getting done were the first ones to give up in fits of depression or to work for their own private survival. For example, Annette used to sit around complaining how lazy everyone was, but never took the initiative of starting a project that would help anyone else but herself. In fact her "bitching" inhibited communal work, making everyone feel like giving up. Roamer, too, was busy stocking his own quarters with goods and materials instead of helping other people. And speaking of Roamer, the street people claimed that his psychotic violence was far worse than that stemming from their drinking.

Roamer did, indeed, flip out over the issues of work and communal irresponsibility. One cold morning he was struggling to build a fire in the stove in the cookshack. Visitors, friends of Arthur's and DT's, repeatedly left and entered the cookshack, letting out the little heat that was in the building. After closing the door four or five times after them, Roamer started screaming at people and smashing objects on the floor. Running outside, he turned over kerosene cans stacked for the winter and began throwing tools at the house. As people emerged from the cookshack to calm him down, they quickly ducked back in as missiles started flying in their direction. A pitchfork and a hammer narrowly missed hitting a couple of people. All the while, Roamer loudly cried that no one cared about the commune, about the land, about each other, and about themselves. Patrick tried to reason with him, pointing out that he might kill somebody. Roamer replied that he didn't care if he killed anyone, didn't care about life at all, and might kill himself. He defiantly screamed that life was meaningless and senseless to preserve if nothing constructive could be done with it. While the intellectuals tried to reason, and others passively mumbled that because of this incident they were leaving JM, Claudius, Arthur's quiet friend and traveling companion, jumped him, knocked him down, and shocked Roamer into abruptly ending his episode.

Later Roamer was castigated by the rest of the group for generalizing the fact that the door was left open one morning into a vague assumption that nothing at all was being done to prepare for winter. Moreover, they indicated that people who threatened to kill one another should not live together. Roamer's status as a leader of JM, painfully built up over the summer, was now destroyed, and he was even threatened by expulsion. Arthur took over as smooth-talking peace maker, and being a very recent convert to the CC, he spoke of the need for peace and love. While CC veterans winced at his naiveté, they didn't argue with Arthur's words because they wanted an understanding to be reached. Roamer admitted that perhaps he was being too negative, but that he was the only one there who had gone through a winter at JM before, and was "plain scared." Others were belittling the dangers of physical survival because they didn't know what was in store. To the charges of killing people, in tears, he answered, "You're killing me everyday, man, little by little. You're killing my mind by paying no attention to my warnings and ideas, going about your business of getting stoned all the time, paying no attention to Peter's wishes or mine." Representing what was rapidly becoming a minority wing as the older intellectuals and hippies left and more street people joined, Roamer felt isolated and alone. Concluding that JM was no longer a commune but a collection of self-indulgent individuals, he withdrew from all efforts at a leadership role from that day forward.

Other members of Roamer's wing agreed, feeling unheeded while their work was taken for granted. For example, while they cautioned against abuse of the vehicles, the street people did what they wanted with them until none of them operated. Those not firmly in the street people or the hippie-older intellectuals camps, namely the younger quasi-intellectuals, wavered back and forth, while Arthur took a kind of mediating role that gave him a semblance of leadership in the commune. But as Roamer pointed out, there could be no leadership without consensus. People on both sides began to resent Arthur's inflated sense of self-importance and cavalier attitudes. They were irked by his assertion that the truck did not belong to JM collectively, but to him. Moreover, other members were particularly upset when they heard that he had told someone at Walnut Hill that he was now the real inspiration and leadership behind the commune.

The women, as a separate entity with independent needs and directions of their own, emerged as a powerful force. This surge was probably not influenced by the area women's movement, though they sometimes participated. Women's consciousness or not, JM women increasingly realized that most of the males there were incompetent, unreliable, and immature. Not questioning why they chose these men as mates, they complained that the men always "took" from the women as individuals, "took" from JM's collective efforts such as they were, and "took" from other CC institutions in the area, never contributing anything in return. Moreover, the men were always critical of things they didn't understand or didn't have sufficient skills to participate in. As examples, they cited the Vital Victuals, Liberation Farm, the commune newsletter, and regional CC meetings (including women's meetings) that the street men were blindly opposed to. The JM women saw some value in these things, even if the Free Provincia influence had led to certain extremes.

Also, the men took liberties with the women that the women would never take with the men. They were aware that their men clung to them for emotional support and monetary resources. For instance, Zeke went to great lengths to plot schemes to get Boop to give him money for beer and wine. The men also slept with other women. Although it angered the women, they did little about it. Some friends from DT's hometown once brought a sixteen year old "nymphomaniac" to JM. Rather than objecting, the women simply withdrew from the potential orgiastic scene (which in fact never occurred, because one unattached male kept her occupied all night). The women claimed that most of the men were young, mixed-up people who wanted guidance from a parent figure. Not having close parental relationships themselves, they still craved the freedom to act irresponsibly that loving parents would allow early in life. The men wanted emotional security through the indulgence of women or the illusion of it through alcohol. What these people at JM were looking for, one said was not a new society, but "mommies and daddies."

A few JMers freely acknowledged the commune's directionless floundering. While passing a joint around on the road in front of the cookshack (because the road was technically off the land), Mission Street Mike, who seldom spoke, commented, "We can't seem to get off the ground. We keep going through the same cycles over and over again. The other communes have things to organize themselves around, like farming or the revolution, but we haven't found anything yet." Both the women and the over-30s (when they were there) agreed. By default, life was governed by the daily solar cycle. It consisted of getting up late, doing chores just to survive, thinking of things that would add a little excitement to an otherwise lack-luster day, such as getting high, and going to bed late.

But Claudius defended JM's living pattern, claiming there was no universal law stating that people had to be involved in anything more than minimal survival. In fact, such pursuits had a purifying simplicity about them that made life less complicated and more rewarding. Unlike other communes that seemed to be constantly embroiled in political, spiritual, or interpersonal hassles, he claimed that JM people at least enjoyed experiencing the raw natural environment together, and really needed one another for survival. JM simply couldn't afford the luxury of the interpersonal nit-picking that drove other people apart.

While the substance of this debate droned on, the composition of those engaged in it changed from time to time. Although there had been a turnover in population throughout the autumn, the period from Thanksgiving to Christmas was a watershed. Former members in good standing were always welcome to return, and often did after previous plans and prospects fell through. A few progressive school hippies came back, but left again when they obtained a vehicle. An Alterian working class woman returned after an unsatisfactory stay at Last Ditch Farm, but eventually decided she just didn't fit in with either hippies or revolutionaries, so she got her own apartment in a nearby town. There, she became even more desperately lonely, and had a number of bizarre dream visions that linked indiscriminate sex with death. Feeling she had come to the end of her rope, she made plans to commit herself to a mental hospital, but by chance met a Jesus Freak, underwent conversion, and became a Jesus Freak herself. The fellow who jumped off the bridge while tripping on acid, also from a Catholic working class background, went back to his home town instead, where he also became a Jesus Freak. Lastly, Allen, from Liberation Farm, returned for a few weeks, found the lack of political and intellectual stimulation too stifling, and moved to the Blue House to help form a quasi-commune there. Thus, those who returned and again left were either from middle or upper middle class backgrounds which allowed access to other options, or from a solid working class tradition which permitted them to some variation of the working class life, even if spiritually changed.

Unlike most of JM's permanent residents that autumn, Arthur had verbal and certain manual skills, and took the initiative in starting and finishing work projects. All but a few of the JM people were taken, as Claudius had been, by his energy and ingenuity, and they welcomed him. Pepsi Joe began to model his behavior after Arthur, working harder than he had all summer. After a month, however, people began to notice Arthur's emotional inconsistency, his driving need for drugs that at times made him more disruptive than the street people, his possessiveness, and his vanity. JM got its first mirror, brought in from some "unoccupied house" found by Arthur, who used it more than anyone else because he was the only one who regularly combed his hair. When his erratic behavior was pointed out to him by the women and Roamer, he admitted he lacked a stable point of reference; something to make him act more responsibly and with more forethought.

His solution for his own erratic behavior was to bring his high school age girl friend from New Orleans, so that he would have "someone to look out for and protect." His reasons for wanting his woman would have outraged any feminist, but it fell on sympathetic ears at JM. He was arranging to have her run away from home and fly to a nearby city where he would pick her up and bring her to the Meadows. Someone warned about the danger of having another runaway on their hands. Everyone at JM could get busted. Boop frankly asked Arthur if his girl knew what she was getting into and if her parents were likely to follow her. According to Arthur, she was fully aware she was coming to a hippie rural commune, and her parents liked him, so that after a period of initial anger, they would probably let their daughter stay.

That he had brazenly lied became evident shortly after her arrival. She ran away from home under the impression that he had a high paying job in the city with a fine apartment. She was a spotlessly clean, all-American girl from the South, and had never associated with hippie types. Moreover, her parents hated Arthur, and had hired a private detective to find her. But Arthur on this and many other subsequent occasions was never really called to task by the others about the fact they had been deliberately misled. People resigned themselves, for what had been done could not be undone, especially when starting divisive arguments within the commune could lead to greater difficulties. He explained to his girl friend that if he hadn't told her the lies he did, she might have been afraid to come to him. That explanation apparently satisfied her, too.

Despite Arthur's girl friend being used to steak and hamburger, daily showers, and balmy weather, she quickly adjusted to the radically different environment. She learned to eat brown rice, put up with the cold, to make love in a room full of other people behind a drawn curtain on a bunk bed, to bathe infrequently, and to shoplift. Despite her SS quirks, everyone liked her, and she developed a close relationship with the other women. Her relationship with Arthur, however, was a stormy one, with both of them evolving familiar lovers' behavioral syndromes that seemed to doom them to mutual destruction. He tried to keep her isolated at the Meadows, forbidding her to participate in certain social activities she might find "unpleasant," and chivalrously vowing to protect her from potential dangers, such as Roamer's flipping out. He would even tell other women in her presence that he loved them in an effort to exact greater submission from her. But with support from the other women she became defiant, nagging him, refusing to accede even to reasonable requests, and at times paying no attention to him when he spoke to her, as though he didn't exist.

Eventually Arthur's jealousy and the growing conflict with the hippie anti-drug faction resulted in a chain of events that virtually tore JM apart. One night Arthur commanded his girl friend to come upstairs to bed with him in a private area he had constructed in the upper floor of the cookshack. When she paid no attention, another young member offered her his bed. Arthur stormed downstairs, threatened to kill the other member, and forbade him and the girl to talk to each other. Because they lived in the same tiny building, having to face each other constantly, the atmosphere grew tense for everyone. Shortly afterward, Arthur announced he had received a letter from a friend saying the police knew where he and the girl were, and would arrive in six days. It was another tall story, but everyone nevertheless believed him. Thus, he was justified in making preparations to leave the Meadows. After previously claiming that his car had hopelessly broken down, he put it in working order in a few hours.

Not content to leave the Meadows by himself, however, he made plans to have a number of other people follow him. After sending his girl to Peter's mother's house with Jean so that she would not "get caught by the police," he told DT that his girl, Jean, had told Arthur that she was leaving DT and would not return from Peter's home town. Panicked at the news, DT agreed to go with

Arthur to Peter's home town to convince Jean not to leave him. Others from Peter's home town resolved to go with Arthur, but the hippie pro-work faction protested. The land taxes were due in a couple of weeks, and everyone was running out when hundreds of dollars still had to be raised. Those intending to leave said they would earn the money in Peter's home town and would send it back.

When the carload of JMers reached Peter's mother's house it turned out that Jean had no intention of leaving DT. Arthur had simply lied to DT to get him and Jean to leave the Meadows and travel with him. The money that they picked up was spent on drugs and liquor, consumed during a week-long party at Peter's mother's house during which a mattress was accidentally set on fire, scorching a wall and almost setting the house ablaze. When no money was received back at JM, Suzie, Peter's sister, called up her mother's house to find out what was happening. She was appalled at their taking advantage of her tolerant mother and their wasting rather than earning money, while those who remained behind struggled to prepare for winter and to get money for the taxes. The angry Meadows people resolved never to let Arthur return to JM, took all his belongings, and made a bonfire of them outside the cookshack.

Tempers at the Meadows cooled as the people at Peter's mother's house called to say they had repaired the damage to the house, could still pick up some money, and would bring back a turkey for Thanksgiving. Arthur returned to an icy reception. That Arthur and his entourage had managed to mysteriously raise enough money to cover the taxes was no compensation. And Arthur was crushed to find all his belongings had been burned. Near tears, he spoke of the lack of feeling among people who were supposedly his friends; people who burned childhood mementos from his mother that had a very special place in his life. It was almost as if they had burned and killed part of him, he said. He vowed he would leave JM permanently in a few days.

Although some people weren't speaking to one another, the Thanksgiving party attracted many ex-JMers who were then drawn into the conflict. Some of the over-30s and Mother Humpers showed up. Cindy was not there because she was in the hospital having her second child. A Mother Humper brought cheap wine, and he and Zeke got drunk together in his car, had a short slugging match, and went back to drinking. Seething with hostility, they finally emerged from the car to stumble around the cookshack almost knocking over the kerosene lanterns a number of times. The Mother Humper took a couple of swings at people, deliberately hitting one squarely in the stomach after his turkey dinner. Later, screaming was heard outside the cookshack, where people rushed out to find the Mother Humper and his woman on the ground, kicking and punching her. One of the over-30s intellectuals ran to stop the Mother Humper as other street people warned him that it was none of his business. "They do it all the time. We never interfere, and they work it out by themselves." He went to the woman's aid anyway, but the Mother Humper was so drunk he didn't know what was happening and made no effort to resist the interceder. To everyone's relief, he finally passed out, whereupon only the previous hostile peace and quiet remained.

The next day, Cindy returned from the hospital with her new baby to find that her older child hadn't been washed or had her diaper changed in days. She also heard of the drinking, fighting, the split over Arthur's return, and dope smoking in the house, despite promises to Peter to keep it off the land. She announced she was fed up with JM and was going with Hank and the other Mother Humpers to their house elsewhere in Provincia. This came as a blow because Cindy had been one of those tough street people who seemed to keep an even keel under all sorts of trying conditions and helped to keep the place functioning despite all the antics of the others. It particularly shook the work faction, who concluded it would be nearly impossible to keep the place together without her. At this point two of the strongest members of the work faction, Suzie and Jean's brother Walter, decided to move to her other brother's commune across the country.

The final step in the rash of departures came when Arthur finally decided to leave. Again using his divide-and conquer technique, he first told Jean that he was going to get a house elsewhere in Provincia with heat, electricity, running water, and all things she would need to care for the baby she would have in a couple of months. Now that she was almost due, many of her attitudes were changing, and Arthur had hit a particularly vulnerable spot. She said she might go. Without asking Jean, Arthur then approached DT, who was growing even more insecure about Jean and told him she was going with Arthur and his girl. Would DT like to come along? DT fearfully accepted, and the four of them made plans to leave, which was not disturbing to many at JM, except for the departure of Jean. Arthur borrowed money from one of the over-30's promising to repay (which he never did), and then went to Roamer to "borrow" from the communal funds for gas, not telling him he had already borrowed some. Knowing the smallest bill Roamer had was a ten, he asked for "only five" knowing he would have to get the ten.

Jean and DT had some misgivings about Arthur's plans. How could they afford to buy a house when they had to borrow money for gas? Where would they live until they found one? Arthur told them not to worry because he would take care of everything. They believed him. Picking up another street kid in Centerville, they bought wine and beer, took off that night, and for lack of any place to go, ended up in DT's home town staying at a motel. In a matter of days they were flat broke, having spent all the borrowed money on motels, restaurant meals, booze, and drugs. Everyone was getting panicked, but Arthur, who still insisted everything was under control, suggested they apply for welfare. Because this part of Provincia happened to have few longhairs and the Welfare office was not yet wary, to everyone's amazement, welfare paid for their motel room and meals while they looked for work.

The two women and the high school youth they picked up began to feel this situation was unreal; a bad dream that really couldn't be happening. Instead of looking for work, Arthur used some of the money to buy speed, and sat in their motel room speeding and playing the guitar for hours on end. On one of the trips to the Welfare office, DT's first wife, who still lived in the town and had the police looking for him for non-support, showed up at the same time to collect

AFDC. She, her sister, and their baby strollers surrounded DT, and a loud argument ensued. Just then an old friend of DT's passed by in a car, and he and Jean hopped in to escape his wife. But his wife also had a car, and a slow motion chase scene developed in which DT's car wandered up and down the streets followed by his wife. Finally, he gave up and talked to her, making some promises he never intended to keep just to stop her from hounding him.

Back in the motel, the five of them spent days not even going outside. DT and Arthur were electric on speed the entire time. Arthur started playing the guitar one evening and when the street kid became bored and turned to the TV, Arthur made him turn it off, pointing out how inconsiderate he was to interrupt his playing. Arthur continued to play into the night, keeping everyone else awake until they fell asleep from exhaustion. When the youth awoke the next morning, Arthur was still playing. Again the street kid turned on the TV, but again Arthur angrily began accusing him of being "fucked up" and selfish. The impressionable youth later confided that "Arthur almost convinced me over a period of a few days that I was crazy and self-centered. But it was him who was crazy. I saw him slowly going nuts before my eyes." Finally, the kid couldn't take it any more, announcing he was going back to the Centerville Street scene. He was sexually frustrated, sitting around in the room while the two other couples made love. Disturbed that he was losing one person from his private entourage, Arthur told the youth he could have sex with his girl friend if he would stay. The kid refused, but before he left, he told Arthur's girl friend what Arthur had proposed. When Arthur found this out he became furious, denying the whole story, swearing he would return to Centerville "to get" the kid.

This escalating absurdity was finally interrupted by a knock at the motel door. It was the police asking if Arthur's girl friend was in the room. She was taken by the police to a juvenile home, but to everyone's relief, the parents were not pressing charges. After Arthur talked to his girl friend and to her parents, he too decided to go back to New Orleans to get a job to pay off his outstanding debts and to change his ways. Having no place else to go, DT and Jean returned to JM. Jean admitted she had been willingly misled by Arthur, vowing the whole experience had taught her a lesson about trusting people.

By the time the Thanksgiving dust had settled, only nine people remained at the Meadows. In addition to the core street men, DT and Zeke, there were two women, two quasi-hippies (Roamer and Claudius), and three young people from Peter's home town. Life at the Meadows settled into that of a quiet leaderless community. Roamer lived in his truck, Claudius in his tree house, Boop and Zeke in the cabin they had occupied all along, and DT and Jean moved into the A-frame after Suzie left, leaving the three young bachelors to inhabit the cookshack.

But life did not remain quiet for long. Boop and Zeke were having violent fights, Jean was drifting further away from DT in her concern for her unborn baby (as was Boop, who was also pregnant), and all the unattached males were "terribly horny." To the horror of the Free Provincia people and feminists who operated the Vital Victuals, Mission Street Mike put up a notice on the bulletin board located there under "items to trade or sell." It simply stated, "Women needed at Jackson's Meadows." Visitors still showed up at the Meadows every three or four days. An emotionally disturbed teenager was brought to the end of the road leading to the Meadows by his father who let him off to walk in alone over the hard-packed snow to the cookshack. The boy explained that his father didn't want him, and after asking in town, had heard about the commune "that would take anybody." Straight looking male homosexuals arrived hoping to find willing partners among the hippie communards where the male to female ratio was now so disproportionate. The state police arrived once, causing everyone to scramble about panicked. thinking it was a raid. They had come to find Mission Street Mike, whose sister in a mental hospital was dying and whose parents wanted him to be present when she passed away. Finally, assorted reporters from the *New York Times* and *Time Magazine* among others, also appeared, each buying permission to photograph communal life with some food and wine.

People also left the Meadows from time to time. DT, Zeke, and Mission Street Mike became involved for days at a time in the city street life, but the others returned to the Meadows thoroughly repulsed by urban ghetto life. Zeke at one point left Boop, intending to remain in the city until he heard Claudius was sleeping with eight-month-pregnant Boop, where-upon he decided he had gotten "laid and drunk enough to get it all out of my system," and returned to the Meadows. On these excursions to the city JMers ran into old friends and into trouble. Pepsi Joe was encountered in his old haunts, and once after getting drunk with his ex-commune mates, he passed out on the sidewalk, cracking his head on the curb. A police ambulance took him to the hospital where he remained for a few days. Another time, DT was seen drunk on the TV evening news, leading a mob of longhairs in an attempt to crash a rock concert, kicking a policeman in the shins and getting clubbed in return.

In the city, Zeke ran into four old IBM friends who, to nearly everyone's horror, he invited to come to the Meadows to live. One, called Popcorn, was continually so drunk on gin that he couldn't even leave the city. The three others arrived full of enthusiasm for the new life in the country, swearing they would renew their lives and change their ways. They turned over to the commune $85 they had "found in a wallet," knowing that if they kept it themselves they would fight over it. Don had a bandaged head with nine stitches which he claimed was the result of his falling on a bottle in the gutter. It was later admitted, however, that Zeke sliced him with a broken whiskey bottle in a fight over $5. Despite all their internecine fights, they referred to each other as "brother" and used the word "love" in reference to each other. These hard core IBMs were a strange mixture of outlaw bikers without motorcycles and sentimental hippies who loved children and animals.

Quickdraw was disarmingly uninhibited in his own innocent way and unable to discriminate between what was appropriate behavior and what was not. In complete sincerity and seriousness he would ask strange women in the street to go to bed with him. He would urinate on the floor in apartments and houses he visited and destroy valuable pieces of art, using parts of them for necklaces of trinkets that hung about his neck. Constantly drunk, he would be completely sad or uncontrollably overjoyed. His way of showing gratitude and friendship was to spit in his hand and then grasp his counterpart's hand in an oozing handshake. He occasionally expressed his feelings toward other males by hugging them and planting juicy kisses on their lips.

With the addition of these new people, the future of JM looked bleak, indeed. Peter's worst intuitions were coming true as responsible people with any reasonable alternatives outside JM left, and irresponsible people trying to escape the consequences of their own actions moved in to replace them. The situation might have been disastrous, but for the re-appearance of Yale. During his sojourns at Rainbow Farm and Parson's Crossing, Yale had kept his hopes for owning the Meadows alive. There was talk of Norman, Pepsi Joe, and Arthur buying the land before Thanksgiving, and they approached Yale to see if he was interested in chipping in. He was interested not because of his feelings toward the idea of community or toward them personally, but rather his feelings toward the land. Hopes were smashed, however, when Peter, while desperately wanting to rid himself of JM, refused to sell it to people already associated with the Meadows. JM had to be completely snuffed out, he said, in order to break the cycle of suffering and moral disintegration taking place there. Despite all good intentions, anyone associated with the commune would only perpetuate the evil and contribute to further death and destruction.

But now Yale's interest was rekindled. Not only was there a leadership vacuum on the land that he could fill, Jean's younger sister, an old love, had run away from home and school, and was again living at JM. Yale felt a little out of place at Parson's Crossing because he wasn't the heavy humanist intellectual type and was interested in participating in local straight politics. Feeling more comfortable at the Meadows, he began to talk to the JMers about all the things they could do with the land if they put their minds to it. They could set up a saw mill, plant a large garden, raise cattle, and so forth. While the people from Peter's home town were interested, the street people didn't like the idea of some ambitious outsider coming in and organizing their lives for them. Those in favor of Yale urged him to move to JM saying they would give it a try.

Yale left Parson's Crossing in an attempt to revitalize the Meadows, and to live with Jean's sister. Moving into the A-frame with DT and Jean, the new "couple" deliberately tried not to fall into traditional monogamous patterns, leaving each other as independent as possible to do what each wanted. This led to the two of them spending much time without each other and to an experimentation with a third person. Breaking the history of standard SS patterned sexual relationships at JM, Yale served as a catalyst for the emergence of some new forms. But, the menage a trois led to cooling of his relationship with Jean's sister. Yale, who was bisexual, came to be frozen out as the two heterosexuals would remain in bed together after Yale got up in the morning to do his daily round of chores. Later finding Claudius also unattached and bisexual, Yale slept with him instead. He accounted for his actions by saying, "When in a storm, put in at any port."

Yale quickly became the father figure at the Meadows, stirring up the same love-hate feelings in the others that parent figures usually did in communal situations. He took over the finances, and dealt with outside authorities, such as the food stamp people. He continued to agitate for work projects, eventually making life so miserable for the new IBM members, that they drifted away one by one before two months had passed. Taking an attitude described as "extremely autocratic" by observers, and acknowledged by himself as "very necessary," he demanded obedience, and threatened the IBMers with expulsion if they did not conform. He would give verbal reprimands to some for work not done and praise to others for work well done, an approach that JMers both resented and appreciated. His bedtime stories read in a theatrical fashion served as major midwinter entertainment, particularly for the street people who could not read themselves. When JM visited other communes and alternative institutions, Yale rarely went, attempting to avoid the embarrassment he knew would follow. Or if he did go along, he acted in a capacity similar to a Boy Scout leader, holding articulate conversations with those he regarded as his peers, intermittently interrupting them to look after his brood.

As the winter progressed, relations between Yale and the others at JM deteriorated. The other JMers became more resentful of his high handed approach, and he grew impatient with their lack of enthusiasm, initiative, and self-direction. Finally, Yale went to talk to the food stamp people and returned with the news that he had gotten into an argument with them, and had removed JM from their list of recipients. He claimed JM should be able to get along without food stamps anyway, and those too lazy to work would either have to change their habits or go hungry. Most people didn't react negatively to this immediately, but other events caused them to wonder. For example, some were contributing money toward the purchase of a pickup truck. But when Yale indicated that the truck would not be community property open to use by anyone, but instead would be under his control, the others began to balk.

Meanwhile, Yale had been negotiating with Peter to obtain a lease on the Meadows with an option to buy. It was to be granted for practically no money at the start, the total price to be paid after some income was generated. Peter's main fear was that even autocratic Yale could not control the Meadows' destructive, repetitive cycles. Attempting to prove he could change the character of the place, Yale resorted to increasingly drastic measures, but soon became discouraged with the results of his efforts. Moreover, he and Peter hit a snag on the negotiations regarding the use of psychoactive substances on the land. Yale wanted the freedom to discriminate rather than prohibit. After the idea of the lease faded away, after Jean's sister returned to her home and school, and after tension over his efforts to organize JM became intolerable, Yale gave up. He simply left one day, to move into Grasshopper Farm after Harvey extended an invitation.

JM people then demanded the return of the $50 they had contributed toward the truck, having practically no money to buy food since they no longer had food stamps. Yale brushed off their requests saying he had "lost it." Hank returned to JM to visit, and he, some visitors, and the other street people drank an immense amount of beer, wine, and whiskey over a two day period. Drunk and angry over the money, seven men stormed over to Grasshopper Farm; Roamer and the women remaining behind. Barging into the house, they demanded to see Yale. Hank made threats while Yale vowed to get everyone off the land even if he had to "starve them out" or use his connections with the town. While the argument ensued, the others roamed into the kitchen, and finding entire cupboards stocked with preserves and canned goods, spontaneously attacked the food supply. Taking large pots and dumping in all the vegetables they could find, they heated them and ate ravenously. They dropped jars on the floor, spilled the contents of pans, and ate to the point of engorgement, managing to consume most of the reserves they could find. They walked out the door with food and kerosene lanterns under their arms and in their pockets. While the "raid" was going on, the Grasshopper people, admittedly intimidated and terrified by the mob, huddled together in the living room for mutual protection.

Yale finally agreed to pay the $50 though he didn't have it at the time. The kitchen was in shambles and Grasshopper's stores were decimated. Realizing they were the propertied communal rich of the Wilfred CC compared with the starving JMers who hadn't eaten for two days, they were prepared to grant JM the food. Now living the bourgeois life, many had previously been Marxist radicals in college, and their former political consciences would not allow them to call out the police. But they were quite disturbed over JM's angrily taking rather than asking and being granted. Grasshopper was left with a cleaning-up job that took days to complete and JM was on the black list of yet another commune. The possibility of a rapprochement with Yale was ruled out.

By the end of February 1971, JM was leaderless, broke, cold, hungry, and isolated. Moreover, Peter was still considering selling the land out from underneath them if he could find a buyer. Roamer increasingly withdrew from the group as it took on a distinctly anti-hippie orientation. Mustering his courage to face the outside world that years ago had driven him into a series of mental institutions, he visited friends in the cities, particularly a former woman JMer and her boyfriend with whom he spent a couple of months. Boop and Jean increasingly became proprietresses of their respective houses rather than commune members, complaining to each other that life at the Meadows was not only intolerable for them, but unfit for their babies that were due. Claudius and a fellow from Peter's home town, who both had supported Yale's presence at the Meadows and the work ethic, left to "find some women," intending to return in the spring. The last of the young intellectuals, also from Peter's home town, left permanently, first to his home town drug scene, and then to Chisholm College for a trimester with Pepsi Joe. The third fellow from Peter's home town, Mission Street Mike, remained with DT and Zeke, becoming a member of the "new generation of the IBM's." With only eight members, and many of them floating around the region and the country, sometimes a week could go by with no one on the land.

The living situation continued to deteriorate. Although the people spoke of a tightness and strong communal feelings that grew between them over the winter, much of it resulted from having no other choice but living with each other when they couldn't find opportunities to leave. About the only outside people they got along with were Irwin Street poverty people and alcoholics who shared a similar animosity toward the world and its social institutions. At one point Boop and Zeke actually moved into an apartment rented by a straight welfare couple, but they had to leave after a week because conditions there were far more intolerable than at JM. The husband was a heavy drinker and the wife "was absolutely helpless and ignorant, often not feeding her children, giving them Pepsi and potato chips when she did remember, and never cleaning the toilets, sinks, or tubs." A helpful alliance with welfare people, however, was achieved when an activist woman welfare recipient visited the Meadows to discover that the poverty existing there made her own condition seem like affluence. She illegally collected unused surplus food from her own and other welfare families for JM, but because it was so difficult for JM to get to her town to pick it up, the project was abandoned after a month.

JM's poverty was real and desperate. DT at one point became ill, so ill in fact that Jean got scared and had a visitor drive him to the hospital. Despite his alarmingly high temperature, the staff refused him treatment after learning he was from JM. He was finally admitted to another hospital 60 miles away where the nurse chastised the others for not getting him medical attention sooner, asserting he had almost died from dehydration. At the root of this and numerous other ailments that winter was the poor diet. Contributing to DT's condition, for example, was the fact that the only food there was to eat was brown rice and soy sauce with a high salt content. During another period of three weeks, the only food available was rice and mustard. The incidence of illness was quite high, and people were slow to recover. One genus of disease was affectionately dubbed "Jackson's Meadows egg-fart-and-burp disease." Complaints of physical weakness were also heard.

Starvation and other unpleasant aspects of JM life associated with poverty were genuine and omnipresent. Compounding this situation were their efforts to escape the poverty through unrealistic scheming and constant indulgence in available drugs and alcohol. Despite protestations that the people tried to change, the same repetitive cycles occurred day after day. The women became stronger as they began to lose patience with the entire situation. Money they received from home and welfare even allowed them to consider leaving JM. The men became more dependent on the women, feeling pinched between the women's accelerating demands and the knowledge that the women could survive on their own. Finally, when Cindy and her two children returned from her disastrous stay with the Mother Humpers, the three women had the financial resources (mostly welfare) to rent an apartment in town just off Irwin Street. Thus, they established an independent base operations in which the men became even more peripheral.

As JM's internal situation deteriorated, so did its external relations with both the CC and SS. JM's last tie to other communes was established when in mid-winter JM discovered the Blue House. Though connected with the Free Provincia movement that was by this time quite hostile toward JM, there was much in common between the two communes, such as young age, limited education, and lower class background. But Allen, an ex-JMer living there, knew that conflict was certain to arise if JM were to be welcomed at the Blue

House. Nevertheless, one of the youngest Blue House members invited JM to a party at which JMers overtaxed Blue House hospitality by eating its food reserves, leaving dirty dishes and bathtubs, and harassing the women. After Blue House's resentment was expressed, relations between the two cooled to virtually no contact. During the period from October to February, JM had been declared unwelcome in every area commune. Forays to urban hip ghettoes and friendships with Irwin Street poverty people and greasers remained their only source of contact with the outside world.

The spring and early summer of 1971 saw only five regular members of JM living on the land, and even they were away more than they were there. All were males, and three of the five spent months away from Provincia looking for women to bring back. They eventually returned with no women after having had brief affairs. Roamer spent some time in a nearby city, after he felt he had "gotten [his] head together" to the point where he could again face the cacophony of urban life. DT spent much of his time at the apartment in Centerville, where his increasingly independent minded woman, Jean, still lived with Boop and Zeke, and later Cindy.

The deterioration of the relationships between the men and women continued even further. The women began to react strongly against the drinking at their apartment, too, knowing that it was often more important to the men than they were. And the men then used the women's nagging as an excuse to continue to drink heavily and get obnoxious. "What's the use?" one asked. "Even if I don't get ripped she gets pissed off anyway. So I might as well get ripped." The drinking occasionally led to shooting barbiturates and heroin. Upon discovering this, the women flatly stated that if they continued such behavior, they would leave them. While maintaining a public stance of nonchalance and good-time-Charlie, Jean revealed that in private, DT sometimes sat in tears, agonizing over what was wrong with him and why he couldn't straighten out. One time he and Zeke washed, combed their hair, attempted to sober up, and actually went to be admitted as patients to the hospital where they previously worked so they could "dry out." But federal funding for that particular program had been cut off. A few days later they were back on the street and drinking again.

Finally all the JM women severed ties with their street men. Jean left DT after he smashed the TV set in the apartment while drunk. He hated it, he said, because it symbolized the technology and life of comfort and decadence that led Jean away from the Meadows and away from him. She and Cindy then went to live on a farm elsewhere in Provincia recently bought with a trust fund by a pre-fire JMer. Cindy cut ties with Hank by having an affair with Claudius. And Boop took her man back to a house her father bought them in her home town. Her father also found him a job, but Zeke could not take the regimentation and isolation from his cronies, and after deciding Boop's money was not worth the restrictions placed on what he wanted to do, "ran away from home" back to JM several times. Boop finally left him, returning to another part of Provincia to take up with a rock musician.

Sexual patterns also changed during this period. Having no liaisons with women, some of the men occasionally engaged in homosexual behavior though never publicly admitting it. Jean became very involved with her baby, and after having gone through a period of promiscuity now practiced virtual abstinence. Cindy ended up living with the ex-JMer who bought the new farm, confiding she did it more out of a need for a home than feelings for the man involved. She openly toyed with the idea of bisexuality, jokingly saying that it was the "latest fad" in the CC, but seriously indicating that some women appealed to her physically, while all appealed to her mentally more than men. Claudius developed a very close relationship, this time with bisexual woman from Rainbow Farm. As a way of depressurizing from the intense feminist consciousness that enveloped Rainbow Farm, the woman, Blythe, moved into the tree house with Claudius.

Criminal behavior and run-ins with the police increased. Once DT went outside an Irwin Street bar to find a bottle of wine he had hidden, followed by a fellow he had been drinking with. According to DT, he was just standing there talking to the fellow, but someone inside the bar reported they were fighting and called the police. When they arrived they saw DT in a drunken condition lying on the ground and told him to get up. DT, however, refused to get up. He was taken to the city jail, punched a few times, and dragged down the stairs by his long hair (with scalp wounds to prove it). Another time, the police arrived to find DT drunk in the midst of shattered window glass from a store on Centerville's main street. He claimed that he was jumped by two people from the bar he was in, and pushed through the glass. But because there were no witnesses to corroborate his story and he could not pay for the damage he had done, he was sentenced to a thirty-day jail term. He later admitted in a private conversation that he did smash the window himself. Passing by the window in a drunken, self-hating condition he saw a reflection of himself and literally struck out at it.

The accumulating police record for JM members cannot be blamed solely on drink, drugs, and thoughtless, malicious behavior. Their refusal to submit to what they considered to be police infringement on their rights, their condition of poverty (for example, being arrested for loitering when picked up passing through a town with no money in their pockets on the way to get some food someone was giving them), and police harassment were undeniable factors. DT and Mission Street Mike once were picked up and jailed for hitchhiking and told they could leave after paying a five dollar fine. (If they had the five dollars in the first place they wouldn't be hitching.) When an ex-JMer arrived to spring them, the police, under the pretext of his "speeding" in the parking lot, took his license and kept it while they discussed the new situation they said had arisen. They upped the fine to ten dollars each. Inwardly outraged but outwardly cool, the driver volunteered to go back to his town to get the extra money, and the police agreed, keeping his license supposedly to make sure he would return. When he did return, they nabbed him in the parking lot again, this time for driving "without a license." The police kept the money and the three of them spent the night in jail. It was events such as these that made DT and Mission Street Mike despise all authority even more. Despite having nothing resembling what a radical could call political consciousness, and despising the political heavies in the CC, DT still spoke of the coming revolution, and once ominously remarked, "When it comes, I'm sure going to take some blood."

Not aware of DT's threats, the larger SS community, which had already shifted its initial reaction of curiosity to one of fear, was now developing an attitude of contempt. JM's descent into chaos, degradation, and violence was regarded by the police, welfare, and heath authorities with rising annoyance, and many citizens stated with growing confidence that their opposition to "dirty" hippies and radicals was justified. Oblivious to the fact that their own attitudes and actions had often contributed to the decline, they seized upon JM as the most visible part of the local CC, using its negative example to generate more hostility toward all CC groups, whether religiously or politically aligned or arts or community service oriented.

JM was even used by its former lawyer, now a state's attorney and gubernatorial aspirant, as an election issue. He publicly charged that JM was the main conduit through which new hippies arrived in the area and that it was the center of all local drug activity that was now corrupting the voters' children. The truth was that JM had long lost its magnetic attraction for CC seekers, and that it had only the most peripheral role in drug distribution, itself being a consumer. In fact, it got its drugs from other sources, including the sons and daughters of the local voters. In the end, it was in no one's interest in the SS to defend or help JM, and its only function at this point was as a tool to help justify the various self-interests of its many critics.

The JM situation was not as clear with respect to other segments of the local and regional CC. Nearly all of the other longhairs had some kind of awareness and dream of an evolving alternative society into which all people, especially the poor and oppressed, would be welcome, and in which communes would play a central organizing and modeling role. But here was JM, now an embarrassment to the cultural revolution in the region and, in some cases, an actual destructive force impeding their own work to help create a new life and society.

Religious groups, such as the Brethren, had essentially already split off from the overall movement, despite some vague talk of common goals. They were seeking change and salvation through self-involved personal transformation instead of coordinated community action, and dumping democratic principles, found it most effective to organize around autocratic and authoritarian leaders. They tended to view groups such as JM with particular disdain, as people who at basic levels shared their quite troubled emotional lives and a propensity for self-involved pursuits, but who inexcusably had chosen the downhill road to debauchery over the exalted path of subservience to a higher being or force.

The artistic or literary groups, such as Parson's Crossing, had also disentangled themselves from the movement as such, regarding emergent political and religious activities as increasingly fanatic and dangerous, while also realizing more than other segments of the CC that they all were fundamentally dependent on the larger, more stable, and affluent society at large as the main source of income for the work they produced. They viewed JM with some mixed emotions, feeling some identification with its plight, but more importantly, responded with repugnance at their overall lack of education, middle class etiquette, self-initiative, and culture, and with outright fear of JM's violence and covetousness of their more ample resources.

The Free Provincia people, however, were the most troubled by JM's situation. As part of their political movement to build a new egalitarian society that would simultaneously rely on and empower all people, regardless of background or lifestyle, they had deliberately sought to include JM. They took a supportive position in JM's struggle with the Brethren and welcomed JM's participation in its own fight over Liberation Farm. But the longer the relationship lasted and the further JM slid into decline, the more they agonized over what to do with it. JM was not only revealing itself as a failure of the new society, but as a definite drag on their entire movement, causing many to reconsider their ideological positions concerning the inherent equality of all individuals and the need for "power to all the people." Because of JMers' and other similar longhairs' behavior, some even began to look seriously at the elitist notion of social triage; of excluding and sacrificing some people so as to better channel and increase the chances of those already more likely to survive and succeed in the revolutionary struggle.

The Free Provincia movement had already been badly shaken. First, was the SS community violence directed at it after the Liberation Farm showdown and the escalated police harassment and middle-of-the-night raid by the FBI that followed. But more important, was the knowledge that it was the average and marginal working persons, for whom the revolution was supposedly being waged, who turned on them to cause the most damage. Finally, they were further demoralized when the day care center and the Liberation Garage they established, projects that had initially been genuinely able to serve low income people in the SS, failed shortly afterward. The idea was to get these alternative institutions started, then pass them over to the people to run by themselves for their own benefit. The people, as it turned out, certainly in the case of the garage, mismanaged them to the point of ruin through internal violence, lack of planning and coordination, alcohol use on the job, intimidation by redneck friends, and little evidence of a self-disciplining work ethic.

Now, cracks appeared within the movement itself as well, as similar patterns appeared. After a certain point, the more the movement succeeded in drawing in great numbers of all kinds of people, the more its own fabric was stressed and weakened. JM itself was the immediate cause of the failure of a truly revolutionary experiment in community-based operation of a service enterprise, the Vital Victuals Restaurant, where each day's operation in a weekly cycle was managed by a different commune or political collective. JM's weekly obligation was not always met, and on occasion, money was "borrowed" from the till never to be repaid, leading to unreliable hours and customer distrust and to unexpected financial shortfalls. Although already struggling, this particular enterprise model was finally terminated when the town, which had long been looking for an excuse to close it down as a CC gathering place, eventually found one. It came when a health inspector showed up early one morning to discover that some JMers had slept there the previous night in violation of both the restaurant rules and a town ordinance.

Perhaps more important, JMers and others like them seriously interfered with Free Provincia's community consciousness raising and organizing efforts. At movement gatherings they consistently got the drunkest and most out of control with, at best, annoying or, at worst, dangerous behavior. Examples ran from knife throwing at wall posters in the crowded local restaurant, through badgering for food and lodging from different political collectives Free Provincia had recently established regionally, to driving an automobile around erratically at night in a field of sleeping protesters during the "bring the War home" March On Washington at the national level. Meeting after meeting was interrupted and sidetracked by JMers hustling money for cheap wine or by shouting out irrelevant or derisive remarks. Hank and a few others directly caused the uproarious breakup of a crucial regional organizing meeting and exposed a very deep and growing schism in the movement between dominant strategists and rising feminists, when they were accused of an attempted rape in a nearby room while the meeting was in progress.

DT's comment about taking blood during the upcoming revolution was only symptomatic of the forces causing serious misgivings among Free Provincia people. Their previous strategy of a "people's revolution" might not work after all. Instead, it might serve only to unleash unproductive violence and lead to the retaliative destruction of the still vulnerable new society they were trying to build, both from within and from without. As an alternative, they began to organize through less direct means, working with other competent independent groups and sympathizers at the regional level. This also involved a hands off policy in terms of specific local projects which directly competed with or challenged existing SS institutions, particularly those involving marginal people of either the SS or the CC. Accordingly, instead of efforts being made to integrate JM into this new organizational constellation which could act as a humane social support network for the less fortunate as well as better situated members, JM was left to fend for itself. JM and its remaining friends had really become part of a new CC underclass.

Analysis

DT and most others involved with JM accordingly were representative of the powerless, oppressed people of the local CC. Taking "blood" was about the only way left for many to affect those who always seemed so comfortable, smug, and in control of things. It was clear that even the new society that was designed to be egalitarian by the CC leadership and originally felt to be gloriously free and unrestrictive by participants increasingly developed rigid internal social boundaries. Initially drawing people from all walks of life, shaking them up and comingling them in societal test tubes, now in the settling out process, distinct new layers were forming. Although occurring throughout the Provincian CC, JM provides one of the most graphic illustrations. A review of the evolution of stratification experienced by the commune demonstrates the basic dynamic of this process.

In the early days after the initial fusion phase in the formation of JM, the character of leadership changed significantly, and it became evident that leadership did not rest on spiritual and political awareness or other non-material concerns alone. It will be recalled that a certain cluster of people in addition to JM Peter emerged as a core group around which the rest of the commune revolved. Conceptualized in terms of stratification instead of a central axis, the core groups at JM could have just as accurately been called the group's elite or the commune's upper class. People outside the core largely fed information into the core while the communication from the core to the outside was more often in the form of requests, exhortations, or directives based on the in-flowing information. With the core, there was a pooling of commune-pertinent information such that any single member of the core knew more about the commune than any member outside the core. This pooling of knowledge extended beyond the operation of the commune, as core members were also most active in finding out about town and regional affairs and were most competent in those skills necessary for survival on the land.

Harder to plot was the flow of material resources, largely because the dominant egalitarian and anti-materialistic ideologies served to obscure it. Although never noted or acknowledged within the group, almost without exception the core people were also the people through whom most of the material resources were processed. They contributed the most cash, arranged for most of the exchanges of goods and labor, most consistently contributed the major share of physical labor, and controlled the preparation and distribution of most of the goods and facilities, from food to fuel to shelter and to transportation. The same core people also figured most prominently in recruitment of new people and in the establishment of dyadic social bonds between people who were already members. Certain core individuals proved to be in the center of social structuring activity, as the major networks from which most new members were recruited were anchored by people from the core group. Core members were most often involved in sexually based relationships with one another and the production and care of children. Because the bulk of the information, material resources, and membership flow was channeled by means of well established and significant dyadic relationships, monitoring these relationships yielded important data about the structure within the core itself.

Primary indicators for high status within the entire commune were the large number, the numerous kinds, and high complexity of social relationships maintained by each individual within the group. This led to a relatively high level of structural complexity with respect to what constituted the upper stratum. Conversely, the lower strata exhibited relatively fewer, less diverse, and lower complexity relationships. In addition to the number and complexity of social links, the content and balance of flow of information, material, and human resources along those links was also important. JM's elite performed a redistributive function, with respect to economic exchange, communication, and recruitment. Theirs ostensibly was an egalitarian redistribution in which the quality and quantity of inflow to the leadership was approximately matched by outflow to the lower strata. This differed from the Brethren, whose leadership, through an unequal flow, accumulated reserves for its own personal use. In contrast, the reality was that the JM core ended up providing more cash, goods, and services to the outer people than they received from them, and the leadership approached states of near exhaustion through being drained by the others. Whether rewarding or unrewarding, the upper stratum was defined by the number and breadth of relationships they maintained, in effect encompassing and using all the relationships established between members of the lower strata as well; relationships that were numerous in sum, but fewer for each individual in the lower strata compared to the upper.

It is also possible to examine the behavior of each individual in the context of relationships. Because any individual had to act in relation to other persons and through them, to objects, the form behaviors took reflected the compound structure of all the relationships. By examining individuals' behaviors, one could note differences between those individuals who appeared to occupy positions in the inner and outer circles, or the upper and lower strata, and could better understand from at least a psychological perspective how leaders and groups of co-leaders were formed. Without imputing any intrapsychic drives for recognition and power, it was possible to observe more differentiated and complex behaviors among the leadership, both with respect to space and to time. These individuals were more apt to set instrumental rather than expressive goals, and these goals were more often multiple than simple, requiring a series of differentiated sequential behaviors in order to achieve them.

For example, whereas the people outside the core concerned themselves with looking after personal maintenance, getting high, maintaining certain diets, participating in conversation, engaging in sex, or just finding a place to sleep, the core people, in addition, organized their behavior so that money was earned for taxes and tools, so that buildings were eventually built, and so that town officials were consulted from time to time. In order to get high, one merely had to wait around the Meadows until a visitor with psychoactive substances arrived, or had to convince someone to provide transportation into town. But in order to raise money, people had to leave the land regularly to look for work, and finding it, get up regularly, travel to work, perform tasks, and save the money. Moreover, due dates, deadlines, and work schedules had to be kept in mind, and care taken not to jeopardize the sources of cash for future needs.

Some who exhibited the most negentropized behaviors, the so-called structure freaks, were not always welcomed or recognized as important, however. Many who were considered too structured, even at times including the established leadership, would be frozen out, or would themselves leave in a mood of impatience or disgust. In times of crises whose roots were external to the group, structure freaks rose in prominence as the group mobilized to meet the crises. On the other hand, interpersonal disputes and internal difficulties often had their roots in the clash between structure freaks and go-with-the flow people; with the former urging highly organized behaviors on the latter, and the latter resisting by disrupting the schedules and procedures of the former. Leadership emerged where stress was most evident, and was operationalized through its deliberate attempts to negentropize the rest of the membership. This is not to say that everyone in the group performed tasks reflecting the increased complexity of the overall group situation. On the contrary, individual behaviors often became simpler because specific tasks were assigned to specific people for the sake of maximum efficiency. But even those simpler behaviors had specified definitions and a precise sequential order never achieved before the crises. Somewhere, the division of labor had to be coordinated, and where the complexity of issues and behaviors were considered and decided upon, the leadership surfaced.

This raises the question of who filled leadership roles. Elitism to the extent it existed, was not merely an attitude learned in the SS and carried over to the CC. There were always ongoing situations requiring certain kinds of behaviors so that individuals could adapt and survive. Certain kinds of people stepped in to perform certain necessary tasks. Thus, the dynamic of the CC itself created the conditions whereby leadership elites of some sort became important. But even given those conditions, was it always former members of the SS upper classes and elites, the children of corporate executives, who stepped into the breach? Moreover, did these same upper class SS trained people actually create the crisis situations whereby their particular brand of skills would become necessary?

The answer to both questions is partly yes and partly no. Some highly motivated individuals, by their own admission, did create situations where they would become important, gain recognition, and achieve a sense of power by controlling the behavior of others. A majority, but by no meals all, did have socioeconomic class backgrounds that would have placed them in the upper strata of the SS. By the same token, leadership roles were assumed by individuals who joined the CC in an attempt to escape the restrictive yet complex negentropic behaviors forced on them through schooling and job training. Despite their reticence, these people were literally forced by circumstances to take control of certain situations requiring disciplined and methodical responses.

A significant proportion of the leadership in communes and alternative institutions did not come from the upper strata of the SS. Many active leaders came from working, lower middle and even borderline poverty class backgrounds. But they were people who had had unusual exposure to environments requiring self-discipline, such as private school education, instruction in the arts, or travel. Thus the CC provided an avenue for a kind of vertical social mobility that was not operating as efficiently in the SS. Whereas the relatively unskilled could settle to a lower position in the CC at this point without great stigma being attached, the creatively skilled who found it difficult to conform to SS encumbrances and ritual hurdles could ascend to the uppermost heights in their immediate, if limited, social universe.

As described in this chapter, however, CC downward mobility could be precipitous and brutal. To the extent that stigma and social pressure were critical determining factors in the pain of descent, the CC could provide a benign environment. In this milieu, display of wealth or power was frowned upon, just as signs of social leveling and humility were respected. But abject material conditions could create such a harsh environment that people with the best of intentions would turn upon and injure one another. The dynamics of this CC version of the poverty syndrome was such that anyone could be pulled into its centripetal whirl, regardless of SS class background. The explanation for this downward slide into near collapse for JM and a few other communal groups does not lie solely within the inner dynamic of each, but also within the larger evolving CC as a whole. The potential leadership and upper strata for JM that did not remain, had to be absorbed by other groups or institutions offering greater potential for constructive development. Thus, the precipitous decline of JM could come about through the simultaneous growth and development of other CC structures and the shifts and realignment of the CC population that their elaboration permitted.

This can be illustrated by looking beyond the situation that obtained the first year at JM to that which existed the second year. Internally, the inner-core/outer-periphery dichotomous analogy no longer held up. There developed a more complex organization lending itself more readily to a trichotomous paradigm instead, as hippie, street people, and intellectual factions emerged. This occurred, it will be recalled, through a significant population turnover as well as through the evolving lifestyles of specific individuals. While the defensive, productive, or decision-making functions did not reside exclusively in any one faction, there were definitely by now familiar patterns involved with respect to the distribution of these tasks. When there were no pressing crises, the distribution was relatively even with respect to factions and individuals within each faction. Near entropic states existed with little interdependence tying people together.

However, in the times of stress associated with the Brethren conflict, the Liberation Farm struggle, or mobilization for survival in the winter, strong leadership manifested itself more frequently in those people through whom the most information, material resources, and indirectly, membership, flowed. The same criteria for leadership as in the past re-emerged, but because the commune was more established and its members more committed to certain styles of life, the pattern was more complex. Again, the verbal and intellectual prerequisites for leadership were abundantly clear, but these had to be supported by a significant material input as well. And those most motivated to think and act on behalf of the group were those who had invested the most in it, economically and otherwise. While leadership roles played by the street people and hippies varied from crisis to crisis, the intellectuals were consistently involved in all. Therefore, the full time intellectual wing more than any other constituted the upper stratum of the group.

As previously stated, to understand more fully how this identifiable leadership "class" manifested itself, one must look outside the commune as well as within it. More communes and collectives had been founded after JM, permitting contacts between all of them and the subsequent establishment of informal links that created a new level of social organization. Moreover, these contacts and links were established in a systematic way. Factions appeared within all the communes in the region as the accumulated experiences of individuals gradually made it clearer to many within each the particular kinds of lifestyles they wished to pursue. Movement toward these lifestyles escalated as people in various communes discovered people with similar interests in other communes and exchanged ideas, goods and services. Those people in each commune who had the greatest number of significant contacts and friends in other communes also by and large constituted the internal leadership of their respective communes.

Just as the inner core at JM the first year had the most complex and overlapping network of dyadic links within the commune, so did the leadership faction in the second year, but this time, the network extended to relationships with people in other communes. A new dimension of leadership had been created, concomitant with the establishment of a higher level of social organization (the intercommunal network), and leadership and social dominance became most apparent where the interconnecting links were located. Again, this new order of leadership was materially as well as communicationally based. The same people who had a dominant role in bringing wealth into the intercommunal network through publishing, holding salaried jobs, and pulling in various trust funds and inheritances, also played a leading role in exchanging these resources within the network.

A new overall organizational pattern became apparent. Individuals who had made various inter-communal contacts in many cases began to move about, some joining other communes where they felt more comfortable and others beginning new communes with acquaintances who shared similar lifestyles, values, and backgrounds. Peter went to the Brethren for a while; Patrick and Allen went to the Blue House; Yale went to Rainbow Farm, then to Parson's Crossing, back to JM and then to Grasshopper Farm; Jesse and Jake went to Red Rose, Annette and others went to Moore commune; and many went to Walnut Hill Farm. This population shift was not sudden, but by the winter of 1970-71, a transfer of like minded clusters of people to certain other groups had occurred. In this transfer, the hierarchies that formerly existed only within the separate communes were transformed to a significant extent into a higher order of hierarchy between communes as they were linked together.

Thus, intellectuals with a political bent tended to collect in one part of the Centerville Area CC, and those with a literary or back-to-the-land orientation went to another. Hippies tended to move to another, and street people to still another. The internal organization of each group was made somewhat simpler in the process, with divisive internal conflicts due to clashing lifestyles and behavior rhythms and patterns being reduced through people segregating themselves to a certain extent. As a consequence, intercommunal friction rose as people involved in old animosities and differences tended to become identified with particular communes. After this resorting process was over, a communal pecking order of sorts did emerge, often blurred by a "separate but equal" ideology which asserted that CC growth only occurred through lateral differentiation. But even the most enthusiastic supporters of communal egalitarianism had to acknowledge that floating groups like the IBMs and the Mother Humpers, and JM as a fixed communal locus, represented something of a different order. By universal acclamation, they constituted the lowest stratum of the area CC, the "niggers" of freakdom, Wilfred's own "ghetto."

In order to discuss the precise manner in which hierarchical structure evolved in the area CC as a whole, some details of the lateral proliferation of communal groups must also be recalled. By the time the events described in this chapter had occurred, there were thirteen other communes or collectives in the Centerville area. Each group had taken on a certain character after initial fusion states, followed by the sometimes painful sorting out periods. Some groups primarily focused around political organizing, others around spiritual pursuits, others around the expressive arts of film, literature, and music, one around psychotherapy, and another around women and gender role redefinition. Some, like JM, had little focus other than survival and "partying."

Although gaining less attention, the process of developing alternative modes of economic support was underway at the same time. Ten communes, including JM, relied on horticulture as a major support base. For some, such as Grasshopper, Walnut Hill, and Last Ditch Farms, food production was the focal activity, while in others such as Red Rose and especially JM, it was distinctly secondary. To varying degrees, other support skills were relied upon, ranging from crafts, carpentry, and hired-out unskilled labor to food stamps, welfare, hustling, and outright theft. Each group had its own unique mix, and as such could, in theory, be rated in hierarchical order according to various combinations of weighted criteria concerning inflow and outflow of information, material, and human resources.

With the new, area CC-wide uneven redistribution of skills, resources, people, wealth, interests, and talents, some former problems were solved by some groups while they were exacerbated in others. During the early phases of communal development, a critical problem was the proper balance of membership heterogeneity. Some people argued that as broad a cross section as possible of personality types and people with diverse interests should be maintained, for that would provide a varied pool of potential adaptive responses to unpredictably changing environments. But of the communes that failed or almost failed so far, after economic problems, too diverse a membership was most often blamed for collapse or near collapse. These groups contained people who could hardly communicate with one another and some people always complained about carrying the dead weight of others who didn't contribute. The increase in the number of communes in the Centerville area helped alleviate much of the internal dissension while creating more stable groups. Moreover, through exchanges of members, the chances for survival of individuals in an overall communal context was enhanced as well. Thus, by moving beyond the organizational level of individual communes to communal networks, new possibilities emerged as the dissatisfied minority of each group now had other communes or alternative enterprises to move to.

Moreover, the resulting new and functioning communal network provided for most communes a broader, even if more distant, umbrella for the security of each. Thus, specialization did not necessarily lead to adaptive failure for groups. As long as there was a larger order of social organization (that is, the communal network), the potential for adaptive response to stresses and changing environments through communal specialization became more widely distributed. JM responded to the Brethren threat by being able to tap those resources concentrated at Red Rose and Liberation Farm Collectives, and Red Rose and Free Provincia were most successful in their efforts when they could tap the resources of other communes and CC individuals in the community. In fact, the effectiveness of each communal component in the CC network was enhanced to the extent that it was somewhat specialized, but only if plugged into the network in a way that other specialized resources could flow easily to it from other communal components in time of need.

So much for the advantages of the population reshuffling. Specialization and the uneven distribution of resources at the communal level, for all intents and purposes, also meant the unequal distribution of resources in the entire Centerville CC. After the reshuffle, some communal components could offer little of importance to other communes, and what they could offer, often was not wanted or needed. Moreover, those which had resources that were most universally in demand had to guard them, for it was certain that in the long run they would be depleted with the unfavorable exchange ratio. Whereas the reshuffling greatly benefited those communes who happened to accumulate important skills and resources and which managed to maintain a maximum number of even or favorable exchange links with certain (but not all) other communes, it precipitated serious difficulty for others. Those who gave away too much too soon, weakened and folded, such as the Liberation Farm Collective, and those who had nothing to give became isolated and increasingly pressed to rely on and consume its own rapidly dissipating resources. Such was the case of JM. Thus, although the overall well-being of the intercommunal system was strengthened, it was achieved at the expense of some of its components. While over-specialization, even within the broader context, spelled maladaptive disaster for some groups, under-specialization, as exemplified by JM, was equally as maladaptive.

Although the dynamics at all levels in the CC social hierarchy are important in maintaining stratification within the overall system, those processes occurring in the lower strata, as exemplified by JM, are of primary concern in this particular study. The structural aspects of social systems tell only part of the story. The rest involves the psychologically based behavioral predispositions of the individuals who composed the social structures. As in previous discussions of psychological considerations, individual behavior is not seen as only a manifestation of intrapsychic factors, but is viewed instead as the product of the interaction of, or to be more precise, the exchange between, two or more individuals, each of whom uses intrapsychic structures to guide his or her action in the course of relationship (Homans: 1958).

If certain political, economic, sociological, and psychological factors are taken together in an interaction framework; that is, if natural environmental factors, material support mechanisms, hostile outside influences, hierarchical and vertical differentiation, social bonding, socioeconomic class formation, power wielding (and non-wielding), and childhood socialization are stirred together in JM's cauldron, a complex but comprehensible explanation of real CC poverty emerges.

People came from all walks of life, but a majority did have their roots in the SS middle and lower middle classes. The kind of people initially attracted to the CC was important, however, as it tended to pull in those people intellectually opposed to "the system" as well as those who found it difficult to operate within its confines. Thus, the systems in the CC evolved in response to ongoing situational adaptive pressures in self-regulating systems (the interactive process), but also with the deliberate and perhaps subconscious efforts of individuals behaviorally disposed in certain ways (psychological states). Some of these behaviors, without SS middle class structures and pressures to control them, contributed to the generation of some new elites, but it also led to the creation of poverty.

JM is a perfect illustration of this poverty process. From its inception JM exercised very little control over the type of person who joined, and because of its primitive environmental conditions and virtually structureless state, it was able to accept almost anyone. Initially, it drew people who sought an unfettered life in the wild. But eventually it drew those people most lost and out of touch with the outside world more than it attracted those most tolerant of or predisposed toward an uncontrolled environment. Through a social equivalent of a natural selection process, JM ended up with people who were less reliant on structure, but also least able to control the environment around them in the form of imposed structures even if they wanted to. The result was that constant energy and food supplies could not be maintained, adequate protection from wind, rain and cold could not be mobilized, and proper work sequences other than those dictated by the nocturnal-diurnal cycle could not be organized.

Moreover, each autumn the solar seasonal cycle precipitated major shifts in the commune. While the specter of the oncoming winter caused some to build a house, get a stove, or stack away some dry wood, it also drove others away. Those who left had other options. They had a vehicle to travel with, a job to return to, friends to stay with, a reserve of money to spend, or skills that were employable elsewhere. Even without climatological pressures, there existed the constant "leveling" process by which everyone who remained at JM eventually had their private material resources diminished to the point of depletion. Equality was achieved within the group, but at the lowest common denominator.

Had JM been a group in a loosely organized band or tribal society rather than a communal group in an industrial one, a fixed and constant limit on the leveling process probably would have developed. Those individuals who exhibited slightly more negentropic behaviors would have had no other places to go, instead remaining and cajoling others into renewed or extended efforts as many headmen do. And if survival efforts through self-help and mobilization didn't maintain a certain minimum effort, the group would have perished or disintegrated. With JM, however, it was possible for the bottom line to be pushed progressively further down as SS and other CC wealth intermittently trickled in in the form of panhandled money, shop-lifted goods, services donated by CC sympathizers, gifts, and occasional jobs. JM was indeed a hunting and gathering microsociety, taking what an industrial, rather than natural, ecological system provided. But it turned into a band of scavengers as those most able to maintain a symbiotic rather than parasitic relationship with the socioeconomic context were constantly siphoned off.

People who exhibited what appeared to be predetermined and relatively unchanging behavior dramatically changed within the context of JM as well as within other communes, and although behavior change was most marked at the beginning fusion stages of development, it continued into the latter stages. Whereas the highly integrated and ecstatic periods were instrumental in destroying old patterns of behavior, the continued survival of the commune necessitated the elaboration of new patterns. Negentropized behavioral sequences that were apparently unrewarding or counterproductive in former SS contexts were disassembled by most people, to be reassembled into new sequences befitting the new and evolving CC environment. But given a certain critical mix of factors, the fusion state, after initially diffusing toward entropy, did not always reverse itself to negentropize in order to maintain itself as a productive system in a new context. Instead, except where external threats were involved and resisted, minimal cohesion could be maintained even as the communal system shrank in size, in internal integration, and in the number of external relationships.

What, indeed, was the critical mix of factors and how could behavior continue to disintegrate, if in fact it did "disintegrate"? To begin with, there is no denying the socialization that people experienced before arriving at JM. There was an increasing proportion of people who had emotional or behavioral problems according to just about anyone's definition. Most of them had been exposed to environments as children and young people that left them fearful of extending themselves either by establishing firm relationships or by interacting with elements in progressively broader environmental parameters in space or time. Afraid to go beyond a few initial steps, they apparently found it difficult to make any personal connections with any phenomena that appeared distant to them. Tending to live in the here and now, they would focus on plans for the day, but little more. Some of this was a deliberate effort to reduce the complexity, alienation, distance, and "irrelevance" of their lives as experienced in the SS, but much was not. The incidence of death, divorce, performance failure, and peer group ostracization in early life was extremely high in this latter group, and although a direct relationship between these experiences and passivity with regard to the overall environment cannot be documented with respect to these particular individuals, it is more than substantiated generally in the psychological literature (Hampden-Turner: 1970).

Did these psychologically injurious experiences take place earlier in their lives in the SS lower strata also? To a significant extent, no. When this investigation was first initiated in 1970, most of the literature indicated the growth of the CC was entirely a middle-class if not upper middle class phenomenon. It was a major surprise to find many people whose backgrounds were from a very low middle class, working class, and even poverty class. But these people did not constitute a clear majority, and as individuals they often were somewhat uncharacteristic of the stereotypes for their class background. They had either been adopted into middle class families where they didn't fit, had experienced very rapid upward or downward mobility in the short period from childhood to adolescence, or had otherwise been exposed to and expected to perform in social environments quite different from that which they had originally become accustomed.

The critical mix of situational factors, then, seemed to include, in addition to a high turnover of extensively skilled and resourceful people, the retention of a relatively high proportion of psychologically impaired people and people with lower socioeconomic class backgrounds. These two groups brought limited skills, resources, and social relationships, along with limited ability to create and maintain new ones. These backgrounds were then mixed with those of people from stable environments in the middle class. But the people with stable backgrounds were often either tired of hard and unrewarding work, or they had never been exposed to or made to feel responsible for the processes that materially maintained the social units to which they belonged, namely their families and schools. Or, they were too young to feel they had to take on many responsibilities. Thus, the overall mix was such that those with lower class backgrounds and psychological problems could increasingly create the dominant life mode in the group because the others were either rejecting theirs or searching around for any patterns that at first seemed more rewarding.

Background was only part of the story. In addition, there were on-going situational factors at work. JM had fewer ties to the CC than other groups, and belonged to no major karass. Even when it tried, it could not sufficiently mobilize itself for survival. As it became apparent JM was not able to reciprocate, the charity JM received from other CC groups and institutions dwindled, and the resentment on both sides led to even further deterioration of social, political, and economic ties. JMers turned increasingly to the SS, but here, too, they met with rebuff except at its lowest levels. Their jobs created more difficulties than they solved problems. In addition, there was deliberate bureaucratic and police harassment which caused psychic stress, and whittled away at JM's already shrinking material resources. Although the popular ideology tended to cover it up, material subsistence became increasingly important. The narrower the margin between comfort and mere survival, the more economic considerations loomed as paramount, with friendship, communication, and other interpersonal considerations falling into the background. Whereas a traffic ticket would only inconvenience most SS and CC people, it could destroy JM.

The less resources the commune had, the less able it was to cope with crises, and the more out of hand crises grew, the more these resources were drained. And the more crises occurred and resources dwindled, the more JMers and street freaks exploited other CC people and ultimately on one another in an effort to survive. The process was imperceptibly slow at first, picking up momentum as it went, sucking people into it when they did not know what was happening, then putting them in a position where they had far fewer options and reduced choices than they originally had. As the situation grew worse, people often took supposedly preventive actions, which instead accelerated the process. In its defensive retreat from perceived attack, JM set up further defensive barriers between it and the CC and SS, which also cut off all hope of reversing the processes of disintegration. As its members grew to distrust and even hate revolutionaries, peace and love, hippies, police, and shopkeepers alike, they were forced to rely more on one another. They needed one another, yet the constant stress took its toll. Violence was increasingly easy to precipitate between them as deep rooted resentment surfaced in the form of active hatred under the pressure. The more their need for material resources became paramount, the more they attempted to withdraw because of fear and ignorance of how to work them, from the very situations that could hope to generate these resources. But as they withdrew, hopefully for respite, external forces actively and relentlessly pursued them.

Toward the end, everyone who remained became locked into the pattern. They felt an increasing need to rely on a close set of buddies and escalated their belief that having fewer people to be responsible for constituted movement toward "freedom." They also found that joys and rewards could become more localized and concrete (such as those coming from a wine bottle instead of stemming from a friend or an accomplished task), and in doing so, became even more deeply caught up in the centripetal syndrome. It made little difference what their child rearing and socioeconomic class background was at that point, for it was their immediate situation that increasingly defined them and determined their behavior.

In addition to moving to other communes, there were, however, certain escape routes along the way. Some with a more stereotypical working class background, opted for Jesus. They had conversion experiences, thereafter organizing their lives around established church organizations, providing some evidence that the new religious revivals common in the CC did not stem as much from formerly living in the SS as they did from attempting to live in the CC. Out of desperation, others dropped out altogether, for example, joining the Air Force. A significant common route was that taken by the women who got pregnant. They formed a line of resistance to stress that not only seemed to hold up and to prevent further withdrawal and shrinkage of social space/time, but in a way provided a springboard from which the reversal of the syndrome was possible.

The mother/child unit worked to stop the spiral by forcing the woman into a close and unavoidable relationship with other humans even if she didn't like it. Most women and girls wanted to have children. They wanted someone to need them, someone to remain with them, someone to give them attention, and someone to give them a purpose. Most had either been lonely as children themselves or had been considered mavericks in adolescence. In a sense, they could now biologically manufacture a captive person to be with. At the level of conscious articulation, however, the new mothers stated that they could change the world more by developing a loved and loving child, than they could by fighting revolutions or living out in the woods. Because primitive living conditions were no longer tolerable, being injurious to the child and unduly troublesome for themselves, they began to think of ways to mobilize their behavior and resources to improve those conditions. They looked ahead and set goals requiring complicated, step by step procedures for their achievement.

Almost invariably the women ceased taking drugs and drinking alcohol upon becoming pregnant. And almost invariably their mates accused them of not being able to relax, to "let go," or to have any fun anymore. Mothers also began to conserve resources ("don't eat the cheese now because I need it for the baby tomorrow"), and to become the conduits through which increasing amounts of resources were channeled. Previously angry SS parents of CC daughters who had recently become mothers themselves, began to buy goods for their new grandchildren, while the new mothers became eligible for a constant and sizable monetary reimbursement through Aid to Families with Dependent Children. With this economic turnabout, their mates grew increasingly dependent on them for spending money while the women grew more independent. Arguments and fights escalated as the women became the dispensing agents for money, while increasingly resisting its waste on psychoactive substances, bizarre schemes, and even gambling. The men, feeling their relationships with their women slipping from their grasps, used more psychoactive substances and pursued more bizarre behaviors in reaction, which drove them even further from the women. Ultimately, relationships with these men became so unrewarding that after accumulating enough resources to fall back on, all the women terminated the relationships. Furthermore, toward the end, the class background and level of education and social skills of the remaining JM women ranked much higher than that of their mates. The women clearly appeared more competent than their mates. This could be explained by the off-noted tendency of people not fitting the stereotypes of their own subcultures, in this case SS male dominance and female submission, to select mates from a different subculture where their status or power could be enhanced (Goode: 1964). In this instance, a CC was generated which discriminated less against active women and passive men, making it more likely they would pair up. In any event, aside from a few very talented and dominant males, most of the initiatives and high levels of activity increasingly came to be recognized as emanating from the women.

The greater potential for the JM women to proliferate relationships, to exercise knowledge (none of the women were illiterate), and to mobilize material resources, paid off. Once they had children, women were able to achieve much of what they wanted while the men couldn't, despite the fact that they had to care for the children and partially support the men. While integrating themselves into the SS government welfare structure cannot be considered "liberating" in the usual sense, at least it prevented them from sliding further into poverty. In fact, it gave them the opportunity to drop their old mates and shop around for more capable ones who could help carry them back up the hierarchy while extricating them from a situation of absolute dependence on welfare. They also reintegrated themselves into the middle echelons of the CC by participating in such affairs as the organization of free schools and the publication of the intercommunal newsletter.

The role of psychoactive substances in the whole poverty syndromic process was particularly significant. Their use was the kind of escape route that intensified the process rather than alleviating it. The more unpleasant "reality" became, the more people sought altered states of consciousness, and the less they functioned with a normal state of consciousness, the more unpleasant reality became, and so on. Rather than meeting problems directly and mobilizing thought and behavior negentropically to reduce the stresses by changing the conditions that generated the stress, they entropized consciousness instead, concerning themselves with matters that were symptoms rather than sources of distress. Just as James, Peter, and the JM anti-drug-and-drink faction predicted, taking the more pleasant and immediate way out, getting high, made coming down off the high even worse. When they did come down and the objective situation was seen as getting worse, they were prompted to get high again so they wouldn't have to concern themselves until they came down again. Eventually, they didn't even have to come down from the high to see what was happening, for the high became a direct causative agent. Jumping off bridges, getting into arguments with the women over drinking and drugging, and progressively getting into more fights while high, even attacking one another with broken bottles, were sure signs.

It should be kept in mind, however, that JM was not typical of the CC. Psychoactive substance dependence was not the fate of groups higher in the new social hierarchy. For them, alcohol and marijuana, the substances of choice at that point, were for the most part much better self-regulated and controlled, causing little or no overt damage. In many cases, it could even be argued that use even enhanced adaptation to specific circumstances. Those adaptive circumstances, involving non-physiologically addicting marijuana in particular, didn't just come about by allowing people to get so stoned that they could tolerate otherwise stressful environments longer or better than others could. It was also achieved by helping previously compulsively motivated people and those who felt trapped by certain life circumstances to lay back, feel less pressure, and question many old attitudes and beliefs, which would then allow them, literally, to play with new avenues of pursuit. Often, these pursuits proved to be unrealistic, but many times they led to tangible changes that better suited their particular interests and abilities. And most of these people, who because of better skills, experiences, education, and access to resources, had a modicum of self-discipline and faith in their futures, eventually came to realize that continued indulgence in these substances was actually debilitating. At that point, they served only to interfere with their new paths once they had seriously set out on them. Most of these people subsequently either reduced use of marijuana significantly, or quit altogether (Laffan: 1982).

The circumstances surrounding JM did not permit such redirection. Instead, drugs and, to a greater extent, alcohol, greatly compounded JM's unfortunate situation to the point where its predominant lifestyle at times seem to be founded on them. This, along with all the other factors, led it to apparent self-perpetuating cycles that resulted only in more destitution. It is ironic, then, after the 1960s, when there was much critical discussion of the concept of "the culture of poverty" and many of the politically active people accordingly helped create the CC as a way of distributing wealth more evenly in the country that in the early 70s, in their own back yard, so to speak, there was an apparent "counterculture" of poverty. As evolved by JM in particular, but to a certain extent by other groups as well, it had nearly all the characteristics so often noted. These include: miscellany of unskilled occupations, absence of savings, crowded quarters, gregariousness, violence, and free unions, as well as political apathy, belief in sorcery and spiritualism, cynicism about government, hatred of police, and male superiority (Lewis: 1970)

Static characterizations such as those noted above, had been used by some politicians to label poverty individuals and groups as victims of their own culturally prescribed behavior patterns, rather than as structural artifacts of larger, dominant socioeconomic systems that functioned inefficiently and inequitably. To be sure, especially toward the end, many JMers followed courses of behavior that were clearly self-defeating. But the dynamic was initiated and sustained in many ways by larger, more encompassing systems, including those of both the SS and the CC, that could eventually overwhelm any one small group, creating conditions ripe for many inappropriate reactions. Having so far focused on JM's internal shortcomings, attention must also be drawn to these factors that were often beyond its control.

There are any number of larger, external causes that can be singled out. Some CC critics point directly to the CC itself as attracting only incompetent misfit followers and dogmatic idealist leaders, who despite their rhetoric, could not deal with common folk while urging them to sever supportive ties to the SS. The reverse argument by critics of the SS has it that the SS, because its very foundations were being threatened, locally and regionally, directly attacked, divided, and choked off various weaker parts of the CC. Other arguments blame the SS in more subtle ways for giving birth to the fledgling CC in the first place: CC critics calling it "permissive" in letting people wander too far from proven, reliable norms and CC supporters labeling it "oppressive" by going to certain extremes that drove its progeny away, forcing it to grapple unprepared with monumental issues.

While all these explanations have validity, possibly a more comprehensive way of looking at it is to see them all as artifacts of the overall, ongoing developmental and evolutionary process in human systems as they relate to one another. Specifically, much of the dynamics that generated JM's desperate situation and which might characterize groups in poverty classes in general could stem from its small size, minimal complexity, and consequent lack of integration with other systems around it that would permit support.

The tendency toward immediate gratification, the incapacity to plan ahead, the inability to build up reserves of cash or goods, the quick use of violence in order to affect other people's behavior, and daily face to face relations with the same people, all reflect the fact that social systemic context is quite restricted in scope. To take one example, deferred gratification implies that there are goals that require a series of intervening steps before final satisfaction can be achieved. But these steps actually correspond with lateral and vertical junctures in an elaborated and negentropically organized social milieu through which people must pass as they move their lives through time and space. Only in a large and complex society could a person study for examinations to pass from grade to grade, graduate and go on to college or a job where further sacrifice of simple pleasure is made for the sake of imposed task oriented work and eventual career advancement. Such a progression presupposes a supporting social organizational structure of schools, classrooms, fellow students, teachers, administration, and a university system and job market supported by a productive and commercial economy. Where no such complex structures exist there are few distant goals to which one can aspire.

In a commune in 1971 in Provincia, if one was not struggling in the context of a revolutionary vision and of a new spiritual age, all there was to do was to set goals for eating, sleeping, warmth, protection, sex, drink, singing, story telling, and the like. Agricultural pursuits, however, did require significant planning, and annual cycle/systems were important to many groups. Dedicated practice in order to become a rock star, or writing to become a recognized author, presupposed a vast public and an organized recording and publishing industry to distribute the product and collect the money. To the extent communards had access to such techno-industrial organizations through well-educated and well-to-do fellow members, deferred gratification was not uncommon. But for those who had little access, either because of lack of skill, or knowledge, credentials, or the right social connections, especially in the CC, where their availability was limited, deferred gratification made little sense.

This does not mean that all complex social systems require highly participatory and productive people. The fact that so many in the Provincian CC originally regarded themselves as peripheral or antithetical to SS behavioral norms is sufficient proof of that. Extreme specialization of components and overall negentropization can involve simpler behavior and more limited institutional and social links the lower the position in the hierarchy one occupies. By the same token, so-called asceticism can and does flourish in the same kind of limited social organizational milieu that encourages immediate sensual gratification. However, in this study, the ascetic path was usually followed by individuals who had tried the sensate life, got caught in a downward spiral or otherwise found it unfulfilling, and discovered they had to impose an order on their own lives in lieu of having a complex social milieu that could do it for them.

A strong argument could be made that so-called hippie incompetence was an artifact of the small size and limited organization of the milieu in which people had to operate, first in the SS and then in the CC. Many had left the SS with a minimum knowledge of the ways the broader segments of the social system worked, knowing only the limited and rather peripheral niches they had occupied as young people. Having relied in the past on family, school, or occupational pressures, accordingly being somewhat naive, many were at a loss when it came time to mobilize behavior and resources on their own initiative.

Similarly, many and perhaps a majority of SS people, comfortable and affluent compared to most CC people, would have been equally helpless if thrown into a milieu at such an early stage of its evolutionary development. There would be few material resources pooled for them to draw upon, no systematic way to gain or borrow expertise, and no complex institutional machinery guaranteeing results that could be relied on. Many of the social and technical aids that the most competent and successful people in the SS rely upon are often taken for granted, and if faced with the prospect of originating these same structures, many would prove to be helpless.

Starting new social forms almost from scratch required great skills, perseverance, and creativity that many people in the SS or CC, and particularly those at JM, simply couldn't muster. Some people worked to create new structures. Others moved into CC institutions that had already been created. Still others sought to stabilize their position within their own limited and sometimes shrinking social contexts. Thus, while most of the CC people were naive when they dropped out of the SS, most, even hippies, learned through hard experience to exercise some initiative and control over their environments. At one extreme, the political people in Free Provincia and the Brethren attempted to build larger systems, and at the other extreme, with hardly any structure to rely on, street people learned to survive by exploiting others in a direct manner that required no intervening institutional machinery. The latter learned to cope with a chaotic environment, taking nothing for granted, consequently developing what is often referred to as "street smarts." Unlike the CC elite, who were often made quite successful, JM street people never developed a "system wisdom."

Without going into any further detail, similar arguments could be advanced regarding other characteristics of poverty. Except for those activities resting on the rising, setting, and seasonal trajectory of the sun, how could one plan significantly ahead? For many there were no realistically obtainable long-range goals because of the relative lack of institutional machinery available in the CC so far to aid in their attainment. For others, there were grand plans that constantly had to be revised and reduced as failures became more apparent than successes. Because so many people in the CC had few and tenuous socioeconomic connections between them, though in places they were growing and becoming stronger, and because the SS network of institutional machinery often snuffed out efforts of CC people to achieve certain CC objectives, the overall environment was quite unpredictable.

JM's inability to build reserves of cash and goods could also be seen as an artifact of system size and relative entropic organization. For example, why did SS corporations have more total assets (including property owned by employees) than those of private businessmen or women? Wasn't it because the larger the system was, the greater the reserves, the more easily these reserves were pooled, the easier they were to be selectively invested or deployed to generate more wealth and property?

Also, why was there the propensity toward personal (as opposed to organized) physical violence in the CC? In addition to goal achievement frustration, this could result from the lack of intervening institutions and specialized groups such as the clergy, the courts, and the police, and fewer important resources to distribute, withhold, or otherwise manipulate so as to indirectly influence other people's behavior. And again, why were daily face to face relations with the same people prevalent? Mightn't it be due to there being fewer people to begin with in a limited social milieu where people tended to remain in the same relationships because there were no clear channels to convey people away from one another, laterally or vertically, temporarily or permanently? And so on, ad infinitum.

The impression should not be created, that CC and/or poverty groups were small systems unto themselves, entirely cut off from the greater SS. On the contrary, they were indeed connected, but not well-integrated into it, whether by neglect, by inability, or by design on either side. Some of the upper strata of the CC, despite ideology and frequent protestations to the contrary, were indeed directly and indirectly using education and money obtained from the SS, while returning very little to it. Others, through infrequent jobs, published books, or musical engagements were sporadically returning something to the SS for what they received. The poor in both the CC and SS usually contributed more than they received until they became cynical or unable to contribute any more. Recalling some of the descriptive words in the characterizations of poverty make clear the state of being in, yet being significantly cut off from, the larger society. Terms such as "dependency," "limited," provincial," "marginal," "abandonment," and "local" are used frequently. When institutional ties become weak or severed, the poor in any society attempt to retreat into a high reliance on that group whose membership ties appear to be the most durable. In their case, it is usually the biological family. In Provincia, CC peer groups manifesting themselves as communes, took on much the same function as biological families in this respect, some even referring to themselves as "New Age" families.

Further questions concerning frustration, helplessness, and ineffectiveness seem to have reasonable explanations when the disadvantageous aspects of small, relatively entropic, peripheral social systems are considered. Where a social entity is not properly plugged into the institutional machinery, it cannot make the machinery work to achieve its desired ends. And when this happens, immediate ends become easier to discern while more distant ones fade in perception as well as anticipation. The psychological ramifications for the people involved are obvious: loss of self-confidence, fear of extending oneself into new situations, reduced ability to pick up complicated skills, distrust, anger, general paranoia. If the individuals involved do not maintain the desire for goals defined and/or achievable by behavior in complex social systems, it is easy and, for some, rewarding to set more concrete goals, closer to self. As CC people retreated from complex social systems toward concrete peer groups, and ultimately to individual physical concerns (food, shelter, sex) and consciousness (fantasy, getting high, even psychosis), their instrumental behaviors took on a simplicity, obviousness, and directness that reflected the reduced environmental milieu with which they chose to focus their interactions. With the intervening levels and kinds of social systems in the environment reduced, multi-step instrumental behavior was for the most part also reduced. Because behavior is expressed in a time as well as space continuum, however, repetitive cycles became more apparent because they were smaller, less complicated, and therefore easier to perceive.

JM people complained of going around in circles, never able to get anywhere. This was because there were not many places they could go, and they did not have the ability or the confidence to reverse the centripetal process by making new extensions or building new centrifugal channels. Even many of the rock music lyrics that people sang involved concepts of cycles and coming back to the same point after believing they were headed in a certain direction. Some, of course, used imagery from "acid consciousness" with respect to physiological rhythms and cycles, while others borrowed from Eastern religious motifs (often themselves born out of a sense of existential futility and naiveté with respect to social, political, and economic systems). This is not to say, however, that perceiving the physical, social, and cosmological environment as cyclical patterns of events rather than as linear patterns is necessarily detrimental. Neither does it assert that distant goals are the only worthwhile goals. On the contrary, it can be argued that steps taken in an apparent linear sequence are really steps that make up much larger cycles, in terms of life span, career, institutional developmental longevity, and so forth. Also, short range objectives, including sensual gratification, if combined with long range goals, seem to be necessary for optimum physical and mental health. As pointed out in this study, gradual regression or piecemeal structural disintegration can be seen as an ultimately adaptive response to extreme stress and as a prerequisite for change psychologically (Laing: 1959) and sociologically (Turner: 1969). It permits the pieces to be reassembled into new structures more in line with evolving realities of the overall environment. But somewhere the retreat must be stopped if total disintegration is to be avoided.

The most obvious force that could have helped reverse JM's disintegrative spiral at the time, the Free Provincia movement, was caught up in an adaptive struggle of its own, and could no longer spare the effort or the resources. Many members were suffering from near exhaustion after all the intense efforts at local organizing. Moreover, its funds, generously donated by sympathetic liberals before the Liberation Farm confrontation and directly contributed by its more affluent members who had access to finite reserves, were running out. In its own way, however, it had gained some system wisdom through bitter experience, and set out to correct past errors on a footing far, far different from that of JM. Because JM was still part of the larger CC context at this point, a look at this and other developments beyond JM's immediate experience would be helpful in understanding JM better and illustrative of larger processes as well.

Although claiming to be an egalitarian movement practicing participant democracy, Free Provincia too, eventually evolved a de facto central leadership. One collective, Red Rose, emerged inordinately influential, as associated collectives and communes floundered with indecisiveness or reckless tactics. Within Red Rose itself a leadership inner circle developed, largely involving its older, more experienced, and better educated people with family backgrounds of wealth and privilege. Despite clearly going out of its way not to appear to be dominating the group's decision making, its unofficial members, most notably Charles, had the tools, emotional, social, material, and otherwise, to step into the breech when special efforts and resources were needed.

But in the end, this ostensibly reluctant leadership got so cut off from other influences and sources of information that it made some very poor decisions based on the assumption that it had more committed and articulate support than it did. As a result, some of its followers dropped out of the movement, particularly in the wake of the violence that surrounded the Liberation Farm battle. This disaffection, as well as the events themselves, led the leadership to reconsider its role and the direction in which it was heading.

One way or another, it recognized that challenges to the existing SS system based in narrowly conceived ideology and arrogant idealism was not the way to go. Where it succeeded in upsetting or damaging some part of the SS, destructive forces were set free that were very costly. Where it tried and failed, the much larger SS system with far more resources of all kinds manifested a virtually infinite capacity to strike back legally, extralegally, and illegally. As a result, it was not difficult to imagine the movement being crushed altogether. This was not a case of students taking on a particular university, or civil rights workers challenging particular laws, or anti-war activists organizing around a particular vivid issue. On the contrary, this involved trying to build new individuals and institutions for an entirely new order, while at the same time testing and resisting those of the old.

Despite all the early euphoria over the perceived inevitability of CC growth and impending wholesale societal transformation, many now realized that the regional CC in general, as well as the Free Provincia movement, was too limited in immediate capability given its sweeping goals. If it tried for the most part to work outside the SS by setting up self-reliant alternatives, efforts had been tolerated only if they were either marginally surviving or slowly failing. But there was obviously no purpose in pursing those particular efforts, as they were bound either to have no effect or a negative impact on the future lives of Americans. On the other hand, if these efforts were successful or potentially competitive, the SS had usually managed to undermine or defeat them by one means or another. With this outcome, there was no purpose in further effort here either. What was needed was a more quietly and subtly developed infrastructure to enable eventual florescence of reliable and significant alternative systems that could then someday replace the old exploitive structures.

In its self-critique, a number of things became very apparent. Specifically, it did not yet have sufficient numbers in its ranks, capacity to generate the wealth necessary for physical support, services to offer its current and prospective members, and technical knowledge necessary for the operation of basic systems. Neither did it have adequate ways and means to get its message across to the larger populace nor a balanced institutional network in place to handle and channel the flow of all the human, material, and informational resources necessary for its reasonably independent survival and for serious impact on traditional SS structures. In particular, the leadership that dealt with these larger priorities had been too isolated and too concentrated in the past.

In short, just as was the specific case with JM, its overall sociocultural system was apparently too small, too simple and too peripheral in the context of the massive society in which it was attempting to grow and exercise real power. Unlike JM, however, Free Provincia had much better potential to prosper if certain changes in strategy were made and if current resources were redirected before they ran out. While JM involuntarily sank deeper into ever smaller circles of misery in its state of abandonment, Free Provincia deliberately reoriented itself. It did so in such a way as to become a larger, better integrated system by moving its efforts to the regional arena. It reduced its attention to circumscribed local groups who would not also make at least some consistent contributions at that level, too. At the same time, it became less confrontational with the SS. Instead, it channeled its influence through the many regional groups pulled into a regional CC coalition, each with specific local roots, so it could be more effective for the cultural revolution in the competition for "the hearts and the minds" of all the citizenry.

Thus, as JM was retreating toward the lower strata of the CC as part of a growing underclass, Free Provincia movement participants also retreated, but did so to regroup and reenter with access to higher participatory levels, so as to garner more of the SS resources. As it did, it also closed off the previous hemorrhaging of the resources it did have, one of which was JM, which further accelerated the reintegrative process for everyone. As paradoxical as it sounds, despite the very different circumstances, purposes, and probable fates, Free Provincia and JM were in a fundamental way making the same lateral moves in terms of backing away from original extreme CC ideals. Yet they were heading in opposite directions when viewed from a hierarchical perspective. The probable reality is, that as parts of the same CC systemic phenomenon, they were moving in complimentary directions. And it was happening by virtue of a self-driving mechanism beyond the awareness, intentions, and control of any specific individual, group, or ideology.

In fact, the same kind of transition was occurring in all other CC groups and at roughly the same time. Many of the Parson's Crossing people were moving up in the larger literary and theatrical worlds in terms of status, while at the same time finding that their growing needs for financial support were overtaking their ability to meet them. Those concentrating on self-sufficiency farming were growing weary of the hard work and isolation, some realizing that producing surpluses of unusually healthful and tasty food and marketing them was one path that could lead to an easier life. Others were thinking of trying to take time off to pursue other personal and professional interests. As it firmly established its niche in the CC and its relatively high place in the communal hierarchy, it was also making gestures toward some reintegration with the larger society.

As a matter of fact, its chief author in residence had concluded that the cultural revolution was over and that the counterculture had "won." All that remained was to take the lessons learned and begin to apply them to the still unsuspecting SS, which was still caught up in fighting the old soon-to-be eclipsed battles. To back up his argument, he cited example after example of sudden transformations in the society at large triggered by the CC, including radically different perceptions of health, an explosion of ecological concerns, changing patterns of family life, different genera of consumer goods, much broader career choices, new management strategies, reborn entrepreneurialism, transcendent new communication approaches, greater information access, new environmentally responsible technologies, expanding women's roles, and a public far more aware of the dangers of secrecy and militarism.

The Brethren, too, were reorganizing to allow a better fit with the surrounding society after first having withdrawn from it in order to achieve a firm identity and purpose without external interference. After the conflict with JM and the town of Wilfred, many realized that much of their other-worldly messianic zeal worked against their best long term interests in the necessary and real world of contact with and reliance upon surrounding institutions, CC or SS. Still wanting to attract new members and more financial support, the group was now mobilizing, not for mountain retreats as had been the case while at JM, but for various business schemes to disseminate its message as well as its services for sale. These included a refrigeration and air conditioning unit, a construction unit, a professional recording studio, a rock and roll band, and an entertainment arcade for potentially wayward teenagers.

All this contributed to the perception that the entire CC was undergoing an unexplainable shift at this time that at first glance seemed to be both merely contradictory and coincidental. Upon closer examination, however, it can be seen that the movement of the various parts of the CC was orchestrated by means of their competitive and cooperative relations with one another and by means of their changing links to the SS once their new places in the CC had been more sharply defined. It also gave the appearance to many that the CC was beginning to fall apart; that the dream and the newly achieved reality based on that dream was crumbling. But a review of the developmental process so far reveals that a consistent internal dynamic happened to be leading the still integrated CC as a whole in a direction different from what anyone had originally hoped or anticipated.

In the beginning, individuals and groups were escaping the SS and its supposedly repressive structures (mass education practices, corporate conformity, industrial pollution, racist politics, the military war machine) to establish as different and independent a footing as possible. When it became apparent to each that many others were doing the same thing, then a rational and a material framework was articulated that united them in forward vision and actual progress in developing new ways of living. This, in turn, attracted the attention of additional malcontents, who joined the CC often for a different mix of reasons (divorce, mental illness, lack of education, brushes with death). But it also drew the notice of alarmed and threatened SS authorities, who in many ways proceeded to work to undermine what they feared could become a genuinely popular movement.

This new combination of players led to much conflict and turmoil, professions of peace and love notwithstanding. It also resulted in a better organized CC in which different groups established certain identities and roles. In this differentiating process, social stratification appeared as well. The unequal distribution of all categories of resources resulted in new internal tensions, to be sure, but it also led to the recognition of the overall insufficiency of resources in general for the CC, regardless of distributive inequality. If there was more to go around, then theoretically, at least, a fairer distribution would be easier to achieve for all. With near simultaneous realization by different groups functioning in very different contexts, the SS was now looked to as the most reliable, even if temporary, wellspring of resources, and each in its own way moved to tap it.

Because most in the CC did not have the strength or will simply to take what they wanted in order to keep their fledgling groups and countersociety on track, open confrontation was not only on the decline, but active reintegration was on the rise. Rather than the dream crumbling, per se, it was evolving into a more adaptive, sustainable form. This happened, despite early naive romantic notions of a free and independent new society. Where such changes openly contradicted ideological positions still held by many, some charges of "selling out" were heard, but most regarded these changes as necessary, even if passing, expedient measures to facilitate their larger objectives. As for JM, although it had no capacity to do anything in a constructive sense, because of its particularly threatened circumstances, it saw in its own way, just as most other groups did, that some fundamental changes had to be made.

Whereas their rejection of a rigid, huge, all-powerful society seemed reasonable, even necessary at first, now it was realized that some kind of stable, large efficacious social system was urgently necessary for their survival when surrounded by others of similar magnitude. What then became important was the group's particular character and the kind of responsive organizational pattern that could be achieved without returning to or succumbing to the original one they had escaped.

9. Reintegration: Transformation of Jackson's Meadows and Regional Change

JM, or what was left of it, was finally ready to accept just about anything that came along offering help. In the mist of the apparent final decline and fall, the over-30s once again stepped into the picture, this time to take command of the situation. Throughout the spring, they and other academic and non-academic friends had been meeting with the idea of purchasing land to set up a community of artists and scholars. They had all cautiously explored and studied the efforts of a community so brazenly and often so naively conducted by younger, more radical people. Having seen mistakes made and impossible dreams frustrated, they wanted to set up a community that would go to no social or political extremes, yet would optimize the creation of a healthy, natural, interpersonally sensitive, intellectually stimulating environment. Hopefully, a center could be created where outside scholars, artists, students, and interested people could come to exchange information, ideas, and inspiration as its way of fostering individual and social change.

They had considered buying JM when Peter had it up for sale after the Brethren withdrew, but Peter preferred not to sell it to them. He claimed they could not stop the downward spiral in the lives of the people already there. Only if all the current JMers were removed would he sell it, and like Peter, none of the over-30s connected with the Meadows would plot to evict them. Despite radical differences in lifestyle, the over-30s considered many JMers to be close personal friends. Especially after struggling against the Brethren together, they could not now as landlords evict former friends. Furthermore, many of the over-30s questioned some of the rights of ownership and exclusive rights to land obtained by virtue of accumulated capital. However, months later, Peter changed his mind. The over-30s now indicated that they thought they could reverse the downward spiral, felt a special attachment to the land and its inhabitants, and were willing to take on the disastrous burden Peter had been shouldering the last two years. Peter also had an urgent need for money himself. He had found another farm for sale in Wilfred with a large house; perfect for the school he hoped to set up and for close friends to come live with him. Peter agreed to sell at a very reasonable price, and the only obstacle that remained was coming to mutually agreeable terms with the remaining JMers.

The over-30s believed that the Meadows and its people could be maintained only on a sound economic basis. Moreover, JM had to have some structure that would slow down the wild and chaotic pace of turnover and events. Lastly, some kind of boundary through which "undesirables" could pass out of the Meadows, but not back into it, had to be set up. A get-together between prospective landlords and JMers was arranged at which the over-30s laid down what they considered to be minimal rules which the JMers should consider. If they agreed to subscribe to the regulations, the over-30s (ten in all, including five who had lived at the Meadows the previous summer) would buy the land. If the JMers felt they could not go along with them, then they would not buy the land.

The regulations were simple. No new people were to join JM except as mates of those already there. If anyone left JM for a month or longer, he or she was understood to have relinquished all rights to call it home. Otherwise, people might be diverting most of their energies to affairs not connected with JM, returning when those other affairs fell through. This would have disrupted the new balance that would have settled in after they left. People whom no one knew would be told to leave, and members would not invite casual acquaintances from town. The word should be circulated in the CC gossip network that JM was "closed," so that the common understanding of the last two years (that JM would take in anybody who showed up) would be terminated. Also, it would be understood that the new owners would not lend money to the JMers, would expect them to pay their share of the taxes, and in no way would financially support them. Furthermore, no illegal schemes to raise money would be tolerated, from raising and selling marijuana to ripping off goods from the local stores and people. Finally, provision was made whereby individuals felt to be intolerably disruptive by the rest of the people, JMers and purchasers alike, could be expelled. Similarly, with unanimous approval, JMers could be given legal parity with the new owners by being admitted to the legal corporation set up to hold the land.

The JMers agreed to abide by the proposed regulations, no doubt believing it was better to have friendly landlords who shared at least some of their values, than it was to have straight landlords in the future who would undoubtedly throw them off the land. And they admitted they also felt trapped by cycles of events and their own behavioral syndromes that seemed to drag them down. They indicated they even welcomed a fresh start imposed from the outside.

But everyone knew that such regulations would not preclude eventual conflict. Nor could they preclude patronizing attitudes by the new ruling gerontocratic intelligentsia on the one hand, and resentful attitudes by the ultimately powerless tenants on the other. People on both sides were conscious of the pitfalls; each trying to avoid angering the other and each attempting to include the other in its social affairs. With generally good cooperation between the under and over-30s, the rest of the summer and fall was spent in a determined effort to watch over and control visitors and rowdy behavior in the

Meadows, while patching up public relations with both the SS and CC surrounding communities. Constant vigil was required and delicate judgment exercised in handling potentially explosive situations. The over-30s soon became exhausted in the process, however, for the first time having the legal responsibility for the Meadows and feeling they were sitting on the lid of a pot that could blow off at any time.

The potential visitor problem in the summer of 1971 was at first the overriding concern. But to everyone's surprise, the rush of visitors expected at JM never materialized. The word had been successfully circulated that JM was "closed," and that JMers were actually turning visitors away. Indeed, most of JM's visitors were either ex-JM members or old friends of members who arrived to stay for extended periods of time, aware that while no one would ask them to leave, they couldn't remain indefinitely. Jean's younger sister returned, as did Arthur, who had paid off his debt and broken off with the runaway girl. He got a job in the Centerville area playing the guitar, eventually getting his own apartment. Suzie, Peter's sister, (who was now pregnant) and her boyfriend Walter visited the Meadows, but moved in with Peter in his new house. Bill and others from Walnut Hill put in an occasional appearance, and Allen spent some time camping on the land with members of the new political group he had joined outside Provincia. Pepsi Joe came by (just before he joined the Air Force), saying he was fed up with drifting. What drove him to that conclusion was that he had just stayed at an urban crash pad where someone repeatedly threatened to kill him, and where he seriously considered murdering the other fellow before the other fellow could get him first.

Others, however, could not escape the violence that was increasingly eating its way further into the CC nationally as well as regionally. One of the three IBMs who had lived at the Meadows for a short time the previous winter returned with a new friend. The other two did not return because they were dead. Manny, who had taken to living in the woods in another region and shooting at hippies, had OD'd on heroin, and Quickdraw's body was found weeks after he disappeared, beaten and decayed nearly beyond recognition. A sheriff's deputy was later arrested for the murder. With Mission Street Mike, Zeke, and DT, the two IBMs embarked on two weeks of escapades that had both the SS and CC communities up in arms. Initially all five went to a nearby CC-Third World rock festival. Getting drunk and obstreperous, they were ejected by some burly black bouncers after loudly booing a speech on Movement unity. On the street, one of them passed out, which drew the attention of a passing police car. The police politely asked them to come to the station house, but when one attempted to escape, the police got angry. They all spent three days in jail and created such a disturbance that the other prisoners began to complain. They were brought before the judge who agreed to let them go in order to obtain bail money to pay for their official release if they promised to return (which of course, they never did).

Also, a local eccentric farmer-woodsman occasionally invited them over for a few beers, but they made a habit of returning, staying late at night and consuming what food and beverages he had around. One time, without warning (they claim), he came running out of his bedroom with a gun telling them to get out of his house or he'd shoot them. Feeling that the farmer had flipped out, they ran outside, jumped in the farmer's car and drove off in it, running it into a ditch and leaving it. Another incident involved the Wilfred CC. Some people about to leave Grasshopper Farm to journey to a recently purchased farm outside Provincia, discovered the spare tire and battery were missing from their car. Figuring that JM must have had something to do with it, a few of them cautiously walked into the Meadows where they met one of the over-30s who naively denied that anyone at JM would steal anything from a fellow longhair. Later, a JMer volunteered information on the IBMs "so long as they never find out who told you."

When all the above events came to the attention of the new land owners, they became greatly disturbed. Not only would the IBMs ruin all efforts at rapprochement with SS and CC people, but ultimately they would wreak havoc at JM itself. But only when the JMers themselves, including Zeke and DT, were beginning to suffer from the misdeeds of the other IBMs (e.g., losing potential friends, having to be careful of their movements because of warrants for their arrest), could the over-30s act with effectiveness. Zeke and DT gave the new owners all the details of the escapades, furnishing them with grounds to ask the IBMs to leave. But only the IBMs' "buddies," Zeke and DT, could ask them to leave without their retaliating in some way. The IBMs quietly, though reluctantly, left when DT explained why they could no longer stay. (One of the new owners tried to explain as best he could, but the IBMs kept repeating, "I don't understand what you're talkin' about, man.")

Thus, the antinomian undercurrent of the CC that had much to do with the founding of JM and precipitated its great struggle with the Krishna Brethren, now threatened to destroy it from within. The IBMs not only respected no law, no social authority, nor even consensual agreement, but were guiltless and fearless in disregarding them. Their only reference group was themselves, and apparently no external social influence could pressure them into conformity. The threat of physical harm or incarceration was no deterrent either, for facing such unpleasant possibilities was their way of life, lived every day. "Outlaws" in the most literal sense of the word, they thrived in the CC where the articulate and idealistic had hesitated to impose social restrictions, and where the inarticulate and insecure were unable to.

As spontaneous communal situations elsewhere settled into more deliberate efforts, more formal and clever informal structures evolved. They were supported by those people skilled at operating the structures and even by those not skilled, and by all who had learned to value the stability and the conditions necessary for economic self-sufficiency that structures permitted. Those still opposed on principle or incapable of such structured behavior, such as the IBMers, found that those areas of the CC formerly "open" were withering away, collapsing, or declaring themselves closed. Thus free zones for people like them were steadily shrinking to the point where they only had hip urban ghettoes or rural ones such as JM. But now, they were even being pushed out of JM. Those doing the pushing, however, were always subject to extra-legal retaliation, for in the final settling out process, only the most obstinate and desperate people held on until the end. Hence the term "desperate-does" used by some local freaks referring to the IBMs, Mother Humpers, and some JMers, was literally quite accurate. And the fear of revenge was justified.

Fear reached directly into JM when Hank returned to JM in the fall intending to pick up where he left off with Cindy. After often leaving her and returning in the past, this time he found her living with someone else. After remaining sullen and quiet for a day or so, he began to glare menacingly at Cindy and complain that no children of his were going to be brought up with people who still smoked dope. When her new mate Claudius, was not present, he slapped Cindy around as the other JMers stood by watching and doing nothing. He then threatened "to get" Cindy. An over-30 owner heard of the incident and with the moral support of only Jean and Roamer from among the JMers, told Hank to leave. Fearful for his own safety, the over-30 nevertheless insisted that any new incident of violence would destroy any chance JM had for survival, and for this reason Hank had to go. To everyone's surprise, Hank acquiesced and left the land, saying, however, he had all the time in the world to get Cindy and Claudius even if it meant surprising them off the land.

A couple of days later he got drunk, and virtually berserk, returned to the Meadows. He went into the tree house where Cindy and Claudius were living and smashed out the windows, wrecked the furniture, destroyed the art work Claudius had created, and even poured kerosene over the bed, perhaps intending to ignite it, but later changing his mind. When Cindy and Claudius returned to find the tree house in shambles, Claudius ran to ask the others what had happened. Only a few JMers and young visitors were around, shrugging their shoulders and saying Hank had done it. When he asked why they hadn't stopped him, they were again evasive. DT indicated that it was not his responsibility; that both Claudius and Hank were friends of his, and each had the freedom to do what each wanted, as far as he was concerned. Claudius was appalled to find that DT's neutrality and non-involvement could allow his home and work to be destroyed.

The basic reason for their not wanting anything to do with the new crisis was fear. Hank ate with the others in the cook shack where people avoided him when they could and humored him when they couldn't. Yet he would threaten them for no apparent reason. Once, for instance, he looked up to catch the eye of another and menacingly asked, "What are you looking at? If you keep that up you're not going to have any eyes to look at anything with." Hank had apparently learned that through violence and the threat of violence he could achieve the freedom to do as he pleased. Moreover, he could intimidate others, if not to carry out his wishes, at least not to interfere. One observer commented that if ever there was evil, Hank was it; deliberately and cynically scoffing at all social conventions to the point of death and destruction, all the while knowing fully well what he was doing.

Cindy and Claudius had the most to fear. At dusk after he wrecked the tree house, Hank came out of the woods, stood at the bottom of the tree with an ax, and shouted threats. He was going to chop the ladder down, set fire to the bottom of the tree house, and attack them with the ax if they tried to escape. Claudius couldn't believe his ears, but Cindy insisted he was crazy enough to do it. Claudius got a rifle he had hidden in the house, aimed it at Hank and told him to go away and leave them alone or he would shoot him. Laughing with a maniacal tone "that sounded like mad killers always sound like in the movies," Hank dared Claudius to shoot him, declaring he wasn't afraid to die because his life wasn't worth anything anyway. "That's also why I'm not afraid to kill you," he added. The rest of the evening Hank sat crouched in the bushes, laughing and vowing to "gouge your eyes out," and "cut your fuckin' heads off and watch the blood come out in spurts. There's no way you can stop me. I'm going to jump you when you least expect it. I've got lots of time." By dawn he was gone.

Norman, an over-30s person who had been away during this latest episode, assuming Hank was safely on his way to the city, returned to find Hank in the cookshack bragging about what he had done. Again mustering his courage, he demanded that Hank leave the land permanently, volunteering to drive him into town immediately. And again Hank left without protest, but vowing eventual revenge, for "no one can point a gun at me and get away with it." The new owners began to wonder if Peter wasn't right after all. Perhaps they were unable to control events irrevocably set in motion before they appeared on the scene, events that would drag them down into the abyss of human degradation and helplessness along with everyone else. Claudius was severely shaken, not so much by the threats to his life by a madman, but by the lack of compassion and commitment of his fellow communards to help him when his need was greatest. He discovered that what he thought was finally his "new family," could not be trusted; that those who professed brotherly love could not live it. He was alone, and though others occupied the land with him, the idea of community at the Meadows was dead as far as he was concerned.

Another kind of danger to the new enterprise came from the opposite direction, from capable new people attempting to move into the Meadows. A couple, the male member of which was allowed academic credit for living in a commune while creating artwork, arrived at the Meadows, supposedly to visit. Being skilled and serious, and having articulated goals, the couple was a welcome relief from the lost drifters and seekers who often showed up at JM asking to join. Though having little in common with the street people, they quickly befriended Roamer, Claudius, and Jean. They didn't, however, attempt to befriend the owners and never told them of their intentions to stay.

When autumn arrived, the couple either had to leave or to start making preparations for the winter. Claudius, who felt caught in the middle, finally told the owners of the couple's intentions. The owners informed the couple that they would have to leave, conforming to the unanimously agreed upon conditions for the new owners purchasing the land in the first place. The couple responded with a long open letter addressed to everyone, satirically depicting the owners as self-righteous absentee landlords who had no feeling for the land or its people. Knowing that inaction and time would finally resolve it in the couple's favor, the owners moved to call a meeting to resolve the dispute.

The tenant JMers generally supported the couple, for they enjoyed their company and regarded them as a step in the right direction. But they didn't want to support the couple to the point of jeopardizing their own position on the land. The tenant and landlord groups now antagonistic, had decreased communication with each other to the point where unfounded rumors were circulating on both sides. The JMers had heard that the new owners were going to call in the legal authorities, and the owners had heard that the JMers were prepared to fight the owners tooth and nail with the now familiar extra-legal means at their disposal.

At the meeting the rumors were proven false, but views were clearly and forcefully stated. The street people really didn't care if the couple stayed or not, so long as no one else would be thrown off the land. The befriended middle class hippies at JM wanted the couple to stay because they were talented, ambitious, stimulating people who served as models for a revitalized JM. Moreover, they could not understand why the owners would object to having responsible people on the land when they (the owners) wouldn't even be there most of the time over the winter. This last point was picked up by longhaired visitors and friends attending the meeting who proceeded to mouth all the CC ideals regarding the land being free, how it should be open to all the people, and why it had to be wrested from the control of greedy, competitive, materialist "pig capitalist landlords."

Appalled at the thought at once again struggling over this worn out and often self-serving issue, the owners dismissed it, replying instead that they did not want people living on the land who were deceitful and who made no attempt to befriend them. Furthermore, despite romantic notions to the contrary, the couple was clearly unprepared to survive the winter in a teepee. In that instance they would either have to leave anyway or move in with the JMers, who would then regret having invited them to stay on the land. Then too, no matter how talented and stimulating the couple was, an agreement had been unanimously reached, and now attempts were being made to undermine or reverse it by one side. There was also a matter of precedent involved. By making an exception to the rule, other exceptions would follow, and these might not involve a bright, industrious couple.

The inescapable fact had to be faced that the land was not "free." It cost money to obtain the land and pay taxes. The new owners had savings and jobs to supply the cash for the purchase, and the JMers did not. Rather than being greedy capitalists or typical absentee landlords, the over-30s said they spent most of their time away from the land specifically to earn money so they could make the payments on it. Meanwhile, the JMers had the privilege to remain on the land, enjoying a lifestyle not bound by clocks and calendars. It was actually because the landlords were absentee that the JMers could live free on the land.

If a defined community was to emerge, the land could not be open to anyone who came along, even if he or she had skills and motivation. The new owners had specific aims of their own that potentially conflicted with the lifestyle preferences of the JM tenants, and around which some compromises could be negotiated. But the owners had made clear from the outset that they would be in charge of directing the evolution of the Meadows with the right to bring in only those new people who would fit into their own plans. By closing off recruitment and influences from all social networks except their own collective network, they hoped to radically change the Meadows' orientation and development.

The meeting ended with no firm decisions being made, but as the owners had anticipated, the couple left after the first few freezes. Later one of the JMers suddenly left without telling anyone. In notes he left behind, it was discovered that he thought the land and isolation was driving him crazy, for he heard strange voices outside his cabin and screams in the night. The owners promptly claimed his house (the house on stilts) as their own. The owners also laid claim to two previously open buildings that henceforth only they or their friends could occupy: the cook shack and Zeke and Boop's cabin (who were no longer at the Meadows). These were occupied the first half of the winter by the owners and their friends, but remained empty and padlocked the latter half. The padlocking was criticized by JMers and other local freaks as being a very uncommunal, un-CC thing to do, but the owners defended the action, saying empty space would only attract drifters. By spring of 1972, the land had only DT and his new girl friend in the A-frame, Claudius and Blythe (formerly of Rainbow Farm) in the tree house, and Roamer in his truck.

Relations between DT and Roamer had always been poor, from the day he first joined JM. Relations between DT and Claudius had also chilled precipitously after he refused to come to Claudius' aid during the crisis with Hank. DT was the only street member left on the land, but by virtue of DT inviting all his street friends from Centerville, plus allowing ex-JMers such as Mission Street Mike to stay with him, street people still set the tone at the Meadows. There were constant beer parties, instances of food and objects mysteriously disappearing from both the tree house and Roamer's truck, and people sitting around stoned or drunk. The street people also refused to help Roamer and Claudius in work tasks necessary for winter survival, such as carrying in supplies from the road over the deep snow a mile away. DT and his friends were disrupting their lives and it was made clear to the owners that something had to be done.

Moreover, DT's friends were causing trouble with the town, which disturbed the owners who were hoping to establish good relations with the town. One of DT's friends moved in for a while and left DT with a $28 unpaid bill at the Wilfred Grocery Store. Another group connected with the IBMs walked into the yard of one of Wilfred's most respected residents (a judge on the regional supreme court) to "borrow" a car they saw parked there. Threatening the caretaker with bodily harm if he interfered, they drove off in it promising to return it on the way back from town (which in this case they did).

But only when the new owners moved onto the land with the warm weather of their second summer, was the decision to ask DT to leave JM made. An uneasy feeling was perceived by the individual owners initially, only later discussed in common as a major problem. The owners felt they could achieve none of their goals for JM so long as DT remained. The past summer, the owners could content themselves with stopping the Meadows' precipitous decline and managing to prevent major human disasters. But this summer they wanted to move the Meadows toward their goals of building an edifice and road that would permit their friends and colleagues to arrive and stay with a modicum of comfort.

Yet with DT and his friends there, these plans could not be carried out. The town fathers, who could grant building permits and improve the access road, had hostile feelings toward JM that were exacerbated by DT and friends. Also, the

A-frame was located on the site where the owners planned to build. In addition, no one would feel comfortable about bringing possessions to the land and leaving them unguarded. While DT was to be trusted with regard to theft and destructive or malicious behavior in a new building, his friends certainly weren't. And DT himself indicated that no one could ask him to abandon his street people friends, the only people who understood him and with whom he got along. Some of the new owners whose limited middle class biases had not been tested by thorough familiarity with the CC, claimed that DT's presence on the land made them feel uneasy, disturbed, and tense. They simply could not adjust to his lifestyle and his friends, all of which made it impossible to accomplish their material and work goals. Even if they felt quite comfortable with the remaining hippies who came from backgrounds similar to theirs, DT had to go.

DT already had his back to the wall, with all but one of his options for survival bypassed or destroyed. His one remaining option had been the land at the Meadows and his A-frame there. When he chose to be serious and fully open, he revealed that "it is the only thing I have left. I love this land. It's the only place where I can be myself without somebody always being on my ass." Never permitted total responsibility for anything of his own before, and having failed in social enterprises with partial responsibility, his A-frame was his one success in life, and therefore his life. By his own admission, he drank and partied so much as a way of temporarily blotting out his feelings of inadequacy and worthlessness. But when he was sober, he puttered around the house, improving this and expanding that like a proud suburban homeowner. Living on the land had taught him skills and given him the satisfaction of seeing the fruits of his own work, and the house had literally kept him alive. Many times he felt so depressed that he seriously considered hanging himself from the limb of the beautiful old tree outside his house. It was only his thinking of the tree and the house that prevented him from doing it, he said.

But the new owners and remaining JMers had their own lives to lead, their own dreams to fulfill, and their own urgent (sometimes desperate) needs to find more rewarding lives. The over-30s felt a particular demand for action with respect to their own lives. Unlike the younger DT and other JMers, gray hairs appeared along with their growing realization that they didn't have limitless time to achieve what they wished. Not satisfied to bake bread, plant gardens, or hold down part time miscellaneous jobs only, they organized their individual and collective lives so as to accumulate and employ money, materials, services, and talents in such a way that the scale of the community undertaking and the scope of objectives was far broader than those of the JMers. They unanimously agreed that DT was the locus around which certain social syndromic processes occurred that would prevent the realization of everyone else's personal and collective goals. Thus, top priority went into removing DT from the Meadows.

Patrick, who knew him best, painfully broke the news to DT, explaining as best he could why everyone else was asking him to leave. Fellow JMers were reluctant to tell him because they feared retaliation; for no matter what followed, they had to live on the land with him until either he or they left. DT was stunned by Patrick's words, not knowing what to say or do. He clearly did not understand the reasons given for his being asked to go, but he firmly believed he was being "betrayed, again" by those closest to him. Rather than take his last option away from him, thereby hoping to soften his anger and disappointment, everyone decided it would be best to offer another option in return, although they were aware nothing could really compensate. The owners committed a few hundred dollars, more money than he had seen at one time in years, to get him off to a new start elsewhere. Although it didn't dawn on him at the time, he later realized it was a bribe of sorts, and that offended him.

Other alternatives were suggested as well, such as his enrolling in an OEO (Office of Economic Opportunity) job training program where he would be paid while learning a skill. Patrick tried to point out to DT that it was his lack of skills that had much to do with his lack of self-esteem, and that it was his inability to obtain and hold money that was fundamental in his losing two women he loved and the children he fathered. He replied that he had tried, but was ultimately incapable of organizing and disciplining his behavior to fit a job schedule. He had lived a free life too long to be domesticated and controlled now. He lost his women, he said, because they succumbed to materialism while he had stuck by his principles, all the while maintaining the essence of free human spirit. Patrick countered that DT's supposed freedom was gained by means of other people's loss of freedom. Moreover, DT's retreating from society into the Meadows solely for purposes of refuge was a mistake, for each move to sever ties to people decreased his options until none were left, cutting out contacts who would possibly be helpful by offering new opportunities. The philosophy expressed in the rock song Me and Bobby McGee, "freedom's just another word for nothin' left to lose," was dead wrong Patrick said. That's not freedom; that's abandonment and despair. If that were true, DT should look forward to losing his house.

After each discussion, Patrick, the spokesman for the owners, reexamined the argument he was making, while DT grew more confused and angry. Patrick reported that he realized that in addition to making little sense to DT, he was articulating what sounded like a defense of the law and order ethic he had spent the last ten years of his life struggling against. Was he to his own horror parroting all he learned early in life? Was he now defending the worst of the Protestant ethic, the Horatio Alger myths, and the Victorian assertions that spontaneous behavior, including some drink, drugs, sexual indulgence, and even moderate personal slovenliness, led to the ruination of countless souls? Was he advocating a position similar to that espoused by a decade of American political leaders who insisted that America was preserving freedom in Vietnam by restoring order to the chaos created by communist insurgents; and that the protest Movement in the United States was inherently inimical to the American Way by virtue of its advocacy and creation of anarchy? In the end, he said he was satisfied that he was advocating what sounded to DT like an extreme because it was a clear response to DT's opposite extreme. Somewhere, a balance had to be struck.

While Patrick reflected on his still evolving social philosophy, DT quietly simmered for a couple of weeks, but finding support from visitor Mission Street Mike, he exploded. The only power he had left was the power to disrupt and threaten physical harm. Having little left to lose, he was now fearless of the consequences. After blowing the money that was given him to pay for transportation, rent, or other resettlement expenses, he changed his mind about leaving. He would defiantly remain or go out in a "blaze of glory." When informed that many other area communards wouldn't object to his leaving, he threatened to round up his violent street friends to do battle with any "fuckin' commune hippies who want me out."

Instead of directly threatening the owners, he turned on his neighbor, Claudius. DT had stood quietly by while Hank threatened Claudius' existence, but when Claudius did the same thing with respect to DT, DT became enraged. After getting drunk one evening, he confronted Claudius, declaring that he had always hated him, and was sorry Hank didn't kill him. He then made threats of his own that dripped hate and violence, unknowingly using some of the same vivid phrases Hank had used the previous fall. Claudius could not believe what was happening again. It seemed a nightmarish repeat of the Hank episode, and he couldn't understand why it kept happening to him. DT had taken Claudius' rifle earlier (the one used to defend himself against Hank), and when he refused to return it, Claudius and Blythe were terrified. They fled from the Meadows for their safety.

But the owners held to their decision. They conceded that the A-frame was DT's rightful property and he could take the lumber from the dismantled building with him if he wanted. But this did not prevent the owners from knocking down the house on stilts, which was again being used by crashers and friends of DT. His territory now reduced to the land immediately surrounding the A-frame, like a last outpost under siege, he put up a flag pole on which he flew the marijuana leaf Yippie banner and the upside down US flag of distress.

DT knew that the group was irrevocably determined to have him removed. One of the owners had arranged a meeting with the town peace officer to determine where the town fathers stood if the group was forced to ask the town for help. The peace officer, who knew DT well, was only too happy to have the police remove DT from Wilfred. Others in the group, however, refused to go along with such an approach, maintaining that with patience DT would eventually perceive the uselessness of remaining. In anticipation of a move to call in the police, DT informed everyone that if the "pigs" were brought in, they wouldn't take him alive. He would defend his house even if it meant killing and being killed himself.

Sensing the futility of his position, he made only a few more bizarre threats before giving in. He vowed to commit suicide, and burn his house down, knowing full well it might set the fields and forests ablaze. But his spirit of defiance sparked by support from Mission Street Mike crumbled with increasing fights between the two of them, and between DT and his new girlfriend. Finally Mission Street Mike left, and DT's now pregnant woman convinced him his life would not be a hopeless abyss once he let go of his spot on the land. The same things had happened to her, she said, and though she didn't think she would, she survived it. Having nothing to hold on to would provide a chance to start all over again, differently. DT finally began to take steps to find a path for himself elsewhere. He found someone who agreed to let him stay in a small house on the other side of Centerville. He also went to a psychiatrist at the hospital in which he previously worked and had himself "declared crazy." By getting classified as too emotionally disturbed to work, he was eligible for large welfare payments and a training program in crafts in which he enrolled.

With DT's departure, a new phase began. DT left on relatively good terms with everyone, though he said he could never again trust Patrick, a supposed friend who served as the messenger of his ill tidings. The three JMers who remained were all sufficiently middle class, educated, or cultured to get along with the over-30 academicians and artists who would set the tone for the next phase in the evolution of the Meadows. The three were also economically self-sufficient. Claudius, for example, sold artwork and contracted to build houses for people moving into the area. His tree house was expanded and became such an interesting example of creative architecture that people from hundreds of miles away made special trips to see it. Work also began on a complex of buildings for the new community that had the blessings of the town councilmen; the road commissioner even agreeing to help build a traversable access road. Plans for the community's economic self-sufficiency were also partially fulfilled by some members generating an income through jobs at the local colleges. Thus, JM had apparently finally settled into some kind of quiet, informal order that distinctly contrasted with the tumultuous previous three years of its existence. With the purge of DT, JM's last major struggle in its transformation from hippie commune, to a rural ghetto, to what one sardonic observer called "a radical professor's retirement farm" had occurred.

For the purposes of this study, the story of Jackson's Meadows ends here. The changes brought about by the new owners were so fundamental and the turnover in people (and kinds of people) was so great, that the old commune for all intents and purposes no longer existed. Yet the new enterprise occupied the same space and was undertaken by some who had lived through many of JM's follies and who had learned valuable lessons in the process. If JM, or the idea JM represented, was to be continued, it would be transformed into something quite different, yet it would maintain the clear mark of its past.

Analysis

What role did JM play as a manifestation of a social movement, as an illustration of communal dynamics, as a critical phase (a terminal phase for some) in the lives of individuals, as a small but somewhat unique cog in the wheels of overall societal change, and even as a possible example of sociocultural evolution in microcosm? This study, as a case study, cannot directly demonstrate how JM and other communal groups in their immediate contexts signaled significant changes occurring throughout American society in the late sixties and early seventies. On the other hand, the kinds of events that transpired in Provincia were not at all unique, as readily verified by the many comments of visitors and observers passing through the local area at the time who were also familiar with the Movement elsewhere in the country.

What this study does show, at the least, is the immediate impact the events had on many individuals and on one specific region, suddenly and permanently changing them in many fundamental ways. At the same time, it helps make clearer the specific manners in which people and communities behaved and how they experienced both the pains and the joys found in circumstances of highly accelerated social transformation. Any general conclusions that are drawn can best be derived, not just by summarizing goings on concerning JM and its members only, but also by outlining the simultaneously shifting parallel patterns of those individuals and groups touching JM and touched by JM.

Setting aside JM as a commune for the moment, what about the individuals who happened to be associated with it at various times? Where did they come from, what happened to them, and what might their brush with JM have done for (or to) them? JM's recruits more or less came in three waves. The first was composed of very able though confused people rebounding from various unfortunate institutional experiences (home, school, work, etc.). While these institutions placed demands on them which they could not or did not want to deal with, in many instances they expected too much from institutions. Most had vague visions of psychological, social, and political ideals, and a few had articulated philosophies constantly undergoing change with new experiences. Reflecting a national mood of youthful rebellion laced with quasi-utopian ideals, they created an enclave or social "free zone" that in many ways was independent from the constraints (demands and opportunities) imposed by the composite of social institutions that surrounded them.

This open microsociety attracted a second wave of refugees from the larger social order. They included the injured, the victims of violent happenstance, and direct witnesses of death and suffering. One recalls the words of one college-educated visitor who referred to these people as a "bunch of lames." Often ostracized from peer groups from earliest memories, all were cumulatively affected as institutional rejection and experiences of apparent failure according to SS norms became common themes in their lives. Drawn to Wilfred to escape demands they couldn't meet or cope with, they sought a benign environment which would permit them to live in their own style at their own pace.

The third wave consisted of older, more experienced people exploring the possibility of a safe way out of institutional constraints permitting them to exercise more independence and creativity in their lives without jeopardizing their style of life or rendering useless the skills they had already developed. They experienced an alternative mode of living without having to pay the full price the pioneers did. Though experienced in the ways of the SS, they were naive in the ways of the deinstitutionalized, unregulated life. Unlike the first two waves, they had for the most part neither been at the mercy of hustlers in the urban hip ghettoes, hit the depths of depression and confusion that accompanied drug abuse, nor experienced the feeling of wondering where their next meal was coming from. On the other hand, they never as thoroughly felt the momentary elation and sense of release that initial exposure to such situations often provided. But what they lacked in direct involvement, they made up for in more careful observation.

Thus, all JMers were people whose ties to standard social institutions were either severed or quite tenuous. All were casting about for ways to change their life situations; to find an adaptive response to the amalgam of pressures imposed on them. For some, the search was studied, for others it was virtually random. While some chose JM as a step on the path away from SS constraints, others chose it as a way out of CC excesses experienced in other situations. JM was a kind of experiential furnace that forced its members over various phases either to get out (with some valuable lessons learned), or to be radically changed if they were to remain. For some who remained the longest, the personal transformations ("growth," in the more popular vernacular) could be viewed as quite constructive. But more often, the longer they held on to the original dream, the changes could be seen as destructive. It must be emphasized, however, that JM as a single case did not strongly reflect the situations obtaining in most other nearby communal environments. JM represented one end of spectrum that has to be viewed as a whole if any locus on it is to be more fully understood.

Of the original wave of twenty two people traced from the Dobson House and the early part of the first summer on the land, ten were living either in or near Wilfred five years later. Moreover, all of the ten were still living in quasi-communal settings. Three joined and remained with established communes, but the other seven set up three households of their own with other people. In fact, one consisted entirely of ex-JMers and their mates, and in a very real sense became the new "old" JM, located a short walk through the woods from the original. Half primarily supported themselves by salaried jobs in the local economy, the other half through direct consumption of the goods they produced or sale of their goods and services in the area. Many people developed solid, practical skills, such as carpentry and commercially oriented farming. Although these occupations did not rank in a prestige hierarchy one might have expected from their socioeconomic background, in a recession economy with proportionately high unemployment (especially among the educated) at the time, their apparent "downward" mobility could be interpreted as a lateral one. More important, these people evidently succeeded in carving out a satisfactory and often rewarding mode of life. No one could be heard complaining about what might have been had they remained in school or in jobs before coming to JM.

The other twelve are harder to pin down. It is not known what happened to five after they left the Meadows, but because most of them already had some skills, they probably found niches in their areas of interest. It is anybody's guess what happened to the Menominee Indian. Two immediately underwent training programs in technical skills and had not been heard from since. One became an influential executive in a large nationally-known health food company. One moved to a rural area in another part of the country, another was last heard from struggling to enter the theatrical profession, and yet another moved to Greece as an English language instructor. The last established himself as an important figure in an Eastern religious organization. For this first wave of SS dropouts or push-outs, there was very little, if any, actual or attempted dropping back in. It could even be argued that they helped to create significant alternatives to, or at least broaden the scope of what can be included in, the repertoire of ways to earn a rewarding and respectable living in the overall society.

The second wave, which also included some very talented people, met with a different overall fate. Of the fifty-five discussed in this study, nothing is known about thirteen after they broke contact with the Meadows. As of 1975, twenty were still living in Provincia, thirteen in or near the Centerville area. Of the twenty, ten were living in quasi-communal conditions, ranging from the same established communes that members of the first group had also joined to separate homesteads maintained on a common parcel of land. Four had ended up living their lives little differently from that which they would be living had they never ventured into JM. In effect, these four did drop back into the SS. Three of these four came from solid working class backgrounds, while the other was very young and very abused while at the Meadows. The range of occupations in the group still living in Provincia ranged from factory and secretarial work to crafts, farming, carpentry, and musicianship. Some still received welfare and social security payments because of the need to support their children or various long-suffered emotional problems. Roamer was the only full-time JMer still living at the Meadows.

Of the twenty-two yet to be accounted for here, six died violent deaths. Three, of course, occurred in the fire (four, if the girl who was just passing through the Meadows is to be counted as a member). One, it will be recalled, OD'd on heroin, and another was beaten to death by a law officer. Word eventually came that Zeke was shot to death in a bar room fight over a woman. All of these three were IBMs, and it is for this reason that a prediction of premature death or suffering for others in this group and the Mother Humpers, unfortunately, would not be unreasonable. One young member who appeared so intellectually alive and full of promise when he joined JM, went on to wreck himself with drugs and has been in and out of mental hospitals since. Randy (with the knife) was seen years later at different times and different places in the country, hitching rides, and doing and saying the very same threatening things. Of the remaining twelve, three went back to the straight life; one as career enlistee in the armed services, another as a career woman, and another as a laborer in construction.

Thus, only seven of the forty-three people accounted for in this second wave dropped back into the SS as it existed in the mid 70s, and it is highly unlikely that any of the missing thirteen did. Those who continued to develop alternative life modes outside Provincia retained a quasi-communal rural life and engaged in assorted occupations ranging from music to labor organizing. Again, a small amount of welfare contributed to the livelihoods of some. Religious conversion to fundamentalist Christianity after leaving JM played an important part in the lives of at least four people, and at least one "came out" as a homosexual. It would be tempting to say that genuine downward mobility was evidenced here, but given the wide range in class background, it would be difficult to prove. While the quality of life and social influence of some from the middle classes unquestionably declined, some from the lower classes could be interpreted as having risen.

The third wave, which included the over-30s, consisted of twenty people (not including Roamer or Claudius and Blythe, whose renowned tree house was reduced to ashes in a fire in 1973 in which one was injured). It does include six people in their early twenties. One, an ex-SDSer, left after a few months never to be heard from again, and another, formerly with the Blue House in Centerville, left to form a communal group in Centerville that made and sold crafts and was active in the organization of a regional land trust. Another was a relative of one of the owners, who irked the other owners to the extent that he was asked to leave. Two women, at different times, lived with Claudius and Blythe in their tree house and eventually left the land to settle in Wilfred as members of other communal groups. One went on to become a widely recognized artist in the area, but the other was killed when she was thrown by a horse. Hers was the eighth (known) death of young people connected with the Meadows.

Of the fourteen over-30s, eight were involved in JM before the land was purchased, and of that eight, four did not join the group of purchasers, though one returned to the land to live for nearly a year. Of these four non-owners, one chose to follow a career as an artist exclusively in the city, and another eventually pursued his calling as a poet quite successfully in another part of the country. Two set up a psychiatrically-oriented communal group outside Provincia which included one of the purchasers of JM and the cofounder of Secret Ponds Community. After a period of intense conflict it broke up, the part-owner of JM returning to involvement in JM affairs while the two originators of this communal group also split up, one moving to set up a practice in another part of the country and the other joining a Buddhist community elsewhere in Provincia. The group of seven owners, which grew to ten by 1973, were all still involved in JM to varying degrees in 1975; five managing to settle full-time into Provincia and support themselves. The other spent the summers and parts of the winters on the land.

Except for those who have perished, the life cycles of all are still incomplete. Therefore, it cannot be said that the apparent patterns outlined here will remain the same. Fully three quarters of the people who considered themselves JMers have gone on to pursue interests that were generally unforeseen, given their types of background and general expectations operating in the society at large before JM began. JM cannot, of course, take all the blame or credit for changing people's lives, because many had been exposed to radical desocializing and resocializing experiences before entering the commune, and others were slowly drifting in a direction that made the Meadows only the next logical step in an obvious progression. But nearly all who have been interviewed indicated that the JM experience was something quite out of the ordinary for them; a critical stage in their development. While some praised the Meadows for fundamentally changing their attitudes toward life in any interpersonal or social context (given their own past isolation and alienation), others more cynically gave it credit for opening their eyes regarding their own previous fantasies and naiveté about people in general.

People's own interpretations of their lives, however, are infamously unreliable and certainly limited. Whereas one JMer might see his or her accelerated absorption into a life of subjective sensitivity, reduced material needs, and very flexible independence as very positive, another person (even another JMer) might negatively interpret it as intensified entrapment in a life of narcissistic fantasy, unnecessary deprivation, and a powerlessness that leaves an individual at the mercy of situations always created by other people and institutions. Broad and subjective questions such as these aside, it can be said with greater certainty that JM represented a phase of very rapid transition in its members' lives. Compared to the pace before and after membership, in most cases it reflected an escalated rate of change, regardless of the directions in which particular changes took place. The intensity of various situations called for innovative responses from members. The amplification effect in communal organizational forms, where experience and information from external sources become decreased while internal sources are ramified, was largely responsible.

What kinds of effects did these conditions have on JMers? Older people lost some of their inflexible cautious attitudes while, overall, keeping an even keel. The very young tended to be most susceptible to transitory phenomena, getting caught in the extremes of drug abuse, violence, indiscriminate sex, and the like. By most standards, their life situations deteriorated after their brush with JM. Those youths in their early twenties rebounded moderately well from the experience for the most part, slowly elaborating stable, definitely alternative lifestyles. Those from the upper strata seemed to do quite well wherever they went, apparently having a repertoire of skills and contacts enabling them to make the best of any situation. Those from the lower strata exhibited the widest extremes in outcomes. Many died as we know, and many returned to the SS, but others managed to integrate themselves into an ostensibly superior milieu (in terms of quality of life, not necessarily income) into which they probably never would have had they remained in or returned to the SS. And those from the middle classes traded places with those from the lower strata or managed to carve out a relatively comparable niche in the CC. Unlike class backgrounds, which are so difficult to define and therefore difficult to ascribe in any social milieu, gender is biologically based and clear. Females clearly emerged the better for their JM experience as compared to the males. Though initially often suffering through more abuse than many women in the SS, most emerged with self-confidence and direction that many of the men both envied and feared.

The JM experience and subsequent events lend credence to some broader observations and generalizations as well. By looking at the complex behaviors of a specific group of interacting individuals over time, it is possible to see both psychological and sociological factors at work, simultaneously and systematically. The cumulative effects of individuals' past experiences helped create a situation at JM into which additional personality factors were added as new people joined. But these factors alone did not account either for the behaviors of specific individuals or for the developmental history of the group. The interactive situation, that is the processual forms of the relationships between individuals, jointly determined behaviors in that context as well as in new forms of behavior that continued to reappear in individuals after leaving (or changing) that context. Therefore, neither personalities nor social situational factors alone accounted for the specific nature of the decisions made and the turns of events. Clearly, it was the interplay of both kinds of factors that permitted change to occur, through resocialization and recruitment of specific kinds of people on the psychological side, and on the sociological side, by means of the number, complexity, and degree of interdependence in relationships maintained.

At the individual level as well as at the group level, an evolutionary process was underway. In the interplay between the individual and his or her environment (between intrapsychic/intrasomatic and socioecological factors), the individual was constantly seeking to reach an optimum state of adaptation to external conditions. He or she did so by means of behavioral adjustment to those conditions and by active attempts to change those conditions by leaving some of them, by searching for others, and by creating additional others. For a majority of JMers, the adaptive process can be regarded as successful; that is, most have apparently found or made a generally benign and/or supportive environment after much search and experimentation. Others in the course of adaptation chose paths that though seemingly rewarding in the short run, led them in the longer run into maladaptive syndromes, ending in virtual or actual self-destruction. Thus, in the myriad of possible avenues to survival, emotional and intellectual as well as material, even those people who succeeded in reaching some kind of destination by the mid-seventies encountered many failures on the way. The evolutionary process in general involves far more failures than adaptive successes and the cases of JMers proved to be no exception.

Also in the evolutionary process, there is no clear, direct route from the simple to the complex, from the naive to the sophisticated. Often, in order for change to occur (adaptive as well as maladaptive), there must be regressive development, simplification, and apparent degeneration so that different structures and altered processes can be elaborated in new directions to better match new environments. At JM, the fundamental building units of behavior were laid bare after institutional constraints had been stripped away, making possible, but not necessarily probable, a recombination of those units into new and perhaps more helpful and responsive complex patterns. It would seem that most JMers (some more than others) underwent a behavioral atrophication process at JM before embarking on a reelaborative effort that would continue indefinitely.

Finally, a composite pattern of life cycles for JMers also became apparent. After all people severed or loosened ties with complex institutions to drift as individuals until coalescing in communal form at JM, the process seemed eventually to reverse itself. Individuals, either after leaving the group or through participating in the final transformation of the group, generally reintegrated themselves into more complex institutions by entering into more and varied relationships with other people. Some, of course, continued to drift with even fewer connections and relationships, but they were a minority. Phrased in more psychological terms, it could be said that not only had their identities changed, but that they had become more complex and differentiated after a period of undeniable simplification and possible regression. Their new identities, like everyone else's, were pinned on a combination of factors based on occupations, sexual activities, household arrangements, avocations, political preferences, religious beliefs, and the like.

It is important to note, however, that most of the people did not reintegrate themselves back into the same kind of institutions they originally left. And they did not evolve identities based upon the same varieties of standard factors mentioned above, nor upon the same proportional mix of these standard factors which they could have been expected to earlier, before the advent of the CC or JM. The institutions were for the most part smaller, relatively unstructured, and flexible in operation, yet complex with respect to informal and spasmodic ties to other groups and individuals. Personalities could similarly be interpreted as being more flexible and open to change, and instead of resting heavily on two or three primary factors or beliefs, managed to integrate many aspects of living into a functioning whole. Presumably this could be said of any maturing person passing through a sequence of life circumstances, but the intensity, speed, and significant changes of direction in this case were for the most part extraordinary.

Shifting focus from individuals to groups, communes must be addressed as the fundamental institutional innovation of the time. During the period of study, they superseded family, the work place, school, political party, fraternal/sororal order, and circle of friends by combining all these into one interrelated whole. What role did JM play in the evolution of the Provincian CC, and how did this compare with other communes? Were communes anomalous social cul-de-sacs, were they catalytically instrumental in certain forms of social change, or were they viable over time, representing ends in themselves rather than means to other forms? What was the internal dynamic that permitted their survival, and what distinguished relatively successful from failing efforts? JM, as the lone case history example, cannot answer these questions, but JM taken together with its broader spatiotemporal context can furnish some possible insights.

We have seen how JM served as a kind of net, scooping up institutionally unaffiliated people, creating a context in which they interacted with one another, eventually leading to the creation of the communal group. In the broader spatiotemporal context, JM can be seen as an important institution in that it set the stage for later less spectacular but more substantial changes. It would appear that drifting individuals, had they not been exposed to such an intense social experience as communes provided, could have reintegrated themselves more easily into pre-existing institutions, merely experimenting, as it were, with a freer lifestyle only to return to "business as usual." But having been exposed, most didn't return. Other Centerville area communes, even more than JM, also served to pull in many individuals, reorienting them toward new ostensibly workable ways of life. A majority of the members of the other communes had by the early to mid seventies also gone on to lead relatively stable and comfortable lives in what before 1968 would have been considered unorthodox or unheard of situations and enterprises.

JM and other communes, almost without exception, were the foci of social, religious, political, and economic change activities in the Centerville area in the critical transition period from 1968 to 1972. Red Rose and Liberation Farm collectives became the nuclei for the Free Provincia Movement (only a few of whose many activities have been mentioned in this present study) which spearheaded what some regarded as a virtual secessionist movement that at the time very seriously alarmed local, state, and federal authorities. The Parson's Crossing Karass also began with two communes, proliferating until it became a subtle but major cultural force in the area. And the Brethren attracted people from across the nation who sought salvation, becoming so strong and active as to instill both awe and fear in many SS as well as CC people. Beyond these groups were smaller, more transitory groups somewhat similar to JM that collected strange combinations of talented and unruly and even criminal elements that misdirectedly attempted to elevate self-destructive behavior to the status of a respectable libertarian ideology.

JM provided a tolerant milieu for social outcasts to seek psychological rest and recuperation, for eccentrics who required novel situations in which to exercise their skills, and for lonely people, enabling them to elaborate new networks of personal friends. It also permitted people the opportunity to begin to develop ideologies that served as behavioral guides and to evolve an independence by being in a situation where if they wanted they could be largely responsible for their own actions, and directly and immediately experience the effects of these actions. Many for the first time eventually came to realize that all was not preordained fate; that an active approach to a limited environment did, indeed, have immediate effects. It taught people additional valuable lessons. First, by serving as a social mix-master, it forced people from all socioeconomic class backgrounds to interact, and for those where relative upward or downward mobility did not result afterward, mutual exposure in some cases taught empathy and compassion. In others, it revealed raw exploitation and left a bitter aftertaste. Second, it gave all a chance to learn anew, even if there were great risks, that some of the overall society's rules were, indeed, supercilious and wasteful, but that many others were ultimately necessary for the preservation of human life and dignity. As already mentioned, the lessons learned early through the entropization and disorganization of thought and behavior that JM encouraged was for some an end in itself, for others a necessary prerequisite for reorganization, and for still others, an added step in a downward spiral.

JM illustrated the very direct and systematically organized relationship between states of consciousness, individuals' behaviors, and the structure of social systems; altered or unaltered, entropic or negentropic. As changes in pattern accrued at lower, more exclusive levels of organization, say individual awareness, their cumulative effects apparently manifested as specific kinds of change at the higher, more inclusive levels of organization, such as Movement dynamics and vice versa. This could most easily be seen in instances where fluctuations in external threats requiring changed attitudes of members, shifts in the kinds of people recruited, and changes in the amounts, and kinds of psychoactive substances used, were all systematically reflected as parallel alterations in social process and structure.

Personal and theoretical ramifications aside, JM also performed a significant role with respect to other communes in the area and the regional CC in general. It was the major conduit through which literally thousands of people entered Provincia to observe and to experiment with psychosocial alternatives. A majority, perhaps, passed back into the society from which they came, but a significant number are known to have either settled into Provincia or into an alternative lifestyle elsewhere. More specifically, JM provided significant personnel for other communal groups and alternative institutions. It was, essentially, one of the first steps on the new underground railroad. But in the process, until the final transformation, it regurgitated those people it could least afford to lose. The poverty and despair evident near the end was for the most part not a result of the fact that the CC tended to draw so many naive, incompetent, alienated, and deprived people. Rather, it was more of an artifact of the process by which the communal network, a higher order of social organization, distributed its human, material, and informational resources. The incipient stratification in each communal group was translated into a more obvious social stratification in the CC in which different groups came to occupy different positions. Just as JM became a concentration point for the most unfortunate circumstances, other groups served as the loci for creative art and literature, for emotional and intellectual exploration, and for the elaboration of viable and even profitable economic enterprises and systems. These were based on the essentially accurate CC predictions that partial urban collapse, inflation/recession, decline of the nuclear family, energy shortages, health crises, increasing poverty, and environmental degradation would scar the country in the years ahead.

This leaves another question unanswered, however. It will be recalled that many of the characteristics of poverty referred to in the previous chapter, were essentially artifacts of small social systems, poorly integrated into a larger systemic context. Whereas small systems could account for much behavior associated with poverty, does such a finding also indicate that all small quasi-independent social systems are doomed to a poverty or poverty-like status within a large, complex societal context? Can they or their members survive without eventually facing the choice (if by that time there is a choice) between low socioeconomic class status on the one hand, and all that implies, and on the other hand, full re-entry into the society at large or the creation or larger systems of their own?

Thus, the question as to whether the communal or quasi-communal social form is viable and/or socially important in its own right becomes important, especially if separate individual manifestations of the form might serve as the strands out of which a new kind of social fabric might be woven. A quick look at the state of various Centerville area communes as of 1974 would be instructive.

In the Centerville area in 1968, there were three communes. This number doubled to six in 1969, and by 1970 increased five-fold to fifteen. In 1971 a peak of sixteen was reached, but in 1972 the number dropped to twelve. In 1973, however, the total rose again to fourteen; a year in which two failed but in which four more were begun. By 1974, the number dropped back to twelve, and indications for 1975 were that the total would remain the same, with one closing down and another being started. These figures cover only those groups connected with the major karasses present in 1969 and does not include any communes that might have been initiated outside these networks, networks where news of them did not circulate. Hence a total larger than twelve for the area is almost certain. These figures also do not include the many smaller two and three person households that spun off from communal groups but continued to maintain relations with them, in effect expanding various karasses. Finally, the figures do not include enterprises that changed so drastically that the communal aspect was lost altogether. As of 1975 then, the commune movement was alive and well, even if changing, at least in the Centerville area.

The same factors that appeared with respect to individuals also manifested themselves in the communal context. The most successful groups in terms of longevity and overall productivity were those that had the greatest numbers of people who were older (mid-twenties on up) and people who had upper and middle class backgrounds. Again, woman emerged as a very strong and sometimes dominant force in the most successful groups, but two efforts that were based exclusively on women failed. Also, as in the case of individuals, many of the organizational and operational modes that were experimented with were behaviorally extreme, and a number of groups collapsed because of this. Even those that survived went through a series of small trials and errors that nearly finished them off at various points. Yet, from all the failures there emerged forms that proved to be quite adaptive to the various conditions obtained in their socioeconomic environments. Despite numerous anti- or non-materialistic ideologies, all survivors came to grips with the problems of producing consumable goods and services earning cash.

Relatively speaking, the politically oriented groups tended to fail within a few years, as did the psychiatrically oriented groups whose life span was even shorter. Unlike the religious ones, political groups had very tangible goals whose achievement success or failure was easily measurable and often found wanting. Both they and the psychiatric ones were democratic and equalitarian to a fault, getting bogged down in excruciating decision making processes or volatile internal squabbles. Accordingly, the religious organizations, such as the Brethren, tended to survive, changing drastically in the process. By 1975, for example, the Brethren owned more than 10 buildings and as many businesses in three towns, a fleet of automobiles, and an old movie theater in which it conducted rock concerts and religious services for the community at large. The back-to-the-land groups that manifested competence in skills ranging far beyond farming, such as writing or organizing and administering, built the most solid foundations for stability and continuity. Their rate of change was slow and steady, reflecting and adjusting to changes in the region that they had helped generate.

As with individuals, composite patterns of communal evolution are important to note. The developmental cycle outlined for JM was repeated in other groups as well, each manifesting its own variation, or disbanding, or revitalizing along the way. Generally speaking, the groups in the process of formation moved to a highly fused state characterized by states of near-ecstasy in the individuals, only to shift shortly thereafter into a disintegrative phase. This disintegrative phase became apparent as pressing environmental, economic, interpersonal, and political (with respect to elements in the society external to the group) concerns grew more prominent. Many could not overcome these pressures. Those that survived, managed to develop an organizational pattern which even if not closely fused, permitted more distant and distinguishable components to function as a coordinated entity through exchange and mutual interdependence. They also developed an external focus, involving projects that furthered this shift. Thus, differentiation and specialization appeared within each group, laterally with respect to productive skills and vertically with respect to decision-making capabilities. There was a lag effect at the communal level as changes were manifested as the cumulative result of more rapid changes experienced by members in relation to one another and to outside factors. Often unintended incidences of conflict and cooperation among individuals and factions gave the groups an overall direction that in most cases was not tied to the attitudes or behaviors of any one individual or faction in them. Thus, self-regulating controls as well as the deliberately instituted and managed controls (or the dominance of various personalities) became important in the development of nearly all the groups.

As communes and collectives passed through their different stages, some individuals' behavior changed with them to reflect the shift from relatively fluid and entropic states to relatively structured and negentropic states. But in most cases, change in communal state was accomplished by a population turnover; permitting the group to drop individuals unsupportive of the shift to a new phase, while at the same time allowing it to pull in those who could function well with it. In the end, or at least by the time data was last collected for this study, most groups had a majority of members who were not present during the earlier phases. Some, such as JM, had an entirely different membership. Just as the earliest efforts eventually attracted the unskilled and emotionally unstable, later efforts proving that communes could survive, at least for a while, eventually attracted those whose skills and attitudes permitted the further elaboration of stabilizing structures, yet which changed the original communal focus. Groups became less concerned with their own involuted dynamics, growing looser, but also extending contacts to one another forming a broader-based community.

This raises a third set of questions concerning levels of organization above and beyond individuals and communes. If JM and other area communes, their members, and most of their former members did not return to participate fully in common SS institutional forms of the day, what did they participate in? Did they indeed constitute, if not a counterculture, at least a subculture or paraculture with viable organizational alternatives and relatively independent support systems? What effects did the phenomena described in this study have on the regional society at large, and could they be considered instrumental in overall social change? What are the processes by which social systems grow and decay, in relation to one another and even within one another? Obviously, this case study cannot provide firm answers, but it can lend itself to admitted speculations.

The evidence presented in this study does not contradict the long observed processes of evolution that occur in realms other than those social and psychological (Redfield: 1968). Lateral and vertical differentiation appear to occur with the growth of systems, and if the growth process is not arrested or reversed, it leads to the specialization and interdependence of various component parts. These parts can be observed to be drawn from the outside and rearranged so as to constitute internal structure. Another order of growth is achieved when previously independent systems amalgamate in various forms to create a larger, more complex supersystem, by means of exchange between and interdependence of the formerly independent systems. This process also leads to specialized systems and to a clear hierarchical organizational format at a more inclusive order of magnitude. Social and psychological systems, largely being more dependent on cognitive and affective information exchange than genetically coded biological and natural ecological systems (but no less ultimately dependent on the processing materials and energy) are more open, flexible, and susceptible to rapid and dramatic changes in form. In all the developments, the shuffles into more inclusive orders of structure, transitions, and integrations, are in the end only responses and attempted adaptations to simultaneously shifting and swirling environments. They are responses and adaptations by systems manifested through the capture and conversion of various elements in their environments that permit their own survival and prosperity, if possible.

In this case, the environments were socioculturally determined and the struggling systems were tools of human aggregates hoping to develop a better quality of life based more directly on what they perceived their particular needs to be. These systems were quite diverse, yet existed side by side in the society, some perhaps growing at the expense of others, some growing with the aid of others, all pulling in additional members (lateral and vertical mobility). But some appeared, peaked, declined, or even disappeared in rapid succession, drawing those who escaped too late or didn't escape at all into the downward spiral. Also, unlike biological systems, component individuals belonged to two or more specific social systems at the same time, even at the same level of organization, and by doing so, caused one to have a direct influence on the other. Moreover, competitive or antagonistic groups or organizations often maintained mutually beneficial relations through exchange of services, goods, or cash, thereby influencing one another, even if they shared no members.

These processes extended beyond communes embedded in the CC to these same communes also as part of the larger society. A surface glance at the Centerville area and the region in 1975 revealed that many of the people who had been drawn there to participate in radical experiments were performing important tasks for the entire community while integrating themselves into its many facets. They were still active, however, even if more sophisticated, agitators for social change, focusing on more defined, specific issues where they realized they would have a sharper, more prolonged impact. The ultimate objective of creating a new, separate society had receded, not only because the ultimate futility of the effort was becoming clearer, but just as important, because the changes they had already helped to bring about made it easier and more appealing for them to redirect their efforts back to the society that had originally spawned them. The local society was, indeed, changing, accommodating them as they accommodated it. By 1975, the overall distribution and mix of behaviors and attitudes in the region as a whole had significantly been modified, and it was achieved through a process that consisted of far more than an institutional drift that merely conformed to societal inertia, kept in motion by preceding patterns and trends. The CC, largely through the efforts of communal forms or their spin-offs, had had an undeniable impact.

If the process wasn't a complete revolutionary change, which it wasn't, and if it wasn't a gradual unfolding of slow evolutionary change, which it also wasn't, what was it? More precisely, what was the larger shape and dynamics of change that led to the state of conditions reached by 1975? Trying to answer this question is the final task of this study. In order to accomplish this task, a look at the broader picture is necessary. The examination must go beyond just JM, other groups, or local traditional institutions, to the overall manner and arena in which they all interacted with one another to generate the specific changes that, taken together, constituted regional social change. This, in turn, requires some additional contextual information derived from other areas of the total study undertaken, but not included in this volume so far, and a slightly freer hand at analysis and synthesis. The discussion begins with what people thought they were doing at the time and proceeds to what they actually might have been doing.

JMers and other communards in the region brought with them ways of living that they had come to believe would be more in tune with the times and certainly more amenable to themselves as products of those times. They took a combination of vague notions, injured psyches, and abstract ideals and used them in a deliberate attempt to find or construct a social environment in which they and others, they believed, would thrive. Most claimed, to varying degrees, to be going off to create an entirely new society based on more than "peace and love." They would struggle to achieve universal human basic needs: satisfaction, harmony with nature, spiritual meaning, cooperation, equality, honesty, democracy, dignity, freedom, and justice. It was to be the new American settlement and revolution, finally accomplishing what the original 17th and 18th century colonists and revolutionaries wanted but didn't achieve. Although many were concerned that the dream might be impossible to realize, they nevertheless set about to build a society from the ground up. And this, naive or not, constituted a monumental task.

Some experiments spun off into such extremes, in terms of "new" behavioral modes, that they overstretched human endurance, and were doomed to certain failure in some instances and very major modification in the others. Such was the fate of those based on "getting high," total self-sufficiency, absolute tolerance of any individual's quirks, complete openness of sexual expression, conviction that any imaginative idea could be converted into material reality, unlimited access to resources by everyone, and deliberate unending, elevating struggle, with self as well as with others as a permanent a way of life.

Other experiments came up short not because of unrealistic ideals, but because some basic principles of human behavior previously revealed through past historical and evolutionary process had been neglected, forgotten, or simply never learned in the first place. These groups had too many members who didn't question other people's intentions, didn't realize that even good intentions did not necessarily yield good results, and didn't insist that individuals conform to some extent to an organized approach to problem solving. Neither did they appreciate that mundane chores were just as essential to survival as exciting challenges, that unwelcome feedback was just as important to a successful undertaking as positive, that a material base of support was necessary to give any effort a fair chance, nor that all people do not have equal abilities in all areas. In a professedly anarchistic movement, many did not see that organized institutions can facilitate individual endeavors as well as hinder them.

Problems internal to JM and the commune movement did not, however, constitute all the reasons for various failures to achieve their original lofty goals. External forces, both malevolent and incidental, played a very real and significant part. Illegitimate arrests, trumped-up charges, and well-intentioned as well as purposefully discriminating laws and regulations took a heavy toll. Community jealously of behavioral freedoms, repulsion at (or envy of) imagined debaucheries, resentment of alleged transgressions against their institutions, and anger and fear as a result of calculated rumor mongering cost just as much, even if the process was more subtle. CC groups were hounded for different reasons. Examples of this are: threats and violence by rednecks finding scapegoats for their own problems, harassment by legal authorities to make it appear they were doing their jobs well, refusal of service by business people for fear of losing other customers, or outcry from community leaders in order to gain support for their own personal political objectives. It became readily apparent that if one was going to step outside the surrounding society, that society would not be content to sit by passively permitting it.

If there were so many problems leading to pervasive readjustments and compensatory changes by many CC groups and outright collapse by others who didn't adapt, then what were the successes? Like failures, they largely emerged as a matter of interpretation and degree. The fact that any innovations at all survived can be seen as some success. Many individuals' integration into the community at large in important and influential roles, as cited above, can be regarded as one such success of the local commune movement, whether or not the communes themselves continued to survive in their original form. This is so because these people brought critical ideas and approaches to their work derived in no small part from their communal experiences. They learned, through intense exposure to other human beings in a context that would allow them to see quickly the consequences of their actions, many things directly applicable in the creative management of living in a larger society.

In fact, the previously mentioned areas of frequent failure constituted valuable negative feedback to correct initial flights of fancy and ignorance, redirecting many members of the regional wellsprings of the CC onto more realistic paths. In some cases, reaction became too "realistic" in terms of cynical attitudes and efforts to outdo traditional society at its own games. In a way, it could be said that one huge historical lesson had been relearned through the communal experience. Yet in the process, old boundaries of human intercourse were extended into new areas, so that when both results are viewed together, exploration and correction, there certainly was no overall return to traditional ways. Instead, a different, well-founded, relatively stable amalgam of behaviors was created that was better suited to the emergent conditions of the 1970s and perhaps beyond.

Both concrete instances and harder to prove, abstract examples of this new footing can be cited. On the concrete side, the new JM with its different mix of members after its purchase by over-30s people, established a sound financial foundation, discriminated as to new members and how they could be included, established an order that did not allow events to get out of control, fostered far more privacy, demanded fewer and more reasonable commitments, and above all, stood by its decisions. Its mission, to the extent it had one, was to apply its skills, chiefly intellectual and artistic, to the larger community as best it could.

The Brethren, which by 1975 had decentralized into a full blown karass of its own, followed a parallel line of development. It set up a number of enterprises to serve the region (and the nation, pulling in universally known rock stars as customers for one of them), set up a board of directors for the new "conglomerate," elevated Brethren Peter to a less powerful inspirational position while promoting a Stamford MBA to run the operation, and required less of its members in terms of single-minded devotion and loyalty. On the other hand, the Parson's Crossing Karass, which was the first to embark on this overall course of adjustment, was continuing to spin off new closely associated but independent households and projects. Indirectly, it was also continuing to spread its regional and national artistic and cultural influence further afield than ever; particularly through plays and books.

Although the scope of this specific study of JM does not permit the inclusion of any detail concerning these emergent patterns in the Free Provincia movement, its development is particularly interesting and calls for some comment. This karass began with some fascinating radical experiments which attempted to integrate people's lives in what it saw as an atomized society controlled by a rigidly repressive political order. It did so by trying to foster knowledge of the forces that they saw governing social, economic, and political life, encouraging action based on that knowledge, and insisting on taking responsibility for the outcomes of those actions.

Its specific early projects demonstrate this. The Liberation Garage tried to teach auto mechanics and gender equality in a normally male-dominated workplace to customers so they wouldn't be at the mercy of auto manufacturers and specialists. Day care centers, a very radical idea at the time, attempted to expand children's and mother's horizons through instruction and by freeing parents from child rearing overload, especially in the lower socioeconomic classes. Its Vital Victuals Restaurant tried to demonstrate that a community could cooperate and be responsible for the operation of an enterprise providing low cost good nutrition and an arena for information exchange. Its newspaper, Free Provincia, was distributed cost free, spreading the vision of alternative models for living as well as critiques on what it regarded as failing or destructive SS practices in the region (e.g. nuclear power, pollution, growing poverty, overdevelopment, and worker and consumer exploitation). And lastly, its Liberation Farm was eventually set up to show everyone that concentrated wealth, no matter its claimed beneficial purpose, served to protect the wealthy from real social responsibility, while leading average or low income people to believe that they were powerless to utilize resources more effectively and cheaply to meet their own needs.

All but one of these specific local projects failed, not, however, because the ideas behind them were entirely and outlandishly new and unworkable. Most of these ideals have been around since time immemorial, and many have since been implemented in limited forms and combinations by other people in Provincia and elsewhere. The primary reasons these particular, more global efforts did not succeed were lack of long term financial savvy, the strident ideological packaging that went along with them, a naive reliance on volunteerism, unanticipated verbal, legal, and physical attacks, and eventual burnout by members. The restaurant, as of 1975, though also transformed, was one of the most popular in the area, and was managed by ex-JMer Yale.

Having learned its own lessons, Free Provincia later expanded into regional organizing, using more of an initiating and facilitating approach than direct leadership, thereby minimizing conflict with detractors inside and outside the CC while encouraging broader based participation. Largely because of its early efforts, a film, radio and print news service, a land trust, a region-wide boarding school, a transportation network (free rides), a mobile health service, and agricultural production and consumer purchasing cooperatives were set up. Not satisfied with instigating an alternative environmental, social, and economic infrastructure for the new society, it also took the lead in establishing a fledgling independent governmental order which included a volunteer police force and a tribunal court for conflict resolution within the CC, a revolving series of regional decision-making "gatherings" attended by many group (mostly communal) representatives and relations with other sympathetic movements and nations. In short, by initiating justice, legislature, and external diplomatic systems, it had taken the lead in putting into place initial alternative forms of just about all the major elements of a modern integrated society. And it had accomplished this outside the structure, yet within the space of the regional society it was intending to circumvent and perhaps replace. Ex-JMer Jesse was particularly active in these efforts.

Yet nearly all of these undertakings as originally set up also eventually unraveled, this time more slowly, primarily because the amount of work and responsibility simply overwhelmed the participants, who were insufficient in number and time to articulate an enterprise of such grand scale. In many ways, Free Provincia was still ahead of its time, trying more to convert additional CC ideals into practice than stabilizing those already essentially established. Although the coordinated revolutionary and secessionist aspects of their work eroded, many of the specific projects did evolve more or less independently into vehicles accepted and used by large segments of the overall populace, particularly those concerning health, agriculture, the environment, and consumerism. It should also not be forgotten that some of Free Provincia's most urgent efforts went into enterprises designed to cease operating once their specific objectives had been accomplished. They, for example, played a central role in mobilizing regional and national actions against the war in Vietnam, and depending on one's interpretation of history, accordingly had a definite role in ending US involvement there.

Various members of JM and many close to it participated in most Free Provincia inspired projects, but often, particularly in JM's worst period of decline, the JMer presence was more detrimental than beneficial. Most seemed to create disruption in one form or another, causing legal grounds for harassment by authorities, diverting attention from the task at hand, precipitating chaotic situations from within, or simply not following through on promises made. They were eventually excluded, but too late to make much of a difference one way or the other. Their exclusion also exposed what many charged was the hypocrisy and elitism of Free Provincia, abandoning the people who most needed help in a supposedly all-peoples movement. Perhaps the greatest weakness of this movement and one of the most important lessons relearned was that even the best democratic and egalitarian efforts for change, especially one dedicated to the creation of a classless society, cannot deny the inevitable emergence of social stratification which, in turn, affects and sculpts the outcome of any complex societal undertaking. In its organizing efforts it failed most dismally with blue collar populations, and even if it claimed that it was the SS that permanently and hopelessly scarred these populations and JMers before the cultural revolution ever began, it still came up blank with respect to dealing with the problem effectively.

In the end, Free Provincia, as a formal, organized movement, had disbanded by 1975, though many of its members, subgroups, and affiliates persisted in various forms. Priorities had changed as circumstances had changed. It had, more than others, planted the seed, made sure it sprouted, and nurtured and defended the young organism as best it could until it branched out in directions it could neither determine nor control. Jesse, the author of the optimistic statement that introduced this study, reflected that Free Provincia had done what was historically appropriate and necessary for the times. At this point, it was time for everyone to move on to do what was most appropriate and necessary next. Many of its resulting offshoots, were in fact, part of its final undoing. JM, for example eventually helped to drain it, upping the odds for mutual demise. Others actively opposed it, feeling that as former supporters, they had been callously manipulated by its distant dogmatic ideologues. But others, which also divided members, caused conflicts, and diverted current efforts, channeled activity in new directions. Certain components of Free Provincia's once global ideological blueprint gained prominence over the whole, and eventually helped to destroy it. Environmentalists and media specialists emerged, for example, but by far, the most significant force was feminism, whose growing number of adherents had once constituted at least half the drive behind Free Provincia. Many women became convinced that sexism and adventurism inside the CC as well as out, was the most genuine, urgent, and solvable problem facing them. The rise of feminism, rooted in CC ideals and practices, occurred elsewhere in the CC at this time as well, and was fundamental to the overall decline of the CC's earlier forms and subsequent transition.

Although growing divergent interests and strategies among activists was an obvious factor in the demise of this formal political movement, a similar pattern, even if more subtle, was just as significant as a cause for change in other groups in the whole region. All the communes and collectives were originally formed by pulling in all sorts of people with all kinds of predispositions, but these differences appeared inconsequential when compared to the two overriding initial concerns: rejection of the SS and the sense of starting a new life. Post "honeymoon" distancing and differentiation, however, in addition to teaching new lessons to different people, also allowed these old original predispositions to resurface. They combined to lead people to switch communal groups, then change social change objectives and tactics and eventually lead to the modification of living styles and conditions.

Accordingly, it was in the larger CC rather than in the Free Provincia movement and other specific efforts where more pervasive even if less noticeable influences came to be felt. There is little question in the minds of most residents of the area that many social norms had dramatically changed over the seven year period from 1968 to 1975, doing so at a far quicker rate than was apparent before then. It was also commonly acknowledged that the pace of change had slowed considerably after 1972. Not only had current and ex-communards and their friends and acquaintances subsequently attracted to the area settled in great numbers, but so did many thousands more who were drawn to the region because of its national reputation in many circles. It was certainly renowned for natural and rural beauty, but more than that, it was known for its commune movement and other exciting experiments in social change. These people brought with them certain sympathetic views and proclivities, to be sure, but they were only forged and additional others developed into actual articulated lifestyles as a result of living and testing them in Provincia with other like-minded people. Only after the tests, could more workable and satisfying adjustments be made.

Provincia itself, however, before the first CC hippies and radicals ever appeared there, was known for its relative tolerance and progressive causes. Younger native residents were especially eager to try on new ways of doing things and older veterans of long gone political and cultural movements reemerged as willing observers and participants. Undoubtedly, the regional and national mass media had something to do with the growing openness to change instigated by CC types, but it is not at all clear what the character and extent of its influence was. Much, perhaps a majority, of the publicity was negative. Change in actual behavior beyond only the simplest of acts is almost always accomplished not by media portrayals, but by people interacting with one another and negotiating new codes of conduct in response to new pressures and possibilities, so as to make it a part of their own social and psychological reality.

By a combination of means, then, words and deeds that were originally popularly regarded as irrelevant, fringe, or worse, antithetical to traditional values, were increasingly seen as acceptable or even desirable, and slowly spread over more and more of the region. They concerned basic areas seen as close to personal behavior or perceived as potentially affecting personal well being, yet which required some larger tolerance or support to be practicable. Where some could be fully organized and institutionalized, they were. Many of these efforts provided services that could be utilized as the basis for new forms of financial support for CC people, but which could also, and did, provide an opportunity for exploitation by previously unsupportive SS people. For better or for worse, the following are some examples of these changes.

Physical and mental health emerged as a major area, with two different basic approaches coming to the fore: preventive maintenance and active rather than passive participation in the care process. Meditation and other forms of stress reduction, health and natural foods, access to counseling, outpatient clinics, and holistic medicine suddenly became very important. Along with these came a few quack healers, "snake oil salesmen," as well as spreading drug use and abuse (although marijuana, the substance of choice at first for most, appeared to have few or no perceptible serious effects compared to all others; especially alcohol).

The state of the environment quickly became a very serious concern, focusing not only on health, safety, and aesthetics, but also on the well-being of the entire natural system which ultimately supports human life and gives it so much of its quality. The immediate results were broad-based efforts at recycling, pollution prevention, calls for development controls, and energy conservation. But there also appeared much self-defeating behavior; such as that of brow-beating zealots who focused on narrow issues, like putting the welfare of individual animals and plants over basic human material needs.

Sex and gender issues became matters of first order concern, in that both freer individual expression of sexuality and more equitable treatment for all people on the basis of sexual identity or preference were emphasized. Women's (and men's) consciousness-raising groups, women in established employment and political practices, inclusive family therapies, moves toward a single sexual standard for both sexes, guiltless experience of sensuality, "coming out" events for gays and lesbians, and households not based on kinship all flourished. So, too, did separation and divorce rates (many former partners feeling "free at last") and problems concerning sexual exploitation and narcissistic self-indulgence.

The local landscape, in terms of the life of the mind, was significantly altered with respect to access to sources of stimulation beyond the mass media, especially with regard to the direct experience of indigenous creative and intellectual efforts. The number of locally authored books, theater productions, concerts, art and craft exhibitions, community forums, discussion groups, new religious observances, and innovative educational programs increased markedly. So did the number of pretentious pseudointellectuals, passive culture consumers, status seekers, and reductionistic folk philosophers (e.g. "You are what you eat").

The material world as well, has been changed in the region, particularly with regard to the small scale, decentralized structure, social responsibility, and information/service bases of enterprises. In a new local growth economy that ran counter to the Nixon administration's policy of writing the area off as economically unsalvageable, instances proliferated of entrepreneurial start-ups, cooperative cost saving ventures, worker participation in management decision making, flexible work schedules, new energy and communication technologies, food and health services, and markets for rare and fine specialty items generally overlooked in rural and in mass market situations. On the other hand, there was also a proliferation in lower paying jobs, in the illicit drug trade, untaxed off-the-record exchanges, bogus cure-all and snob appeal items in the marketplace, and the enterprise failure rate.

Probably political changes were the most difficult to see. Provincia was already characterized by a high degree of community level participation and small scale rural access to authority, and as such, was a bad target for confrontative radicals demanding participatory democracy. It was also an accommodating sponge for liberals and moderates who, having been readily absorbed to a certain extent, were nevertheless frustrated by slowness of change. CC people did, however, form many significant interest and watchdog groups concerning such matters as the environment, nuclear issues, outside exploitation by big business, and policies for peace and disarmament. They also had impressive voting power in certain towns, and on certain school committees. As the population shift continued to drift in their favor, there were indications that that power would increase. They fielded very qualified candidates for state and local offices, revitalized a pre-existing left wing party into prominence, and increasingly took up positions in public administrative machinery where small day-to-day decisions had a cumulative effect. However, many also failed to exercise political influence by virtue of ideological nit-picking, preoccupation with their own survival pursuits, other-worldly spiritual beliefs, or disillusionment because of the apparent collapse of a movement that had advocated far more radical measures. And, aside from the fact that they had insufficient wealth to buy their way into power, they were often actively excluded by native locals resenting the sudden influx, and by rural, small town "good ole boys" who were already in control and wanted to keep it that way.

With all the struggle, decisions, and conflicts between various individuals and groups concerning everything from abstract sacred principles to basic self preservation, there was evidence that something larger was going on; something that in many ways was beyond the actual or potential control of anyone. From another perspective, it was as if the aggregate of individuals who were involved had only been interpreting the acting details in the performance of a basic script already written by a subsuming, self-driving process. Movement, revolution, radical innovation, and other purposeful measures for change could be seen as part of a more inclusive design for a shift in social forces that, in turn, constituted only one phase of a still larger, ongoing, cyclical, self-regulating, adaptive realignment process between and among individuals and institutions. Opposing points in intermeshing cycles seemed to be characterized by alternate combinations of cohesion and separation, order and disorder, and direction and aimlessness. Rates of movement also seemed to vary synchronously according to phase.

The Centerville and Provincian CC, its feeder cities and towns, and the areas of the region and beyond that it later touched can all be viewed as part of this apparent pulsing dynamic of social life and change. It has already been pointed out how the growing failure of many SS institutions to manage themselves properly in meeting the needs of increasing numbers of people they were supposed to serve, in turn, led to aimlessness, separation from those institutions, and disorder. It has been similarly shown how this, through recombination of the loose and moving particles of society set free as a result, permitted the coalescence of collectivities to form with their own evolving order and direction as the nucleus of the CC. This cleavage between parent and offspring societies, it seems, set the stage for an eventual, although uneven, synthesis of the two; leading to a still different, compromise order, direction, and integration. In the end, the process might not have yielded the degree of change that appeared so inevitable from the perspective of one side. On the other hand, from the perspective of the other side, it also certainly didn't result in the preservation of the original traditional system that seemed destined to continue on so indefinitely.

The "end" of this process, however, is still unfolding and is not the main focus of this study. It is the "setting of the stage" aspect of the process that is; the conversion of loose social particles into surprisingly potent, potentially reconstructive sources of energy. Communes and collectives were the means by which the stage was set. As part of a larger process, they did not appear on the scene entirely as the result of great human imagination or as part of a grand premeditated plan. They arose mostly as the natural consequence of the intersection of a series of forces in time and space which was particularly conducive to their formation. A hodgepodge of ideas and people were able to converge in an area of least initial resistance to them, reach a critical mass and then fuse; generating a power that was bound to have significant impact. Communal ideals largely emerged from the nature of the collision and fusion itself; undifferentiated, whole, and gloriously, even if momentarily, free from the burdens of both conformity to organizational demands and vulnerability to random caprice.

Conclusion

Just as communal principles emerged from the fusion process itself, so did they also become the main reference points for subsequent organizing efforts. These efforts were essentially threefold: to keep communes operating after the initial communal experience, to build a broader support base in the form of the local and regional CC, and eventually, to change certain aspects of the SS when necessary or feasible. Seen from the point of view of social system self-correcting dynamics, communes and collectives, and the principles generated by virtue of their very creation, served as templates for the subsequent differentiation and extension to follow. Stretching an analogy from the physical sciences, it was as if communes were little "big bangs" which started a social micro-universe, carrying along evolving structures and processes as they expanded. These bangs became embedded in the initial fused states, becoming more articulated and stabilized only as they reached wider into societal space and time. Hence the urgent and integrative anarchic egalitarianism and volitional ideals that were sought after can be viewed as inevitable reflections of inherent attributes of social system dynamics themselves, becoming modified as the cycles of change progressed through new circumstances.

While most social scientists and careful observers of the overall CC movement would agree that more was going on below the surface than any of its active protagonists and antagonists could see, and that there was a process at work which went beyond the mere cumulative effect of all their intentions and plans, far fewer might agree that the process was part of the social system's dynamic itself. All sorts of hypotheses have been offered emphasizing primary operating forces at levels transcending various individual's or group's consciousnesses or ideologies, but they do not seem to get directly at more basic, universal principles.

For example, many social philosophers, though sympathetic to the CC, stood above the tumult, seeing instead into root causes and patterns of the societal transition underway. Marx's concepts of class dialectic and alienation, Durkheim's anomie and organic solidarity, and even Weber's categorical juxtaposition between charismatic/transitional and bureaucratic/routinization modes have been cited in an effort to point out that a humanizing "reordering of priorities" was needed and was indeed taking place in our modern society. The war in Vietnam and civil rights violations were only symptoms of the larger problem; serving merely as catalysts around which to organize the reordering process. Some academicians went so far as to couple their critique of society with uncritical glowing praise of the CC. They emphasized the psychic and social price paid by those who lived in a system that focused on so much material abundance: loneliness, exploitation by schools and corporations, crowding, pollution, urban decay, the squandering of resources, and the concentration of power in the hands of increasingly fewer people as production increased (Reich: 1971). But praise for the utopia foreseen as a result of the development of anti-establishment alternatives made no mention of the different kinds of human suffering and failures encountered as a result and as amply demonstrated in this study.

On the other hand, there were hypotheses equally uncritical of the SS. Perhaps most notorious was touted by the then American Vice President, Spiro Agnew, which held that the movement was in reality not a counterculture, but an "anticulture." Spawned by "kooks, misfits and effete snobs," its supposed sole, real aim was to subvert all that was right and good in the traditional order. Similar themes, though less simplistic, also emanated from academia. One example asserted that the CC movement was really a "death rattle"; the last feeble gesture of people ill suited for life in the coming technological society and who seemed to sense their own historical irrelevance. Accordingly, it was clearly counterrevolutionary, not revolutionary, in that it sought to prevent or forestall the inevitable transition to the cybernetic age (Brzezinski: 1971). Aside from essentially failing to recognize that the CC's supposed human anachronisms were pushing the limits in many areas of society rather than resisting them, evidence from this study would suggest that many of the components of the new society were actually being crafted by these very people.

More balanced and perhaps more benign explanations were offered by other social and behavioral scientists. The most acceptable and popular of these appeared to be the "baby boom" approach of demography. It proposed that the dislocation and attempts at alternatives concerned only a narrow range of the population; the relatively high number of people born immediately after World War II who were approaching adulthood in such a compact time frame that society's institutions and economy could not adequately occupy or absorb them (Trotter: 1973). If this were the fundamental explanation, how does it by itself account for the large percentage of over-30s encountered in this study? This explanation also did not address the reasons the CC took on the particular forms it did.

Closely related, but derived from a psychological viewpoint, were hypotheses having to do with the concept of psychosocial moratorium: that period of life before adulthood when individuals are allowed to explore and experiment before embarking on a chosen path (Erikson). Although broadened by some to include the possibility that such moratoria can be experienced more than once and at different ages, depending on historical circumstance, this approach still has many of the same limitations associated with the baby boom analysis (Keniston).

A different approach, one based on a social class analysis rather than age, proposed that a CC, based on people dropping out of the SS, was essentially a healthy self-regulating societal mechanism allowing vertical social mobility. Specifically, as the unmotivated, "spoiled" progeny of affluent groups left the system, room was created for the previously excluded blue collar groups to rise and fill their vacated slots (Berger: 1971). Assuming a rather static class structure in the face of social change, mobility notwithstanding, this hypothesis is not consistent with the evidence from this study which suggests that only a proportional minority of CC members had affluent backgrounds, and that with time, a significant proportion came from the blue collar classes or lower. Moreover, the affluent did not become downwardly mobile in the overall society. Instead they used their resources to create new kinds of niches in which they still constituted an upper class, at the same time permitting some relative upward mobility for others through the creation of these new niches. Most of the ones who did spiral down after a brief social class fraternization period allowed by communal fusion and social leveling were predominantly from the lower classes to begin with.

The standard social movement literature, largely composed of historical, sociological and social psychological contributions, is of course directly relevant as far as it goes, providing essential understanding, usually with respect either to movements' relationships with the larger and more powerful surrounding societal contexts that gave rise to them or to principles of internal dynamics (e.g. McLaughlin, Toch, Zald and Ash, and Melville in particular). Among these are at least two approaches, both based in the sociocultural anthropological tradition, that appear to go further than most others toward a more comprehensive, unified theory of social movements as part of a larger, universal process of societal transition. While necessarily global and general in perspective and ordinarily not applied to the particulars of modern complex societies, they can yield some interesting insights.

One, the revitalization theory, takes the position that different social, political and religious movements, no matter their specific contents and purposes, are reflections of an incipient mechanism present in all societies for renewal. They are basically attempts to reverse stressful or disintegrative processes; sometimes being successful, sometimes not (Wallace). In complex societies, they often are only partly successful. Accelerated change, one way or the other, is the result.

The other approach referred to here as the structure/antistructure approach, specifies that groups and societies either by means of deliberate ritual or by default and turmoil, manifest attempts to reach optimum stability and continuity. They do so by constantly alternating emphases between strict and rigid organization, good for controlling the flow of forces that bind people together in task performance, and relief from that organization, good for the member's freedom and creativity in dealing with hitherto unpredictable or uncontrollable forces (Turner: 1969). Both approaches rely on dynamic cyclical patterns, social systemic adaptation, dialectical feedback process, and of particular interest to this study, communal forms as inherent and central concepts.

This study has utilized nearly all of the approaches catalogued here so far, to varying degrees in an effort to interpret the complex and confusing events depicted in and around JM. While reductionistic notions of single and linear cause/effect were avoided in the process, revitalization and structure/antistructure explanations were particularly useful in the effort to gain an overall, coherent perspective; organizing all the different analyses into some kind of an integrated whole that hopefully made consistent sense. But in the end, a general systems theory framework, developed originally outside the social sciences but sufficiently general to be helpful to them, seemed to provide the best fundamental organizing rubric for all the different perspectives. It permitted their inclusion and combination in ways that teased out more hidden, underlying principles while keeping different elements in relation to one another, thereby allowing the entire phenomenon to remain reasonably comprehensible (e.g. Hampden-Turner, Buckley, Harris). While denying neither the essential humanity of a social system nor the fundamental role of individual human perceptions, beliefs, or aspirations in social dynamics, it does provide the larger material and informational conceptual context within which all human systems can best be understood to operate.

Thus, at a most general level of explanation, the systems approach and all it encompasses here lends itself to the argument that the rise, sputter, fall, and metamorphosis of JM, other communes, and the regional and national CC were all a part of American society's greater renewal mechanism at work. These transitory forms could have been multilevel manifestations of a re-energizing, redesigning and reconstituting process that achieved some redress in social norms and institutions that were increasingly becoming maladaptive in adjusting to shifting changes in circumstances. If these norms and institutions were not protecting society as a whole from threat or stress, which is a matter of debate, they certainly were not doing so for at least certain significant segments of it. Although perhaps differentially felt, depending upon one's status in society, the shifting pressures stemmed from changes in common elements ranging from technology to birthrates, from geopolitics to environmental integrity, and from educational practices to employment demands. Perhaps the overall factor was that the sheer complexity and confusion of the society itself had outstripped the capacity of those not in control of it to cope with it. The mounting pressures might not have been an artifact of the blind drift of general change as much as it was the result of measures by other, more powerful segments of society seeking to strengthen their own positions at the cost of those peripheral to centers of power.

In order to reverse this potentially self-destructive positive feedback syndrome facilitated by entrenched interests in the established order, various components of that order had to break away. The breakaway process accelerated until such time that separate centers of counter-syndromic processes were created and protected in their early stages of development. Communes were ideal in that they generated the social internal intensity and external isolation required for initial survival in hostile environments. It mattered not what particular direction each took in terms of ideological objectives or support base, so long as some lasted long enough to formulate and refine different alternative modes that would eventually be tested in a broader context. Many experiments failed, generating their own destructive syndromes of a different nature, reinforced by external circumstances. But to the extent that any survived, their trials intact and/or in some adaptable form, then they served as the nuclei for more successful, though modified, responses to societal stresses, becoming themselves more entrenched and permutated through time, eventually reaching a point where they essentially constituted new, reformulated suborders within the overall social order.

In the long term, these kinds of cycles have probably repeated themselves in one form and to one degree or another, and will continue to do so as certain changes are eroded by eventual countermeasures or as a result of society's central institutions' inability to adapt to unforeseen new future circumstances. As demonstrated in this case study, it appears that the underlying drive of the entire process is to permit a complex social system, in all its diverse manifestations, to perpetuate itself for the benefit of some optimal critical mass of constituent individuals within the system. But as the system seems to be its own highest priority, even as it is constantly recreated moment to moment by human cooperation and conflict, the renewal process can also be quite inhumane; sacrificing many individual and group beliefs, aspirations, livelihoods, and lives along the way.

General theories and hypotheses aside, at a far more concrete level it can be said with some certainty that JM was one of many communes generated as the result of the conjunction of critical requisite factors stemming from the stresses and strains in America at the time. At the peak of their cycles in Provincia during 1970-7l, these communes also served as the focal points around which people beyond their membership were encouraged to behave and affiliate as if there were two distinct societies in the making, even if in a more objective reality there actually weren't. If the people in this study hadn't banded together as they did, and created some kind of mutually supportive momentum, it is doubtful that changes concerning humanistic responses to individual vis-a-vis institutional needs in the Centerville area and Provincia would have occurred to the extent and in the direction they did. Eventually, the consciously communal forms withered or drifted slowly toward organizational patterns more compatible with a larger social order that was also moving toward mutual compatibility, thereby creating a rather sudden new composite.

Should JM, the commune movement, and the CC be regarded as a failure? If their perpetuation as lasting societal institutions is the criterion for judgment, then the answer is yes. If, however, viewed as vehicles for social readjustment and improved adaptive capacity, they can be regarded as qualified successes. Based on the events described in this study, at least, they should not be disowned, ridiculed or forgotten by former proponents and opponents alike. There are valuable lessons to be learned from their existence and experience that will permit a much greater understanding and appreciation of these kinds of phenomena when a low point in our society's next adaptive cycle comes around.

Epilogue

Being a poet and a somewhat mercurial professional, I was honored and somewhat surprised when asked to write an epilogue to this study. I suspect I was so honored because Barry was, until his premature death, my intellectual mentor, life chronicler and dear friend, as well as the only person I have known who shared my June 16th birthday. Also, I was one of the many political/countercultural wanderers whose life was touched by Jackson's Meadows and the Free Vermont movement and was one of the very few with whom Barry stayed in regular contact over the years. Perhaps most importantly, I am a headhunter for lawyers, a person finder, and as such better able than most former counterculture types to locate many of the eclectic women and men who passed through Jackson's Meadows. Whatever the reason I was chosen to write this epilogue, this will be the first time in my life that I am going to have the final word in the Barry Laffan/Howard Lieberman banter, which, although I dearly miss Barry, I find quite appealing. I hope the modest thoughts that follow do justice to Barry's prodigious work.

I began writing this epilogue armed with a list of names and obsolete telephone numbers given to me by Barry's friend and widow Joanna Mauer. Most of the people on her list were people from my own past; fellow denizens of the political/countercultural miasma of the 60s and 70s. The possibility of reconnecting with my past to write the epilogue was both intriguing and disturbing. Although curious, I wasn't altogether sure that I wanted to tamper with my memories of that era. I have been convinced in these last 30 years that the activist movements of that era were, as we would have said, righteous, and in some way actually transformed some aspects of society for the better. What if my research discovered that the old communards and politicos were now sold out bourgeois yuppies, born again Republicans or worse: 40 and 50-something women and men with TV remotes in their hands instead of ideas in their minds? Undaunted by my fears, and with notepad in hand, I began the tedious process of tracking down 92 lost and not-so-lost souls.

After many hours and a growing long-distance bill, some patterns began to emerge. First, although I fled Southern Vermont after being beaten by an infamous undercover police officer by the name of Paul Lawrence, and being shot at on more than one occasion by militant members of the lunatic right, many former Southern Vermont communards have stayed in Vermont and actually formed the base of Vermont's economic and political renaissance (I write these words with a dish of Ben and Jerry's chocolate sorbet at my elbow). Vermont may not have become the revolutionary state that the leadership of the Red Rose Collective had predicted, but it has, as far as I can tell here in Stillwater, Minnesota, become quite a vibrant little counterculture capitalist haven. Whether this has been a good thing for Vermont as a whole or old time Vermonters in particular, I leave to others to discuss. My only point being that many who came to Jackson's Meadows and the other communes and collectives in Southern Vermont in search of a better, more meaningful existence became more than mere transients. They stayed and built, becoming stable members of the Vermont community.

Second, as Barry observed, there evolved in the Jackson's Meadows/counterculture community class differentiation that in most ways mirrored the stratification found in so-called "straight" society. My follow-up research has indicated that all too often the class distinctions that existed within and among the diverse communes and collectives has continued today. Those who arrived in paradise from working class backgrounds are pretty much still working class or worse or met violent death. Those who flew in from prominent families with significant trust funds or other independent means and at least a college education are still pretty much ensconced at the head of the class. Those in the middle seem to have gone in both directions: some moving into successful careers or achieving artistic or other fame, some (a minority) falling into a more marginal existence.

Third, most of what happened to other baby boom generation women and men seems to have happened to former members of the Southern Vermont commune/collective community. Some examples are:

• Many of the women who chose to have "communal" children have gone on to become single mothers when the fathers lost interest and the communes disintegrated.

• One of the original founders of Jackson's Meadows died of AIDS some years ago, surrounded, I am told, by family and friends.

• One of the longest-standing members is today a dishwasher at a restaurant in Putney, Vermont, and a surprisingly functional member of society.

• The young woman who first brought me to Jackson's Meadows the morning after the fire and with whom I first encountered a sexually transmitted infection, became born again and is active in a religious community.

• One hard-headed New York radical feminist ex-junkie is now an attorney in New York, active in attorney discipline and she is a mother of two children. Her husband is a senior attorney at a major financial institution.

• One former college drop-out radical leftist went on to become a successful corporate attorney in New York.

• The charismatic leader of the Red Rose Collective went on to become a prominent film maker in Europe.

• One of the more militant leftists is now a successful professional active in Republican politics (be not too radical in your youth lest you become too conservative in your old age?)

• One over-30 New York intellectual, interested in communal life, became a college professor and author.

• Others own small businesses, practice in the professions, are married with kids, and some have yet to find a mainstream niche, either through bad fortune or wanderlust, or because they never got the urge to become mainstream.

• Several wound up as homeless people or town drunks.

In short, people passed through Jackson's Meadows, Parson's Corners, Red Rose, Liberation Farm and the panoply of communes and collectives that took root in Southern Vermont, then moved on to some other existence, often to lives that look amazingly similar to the lives of most others of their generation. Does this mean that the Jackson's Meadows/counterculture experience was just youthful rebellion with little or no lasting impact? Perhaps, but I don't think so. With some exceptions, the people I have been able to locate, regardless of occupation or economic situation, share a view of the world that is community oriented; looking beyond the merely expedient to something more global. Even the Republican activist was passionate in her belief that only minimal government and an unregulated marketplace will allow people of all backgrounds to achieve success and societal equality. A jaded old legal headhunter like me still takes an active role in politics and community affairs, and fights social justice battles both large and small. This broader view seems to be a common thread that runs through the lives of all the people I was able to find.

Can I justifiably conclude then that the commune/collective world Barry Laffan chronicled has had some lasting impact on the world? As I read about people slaughtering other people because of religious or cultural differences, or think of any number of other unspeakable evils that seem to always exist, I don't really know. I hope so. What I do know is that my dear departed friend Barry Laffan never once wavered in his compassion for humanity, his attempt to bring order to chaos, and his undying love for friends and family, which makes me proud to have been his friend, and grateful for the opportunity to write this brief epilogue.

Although you didn't really believe in an afterlife, Barry, wherever you are, even if only in the memories of friends and loved ones, don't stop fighting for what's right and just.

Howard Lieberman
1997

Bibliography

Berger, Peter and Brigitte. "The Blueing of America." In *Intellectual Digest* 9: 25-27, 1971.

Brzezinski, Zbigniew. *Between Two Ages*. New York, Vintage, 1971.

Buckley, Walter. *Sociology and Modern Systems Theory*. Englewood Cliffs, Prentice-Hall, 1967.

Erikson, Eric H. *Childhood and Society*. New York, Norton, 1963.

Goode, William J. *The Family*. Englewood Cliffs, N.J., Prentice-Hall., 1964.

Hampden-Turner, Charles. *Radical Man: The Process of Psychosocial Development*. Cambridge, Schenkman, 1970.

Hardin, Garrett. "The Cyernetics of Competition: A Biologist's View of Society." In *Modern Systems Research for the Behavioral Scientist: A Source Book*, edited by Walter Buckley. Chicago, Aldine, 1968.

Harris, Marvin. *Culture, Man, and Nature: An Introduction to General Anthropology*. New York, Crowell, 1971.

————. *The Rise of Anthropological Theory*. New York, Crowell, 1968.

Homans, George C. "Social Behavior as Exchange." In *The American Journal of Sociology* 62:597-606, 1958.

Keniston, Kenneth. *The Uncommitted: Alienated Youth in American Society*. New York, Dell, 1960.

————. *Young Radicals: Notes on Committee Youth*. New York, Harcourt, Brace and World, 1968.

————. *Youth and Dissent: The Rise of a New Opposition.* New York, Harcourt Brace Jovanovich, 1971.

Laing, R. D. *The Divided Self.* London, Tavistock, 1959.

Laszlo, Ervin. *The Systems View of the World: The Natural Philosophy of the New Developments in the Sciences.* New York, Braziller, 1972.

Laffan, Barry. *The Psychosocial Effects of Drug Use on a US Population.* Report to the National Institute on Drug Abuse. 1982.

Lewis, Oscar. "A Puerto Rican Boy." In *Culture Change, Mental Health, and Poverty,* edited by Joseph C. Finney. New York, Clarion, 1970.

McLaughlin, Barry (ed.). *Studies in Social Movements: A Psychological Perspective.* New York, Free Press, 1969.

Melville, Keith. *Communes in the Counter Culture: Origins, Theories, Styles of Life.* New York, Morrow, 1972.

Moore, Wilbert. *Social Change.* Englewood Cliffs, Prentice-Hall, 1963.

Redfield, Robert. "Levels of Integration in Biological and Social Systems." In *Modern Systems Research for the Behavioral Scientist: A Sourcebook,* edited by Walter Buckley. Chicago, Aldine, 1968.

Reich, Charles. *The Greening of America.* New York, Random House, 1971.

Toch, Hans. *The Social Psychology of Social Movements.* Indianapolis, Bobs-Merrill, 1965.

Trotter, R. J. "Good-by Cruel Sixties, Hello Calm Seventies." *Science News* 104: 88, 1973.

Turner, Victor. *The Ritual Process: Structure and Anti-Structure.* Chicago, Aldine, 1969.

Wallace, Anthony F. C. *Culture and Personality.* New York, Random House. 1961.

————. "Revitalization Movements." In Barry McLaughlin, ed., *Studies in Social Movements: A Social Psychological Perspective.* New York, Free Press, 1969.

Index

BARRY LAFFAN taught at Florida State, Columbia, and Antioch universities as well as at Marlboro College. He received his doctorate in anthropology from Columbia University where he studied under legendary anthropologist, Margaret Mead, his master's in education from Hofstra University and his bachelor's in zoology from the University of Colorado. During his lifetime he received an array of research grants and was founder and director of the Northeast Center for Social Issue Studies, the Association for the Apalachee Culture and Coastal Wilderness Area, Inc., and Gulf Coast Excursions, Inc. His publications include coauthorship of *Community Process and Planning in a New England Town,* major contributions to *Energy Alternatives and Human Values,* as well as articles and reviews in professional journals. This study of a 1960s New England commune, *Communal Organization and Social Transition,* was published posthumously.